FALLUJAH
AWAKENS

FALLUJAH AWAKENS

MARINES, SHEIKHS, AND THE BATTLE AGAINST AL QAEDA

BILL ARDOLINO

Naval Institute Press
Annapolis, Maryland

Naval Institute Press
291 Wood Road
Annapolis, MD 21402

Library of Congress Cataloging-in-Publication Data
Ardolino, Bill.
  Fallujah awakens : Marines, sheikhs, and the battle against al Qaeda / Bill Ardolino. — 1
    pages cm
  Summary: "Attacks in the Fallujah peaked in 2006 when American and Iraqi government forces struggled with a reinvigorated insurgency and the prospect of premature withdrawal by U.S. forces. Fallujah Awakens tells the story of the remarkable turnaround that followed. Journalist Bill Ardolino explains how local tribal leaders and U.S. Marines forged a surprising alliance that helped secure the famous battleground. It is one of the few books to recount events from both American and Iraqi perspectives. Based on more than 120 interviews with Iraqis and U.S. Marines, Ardolino describes how a company of reservists, led by a medical equipment sales manager from Michigan, succeeded where previous efforts had stalled. Circumstance combined with smart, charismatic leadership enabled Americans to build relationships with members of a Sunni tribe who pushed al Qaeda and other insurgents from their notoriously rebellious area"— Provided by publisher.
  Includes bibliographical references and index.
  ISBN 978-1-61251-128-3 (hardback) — ISBN 978-1-61251-129-0 (e-book) 1. Iraq War, 2003–2011—Campaigns—Iraq—Fallujah. 2. CounterInsurgency—Iraq—Fallujah. 3. Civil-military relations—Iraq—Fallujah. 4. Iraq War, 2003–2011—Civilian relief. 5. United States. Marine Corps—Civic action. 6. Tribes—Iraq—Fallujah. 7. Qaida (Organization) I. Title.
  DS79.764.F35A74 2013
  956.7044'345—dc23

                                                                    2012047848

♾ This paper meets the requirements of ANSI/NISO z39.48-1992 (Permanence of Paper).
Printed in the United States of America.

21 20 19 18 17 16 15 14 13   9 8 7 6 5 4 3 2 1
First printing

To the Iraqis and Americans who risked everything to defend others

To Ensign William H. Martin (RIP), Captain Daniel Eggers (KIA),

Major Michael Mundell (KIA), Corporal Joshua Hoffman (WIA),

First Lieutenant Travis Manion (KIA), and Sergeant William Cahir (KIA),

for their examples of honor and sacrifice

❖ CONTENTS ❖

List of Maps		ix
Introduction		1
1	Dark	7
2	Chasing Shadows	17
3	COIN	29
4	Alliance	54
5	The *Diya*	65
6	Pulling Threads	84
7	Adilah	92
8	Civil Affairs	100
9	*Wasta*	108
10	A Macy's Thanksgiving Day Parade	113
11	Down by the River	128
12	Hawa	132
13	Score	147
14	"Because the Language They Use Is Killing": Al Qaeda and the Sunni Insurgency	157
15	Gas	173
16	MassCas	189
17	Endgame	204
Afterword: A Note on COIN		219
A Note on Research Methodology		221
Acknowledgments		227
Notes		229
Index		279

❖ MAPS ❖

Map 1. The Fallujah Peninsula   7

Map 2. Morning Ambush, Albu Aifan, November 4, 2006   31

Map 3. Afternoon Ambush, Albu Aifan, November 4, 2006   42

Map 4. Marine Ambush along Route Boston, March 11, 2007   153

❖ INTRODUCTION ❖

Fallujah is iconic in the history of the Iraq War. For most western-ers, the "City of Mosques" conjures images of brutal house-to-house fighting, the killing and mutilation of American contractors, and the birth of an insurgency that prefaced years of chaos. Several authors have documented the two hard-fought U.S.-led offensives in the city in 2004, colloquially known as the First and Second Battles of Fallujah. Insurgent attacks in the area peaked more than two years later, however, severely test-ing U.S. and Iraqi security forces before a remarkable turnaround. I decided to write a book about this "Third Battle of Fallujah" after witnessing the dramatic transformation during two visits there as a reporter in 2007.

In January 2007, eastern Anbar province was still gripped by violence. Despite the killing and capture of thousands of militants by coalition forces during the famous battles of 2004, and the subsequent cordoning of the city with entry control points, the insurgents still managed to infiltrate and stage daily attacks. Within days of my first visit, two Iraqi policemen were griev-ously wounded by gunshots, a U.S. Marine was shot by a sniper and para-lyzed from the neck down, and insurgents destroyed a multimillion-dollar M1 Abrams with a firebomb. A U.S. soldier was killed while accompany-ing Iraqi soldiers attempting to evacuate civilians from the area around the burning tank. Roadside bombs were detonated against American and Iraqi patrols several times a day, and insurgent mortar teams and snipers prowled the area. The situation was arguably even more "kinetic" outside the city. A trip to the town of Ameriyah through the rural peninsula south of Fallujah was the surest way to get attacked by insurgents, according to a U.S. Army advisor to the police. In terms of sheer numbers of attacks, winter 2006 and early spring 2007 would be the most active period in Area of Operations (AO) Raleigh, Fallujah and its environs, during the war.

Perhaps most troubling, however, was U.S. strategy, which seemed at odds with the reality on the ground. American forces were stepping back to encourage Iraqi security forces to take the lead even though the local cops and soldiers were unready. The police had hunkered down in defensive positions within their stations, yet they were still being killed and wounded at an alarming pace; in addition, their families were targeted by assassins when their identities were discovered. The Iraqi soldiers, many of whom were Shia Muslims from other parts of the country, were considered outsiders in Fallujah, a Sunni enclave, and their ranks were undermanned due to a counterproductive leave policy, missed paychecks, and corrupt leadership that claimed a full roster in order to pocket the pay of nonexistent "ghost soldiers." U.S. attempts to push these security forces into the lead were premature.

The situation seemed dire, but there were glimmers of hope. To the west of Fallujah, the tribes around Ramadi, the provincial capital, had "awakened" the previous year to fight al Qaeda insurgents and form an alliance with the Americans. Some Fallujans had heard of the development and hoped that a similar arrangement could be made in their area. In addition, the Iraqi police hired a competent new district chief, and the corrupt leader of the local Iraqi Army unit fled from his command after stories about his thievery surfaced in the Western and Arabic media. And in January 2007, U.S. president George W. Bush announced the appointment of Lt. Gen. David Petraeus to head coalition efforts in Iraq along with a "surge" of U.S. forces and a counterinsurgency strategy that would attempt to stabilize the burning country. When I left Fallujah at the end of that month, I thought that security progress was possible, but that it would take a major commitment from U.S. forces and a great deal of patience. In retrospect, I underestimated how quickly things could change.

By late May, news of positive developments began to trickle back to the United States. The tribes around Fallujah had risen up to fight the radical insurgents. The Iraqi police and army were operating more effectively, and the Americans had reversed course and doubled down on their commitment to the Iraqis by aggressively projecting into the population to support local tribal militias, police, and soldiers. As a result, security had noticeably improved in Fallujah and across Anbar province by the late spring and summer of 2007.

Nothing had prepared me for the improvement I witnessed when I returned to Fallujah in September 2007, however. The Marines seemed almost relaxed when driving along formerly explosive stretches of highway. The area was being rebuilt; the power grid was more reliable; and many more civilians were venturing outside their homes, cleaning up rubble, hawking wares, repainting medians, and interacting with the Marines and the Iraqi cops. The insurgents still staged attacks, but with far less frequency. Whereas in January small-arms fire, mortars, and explosions from roadside bombs had been routine background noise, only a few scattered gunshots broke the peace on my visit seven months later. The change was stunning.

I initially planned to write a book about all of the factors that had contributed to this dramatic turnaround, including the "Awakening" of major tribes south and northeast of Fallujah and the urban counterinsurgency campaign that secured the city proper. After interviewing Maj. Brian Lippo, however, my focus narrowed. In discussing the progress of the war, Lippo, a Marine who had been an advisor to the Iraqi police in late 2006 and early 2007, assigned key credit to the tribal Awakening that had taken place on Fallujah's suburban and rural southern peninsula. He regarded the U.S.-Iraqi alliance as a turning point that jump-started progress and injected sorely needed manpower into the Iraqi security forces. Lippo advised me to speak to Maj. Dan Whisnant, the man who had served as the Marine Corps commander on the peninsula, and who, Lippo said, "did some great things down there." The result is *Fallujah Awakens: Marines, Sheikhs, and the Battle against al Qaeda.*

The story told here is not a holistic view of all the factors that secured Fallujah. It does not deal with the Awakenings among other tribes outside of the city, nor does it fully detail the campaign that secured the city itself and the pivotal contributions by several successive Marine units, the Iraqi police, and the Iraqi Army in those efforts. In addition, this book does not attempt to address the decisions at high levels of U.S. command that shifted the strategy and tactics around Fallujah. Many American and Iraqi leaders, most notably the U.S. Marine regimental combat team leadership and the Fallujah district police chief at the time, Colonel Faisal Ismail Hussein al-Zobaie, played key roles that are not the focus of this book.

This book offers a glimpse of the first tribal Awakening around Fallujah by one of the area's most important tribes, the Albu Issa. It also documents key actions at the company commander level and lower, highlighting how individual decisions by a major, captains, lieutenants, sergeants, corpsmen, corporals, and lance corporals affected the outcome of the war. Finally, it is an examination of aspects of counterinsurgency doctrine (COIN) and how this strategy capitalized on changing local politics.

COIN has been the subject of controversy in punditry and military circles. Its supporters credited the doctrine with saving the Iraq enterprise, and they later sought to impose a similar strategy in Afghanistan. Its detractors claimed that local dynamics—not the change in U.S. methodology—were responsible for Iraq's turnaround. Both camps made valid points, but ultimately the U.S. military supported community developments with the effective use of COIN to halt the growth of radical insurgent groups and Iraq's slide toward civil war. *Fallujah Awakens* demonstrates how individual components of the doctrine were applied around Fallujah even before it became an official strategy for the overall U.S. effort in Iraq.

Beyond an examination of doctrine, I've attempted to communicate something that is more abstract, but no less essential: the importance of personalities in shaping the course of a war, especially a counterinsurgency involving actors from vastly different cultures. People matter. Strong leadership, patience, and intellectual and emotional flexibility are necessary for success in an environment as chaotic as Anbar province was during 2006–2007. To this end, much of the book is written in a narrative nonfiction style to closely re-create the events, backgrounds, and motivations of the Iraqis and Americans who took up the fight.

After the famous 2004 battles in Fallujah, the city became a powerful symbol of resistance against foreign forces in Iraq and throughout the Arab world. By 2007, however, proudly nationalistic tribesmen had begun working with the Americans. In doing so, their mindset changed dramatically. It shifted from the idea of fighting an invader from a foreign land and with a different religious background to working with it against religiously radical former allies who had turned murderous (and greedy) in their bid to consolidate power. Many Americans wonder why the Iraqis who eventually came to work with U.S. forces didn't do so earlier in the war. This book attempts to answer that question, among others. It also seeks to give voice to the tribesmen, who are often treated as abstractions in the Western media coverage of Iraq. Most of these individuals had rational motivations and had to navigate an ultraviolent environment unfathomable to most westerners. From dealing with the deaths of family members killed in the crossfire between Marines and insurgents, to the risky decision to take a public stand against criminals and radicals, many Iraqis faced difficult circumstances. The individuals who stuck their necks out took on an astonishing degree of personal risk. Many of these decisions were heroic.

From the American perspective, this book examines how war fighters—primarily U.S. Marines primed for conventional battles—were tasked with a job that often resembled police work as much as it did traditional combat. This adjustment was not easy for many of them, especially when the job called for aggressive young men to show patience and restraint after their friends had been wounded or killed by snipers and booby traps. Five men assigned to Alpha Company 1/24 Marines were killed in the deployment to Fallujah's peninsula, and more than thirty men were wounded. Of the former group, two—Sgt. Thomas M. Gilbert and LCpl. Jonathan B. Thornsberry—feature in this book's narrative. The others are PFC Brett A. Witteveen, PFC Bufford "Kenny" VanSlyke, and Cpl. Jacob H. Neal.

Witteveen was killed by an improvised explosive device on February 19, 2007, while conducting a foot patrol. The PFC's former high school principal described him to the Associated Press as "a fun-loving kid, with a great smile, [who] knew that he wanted to serve his country." Witteveen's squad leader at the time of his death, Sgt. Michael Moose, spoke haltingly with emotion as he described the circumstances and aftermath of the explosion five years later.

VanSlyke was killed by a sniper on February 28, 2007, while manning one of the entry control points that monitored traffic into the city. According to one Marine, he had enough time to say "I've been shot" and "I can't feel my legs" before slipping into unconsciousness. VanSlyke had always been friendly with Fallujans who passed through his checkpoint, so much so that some regular passersby expressed condolences to the Marines when they learned of his death.

Neal was killed by a buried roadside bomb during a night convoy on January 19, 2007. He was a popular Marine, and his platoon took the death hard. The corporal's home unit hadn't been slated to deploy to Iraq, but Neal volunteered to go when his good friend LCpl. Matthew Teesdale was ordered to Fallujah. The night Neal was killed, Teesdale "just crumpled, fell to his knees and started crying," according to Cpl. Elijah Villanueva, another member of the squad. Neal was so well liked that four Marines later named their children after him to honor his memory. After the corporal's death, it was difficult for some American troops to accept the fact that the people they were trying to help had failed to warn them of the bomb or had possibly even sheltered the men who attacked the convoy. Years later, Villanueva commented on how it affected his deployment.

> The guys who put that IED in the road lived in a village that we had been . . . bringing water, school supplies, asking them if they needed help. We were doing the right things for them, and that's how they repaid us. We were trying to do the whole "No worse enemy, no better friend" thing. The guys used to tease me sometimes because I would carry extra stuff for kids—teddy bears, candy, whatever. [After Neal's death] was the first time I actually felt bad about it. . . . It changed the way I felt about the country and what we were doing . . . how I wanted to act while I was there. After that night I stopped carrying that extra stuff, I just did the mission, did the job and stopped doing anything else. I didn't go out of my way to be anybody's friend. I didn't become a monster or anything, I just wasn't interested. It was the worst kind of reminder that you're not at home, you're not safe, you can't trust anybody. I know there are good people [in Fallujah], but I went from being open to completely closed.

Some Marines hardened their hearts to the Iraqis after their comrades were wounded or killed. Others had arrived in Fallujah with an aggressive attitude and a closed mind, and they stayed that way. Still others showed great compassion, and they were able to keep an open mind in the bewildering ethical and emotional environment inherent to fighting an insurgency. In the end, despite many tragic errors and challenges, the Marines maintained enough professionalism to cement a key alliance that improved security.

This fundamental test in Iraq offers an important lesson for future small-unit leaders tasked with fighting an insurgency. Beyond the dictates of strategy, tactics, and logistics, and platitudinous ideals about protecting civilians, key questions loom: How do leaders instill enough restraint in young Marines and soldiers to have success in a frustrating, asymmetric conflict? How do squad leaders, platoon leaders, and company commanders compel troops to exhibit the requisite patience and professionalism in political and media environments that are unprecedented in the history of warfare? In meeting this critical challenge, individual personalities and decisions matter. I hope this book conveys how these factors shaped the history of Fallujah.

1

❖ DARK ❖

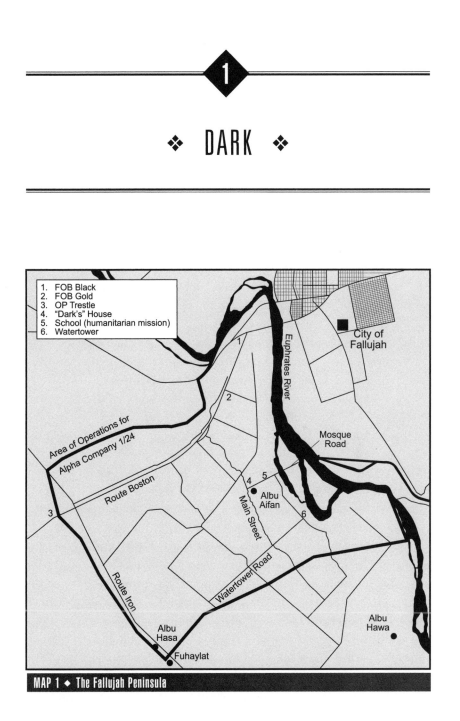

1. FOB Black
2. FOB Gold
3. OP Trestle
4. "Dark's" House
5. School (humanitarian mission)
6. Watertower

City of Fallujah

Euphrates River

Area of Operations for Alpha Company 1/24

Mosque Road

Route Boston

Main Street

Albu Aifan

Route Iron

Watertower Road

Albu Hawa

Albu Hasa

Fuhaylat

MAP 1 ◆ The Fallujah Peninsula

O n the walk to the meeting, Maj. Dan Whisnant thought about what he would say to the sheikh. "What will he ask for?" he wondered. "What are we prepared to give?"[1] Accompanying Whisnant to the midnight parley were an Iraqi interpreter nicknamed "Caesar," a military intelligence Marine, and five well-armed infantrymen. The small party was leaving the security of their base for one of the sheikh's houses a few hundred meters outside the wire.

A crescent moon and a quilt of bright desert stars barely illuminated a wall of twelve-foot concrete barriers and sharp rings of razor wire that guarded the eastern face of the American compound. The men picked their way through a maze of lower barriers crisscrossing a section of road running through the entrance, the serpentine configuration preventing suicide car bombers from penetrating their lines. A young Marine manning an M-240 machine gun atop a wooden observation tower silently watched as a member of Whisnant's detail held up a coil of the edged wire and replaced it behind them after all had exited the gap. The group turned sharply left along a grass and gravel path hugging the fence line running due south. They moved in silence broken by an occasional softly spoken command, the crunch of boots, and the rustle of weapons and body armor.[2]

It was a chilly evening on December 26, 2006. From Forward Operating Base Black, Whisnant commanded a company of Marines in charge of the rural peninsula south of the famously restive city of Fallujah. He and his men were tasked with leaving an eighty-square-kilometer area at the heart of Iraq's violent insurgency in better shape than they had found it. About three months into their tour, Whisnant's Marines had detained and killed some of the enemy, lost some of their own, and made fitful progress. But the clock was ticking on their six-month deployment.

Whisnant believed that the key to beating the area's resilient insurgency was information. His men needed to win the cooperation of the people, or at the least alienate them less than the rebels did. To this end, he prioritized getting to know the locals. His men were ordered to be respectful and follow sensible rules of engagement to minimize civilian casualties in their frequent battles with insurgents. Regardless of conscientious doctrine and careful execution, it was exasperating, uncertain work. The population of the area of operations (AO) had proven apathetic, uncooperative at best, and enthusiastically deadly at their worst. The major couldn't discount the possibility that his Marines were wasting their time.[3] The visit to the sheikh might produce a breakthrough.

It would be Whisnant's first chance to negotiate in secret with one of the sheikhs of the Albu Issa, an old and quarrelsome tribe that effectively administered the Fallujah peninsula and represented a large share of the citizenry within the city.[4] Then again, the late night conference might wind up in the familiar fashion of more public meetings with tribal leaders: sweet tea and cigarettes, flowery Arabic rhetoric, inexhaustible complaints, and ethereal promises of cooperation that would evaporate with the morning sun. Whisnant cautiously hoped for the best.

Intelligence documents were murky, but hinted that the man they would meet, Sheikh Aifan Sadoun Aifan al-Issawi, might have ties to the insurgency. One of the Iraqi's older brothers had certainly funded it, and Aifan himself might have even fought the Marines. The sheikh had even claimed to have been shot by Americans, under unclear circumstances, before being jailed for a time in the Abu Ghraib prison.[5] A dodgy past wasn't, however, a disqualifying concern for negotiations with the Marines. Many proud military-age men in Fallujah had supported "the resistance against the occupiers" in one way or another during the early years of the war. The "City of Mosques" had been a town filled with and surrounded by barely governable hard cases long before Iraq's Ottoman era, and the citizenry's characteristic independence along with a series of unfortunate events had bred rebellion that arguably rivaled soccer and prayer as local pastimes after the U.S.-led invasion.[6] The only things that might make Sheikh Aifan stand out in this regard were his noble tribal lineage and wealth.

Whisnant's well-armed security team and the proximity of the sheikh's house to his base meant the major wasn't particularly concerned for his safety, even while meeting a possible insurgent in the middle of the night on the Iraqi's terms. No, what occupied the 42-year-old company commander was sorting out his new contact's status and motives. He wondered, "Who is this guy? What kind of influence does he wield?"[7]

Aifan was a notable sheikh, but in the bigger picture, he was merely a nephew of the paramount sheikh, the acknowledged leader of his tribe. In addition, the leaders of the Albu Issa are not, in any case, omnipotent. Tribes in Iraqi society are not monolithic, cohesive entities. Rather, they are loose confederations of subtribes, or *hamulas*, that roughly correspond with individual villages. The subtribes alternately compete with one another for resources or work together against outsiders in shifting patterns of seg-mentation and collectivism bred from their nomadic ancestors' struggles to survive a harsh social, political, and desert environment. The paramount sheikh of the Albu Issa tribe nominally presides over twelve subtribes. This leader typically descends from one of the most prestigious *khams*, an extended family unit consisting of male children who share the same great-great-grandfather. Even under ideal circumstances, the authority of the paramount sheikh is limited, however. His tribe views him as the "father of his people," influential and responsible for their well-being, but he is still required to consult with a council of sheikhs representing the various subtribes. The complete societal upheaval and loss of basic security after the 2003 invasion had weakened this delicate hierarchy and essentially threw the Albu Issa into chaos.[8]

The moneyed, foreign Islamist fighters who arrived to confront the Americans and their allies were initially welcomed, or at the least tolerated, by many of Anbar province's Sunni tribes as allies. The newcomers' thirst for power, however, soon threatened the traditional structure. They siphoned tribal manpower, co-opted or intimidated entire subtribes, casually plundered resources, and murdered competitors.[9] As the insurgency against U.S. forces persisted, the Albu Issa descended into a parallel civil war for control of the Fallujah peninsula. Some local tribesmen sided with the Islamist radicals in grasping for a new order, while others clung to the status quo. By late 2006, no one sheikh appeared to speak for the tribe. The paramount sheikh and his family nevertheless remained influential figures among an intimidated population caught in the middle of a complex war between insurgents, criminals, Americans, and fellow tribesmen.[10]

Gen. David G. Reist and other Marine leaders had recently courted Khamis Hasnawi Aifan al-Issawi, the Albu Issa's paramount sheikh and titular leader, in Jordan, where some of the tribe's leadership had taken refuge when al Qaeda began assassinating those who did not bow to the authority of the Islamic State of Iraq, their shadow government. The Marines had attempted to convince Khamis and his family that the United States would support and protect them if they returned from exile and formed an alliance against the radical insurgents.[11] Khamis, Sheikh Aifan, and other sheikhs of the Albu Aifan, a subtribe of the Albu Issa, had come home only days prior to the meeting with Major Whisnant. Their return was motivated by the American promises, a sense of duty, and fear that their influence would disappear permanently as other tribes in Anbar province grew in stature and bargained with the Americans, while al Qaeda–backed elements expanded control of the peninsula in their absence. Consummate survivalists, most of the sheikhs remained aloof from U.S. overtures as they assessed prevailing winds.[12] The man Whisnant set out to meet on the night of December 26, however, claimed to be different.

Sheikh Aifan had been actively petitioning to fight the radical insurgents. Unfortunately for American interests, he was only the paramount sheikh's nephew and the fifteenth of sixteen sons within his *kham* at that.[13] The Marines didn't really know him, wondered about his motives, and were skeptical about his influence within the tribe. Whisnant and his military intelligence sergeant were intrigued, however, by Aifan's unusual request to meet secretly and considered him a possible inroad toward gaining his powerful uncle's confidence. They were willing to "keep an open mind" and engage the upstart as a first step toward generating local support.[14]

More than three years into the war, the sheikhs of the Albu Issa remained an enigma to the Americans. While a number of them had courted the U.S. military after the invasion, some of these same individuals concurrently supported the then-nascent insurgency.[15] Such double-dealing is a common characteristic of Middle Eastern politics and tribal relations. Nonetheless, the authors of a study on tribes published a few months prior to Whisnant's deployment had singled out the Albu Issa for their alleged duplicity. The researchers, a group of academics and former military officers, used an old Middle Eastern proverb to describe the tribe: "Put a black turban on a scorpion and you still have a scorpion."[16]

The Albu Issa included some conservative religious firebrands, but the everyday tribesmen weren't particularly radical in their practice of Islam, and they had no great love for the memory of Saddam Hussein or the Baath Party. They were, however, fierce Iraqi nationalists and members of the newly disenfranchised Sunni minority. Thus, the tribal study determined that the Albu Issa would maintain some support for the insurgency and cynically play both ends to achieve its overriding interests: the economic and political welfare of the tribe and the hasty ejection of foreign forces from Iraq. The authors regarded the possibility of successful cooperation between the Americans and sheikhs of the Albu Issa as unlikely.[17]

Past meetings with tribal leaders almost always took place in public and tended to run in rhetorical circles. The superficial dialogue frustrated American—and especially military—sensibilities. Sheikhs would make vague promises while issuing a litany of requests and platitudes, rarely offering actionable intelligence or assistance against the insurgency. Experienced

U.S. negotiators had learned to limit promises and obtain concrete support before making significant concessions.

Whisnant knew the game, and on this first visit to the sheikh, he couldn't promise much anyway. The major had no instructions on how to play things. In fact, the chain of command had not even briefed him about the U.S. mission to woo the tribe's sheikhs in Jordan. Thus, Whisnant was neither sure of Sheikh Aifan's position within the tribe's leadership nor what he was authorized to offer him. Their meeting would be limited to tentative overtures and appraisal. Whisnant later recalled that he was simply there to "assess the man. Get something of value before promising anything of value. And keep an open mind."[18]

The group of Marines and the interpreter walked by a row of houses situated in the village of Zuwiyah. The loosely spaced residences were typical, if relatively affluent examples of the area's architecture. One- and two-story concrete block structures of muted earth tones lined the road, surrounded by tall brick walls usually split by a metal gate. Here and there palm trees flanked or peeked over the courtyard walls, and scraggly green bushes of hardy flora burst from the powdered dirt shoulders of the road. Whisnant's delegation soon arrived at their destination—a simple two-story house. Oddly, all of the lights in the neighborhood were out.

The major posted his security element around the building and crossed the courtyard to the front door with his interpreter and the military intelligence Marine whose radio call sign was "Saint One." One of the homeowners, a tall, reed-thin man named Ma'an Khalid Aifan al-Issawi, was waiting at the door. A smile flashed from his dark brown skin, and the young man gave each of the visitors a soft handshake. "Welcome," he said in thickly accented English.[19]

Ma'an was glad to be hosting the meeting. It might mark an opportunity to fight back against the groups who were threatening his tribe and close family members. Ma'an's grievances were many: the insurgents practiced a radical form of Islam alien to the local tradition and killed all who disagreed with them; his tribesmen considered themselves to be pious Muslims, but the radical insurgent *takfiris* (those who accuse others of apostasy) considered any Muslim who failed to meet their draconian litmus test to be *kafir*, a nonbeliever. And they murdered *kafirs*, often in creatively cruel ways. The radicals had even forced marriages between foreign insurgents and women of Anbar province's tribes.

While many of Ma'an's fellow tribesmen had hesitated, the twenty-four-year-old lawyer by training had joined his cousin Aifan's lonely vanguard of fighters itching to wage war against al Qaeda and traitorous tribesmen working on its behalf. The enemy, however, was strong. The foreign radicals had plenty of money to back their murderous ideology, and corrupted some Iraqis with it. They also wielded the sword with ruthless impunity at a time when local fighters could not openly carry weapons to defend themselves, lest they get shot or imprisoned by Marines as suspected insurgents.[20] Ma'an and Sheikh Aifan wanted U.S. military resources to launch their fight against the radicals, to be sure. More fundamentally, they *needed* the Americans to let them openly carry arms and recruit fighters to guard their village and attack the *irhabiyin* (terrorists).[21]

Ma'an hoped that the meeting with the Americans would go well, although he had skepticism borne of experience. Previous U.S. units had failed to deliver on their promises, and it seemed that one group of soldiers had barely arrived before new ones replaced them. Still, he held out hope that a deal was possible. His cousin Sheikh Aifan was strong willed and easy to anger, but he was willing to fight. And the sheikh also wasn't shy about telling anyone who would listen what he needed to begin that fight. From Ma'an's experience with Americans, he had a feeling that they would like his cousin's aggressive style.[22]

Ma'an led the men into his darkened house. A smattering of candles flickered low light over a typically hospitable Arab spread of dates, fruit, vegetables, and bread atop a row of TV trays in a main room. The visitors removed their gear and placed their rifles against a wall as a show of good faith; they kept their sidearms. Ma'an motioned them over to chairs set up in front of the trays, putting their backs to the entrance of the house. A man got up from his position on a low couch opposite the chairs. He wore pale robes under a dark suit jacket, and his head was enigmatically wrapped in a red-and-white checkered *shemagh*. Only passionate brown eyes and the top of his nose remained visible. He offered a loose handshake and spoke in surprisingly good English.[23]

"Greetings sir, welcome sir. Thank you for coming. Call me 'Dark.'"[24] Sheikh Aifan, now "Dark," was doing his best to cast an atmosphere of secrecy and intrigue over the late-night rendezvous. This was an understandable precaution. Al Qaeda inevitably attempted to kill (brutally, if possible, to set an example) anyone openly meeting with Americans. Regardless, Whisnant still chuckled to himself at the cloak-and-dagger theatrics. The odds of neighbors failing to notice the retinue of armored Marines traipsing through their village and entering this house defied any prospects for secrecy.

Everyone sat, and the Americans politely sampled the food. Dark began speaking in an Arabic that even the Marines recognized as a particularly formal dialect. Caesar translated the sheikh's brief pleasantries, which were followed by a list of grievances against al Qaeda and his other enemies. Dark said he hoped for U.S. support and an active alliance with his men, who would provide intelligence and identify the insurgents for the Marines. He enthusiastically handed them leaflets he had created denigrating the foreign radicals and "traitors." As the sheikh continued, his formality ebbed. His words became casual Arabic, then English, and the forthright passion of his nature surfaced. He removed his head covering, revealing a neatly trimmed beard bordering the full face of a man who looked to be in his thirties.[25]

"Give me the support I've been promised [by Americans] in Jordan," Dark said. The Marines were perplexed. They knew of no specific promises. The sheikh also expressed that he needed his men to be able to carry weapons, and he asked for the release of some tribesmen who had been detained by the Marines.

"What authority do you have to speak for the tribe?" queried Saint One, the military intelligence Marine. He then specifically asked Dark whether he had the support of the paramount sheikh, Khamis. Dark bristled at the question. The American continued probing along these lines, asking the young sheikh about his motivation and placement, while Whisnant silently observed.

"Sheikh Khamis is an old man," came the response. "He doesn't have the will to fight al Qaeda like I do," said Dark. Still, the Marines emphasized that they would need assurances from Khamis about the younger sheikh's authority to speak for the tribe.[26]

Ma'an had considered how he might help deliver what the Americans were requesting. Dark and Khamis weren't close and didn't see eye-to-eye on how to deal with the mujahidin. Khamis was indeed old and careful; he was shrewdly hesitant about the idea of openly declaring war on the radicals and doubted Dark's enthusiasm. Ma'an, however, was favored by the paramount sheikh, his uncle. He could serve as a link between Khamis and Dark, and believed he could even help persuade Khamis to show enough support for his cousin to set in motion a deal with the Americans.[27]

Dark was as eager to work with the Marines as Khamis was hesitant. The young sheikh wanted weapons to destroy the *takfiris* and business contracts to increase his stature within the tribe.[28] As only the fifteenth son of the first son of Sadoun Aifan, the patriarch of the leading family, he lacked the lineage and experience of the paramount sheikh, his other uncles, and several older brothers. At the same time, while birth order is important in Arab tribes, it is not the only thing. Three idealized, traditional virtues signify great men: a sheikh's courage, leadership, and luck (*hadn*). Dark's burning ambition fueled the first two traits. God's will would determine his luck.

A sheikh is also elevated as a leader based on the unspoken criteria of the security and largess he can obtain for the tribe. Dark had a plan to acquire both.[29] He had followed the meteoric rise of Abdul Sattar Abu Risha, an ambitious sheikh to the west, near Ramadi, the capital of Anbar province. Sattar was a relatively young sheikh heading the Abu Risha, a historically minor tribe, but was transforming his cooperation with the Americans and his brave willingness to stand up to al Qaeda into victories against the radicals and rapid advancement for himself and his people. His name rang out in Anbar.

Dark knew Sattar personally and admired his path, while undoubtedly viewing him as a competitor for regional power and business. While some of the Albu Issa had stood up to insurgents at about the same time, Sattar's formation of the Anbar Salvation Council, a confederation against al Qaeda, had obtained license from both the Americans and the government of Iraq to organize and fight. In the near term, Dark hoped to borrow some of Sattar's "emergency response units" for a nearby fight south of Fallujah while building his own local force modeled on the Abu Rishas' example.[30] God willing, he would be the man who killed or drove the hated *irhabiyin* from Fallujah, claiming security and stature. If only the Americans—who bumbled and missed as often as they fought or imprisoned the right people—would let him and his men loose on his enemies. Release some of his detained tribesmen and allow them to openly fight al Qaeda, and the insurgency would be finished. He had to convince the Marines, make them understand. They must act, *now*.[31] That sentiment—expressed in Dark's formal preamble, itemized list of demands, and conclusion—ultimately defined the two-hour meeting. The garrulous young sheikh reminded Whisnant of a phrase from Alec Baldwin's aggressive salesman in the movie *Glengarry Glen Ross:* "A-B-C. *Always* be closing."

"I am tired of waiting. I am tired of sitting around in circles and talking. I want action now," said Dark.[32] The meeting ended with smiles, handshakes, and a cordial agreement to hold a subsequent parley with paramount sheikh Khamis. The Marines gathered their weapons and armor and left the house. Whisnant's security element formed up and spread into a small protective column for the short walk back to the base.

The major had been careful to promise little, only to follow up on the support of radios and weapons allegedly promised by Americans in Jordan. He was too cautious to be overly optimistic, and he couldn't suppress thoughts about the oddness of his situation and the man he had just met. The Reservist Marine officer was worlds away from his civilian life—a Baptist family man from Michigan was cutting midnight deals with an upstart sheikh from a dangerous and ancient tribe rooted in the "Cradle of Civilization."

Whisnant and Saint One compared notes. They both had a good feeling about Dark. He was smart and motivated. The Marines dared to wonder if they had finally found an effective local partner.

"Here is a guy who wants to get something done," Whisnant thought. "Let's hope it pans out."[33]

2

❖ CHASING SHADOWS ❖

The Marines could have used some help over the previous few months. Alpha Company of 1st Battalion, 24th Marine Regiment took over its area of operations on the Fallujah peninsula on October 7, 2006. It did so with resolve, but only limited direction—a missive to improve security and somehow snuff out the local franchise of Iraq's resilient insurgency.[1]

Alpha 1/24 is a Marine Reserve infantry unit based in Grand Rapids, Michigan. It was filled out for this tour by augments from the 3rd Battalion, 24th Marines from Indiana, Missouri, and Tennessee and a smattering of active duty volunteers and Navy corpsmen from across the United States. Its ranks were generally dominated by working- and middle-class young men from the Midwest and a significant minority of hardy Jacksonians from the South. The vast majority attended school or worked civilian jobs, but had joined the Marine Reserves looking for something extra.

For some it was the chance to proudly serve their country or continue a family tradition. Many sought action and adventure, and more than a few wanted to be a part of something that officially minted them as mentally and physically tough. Others had drifted through life before grabbing on to the disciplined structure of the Marine Corps for direction. Some were the sons of immigrants who wanted to pay back the United States for the opportunities afforded their families. A few admitted to being lured into the Corps after falling for the Dress Blue uniform as a kid. One man signed up on a whim, after stopping for Chinese food next to a recruiting station in an airport.

Some of the Marines had previously been on active duty and felt a little out of place in the civilian world, and some needed the extra money that came with two days a month of Reserve duty or the combat pay of deployment. Regardless of the reason, all who volunteered for the Marine Corps shared the perception that they were part of the best, toughest branch of the U.S. armed forces.[2] This reputation, and the ambitious people it attracted, helped define the attitude and quality of Marine Corps recruits. Many proudly believed in a description of the Corps as "America's shock troops." This pride was reinforced by a pervasive, particular culture in the expeditionary service branch. In contrast, Marines thought of the Army as a bloated, pampered institution with more room for hard warriors and soft office workers to coexist without cross-pollinating values. The Marine Corps was smaller and leaner. From the truck drivers derisively nicknamed POGs (pronounced "pogue," persons other than grunts) to the elite Recon warriors, every Marine was somehow touched by an insular culture of macho one-upsmanship and reinforcement of their idealized values: "Every Marine a rifleman." "No better friend, no worse enemy." "Always Faithful" (Semper Fidelis).

There also was an attitude that any given Marine unit would "get shit done." Army units might vary from stellar to awful in the motivation department. To hear Marine grunts tell it, most members of the "blue-side" Navy and all of the Air Force would have issues if they missed a hot meal. But the odds of coming across a pack of hard, motivated men in any group of Marines were a lot better, if admittedly not assured. That said, the Corps also had no shortage of sarcastic generation-Y commentary lampooning the "moto" (stereotypically motivated) ways of true-believing contemporaries and certain squared-away, cigar-chomping superiors appearing to endlessly audition for a recruiting poster. One need not look far for some wise-ass junior Marine poking fun at officers or his fellows' "Oo-rah" mentality, a mockery usually accomplished with a burst of creative profanity. And the unofficial Marine motto of "Improvise, Adapt and Overcome"—a legitimate educational device in a service that relied on hand-me-down equipment from the Army—could be expanded to "Improvise, Adapt, Overcome and Bitch about It the Whole Time."[3] Careful observers weren't fooled by the cynicism, however.

Many Marines could be disillusioned by the infamously soul-killing military bureaucracy or by the political machinations of careerist noncommissioned officers (NCOs) or officers. For them, the superficial idealism was gone. If one scratched a Marine with the most cynical strut, underneath was often a romantic. Most were men who yearned for meaning, and for many, the Corps met that need, whether via a belief in the institution, the development of rare friendships under duress, or the satisfying knowledge that they were going places and doing things that most modern, soft Americans just didn't have the stomach for.[4]

In the macho hierarchy of the Marines, the men of Alpha 1/24 might fall somewhere around the middle of the pack. In their favor, they were infantrymen; the infantry was the military occupation specialty of those who sought spartan hardship and danger as features. They were Reservists, however, a status that sometimes garnered eye rolls and patronizing comments from active duty Marines, who questioned the tactical proficiency and aggressiveness of "weekend warriors."[5]

Jerome Greco, a first lieutenant and commander of Alpha Company's 3rd Platoon, came to reject this stereotype. An active duty Marine who had volunteered to augment 1/24's shortage of officers, he had plenty of experience to render judgment. Greco had previously deployed to Afghanistan as well as Iraq, and had led a rifle platoon during the brutal Second Battle of Fallujah in 2004. Often considered the most difficult of the few set-piece battles during the war, Operation Phantom Fury—also known as al-Fajr (the Dawn) in Arabic—was one of the few engagements to penetrate the American consciousness, through dramatic, extensive media coverage of the campaign. By the time the city was taken, and average Americans' disinterest in news from Iraq had resumed, Phantom Fury had shaped a cadre of young officers like Greco into experienced veterans with an understanding of combat.

As he began to work with his men on their new deployment, Greco discarded the idea that his Reservists were inferior. He came to believe that active duty and Reserve units each had unique advantages. For one, the slight defensiveness about their status seemed to drive his men from 1/24 and 3/24 to excel. They had something to prove to him. In addition, their varying experiences in civilian employment gave some a skill set that let them more naturally adapt to counterinsurgency, which could resemble social work and police duty as much as it required closing with and killing the enemy. A Reservist's advantages were also evident in the company leadership. Greco speculated that Maj. Dan Whisnant's experience as a civilian sales manager granted an intellectual flexibility that helped him juggle demands from higher command and work with difficult local sources from a different culture.

It also didn't hurt to have a major as a company commander, a slot usually filled by a captain. Reserve units often had more-senior officers filling traditional billets, and the gold oak leaves gave Whisnant more influence when he dealt with higher command. Combined with the major's background in Marine intelligence from a previous deployment to Iraq, these traits set the tone for Alpha Company's initial, ambitious, and nominally successful efforts to take a crack at counterinsurgency doctrine (COIN).[6]

The doctrine of COIN comes from a school of military thought that is conceptually simple but achingly complex to execute. The strategy has no shortage of clever slogans to describe it in academic circles filled with professional officers and military studies geeks. It's been likened to "playing three-dimensional chess in the dark while someone is shooting at you," and it sometimes exemplifies the idea of the "three-block war," a pithy description of modern conflict coined by Gen. Charles Krulak in a 1997 speech. Then commandant of the Marine Corps, Krulak was attempting to describe "fourth-generation warfare," which is often carried out in an urban battlefield, by outlining its various demands beyond destroying the enemy. In a conflict like the Iraq War, soldiers and Marines may be called on to wage classic combat on the first block, conduct peacekeeping operations on the next, and deliver humanitarian aid to a third within a matter of hours or even minutes. Some analysts later insisted the "three-block war" analogy was insufficient for describing modern conflict; it needed a few more missions, on a few more blocks.[7]

The complexities of counterinsurgency can be distilled to an even simpler shorthand, however: In COIN, the people are the prize. Insurgencies rely on the ability to blend into, intimidate, and utilize civilian populations. According to the theory, if one can protect the population, kill the "right" people, and provide alternatives more attractive than fighting the government, the rebellion will lose popular support and deprive its fighters of their natural camouflage and freedom of movement. The insurgency will wither on the vine. Easy in theory, hard to execute.[8]

In this type of struggle, information is at least as important as military proficiency. Unfortunately for Alpha Company, it arrived on Fallujah's peninsula with almost none of this vital currency in the bank account. Whisnant quickly directed his platoons to learn about the residents in their area of operations (AO). This effort took the form of security patrols and census operations, so the company was reorganized according to the mission. Marine companies are typically composed of four platoons, each with about thirty-six men split into three squads. Usually, three of these platoons fulfill the role of light infantry, while the fourth is a weapons platoon, dedicated to bring mortars, rockets, and medium machine guns to bear in conventional battles. The operations on the peninsula, however, called for each platoon to be capable of independent operation. Thus Weapons Platoon, which had been assigned to operate from FOB Gold, a forward operating base about a kilometer away from FOB Black, was retasked primarily as light infantry with the option of fulfilling its traditional role as needed.[9]

First Lt. Rob Lehner led 1st Platoon. Like Whisnant, Lehner was a "mustang." He had started his career as an enlisted Marine before his recent promotion to the officer ranks. Company officers and staff NCOs offered generally positive reviews of Lehner's leadership and the resulting performance of his platoon. He was slower to undertake the aggressive intelligence gathering and subsequent operations against the insurgency embraced by two of his peers, but eventually "got up to speed" as the deployment progressed.[10]

The 2nd Platoon was led by GySgt. Brian Ivers. An Australian who had already served two tours in Iraq, Ivers drew criticism, especially from officers and senior NCOs, for hesitating to throw his men into their mission. Some officers speculated that "Gunny Dingo" lacked the initiative instilled in prospective lieutenants during Officer Candidate School. Others gossiped that he was gun-shy after his previous tours. Some Marines, however, especially those under his command, claimed to know the real deal: Ivers was highly competent, even aggressive in combat, but he simply didn't buy into the mission. According to them, the Gunny had lost some men on previous deployments, and he didn't believe in losing more while wandering around like bait, waiting to get shot at.[11]

While all four platoons conducted similar missions and had their share of good and not-so-good officers, NCOs and grunts, 3rd Platoon and Weapons Platoon soon proved themselves company standouts. Led by a pair of ambitious hard chargers—1st Lieutenant Greco at the helm of 3rd and Capt. Jeremy Hoffmann at Weapons—each worked a preternaturally punishing schedule of ambushes, roadblocks, "census ops," and security patrols. Greco was tall, athletic, and had the rough features of a boxer, while Hoffmann was diminutive and youthful-looking and had a higher voice. The pair, however, had a lot in common, including elite educational backgrounds—Greco had attended Dartmouth, Hoffmann the Naval Academy—knowledge of counterinsurgency doctrine, and, above all, aggressiveness. Both men epitomized the Alpha male personality of a Marine officer, and as a consequence, brutally drove their men to "get after it." Some of the lance corporals grumbled bitter jokes about Greco and Hoffmann running a competition to kick more ass and to impress superiors on the backs of their men. The rivalry was reflected in the pair's occasionally brusque interactions at planning sessions. Greco, nicknamed "Greco Fury" for his intensity during volleyball matches prior to deployment, caught wind of the "dueling platoon commanders" scuttlebutt, and told his men it was ridiculous. The enlisted Marines under Greco's and Hoffmann's command didn't consider their leaders' competition reckless. Most had no doubt that the pair would have worked them like mules anyway, regardless of any officers' pissing contest. But the young Marines also didn't quite buy Greco's denial, mostly because they had their own rivalries with enlisted counterparts in the sister platoons. Some exchanges were typical:

"How long were you pussies on long ops? We were out for weeks."

"Hey, we just walked 28 fucking clicks today. . . . How far did *you* go on that patrol?"[12]

Ongoing critiques of Greco were also mitigated by the fact that he worked as hard as his men did. He impressed his squad leaders by regularly joining them on patrols and sometimes exposing himself to dangerous situations in place of others. In one case, Greco took point on a foot expedition to find an IED known to be buried in a certain area. The lieutenant found the wires of the hidden bomb while scratching in the dirt with his Leatherman tool and could have been killed by an alert insurgent manning its trigger. Enlisted and NCO ranks always subject officers to harsh appraisal, but actions like these earn valuable credibility.[13]

Hoffmann was commonly regarded, and often critiqued, as something of a merciless hard-ass. The captain was also considered smart and hardworking, and he was an enthusiastic student of counterinsurgency. He repeatedly stressed two goals to his men, the latter explaining why he worked them so hard: First, their success was contingent on getting to know, respect, and protect the people in their area. Second, they would deny the insurgents any rest or safe haven on the peninsula, even if his Marines had to walk fifteen miles a day to do it.[14]

The operational pace was brutal: up to twenty hours a day (on missions), six and a half days a week, for months, with little downtime. All four platoons divided their time between "short ops," within walking distance of their forward operating base (FOB), and "long ops." Short ops usually consisted of foot patrols, running overwatch on the main supply routes to prevent emplacement of bombs, launching targeted raids, and serving as a quick reaction force (QRF) to assist any Marines in trouble. On long ops, a platoon would travel far afield of the FOB, setting up a temporary patrol base in whatever commandeered local structure had the requisite defensive capabilities. Each of a platoon's three squads would then rotate through a schedule of conducting patrols, manning ad hoc checkpoints, protecting the patrol base, and sleeping on cement floors, a respite that seldom exceeded four or five hours at a time. Census ops became the cornerstone of Whisnant's information-gathering campaign during the longer outings. Marines would project into a village and introduce themselves, asking civilians a half dozen mostly fruitless questions about who and where the bad guys were.[15]

Sgt. Christopher Dockter quickly grew frustrated by the question-and-answer sessions with local villagers although by most accounts he was a patient man. The leader of 3rd Platoon's 2nd Squad, Dockter had been dubbed "Manbearpig," after the chimerical beast from the show *South Park*. The unflattering nickname, along with a second one, "Lunchbox," were his men's tribute to the dark-eyed squad leader's hairy girth. The laconic Tennessean took it in stride. Dockter was a volunteer who had requested deployment to watch over younger augments from his home unit of Reservists with 3/24, and he knew that few Marines could expect to escape deployment without a rude nickname or two.

The newly married twenty-six-year-old's easygoing nature permeated his management style. Only rarely did Dockter yell, barking at his guys when he had no time to baby the naturally unruly nineteen- and twenty-year-old PFCs and lance corporals. Usually he would ignore his men's endless complaints about whatever facet of the "colossal suck" of being in Iraq had drawn their ire. After all, according to him, "Marines ain't happy unless they're bitching."

Sometimes, however, Dockter took the time to outline the rationale behind orders when the youngsters bucked, because enlisteds often gripe due to being kept in the dark. The most common response offered by a lance corporal when asked why he was doing something was a blank stare followed by, "Because Gunny told me." Dockter found that by occasionally explaining important things to them, he could get the men to quiet down and perform even the most difficult or boring tasks with workmanlike efficiency.[16]

Indeed, the sergeant's unusual patience, along with requisite tactical proficiency, made him a well-liked squad leader in the company. But even this southerner's laid-back temperament was sorely tested by a legion of Fallujan farmers in the early months of the company's deployment. His interviews with them often resembled an exotically exasperating rendition of Abbot and Costello's "Who's on first?" comedy routine.[17]

Greco would direct Dockter's squad to move into a village and go from house to house, knocking on doors like heavily armed vacuum cleaner salesmen. They would conduct a light search of the residence, followed by an interview. Dockter took pictures of all military-age males, and then he would launch into a prepared set of questions, sometimes with the aid of an interpreter, other times without one. A typical interview might go as follows:

> "What is your name?"
> —*So far, so good. This typically yielded names.*
>
> "Who lives here? Who exactly is in your family?"
> —*Complete answers to this question were hit or miss.*
>
> "Do you need anything? What can we do to help?"
> —*Local residents had no problem offering up a list of complaints about the economy, infrastructure, and especially security.*
>
> "If you want us to help you with security, you need to tell me who Ali Baba [Marine slang for "the bad guy"] is. Do you know anyone bad in the area? Who's bad?"
> —*Here the interview would hit the wall.*
>
> "Do you know anyone putting bombs in the area or fighting Americans?"
> —*The answer to this question was usually, "No one bad lives around here, the bad guys are all from [insert random village or city]."*

If Dockter got lucky, he would be entertained by garnishment with a fanciful story. The sergeant would then try to reason:

> "We want to make things safer for you, but we can't help you unless you help us."
> —*The response was usually polite smiles, shrugs, and no dice.*[18]

After a couple of weeks of frustrating census ops and near-daily contact with insurgents slinging mortars, bombs, and small-arms fire, LCpl.

Alan Webster would become the first Marine in the platoon to be wounded. A sniper shot him just above the knee, shattering his leg and stealing vital muscle. It was an injury that would initiate a years-long odyssey of surgeries and rehabilitation in the young man's quest to regain full mobility.[19] In response to the shooting, an angry Greco ordered his men to start confiscating all the weapons in the area of the attack, a move that contradicted the usual regulations allowing each family to keep one rifle to guard their home. During the confiscations, some of the exchanges became contentious. A middle-aged farmer argued animatedly as Dockter took his AK-47: "He asked 'How am I supposed to defend myself and my family?'" said an interpreter, distilling the agitated flurry of Arabic. "Tell him that when he starts using it to fight Ali Baba, we'll give it back," responded Dockter.

This generated one of the more original reactions the sergeant encountered in his conversations with the locals. The sun-wizened resident of the Albu Aifan village looked stunned as he listened to the interpreter's translation. He turned toward Dockter with a face that seemed to indicate that the idea had never occurred to him.[20] In retrospect, the farmer probably never thought the Marines would *let him* fight Ali Baba without shooting or imprisoning him for brandishing his rifle outside his house. And in a few months, it would be Dockter's turn to be shocked, as he and his men handed these weapons back, and provided additional ones, to the people of the village.[21]

Some American-Iraqi miscommunication was inevitable. Arabic speakers have unique linguistic traditions. Carefully crafted metaphors and eloquence are often intimately tied to an individual's identity, though expression widely varies with a speaker's background and education. Arabic's lyrical phonetics and grammar can make even everyday conversation resemble poetry, with exaggerations and allusions popularly exemplified by Saddam Hussein's exhortation to fight the "Mother of all Battles" during the Persian Gulf War. These flourishes and stretches, coupled with what often seems like a winding, circular path toward a point, do not always translate well into English, especially into the American "dialect" spoken by military men, who value plain answers to blunt questions. To many Arabic speakers, the rhetorical journey *is* sometimes the point. These cultural differences can result in poor communication and misunderstanding, depending on the sensitivities of the Arabic and English speakers, and the skill of their interpreter.[22]

Alpha Company's interviews were usually hampered by something a lot simpler and more powerful than linguistics, however: the survival instinct. The lack of helpful information from everyday citizens was intentional. While the population included some hard-core insurgents and many more casual rebels for hire, the majority of residents were generally neutral noncombatants. Many of them had soured on rooting for the splintered insurgency against the invaders, and even a few rare souls were inclined to support the Iraqi security forces or deal with the Americans. But with the exception of hardened criminals and radical fighters, first and foremost, most Fallujans were intimidated survivalists.

Some of the hard-core insurgents—most of whom were local men between the ages of sixteen and forty along with a minority of foreign fighters—had a penchant for shocking criminality and barbarism. If a collaborator with the Americans was lucky, his or her discovery meant violent death by a simple explosion or a bullet to the head. Often, the punishment was more gruesome. Beheading, dismemberment, torture with drills or acid, or being burned alive were some of the brutalities that potentially awaited those caught cooperating with the infidels—anything to make the point. Innocent family members, including children, could be targets.

The Americans could come through a house for a few minutes and ask their questions, but after they left, who would be there to protect anyone who cooperated? Even if a tip led to the arrest of a local criminal, there was no guarantee that "Ali Baba" wouldn't be released from prison in as little as a few months or a year. And when the bad guys came back, they came back hard, exacting revenge on as many people as necessary to be satisfied that the rat had been killed, and others had learned the lesson. Given a choice between a potentially torturous death and helping Americans who didn't stick around to protect anyone, it wasn't much of a choice at all.[23]

Even so, the men of Alpha 1/24 were angry and frustrated when a buried roadside bomb made from two massive 155-mm howitzer shells exploded in the midst of one of their convoys, and a dozen or so locals living yards away would swear that they knew nothing about who had laid the elaborate trap.[24] Greco tried to mitigate his Marines' frustration by telling them to "put [themselves] in the [Iraqis'] shoes" and to imagine what they had been through in the past three years. Above all, most civilians merely wanted to survive, and helping Americans had proven to be a terrible survival strategy.[25]

The most useful information gleaned from the early census ops were names, which fed a database designed to track and identify insurgents and their families, distinguishing them from the rest of the population. Though the database failed to yield quick results, it would pay dividends down the road.[26]

To compensate for the scarcity of local support and the slow pace of the census ops, Alpha Company also launched an offensive relying on aggressive "paper shuffling." Whisnant and his platoon commanders combed through old intelligence reports filed by "human intelligence exploitation teams" that on earlier deployments had run sources and "targeting packages" against "high value individuals" in the area. This wasn't standard operating procedure for all units; there was sometimes a disconnect between the archived work of the intelligence specialists and units running ops on the ground. Whisnant's background as an intel officer, however, and the utter lack of local cooperation naturally led him to grasp at the reports; Hoffmann and Greco immediately recognized their value and enthusiastically joined the effort. The officers would comb the old reports to find names and locations of identified insurgents and propose and execute raids to snatch a suspect or simply knock on a man's door to ask questions.

The success of these efforts without local help was measurable, but limited. In the early months of Alpha Company's deployment, only one or two of every ten raids led to the detention of a legitimate insurgent or to actionable intelligence.[27] And while some, though not all, of the Marines attempted to show respect for the occupants of targeted houses, tossing someone's home with a no-knock raid in the dead of night inevitably angered civilians. In a tribal society, this insult demanded redress or invited revenge.[28]

The question that nagged at the Marines was whether they were making more progress than any damage caused by their presence. It was hard to say whether their efforts were diminishing or fanning the peninsula's insurgency, especially since they had been getting shot at and blown up almost since their first day in country.[29] This violence, coupled with the seeming apathy of local civilians, made it feel like they were starting at zero. It was hard for some Americans to fathom how they could make things much worse.

Of everything that confronted Greco on this deployment, the volume of attacks was the biggest surprise of his new command. He thought he had seen the worst possible violence during the brutal urban house clearing of Operation Phantom Fury, but this tour on Fallujah's southern peninsula had its own twists on war. His men were getting engaged regularly by small arms and mortars, and the roads were studded with hidden bombs. The IED booby traps were the biggest threat to his Marines, showcasing the irrepressible and deadly creativity of the insurgents who wanted to kill them.[30]

On October 25, Alpha Company lost its first Marines. LCpl. Jonathan Thornsberry and Sgt. Tommy Gilbert of Greco's 1st Squad were killed instantly when their Humvee drove over an IED. A massive artillery shell had been buried in the middle of the road and rigged with small, bulbous trigger mechanisms nicknamed "Christmas lights." LCpl. Brad Bueno was blown twenty feet from the Humvee's turret and was medevaced with a broken leg.

Thornsberry had been a dependable "good country boy" from Tennessee.[31] He had always made it a point to look after his fellow Marines' comfort and constantly bragged about his young daughter. Gilbert was a twenty-four-year-old raised in middle-class Illinois. He liked to go out drinking with his buddies, but would sit quietly in a corner, sipping a Jameson's whiskey and reading a newspaper while his friends raised hell around him. Gilbert would just smile and shake his head occasionally or stop what he was doing to drag them out of whatever trouble required his undivided attention. The company took their deaths hard.[32] These losses happened only three weeks into the deployment, and there would surely be more casualties to come.[33] The Marines grieved, but moved on with their work.

From day one, seeking out this violence was a component of attempts to defeat the enemy. The routine was simple: leave the FOB or ad hoc patrol base; get attacked while conducting a mission; fix, counterattack, and kill the enemy. Some reactive posture was inevitable when fighting an insurgency. It was dangerous work.[34]

3

❖ COIN ❖

Sgt. David Kopera's men moved in zigzag formation through a lush field on the edge of Albu Aifan village. Barely midmorning on November 4, 2006, the strong Fallujan sun warmed the dry ground and desert air. Sweat ran down the men's torsos under heavy armor and equipment, applying a fresh coat of grimy ochre stain to their faded brown Kevlar vests. The Marines had good dispersion but little cover among the leafy green shoots that brushed their shins and stood in uneven clumps atop grayish-brown sandy soil.

Kopera had deployed his undermanned squad—those who remained after the loss of Tommy Gilbert, Jonathan Thornsberry, and Brad Bueno on October 25—into two staggered columns. Ruben "Doc" Muñoz, the medical corpsman, trailed about fifteen feet behind the squad leader. Kopera's team methodically approached the backyards of a cluster of muted tan, concrete-block houses lining a main road. Cpl. Matthew Zofchak's second team traveled along the edge of the field, parallel with them, less than one hundred meters to the southeast.[1] As the Marines moved along, they saw a robed woman and a teenage girl harvesting a crop along a deep irrigation ditch.[2] Nearly twenty meters from the village, Kopera's world erupted.

Incoming bullets rent the air with cracks; the muffled sound of rounds churning the ground around him mixed with the stuttering of at least two RPK light machine guns and the chatter of AK-47s.[3] The crackling boom of a rocket-propelled grenade (RPG) echoed from somewhere to the left.[4] The rounds were landing so close that Kopera knew they were shooting right at him. Exposed in the open field, he had to move. The sergeant sprinted to a concrete outhouse in the backyard of the nearest house.[5]

When the shooting began, Doc Muñoz had been looking at the ground in order to carefully choose his footing in the field's sinking, uneven soil. His worries about twisting an ankle evaporated when he saw the powdery dirt begin to hop, and the air around his ears exploded with the familiar sound of flying metal shredding the sound barrier. Ahead, he saw small puffs silhouette Kopera as the rounds landed. It was obvious to him that they were targeting his team leader, who had a prominent radio antennae jutting skyward from his back. "God! That's close!" Muñoz later recalled thinking.[6]

The corpsman hit the ground hard, crawling for cover behind a small berm that rose less than a foot above the rest of the field. He raised his weapon to return fire and willed himself small as bullets zipped around him. He saw Kopera make a play for the outhouse. "Shit, that's a better idea," he thought. "I have to get the hell out of here. . . . My luck is going to run out." Adrenaline surged through his body, lifting him off the ground and into a pell-mell sprint for safety as rounds slapped around him. He leaped behind the outhouse, joining Kopera with a thud as the ceramic plate in his carrying vest smacked the concrete wall.[7] In the first few seconds of the engagement, it seemed like hundreds of rounds had hit in a terrifyingly close cluster around the two men. Even though it was clear the attackers knew how to shoot better than most of the others the Marines had run into, they somehow had missed. The insurgents maintained their fire, with bullets chipping the concrete structures in front of the pair.[8]

Kopera tried to get a handle on the situation. The members of his squad that he could see had found good cover behind a house. He then tried to figure out where the fire was coming from. About 125 or 150 meters to the southwest stood a group of low buildings fronting a single-story peach-colored mosque. Peeking around the outhouse, Kopera spotted muzzle flashes above the low walls bordering the roof of one or two of the buildings.[9] "The fire is coming from that side," he told Muñoz, pointing. After unsuccessfully trying to raise his other team on the radio, Kopera and the corpsman started returning fire.[10]

Before "the shit hit the fan," Cpl. Matthew Zofchak had been walking along the raised berm of the wide irrigation ditch bordering the field. His team was moving to the right of the watery trench in a staggered southwest-northeast column spread out over ninety meters. Only Sgt. Caleb Inman, an artilleryman and truck driver who had volunteered to augment the undermanned infantry squad on this patrol, was close to Zofchak.[11] Although Inman had

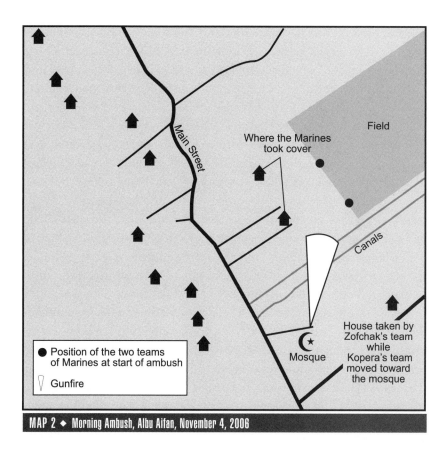

Field

Where the Marines
took cover

Main Street

Canals

House taken by
Zofchak's team
while
Kopera's team
moved toward
the mosque

Mosque

● Position of the two teams
of Marines at start of ambush

▽ Gunfire

MAP 2 ◆ Morning Ambush, Albu Aifan, November 4, 2006

already served a 2004 tour in Fallujah, non-infantry augments were always assigned to a team leader, who would closely watch their performance. Zofchak drew the assignment. They were walking in tandem, less than ten meters apart, while LCpl. Eddie O'Connor, the squad's lone machine gunner, pulled "tail-end Charlie" at the rear of the formation.[12] Zofchak took advantage of Inman's proximity, joking that the twenty-five-year-old Texan was a "damned POG [person other than grunt]." Then the crack of small-arms fire pierced the air.[13]

Zofchak and the others hit the ground as rounds began landing near them. The woman and her daughter who had been working in the field bolted for the cover of a house.[14] Zofchak saw a distant Muñoz and Kopera get up off the deck and do "the chicken little dance" as they ran through incoming bullets to the safety of the concrete outhouse. Zofchak and Inman watched bursts of dirt spring into the air maybe a dozen feet away. The loud crumple of an explosion washed over the pair of Marines. An RPG had overshot them and landed nearby. O'Connor saw the rocket explode near the two men, front and to the left of him, as he took cover behind a mound of dirt.[15] Zofchak and Inman looked at each other incredulously, momentarily stunned by the sudden explosion. Zofchak's surprise mutated to anger. The corporal took to a knee and oriented himself south toward the attackers, looking for a target through a tangle of reeds that lined the canal.[16] "Hey, Tyink! Tyink!" Inman yelled to Cpl. Andrew Tyink, the man ahead of him in the column. For some reason, the prone Marine, another augment, this one from the company's intelligence cell, didn't answer. Tyink raised his weapon and started firing off rounds at a target.[17]

Zofchak shouldered his rifle and scanned for the source of the fire through his advanced combat optical gunsight. He spotted movement on the top floor of a low building maybe twenty degrees to the left of the mosque. He thought he saw a man briefly profiled above the low wall bordering the roof. The corporal fired off a quick couplet of rounds toward the target to try and suppress any attackers.[18] "What are you firing at?" yelled Inman from his newfound cover behind a narrow tree alongside the ditch. The trunk's three- or four-foot radius had barely obscured his body. Bits of foliage fell as bullets whipped through the cattails covering the trench. Inman soon thought he gained "positive identification" (PID) of a target, and he fired back as well.[19]

Zofchak looked for the rest of his team. LCpl. Scott Serr had been near the head of the southern column when the gunfire erupted and quickly crouched behind one of the brick ovens found in the backyard of many residences.[20] Others had sprinted or were now sprinting forward for the cover of the nearest house at the back of the village.[21] After getting his bearings behind the oven, Serr moved inside one of the houses to look for a concealed angle of return fire.

Zofchak soon made out muzzle flashes next to the mosque, raised his weapon and fired maybe three to five rounds. He then pulled out a 40-mm grenade from his ammunition harness and loaded it into the M-203 launcher slung under the barrel of his rifle.[22] He shot two grenades at the structure. After gaining PID and "going trigger happy," Zofchak, Inman, and O'Connor executed a bounding leapfrog movement toward the rest of their team behind the house, using the cover of the trees and a raised berm next to the ditch.[23]

Still behind the outhouse, Kopera could not see Zofchak and his team, who were closer to the attackers. He suspected the raised profile of the canal's berm and cattails must have screened them from the clear view of the insurgents as well. He failed to raise them on his radio, but soon heard the high-pitched, nearer banging of their M-16s mingle with the throaty chatter of RPKs and AK-47s. The pressure on Kopera's position lessened as some of the insurgents shifted their fire to the other group of Marines. Another RPG whooshed and exploded to his southeast.[24]

Whoomp! His second team had started slinging grenades onto the insurgent position. Kopera again peeked at the enemy. He thought he glimpsed tiny figures crawling to their feet, running, and then dropping over the opposite side of the lower roof of a building. Two "40 mike-mikes" (grenades) had sealed it. The attackers seemed to be retreating. Kopera moved his group southeast to consolidate the squad. Sporadic outgoing fire continued as they moved toward the other Marines. The firefight only lasted a couple of minutes at most, but to some it felt like ten, to others about one. It "was one of those things that could have been two seconds or twenty minutes," O'Connor said, recalling how adrenaline had warped his sense of time.[25]

Kopera had allowed himself a brief moment of pride in his Marines' performance. Zofchak's team had taken initiative, quickly grabbing cover and gaining "fire superiority" by dousing the enemy with bullets and grenades. The appraisal was brief, however. Kopera's mind returned quickly to the task at hand. He felt alert, but fought a sick feeling in the pit of his stomach. At least one RPG had landed close to his second team, and someone on his side of the formation had speculated that a Marine had been injured.[26] The squad leader had been unable to raise them on the walkie-talkie, but once the squad was consolidated, he was relieved to discover that everyone was OK.[27]

The Marines had been surprised, with several of them caught in the open. More than a hundred rounds had hit within feet, even inches, of Kopera and Muñoz. At least one of the exploded RPGs had flung its cloud of shrapnel just a few meters from Zofchak and Inman. None of the Americans were injured, but one of the Marines told the others that he had seen the attackers "pulling wounded with them" when they retreated.[28] The squad leader had little time to bask in relief or contemplate the vagaries of fate. He successfully radioed Lt. Jerome Greco back at the patrol base, reporting that the enemy had broken contact, and his Marines were moving in pursuit along the main road.[29]

A kilometer and a half away at the patrol base, Greco was concerned but pleased with the performance of his squad leader. Kopera already had proven himself in garrison and under fire. Somewhat of a "profane intellectual," the lanky sergeant was reliably sarcastic but turned serious when it came time to run his teams. Having now experienced what sounded like his first sustained contact (relatively speaking), the sergeant was calmly telling his platoon leader what he planned to do, rather than asking for instructions. Greco liked the initiative. His sergeant was getting after it.[30]

The Americans didn't know it at the time, but intelligence sources later revealed that one of at least six insurgents had been wounded, and another, a member of the Abu Yousseff subtribe largely based in an area south of the village, had been killed by the Marines' return fire. The dead attacker's compatriots had withdrawn to remove his body and lick their wounds. Islamic tradition stresses that the dead receive a proper, ritual burial as soon as possible. Muslim fighters and even noncombatants strive to fulfill this sacred mandate, snatching up and carting off bodies in the middle of terrible fighting. Some Americans grudgingly admired their opponents' efficiency at recovering the dead, a cultural sensibility that resembled their own ethos of "leave no man behind."[31]

Occurring after the Marines had barely been in country for a month, this engagement was a first for most of them in its immediacy and duration.[32] The insurgents had learned painful lessons from the all-out frontal melees waged against the U.S. military during the early phases of the war. Blood-soaked blankets filled with dead insurgents had been stacked in grim piles in front of the mosques of Fallujah and Ramadi during the battles of 2004.[33] Most serious rebels were either clever or dead, and the smarter ones had adapted by shunning stand-up fights in favor of more tentative guerrilla tactics.

By late 2006, the peninsula's insurgents were usually engaging Kopera's men from at least two hundred yards out, if not more, and would then pull back immediately after the initial volley. Marines called it the "shoot and scoot." This attack in the field had been mildly sustained and had been launched from little more than a football field away, causing Kopera to speculate that either they had run across a particularly brave group of jihadists or the sudden appearance of the Marines had surprised them.[34]

Before issuing orders, Kopera instructed his squad members to quickly brief him on what they had seen and to check their ammunition and equipment. His team would head south, along the main road splitting the village, for a direct assault toward the mosque and the lower row of buildings in front of it that may have housed some of the attackers.[35] Zofchak's team was to move along behind the backyards of the homes on the eastern side of the road and commandeer a house to the side of the mosque. The position offered fields of fire that would cut off the enemy's escape if the main assault drove them to flee toward the network of irrigation ditches that crisscrossed the fields. Zofchak's team would serve as an anvil for Kopera's hammer. The Marines moved out.[36]

Zofchak's route offered the better cover and was supposed to get his team into position faster than the other team, but it also involved crossing two seemingly small irrigation creeks. Unfortunately for the Marines, the roughly three-foot-wide trenches held water four to five feet deep, were covered in cattails, and had mushy bottoms of thick sticky mud.[37] The men grunted or yelled in surprise as they plunged into the ditches, thrashing and churning their legs across the grasping bottom. At least one of the Marines lost his footing and went under. Inman became angry when his cigarettes got soaked.[38] "Fucking Zofchak," several muttered in disapproval of their leader's navigational decision.[39] Some seventy-five meters that should have taken less than a minute to travel took several. After emerging from the steep bank of the second channel and finding firm footing, the five muddy Marines hustled for their destination—a tan, two-story house that offered fields of fire over the likely escape routes from the mosque.

The team lined up in a wet "stack" in front of a door before rushing inside the house. The wet clomp of boots was met by high-pitched screams from the women and children inside—three little girls between the ages of four and eleven, three middle-aged women, and two elderly women, the latter of whom wore conservative black robes and head coverings. The Marines fanned out past them and throughout the house to look for threats. Some of the Iraqis cried or screamed as they were herded into the house's main room. The muzzles came down. The weathered, older women, whom the Russian American Zofchak referred to as "babushkas," moved forward. The eldest female quietly confronted the invaders with a look that was at once confused, scared, and resigned.[40] The Marines tried to calm the kids because "they were freaking out."[41]

Zofchak attempted to communicate with calming hand gestures and stilted Arabic. "Ali Baba [bad guys]?" The older babushka looked at him, shook her head, and said, "Laa Ali Baba. Laa Ali Baba" (No Ali Baba). Zofchak felt bad for kicking in their door and frightening them, but didn't give it a lot of thought. They needed this house, and that was that. Eventually the civilians quieted to a state of wary alarm. With the residence secured, one of the Marines was assigned to watch over the women and children clustered in the main room while the rest of the team deployed around the property. The kids were "glued to the women's hips." The women remained standing and quietly murmured to each other as they kept an eye on the wet, dirty Americans.[42]

❖

Nearby, Kopera's team of Marines had been rushing in accordion-like bounds across the front yards of homes lining the road during their move to the mosque. A group of two would run from the safety of one residence to the next under the cover of the others' poised weapons. Along the way, half the team was put on a rooftop for lookout, while the other Marines quickly bounced in and out of the low tan and gray residences, conducting cursory searches and asking the occupants about the insurgents.[43]

Most of the local men were typically out and about at mid-morning. The Marines encountered a smattering of old folks; women of varying ages cooking, folding laundry, or doing yard work; and children sitting inside waiting out the gunfire. Reactions to battles in the community varied, but to the Americans, Iraqis could be a strange bunch.[44] When firefights broke out, as long as the bullets weren't directed at them, many families would ignore it or move inside, but then quickly return to hanging clothes or performing whatever chores had been interrupted by the sounds of explosions or rifles. Many were used to this: Whatever God willed—*insh'allah*.[45]

Whether it was bravery, Arab world fatalism, or something else that drove the Iraqis to carry on, Kopera admired and sympathized with them. His men tried to show respect in their dealings with the locals and executed what he thought of as well-considered rules of engagement and detainee-handling procedures. But no amount of good intentions and careful execution could blunt the terror of war and the disruption to their way of life, perhaps especially for Iraq's politically displaced Sunni minority. Kopera thought Americans should try to imagine how they would feel if a superpower invaded the United States and dismantled the government, directly or indirectly causing the deaths of tens of thousands of fellow citizens.

Complicating matters were the tragedies, abuses, mistakes, and public relations disasters since the 2003 invasion that had consumed the local consciousness. The stories of prisoner abuse at Abu Ghraib, the confused shooting of Iraqis during a protest outside the Fallujah Government Center on April 28, 2003, and other terrible stories were told and retold, often with embellishment, while the Americans' acts of kindness and attempts to establish security were little acknowledged, poorly understood, or overlooked. It seemed that the good the Marines and others tried to do had little chance of competing for a place in the narrative.

On top of that, the tempo of rougher operations, including raids and mass detentions of military-age males, had been especially high in the early years of the war, as the U.S. military reacted forcefully to the growing insurgency. If an American unit had treated locals with disrespect, and some had, it made Kopera's job exponentially harder. This was especially true in the context of a tribal society that demanded restitution, or revenge, for an insult. The challenges could be depressing, but they were simply the products of culture and human nature. These were facts Kopera understood, even as he struggled with them.

Kopera had come to respect Iraqis' way of life, even to admire them. The heritage of the Middle East dates back thousands of years, he mused, and there was a decency in most Iraqis' personal standards and civility, even to invaders. Kopera could go to a restaurant as a paying customer back in the States and find the hospitality worse than what he experienced after forcing himself into the house of a surprised Iraqi, abruptly face-to-face with Marines bristling with helmets, armor, antennae and weapons. If only he could somehow show other Americans what was happening in Iraq. Let them walk in Iraqi shoes for a minute, and they might want to help these people too.

Fallujan tribal society is based on the concepts of shame and honor. Everyone must live by a code. As a Marine, the thirty-year-old Kopera understood the idea. He had joined the Corps while attending community college in 2000. An avid painter, he had dropped out of art school after deciding he didn't want to try to make a living as an artist, opting instead for a more practical associate's degree in auto repair technology. He ran into a military recruiter while drifting through a couple of courses and living week to week on his modest income working a few shifts at a restaurant. Patriotism was part of it, sure. But he also didn't really have a plan and craved direction, something military life offered in abundance. Kopera chose the Marine Corps, figuring that if he was going to take such a drastic step as joining the armed services, he might as well go with the toughest branch. He also liked the Marine Corps ideals. It demanded high standards of physical fitness, training, and personal discipline, and the challenge of achieving something noble and difficult appealed to him. Kopera wanted his own code.

Six years in the Marines had mostly validated his choice. Yeah, it was tough, and there were occasional disappointments. One of them was that some of Alpha Company's Marines had opted out of the tour in Fallujah after a short-lived order stipulated that Reservists who had already deployed in support of Iraq or Afghanistan could not be forced to deploy again. His battalion had already conducted a quiet rotation in a combat zone, pulling security on a Special Forces base in Djibouti. Although the majority of the men from Alpha Company 1/24 had embarked on this subsequent, far more dangerous trip to Iraq, about twenty-five Marines had taken advantage of the decree and declined deployment. Kopera was shocked that the government would let members of the service "cop out like that," go back to college or do whatever they pleased. "When you join the armed services, you swear an oath to serve a time commitment and do your job, regardless of personal" preference, he thought. For someone to voluntarily sit back and watch fellow Marines go off to a combat zone—"with some of them almost certainly coming back in a pine box"—was anathema to Kopera.[46] The great whys and hows of the invasion of Iraq hovered distantly outside of his job description, which at the moment simply consisted of finding and killing the insurgents who had just tried to kill him.[47]

Many of the locals Kopera interviewed on the way to the mosque were less than helpful. In most of the eight or nine houses they briefly searched during roughly twenty minutes, the eldest woman would come forward to meet them, answer questions, and then shadow the Marines as they quickly peeked inside her house to look for insurgents, bullet casings, weapons, or blood trails.[48] Almost none of the civilians testified to having seen much of anything. Toward the end of their movement, an old man proved to be an exception by providing a lead.[49]

The witness told the Marines that he had seen the ambush party—five young men who weren't from the village. The attackers had fled the buildings around the mosque in two cars, traveling south. Kopera thought the man seemed genuinely agitated by outsiders picking gunfights with Marines in the middle of his village; he probably didn't want Americans to blame his neighbors and come down hard on anyone.[50] The Iraqi's stooped shoulders and wrinkled face also conferred that elderly aura of just not giving a damn. He seemed to disregard the possible consequences of feeding actionable information to the Americans. Kopera bought the man's story.[51]

Widely dispersed and moving briskly, his men soon arrived at their target, the al-Shahid mosque. The small, single-story building whose name translates as the "witness" or the "martyr," was surrounded by a low wall and a southern border of trees that blocked the view of an open field behind it. The simple concrete edifice was covered with stucco and a fading coat of light peach paint. On the roof was a small square turret crowned with speakers.[52]

The team had taken no gunfire during their movement toward the building. It seemed that the insurgents had fled. The sergeant consolidated his squad a second time and consulted with Zofchak when he reached the mosque. Members of the squad thought that the insurgents might have been shooting from behind the low wall that edged the roof and from the reeds in a field next to the building.[53] But standard operating procedure stipulated that unless taking direct fire from a holy site, Americans couldn't set foot on the grounds, much less search the interior. Procedure also dictated calling headquarters and asking for Muslims from an Iraqi Army unit to come to the village and case the structure. That might take hours, however, and the Marines did not trust the Iraqi Army units anyway.[54]

Zofchak's blood was up, and he wanted his prey, which might be hiding, or dead, inside the mosque. His thought process consisted of an equation involving three parts adrenaline, plus three parts "We need to investigate," minus four parts "Shit, we can't go in there, otherwise our ass is grass." He did the math and concluded, "I don't care if it's a mosque, I want to go."[55] Kopera wrestled briefly with what to do. He weighed the politics but ultimately decided he didn't have time to call for an Iraqi unit if he was going to find any trace of the insurgents. "Fuck it, I'm jumping," said the sergeant.[56]

Without informing his platoon leader, Kopera opted to split the difference by climbing the mosque's exterior staircase to look for shell casings on the roof, thus avoiding setting foot inside the building itself. He leapt over the courtyard wall and bounded up the stone stairs, but found no rebels or remnants of their presence on the roof. At the top, Kopera peeked through an upper window to verify that no attackers were hiding inside. He scampered back to the ground. The Marines found a few bullet casings on a road by the mosque, but it looked like the locals had already mostly picked the scene clean of brass, and the ambushers had made their getaway.[57]

Kopera formulated a new plan and informed Greco: His squad would move south to the abandoned house of a wealthy sheikh that stood on the well-traveled intersection of Water Tower and Main Street. They would run a roadblock along the heavily trafficked thoroughfare and, with any luck, catch the insurgents if they were dumb enough to move back through the area.[58] First Squad formed up and moved out along the front yards lining the road, ready to duck quickly behind the courtyard walls if they were engaged a second time.

They approached the sheikh's white, tan, and peach house, a large, lavish structure surrounded by a high elliptical wall on three sides and a thick row of hedges on one. The wall of the front courtyard was split by a wide, sloping driveway, and the roof was blessed with the standard low wall, which gave great cover while Marines capitalized on panoramic views from the unusually high third story. The residence resembled a mix between a small fortress and one of the stylized theme restaurants that dot the fancier strip malls of south Florida and California.[59]

Kopera ordered the majority of his squad and the Navy corpsman into the house to begin overwatch and get a Squad Automatic Weapon (SAW), a general purpose machine gun capable of laying down a steady wall of suppressive fire, set up on the roof. Meanwhile, Kopera, Inman, and Serr moved to initiate a "snap vehicle control point" at the intersection.

Almost immediately, a sedan with three young men drove toward their position from the southwest.[60] The Marines snapped up their weapons and "drew down on them." The car and its occupants matched the old man's general description of the attackers—sedan filled with young males. Kopera waved at the car to stop and looked at the men, searching their faces for signs of aggression. No visible weapons, and something in their manner clicked with the sergeant. He made an instinctive decision that they were of no immediate threat. Such snap judgment calls about who might be trying to hurt you, and over life or death itself, were played out millions of times across Iraq as coalition forces struggled to find the balance between self-preservation and sparing the innocent. Outcomes were varied, and sometimes tragic.

Despite having been terrifyingly ambushed less than twenty minutes before, now conducting a hunt for his attackers, and seeing a car whose make, color, and occupants roughly matched a witness's description of the insurgents, Kopera made the accurate call and eased off the trigger. He cautiously moved to search and speak with the young men. When the Iraqis exited the car, however, Inman didn't like their attitude. To him they seemed too jovial, almost taunting, as the Marines searched the vehicle and found nothing. The trunk was empty but fresh grass and soil were scattered about it. Something about that and the men's cocky demeanor struck Inman as "not right." But a hunch was insufficient evidence. The men had no weapons, explosives, or other contraband.[61] Serr disagreed with Inman's take on the situation. He thought Inman was "still pissed" about the previous firefight and therefore took the Iraqis' casual attitude as a threat or perhaps a sign that they "knew something we didn't." Serr's instincts told him the men had no knowledge of the shooting.

Meanwhile, O'Connor and another Marine had sprinted toward the back of the house to clear it and set up a rear watch and field of fire, as others cleared the structure. LCpl. Steven Auton moved toward the front of the house. The dark-haired lance corporal was a compactly built "tough kid" described by one Marine as "a little ball of fuck you up." According to some of his squad mates, Auton showed little regard for authority in peacetime and made a lousy "garrison Marine," but his aggression made him a good "combat Marine." Auton was not the type of guy one would choose to conduct a gentle detainee interrogation, according to Serr, but once someone won his respect—a rare occurrence—his loyalty was absolute. He was "the type of guy who would punch a sergeant major in the face for you."[62]

Auton jogged over to the staircase leading up to the front porch of the house. As he reached it, all hell broke loose, again.[63] The familiar growl of an RPK erupted from a surprisingly close position less than a hundred yards away, somewhere to the southeast.[64] Rounds cracked the ground and cement around the SAW gunner, who barely had time to dive under the staircase. O'Connor saw bullets landing "literally inches from him" as the stairs were riddled with impacts.[65] O'Connor let off a couple of long bursts from his SAW to quickly "get something going" because Auton "was in a bad spot."[66] Someone yelled at the Marines to "get in the house," where they could set up a field of fire from the roof. O'Connor recalls telling LCpl. Jeff McAlinden "let's get in the house," but as they moved toward the porch, he saw "a line of [bullet] impacts between us and the front door along the outside wall" and thought better of the idea.[67] He could tell from the angle that the fire was emanating from a field catty-corner to the home. The SAW gunner recalls shooting back with a series of "short five-to-eight round bursts" while McAlinden started returning fire with his M-16, as little bits of concrete knocked loose from the incoming bullets "landed on [their] heads."[68]

Muñoz recalls moving toward the residence with Tyink, Zofchak, and LCpl. Brandon McCarty when they suddenly came under fire. Muñoz was in the road in front of the circular wall when bullets started hitting the stairs at the front of the house. The laconic corpsman thought the insurgents had left the area, so he was surprised, and maybe a little angry, that the Marines were getting ambushed again. "These guys want to kill my ass," he thought, as the men sprinted the remaining few yards toward cover. Zofchak and Tyink

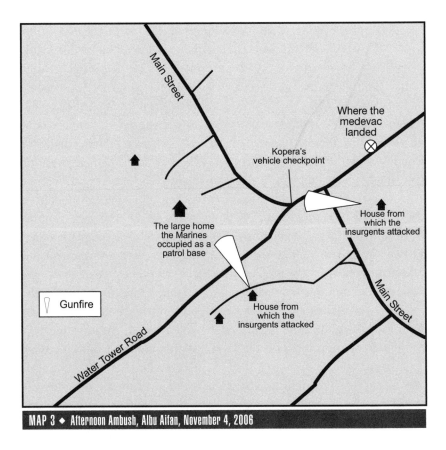

MAP 3 ◆ Afternoon Ambush, Albu Aifan, November 4, 2006

moved behind a concrete outhouse that stood next to a ditch lining the front yard while Muñoz ducked behind the courtyard's curved brick wall.[69]

Zofchak tried to establish the locations of his team and the source of the fire but couldn't immediately figure out "where the hell" it was "coming from." Gaining situational awareness under fire can be difficult, even for experienced combatants. The snapping air and impacts of bullets told the Americans that a heavy volume of machine-gun fire was aimed at them. The directional echo of the firearms and the path of landing bullets can orient an observer only to the general source of the attack; there's not much else to go on in the first few seconds.[70] In an instant, the body floods with adrenaline, and time seems to slow down or speed up. Some people feel numb, undergoing a vaguely out-of-body experience as their senses become selectively sluggish and sharp at the same time. And there is fear. It's not the slow, creeping variety felt when anticipating hidden roadside bombs from the seat of a Humvee, rather a stabbing terror that promptly gives way to something else, or sticks around and incapacitates.

With Marines, their training usually kicks in, making the first, crucial order of business to discern the source of the incoming rounds and to quickly return a large volume of fire to subdue the ambush and eliminate the attacker's advantage—that is, "suppressing them to gain fire superiority." The problem is that the men shooting at you already know where you are and are *suppressing you.* And doing what needs to be done to obtain eyes on a position in a firefight—exposing oneself, even a little bit—might mean catching a bullet. Even wildly aimed machine-gun fire is unforgiving.

Muñoz crouched behind the courtyard wall and watched as Zofchak twice shifted from the cover of the outhouse to find the enemy's position. "That's pretty crazy," the corpsman thought. Zofchak spotted muzzle flashes at two houses merely seventy-five to a hundred meters southeast, along Water Tower Road. He focused on flames he recalled blinking in the window of one of the houses. The corporal popped from cover, shot at the insurgents, looked around or yelled to someone, stuck his neck and shoulders out, and shot again.[71]

Tyink was next to Zofchak behind the outhouse, his legs still sprawled in front of him after an urgent slide for cover. According to Zofchak, Tyink was momentarily frozen. He had a distracted look on his face. Zofchak glanced at him, thinking, "What the fuck are you doing?" and then returned to shooting at the insurgents. At the renewed gunfire, Zofchak recalls that

Tyink seemed to shake himself from his open-eyed slumber. He too raised his weapon and started peeling off rounds toward the attackers.[72]

During a lull in incoming fire at the front porch, Auton escaped the space under the stairs and ran into the house. O'Connor and McAlinden followed "maybe twenty or thirty seconds behind him, at most," according to O'Connor. When the two men entered the house, Auton was nowhere to be seen, and they later surmised that he had gone "straight to the roof." The two following Marines rapidly cleared the large house room by room to make sure no one was hiding in the building. By the time they made it to the top, Auton had set up a field of fire.[73]

From his spot behind the courtyard wall, Muñoz looked for something to shoot at and watched Zofchak for clues to get PID of a target. He admired the team leader's calm.[74] Muñoz tended to be pretty calm himself. In the social hierarchy of Alpha Company, most everybody seemed to like the quiet Navy man, who rotated in and out of the three squads as one of the platoon's two overworked medical corpsmen.

The amiable Colombian American was known as "the Puma." Their platoon sergeant had coined the nickname on an earlier deployment to Iraq in 2005. Some claimed that comparing the short corpsman to a jungle cat was a play on his South American heritage, but others speculated it might be because of his graceful movements or the way he "pounced" on injured men to render treatment. Whatever the actual etymology, the serene Muñoz merely smiled when he heard "The Puma" and an accompanying *Rawr-rawarrr!*—a stream of terrible, throat-cracking impressions of a cat's roar. He had also been christened with the ethnically incorrect handle of "Ruben the Cuban," which played on his Hispanic lineage and the bottomless cups of strong Cuban coffee he drank and shared with the Marines.

Muñoz was no "shit talker," but he had to occasionally bare his teeth in the never-ending cycle of abuse that Marines and corpsmen heap on one another. While some guys flung endless volumes of crap at the wall and hoped that some of the insults stuck, the Puma would quietly observe or endure "beaner" jokes with a slight smile, waiting for an opportunity. When the right moment presented itself, he would strike, slipping a rhetorical knife through an attacker's ribs in the form of a quiet insult, often followed by everyone bursting into laughter. His low-key put-downs gained authority from his selective use of them. Most of the Marines liked the chubby-cheeked corpsman, but more important, they respected him as possibly the best medic in the company. The thirty-five-year-old had seasoned himself as a first responder in his eleven years as an EMS technician and then as a fireman in Miami, Florida. He inspired confidence when the Marines witnessed him leap into action when people were injured. Assessed one man, "The Puma was unflappable."[75]

For four years before leaving the service in 1995, Muñoz had been an active duty Navy man on the ship-based—"blue side"—of the corpsman hierarchy. After the September 11 attacks, he volunteered to resume his work as a Navy medic, but on the "green side"—Marine infantry. He wanted to do his part, and serving with the Marines guaranteed him a crack at the combat he had missed during the Persian Gulf War. Muñoz wanted to test his skills in action.[76] He was getting plenty of that now, being shot at by a machine gunner for the second time in a day. He projected calm, but incoming bullets imbue anyone with great turmoil.

Firefights happen impossibly fast and generate a jumble of conflicting emotions. For Muñoz, there was excitement; there was piercing fear. He was sure that everyone was scared to some extent, but there was an unspoken, often successful struggle among the Marines not to show it. You had to display confidence to avoid making your buddies think you might crack up and fail to do your job. In the end, the fear of letting down friends and looking weak before alpha male competitors tended to eclipse the stark terror of being shot at.[77]

At the sheikh's house, everyone, according to Muñoz, seemed to keep things cool as they returned fire on the insurgents. He perceived the men they were fighting that day as acting professionally as well. In the first ambush, the insurgents had set up impressive fields of fire and then successfully retreated, only to position themselves to surprise the Marines a second time. Maybe these guys knew what they were doing. Muñoz waited for the call to treat any wounded.

Back at the checkpoint, Kopera, Serr, and Inman dropped behind the white car for cover when they heard the stutter of RPK fire directed toward the men at the house. The young Iraqis they had stopped and pulled from the vehicle were scared and unsure about what to do; they panicked and ducked in the middle of the road as bullets passed high and wide of their position.

Kopera called to them and motioned toward a reed-filled ditch along the road's right shoulder. One of the men eagerly complied and sat down in the dirt with hunched shoulders. Another ducked behind a shack in someone's front yard, and the other man remained behind the car with the Marines.[78]

Kopera heard his men at the house returning fire toward a target somewhere to his south. Peeking around the hood of the car, he determined the enemy's general location from the close staccato of their weapons, but his line of sight was blocked by tall rushes lining the edge of the road. After a few seconds, he discerned the flicker of muzzle flashes through the high green shoots. Kopera carefully aimed and shot toward the insurgents, but his men around the house had a better line of sight, so he let them do most of the shooting.[79]

Through his scope, Serr saw "four or five . . . men with guns" in the yard of a house catty-corner to the building the Marines had moved to secure; he shot maybe twenty rounds at them.[80] Inman, taking no chances, quickly burned through two magazines shooting at the enemy.[81] Once the Americans at the car heard covering fire from their teammates near the house, they took the opportunity to jump into a roadside ditch for better cover. The young Iraqis from the car joined them.[82]

For Kopera, time slowed during a gunfight. He had seen a few Marines panic when they were shot at, losing their minds in an instant. Some got angry and yelled. He and many others just responded. The sergeant explains that he never encountered a feeling he identified as "fear" during a battle; he never felt the instinct to flee, and he never got particularly excited. He just acted. Only after an engagement, after his adrenaline had surged and crashed, would thoughts of what had just happened or almost happened suffuse him with excitement and dread.[83]

The Marines on and around the sheikh's house could see their attackers firing from inside and around a couple of smaller homes no more than about 100 meters away. Over several minutes as the firefight progressed, the insurgents initially "held their ground," but then moved to break contact. They tried to escape through a field of thigh-high green crops behind the houses. Two of the Iraqis were cut down before their companions managed to retreat through the series of irrigation ditches that split the field.[84] Subsequent intelligence reports identified one of the dead as a local man whose family lived in the modest house next to the scene of the original ambush in front of the al-Shahid mosque.[85]

The gunfire tapered off. This second exchange had probably lasted two to five minutes, though again, no one could tell for sure.[86] Within seconds of the stillness, the Americans on the roof heard women screaming and wailing.[87] Another sedan generally matching the description of the insurgent getaway vehicle could be seen rolling toward the Marines. Kopera quickly glimpsed at one of the men from the first car sitting among the weeds in the ditch. He had a panicked look on his face. The Marine then refocused on the new vehicle.[88]

As the car slowly approached the Marines, Kopera recalls seeing two men in their fifties or early sixties waving their arms from the front seat, trying to communicate with the Americans. Kopera motioned them forward. He briskly moved toward the car. Peering inside, the sergeant saw four middle-aged and elderly men with agitated looks on their faces and a barely conscious woman in her early thirties lying across the back seat.[89] She was wailing, in pain.[90] A small bloodstain across the front of her dark abaya marked a wound in her upper chest.

There was no interpreter available, but the sergeant could tell that the Iraqis wanted permission to drive her to the local hospital. Kopera didn't think that she would make it without first being stabilized.[91] He yelled for Muñoz and directed the driver to move the car up the driveway to the front porch of the house. The sergeant had Inman round up the men they had initially stopped at the checkpoint and motioned that they were free to go. Their faces filled with relief as they jumped in their car and sped south.[92] Kopera ordered all the Marines into the house to plan their next moves.[93] "I'm tired of getting shot at," Kopera said matter-of-factly to Zofchak.[94]

From inside the house, Muñoz heard the call that "somebody is shot."[95] The Puma rushed outside, meeting the car as it drove up to the porch. The Iraqi men left the vehicle and opened the door of the beat-up old sedan, giving the medic access to assess the patient. He saw a slightly heavyset woman slumped but conscious in the backseat. Her breathing was labored as a Marine and the corpsman helped her out of the vehicle and walked her up the stairs and into the house.[96]

They sat her gently on the off-white marble floor, and Muñoz began a culturally delicate attempt to assess her wounds while allowing her to retain her modesty. He incrementally uncovered small swaths of her layered dress to probe for entrance and exit wounds. She didn't object, realizing he was a "doctor" trying to help her. There was a small entrance wound in her left upper chest below the clavicle, with a slightly larger exit wound through her back.[97]

The woman's dress was soaked with blood. It wasn't life-threatening, arterial bleeding, but instead pulsed steadily from her body.[98] The woman's breathing was ragged. A lot of chest wounds eventually result in a collapsed lung, but Muñoz knew that this was not an immediate threat as "she had good lung sounds" and she wasn't rapidly "decompensating." The corpsman cut off a portion of her clothing to access the wound and applied an occlusive dressing and a trauma dressing over that to prevent air from entering the space around her lung and crushing it.[99] He secured the elastic bandages with duct tape and continued to check her airway and pulse. Muñoz didn't think the woman would die anytime soon, but she would have little chance of surviving the day without more sophisticated medical attention, including insertion of a chest tube to prevent her chest from collapsing in on itself.[100]

The woman's male relatives realized he was a medic and quietly observed her treatment. They stood in the living room, concerned and watching, occasionally murmuring to each other in Arabic. In the distance, the Marines could hear the high, mournful wailing of a group of women who had gathered in a nearby house to lament the shooting.[101] The men in the room looked upset but didn't panic. Once they had judged the Marines' intentions as being helpful, they relinquished control to the will of God (albeit through the Americans) to help her.[102]

A couple of Marines sat on a half-circular staircase and smoked a cigarette as they watched Muñoz at work. Inman looked at Zofchak, who stood nearby.[103] "She's bleeding a lot," he said. "Yeah. She's bleeding, a lot," repeated Zofchak.[104] The injured woman occasionally moaned but she had otherwise become quiet. Inman was impressed with how she handled the injury. "Man, she's a little bad-ass," he said to another Marine.[105]

Muñoz offered his assessment to Kopera that she was "stable," but she "would die without better treatment."[106] Serr recalls that the corpsman was "really firm" as he made his case. The squad leader paused for a second. "We have to get her out of here," decided Kopera, radioing his intentions to Lt. Greco: No U.S. casualties; one critical civilian casualty; calling a medevac or casevac.[107]

He then tried to raise an on-call medical helicopter on the predetermined frequency, but couldn't get through to the pilot. He later found out that the frequencies, which were regularly changed, had been incorrectly set up to transmit as text.[108] The helicopter's crew could hear him, but he couldn't hear them. The sergeant called back to Greco and asked his lieutenant to direct the bird to his location. Marines weren't required to evacuate civilians to U.S. care unless they had been directly injured by Americans. Kopera was unsure how the woman had been shot; her entrance wound did not reveal the guilty round to be a 5.56 mm used by the Marines or the 7.62 employed by insurgents. The insurgents had started shooting at the Marines from a field behind and to the side of her house, and several women had been standing in the yard, almost directly in the middle of a withering crossfire.[109]

Kopera's training had instructed him to prioritize the care of Marines, and after that treat both wounded civilians and insurgents as they would their own. He didn't know how well others took that directive to heart, but making the attempt to save the woman was an instinctive decision. She would certainly die from her wound otherwise. If the slow ground travel through multiple checkpoints didn't kill her, he thought the conditions at the local hospital most likely would.[110] Evacuating her was not, however, without risk. A helicopter might make an attractive target for the group or groups of insurgents undoubtedly still lurking in the area, and the roads, sometimes used as landing zones for the helos, were studded with IEDs. The last thing anyone wanted was for his Marines to get killed evacuating a civilian or for a helicopter to take a catastrophic hit. Back at the patrol base, Lieutenant Greco deferred to Kopera's call.[111]

The Marines in Kopera's squad prepared to execute the order. Some supported the decision, but others grumbled about it.[112] Serr assumed that the woman's family "was forced to use her yard as a battlefield" and consequently he "thought it was the right thing to do." Inman nonchalantly followed orders, but he recalled the times he had had to drive a seriously wounded Marine to the hospital at high speeds on a road potentially packed with bombs. It didn't seem quite fair that an Iraqi would be rushed out on a medevac bird in only a few minutes.

Zofchak tried to fix the radio and raise the helicopter, but it was a lost cause. To compensate, the Marines played a high stakes version of the game "broken telephone." Their walkie-talkies were unreliable and had a very limited range, so Muñoz used his personal role radio to relay instructions to a Marine on the roof. The altitude allowed the second American to switch frequencies and project a message farther, to Sgt. Christopher Dockter's 2nd Squad, which had moved into a position a few hundred meters away.[113]

Dockter's radios to air support had also failed before they rushed out to back up Kopera's squad after the first engagement, so he was relaying instructions via short-range radio to Greco. Mercifully, the platoon leader's encrypted line to the helicopter still worked, and one of his Marines interpreted these instructions and tried to direct the inbound helicopter toward a field set up as a landing zone immediately northeast of Kopera's house.[114] Muñoz, Kopera, and three Marines waited near the front of the house, while the rest of the men maintained security and overwatch from the roof.

The Americans were annoyed by how long it took for the helicopter to arrive.[115] Some became concerned. After two ambushes in the last hour, they could not rule out a third attack as the vulnerable helo landed in an open field and the Marines escorted the patient to meet it.[116] Within a few minutes, a distant hum gestated into the unmistakable beating of the large, tandem rotors of a CH-46 Sea Knight. The ancient airframe resembled a light gray-blue beetle that had been grabbed at both ends and stretched out. The pilot made a low pass over their position. A sleek AH-1 Super Cobra attack helicopter circled nearby as an escort.

The Marines had thrown a dark smoke grenade on the road next to the landing zone to signal the pilot. After spotting his destination, the CH-46 pilot banked sharply and circled back through the blue midday sky toward the field. The helicopter's lumbering outline grew and then receded as it flew toward and then past the marked landing site.[117] "What are they doing?" wondered Muñoz, as the pilot cut speed and raised the bird's stubby nose to descend 75 meters to the south of the field. "That is the dumbest fucking thing in the world," thought Zofchak. The chopper was landing in the middle of the frequently bomb-sown street, where Alpha Company had lost Gilbert and Thornsberry to a massive IED. The large crater left by the deadly bomb was still visible less than twenty meters from where the helo was setting down. For all anyone knew, there were other bombs hidden beneath the surface.[118] "Oh God, please don't let them land on an IED," thought Muñoz.

When the helicopter touched down and nothing exploded, the Americans directed one of the Iraqi men to start the sedan and slowly drive the wounded woman toward the nearby intersection. Some of the Marines and the corpsman jogged in a loose cordon around the white car, weapons poised and eyes peeled for ambushing insurgents or bombs along the road's shoulder. At least three Marines fanned out to form an ad hoc perimeter.[119] Once in the open, they were "sitting ducks," according to Inman. Others weren't worried much at all, because the presence of a Cobra attack helicopter escort overhead tended to scare off insurgents.[120]

Through the dust-filled air, a female corpsman or nurse commanding a stretcher crew emerged from the back of the helicopter to meet them.[121] Inman saw blonde hair and for a moment, he forgot his surroundings. She was "really hot," he recalled. The thirty-something-year-old medic, whose gender and attractiveness were apparently distinguishable in a bulky helmet, vest, and flight suit, jogged to the vehicle and yelled a brief report to Kopera. Muñoz shouted an assessment of the patient over the deafening engine whine and rotor wash. Two crew members set down the litter and gently loaded the Iraqi woman onto it.[122] Her four male relatives, who had been projecting resignation and quiet gratitude despite lacking an interpreter, now made agitated gestures and raised their voices.[123]

"Can we send someone with her?" Kopera yelled in the ear of the medic. "We can take one," she replied. Kopera made eye contact with the worried men, pointed at them, raised one finger, and pointed at the helicopter. The eldest male, who might have been her relieved father, uncle, or husband, moved to the side of the litter and trotted along with the crew members as they loaded the injured woman onto the chopper.[124]

The engine whine became urgent as the rotors gathered speed and beat rolling clouds of dirt over the Marines and remaining Iraqis. The Sea Knight strained its cylindrical bulk into the sky, gaining altitude and speeding the injured woman northeast, to the care of doctors in the surgical shock trauma unit at al-Taqaddum Airbase. Her journey would end at a U.S. hospital in Baghdad. She would live. Kopera never met her again, but he later learned that she had been able to return to her home about a month later.[125]

Kopera bid the remaining Iraqi men goodbye and consolidated his squad back at the house. They were to hole up in the home until thirty minutes after sunset and then make their way back to the rest of the platoon at the patrol base. The men had time to review the day and fill each other in about what they had witnessed. There was still a lot of confusion. They itemized their close calls: the rounds hitting the ground near Muñoz and Kopera, the accurate RPG near Inman and Zofchak, bullets chipping at the stairs over Auton's head. Some thought they may have cut down some of their attackers.[126] Firefights were exciting and to some could almost seem like fun when no Marines were seriously hurt.

Kopera reflected on the day's events. It was never a good thing to have a firefight blow up in the middle of someone's neighborhood and wind up with a wounded (or dead) civilian. They did, however, fight off two ambushes, possibly kill some insurgents, and give the wounded woman a fighting chance—all without an injured Marine. He liked to think that the care they had shown the civilian differentiated them from the insurgents and would help win local favor, but he knew better than to expect it.[127] The sergeant and the members of his squad didn't rehash things long. They had had a lot of enemy contact in the past few days, and certainly more would come. It was almost always time to get back to work.[128]

The officers at the platoon and company levels were pleased with the day's engagements. Subsequent intelligence reports relying on Iraqi sources drily quantified the squad's effectiveness: three enemies killed, one enemy wounded, one civilian wounded, and no Marines injured or killed. In Alpha Company's growing tally of good, bad, or downright confusing days on the peninsula, this was considered a small victory.[129] Other battles ended differently.

Three weeks later, near the southwestern village of Hasa, Kopera would be shot in the head. His Marines were conducting a patrol when an insurgent's bullet penetrated his Kevlar helmet and embedded itself in his brain, briefly knocking him down and out cold. Zofchak was about twenty meters away and had immediately jumped into a ditch for cover. When he turned around, the corporal watched in horror as a now conscious Kopera stood up and began stumbling around in the open, dazed, as machine-gun fire cracked around him. Zofchak ran to his squad leader and pulled him into the safety of the ditch.

Muñoz assessed the injury.[130] "My head hurts," slurred Kopera.[131] The sergeant tried to take his helmet off but Muñoz stopped him; the corpsman feared it was the only thing keeping his head intact.[132] A mostly lucid Kopera was quickly medevaced, walking onto the helicopter under his own power. He survived after having a nickel-sized piece of his brain removed. Now medically discharged, Kopera suffers short-term memory loss and loses his temper a little more often than he did before his injury. It sometimes strains his marriage. He jokes that he's "the same asshole, but now [he has] an excuse." He voices no regrets about his days as a Marine.

For his actions during several engagements prior to his injury, Kopera was nominated by Greco for the Bronze Star with Valor Device, which the sergeant received. The lieutenant was impressed with his squad leader's ability to maintain focus, go after and kill attackers, and successfully conduct the difficult symphony of decisions demanded by counterinsurgency. Quickly ramping up to kill and then just as quickly making the choice to hold a trigger finger is difficult. And helping the civilian woman, although it carried risk, was a proper call, from a COIN perspective: "Protect the people." But in retrospect, Greco thought it probably never occurred to Kopera *not* to call for the medevac. For a guy with a code, it was just the right thing to do.[133]

◆ 4 ◆

❖ ALLIANCE ❖

The war in Anbar province was complex. The Americans were fighting an enemy who ruthlessly intimidated civilians, wore no uniform, and operated under an effective camouflage of a culture and language exotic to them. Reacting to attacks, combing intelligence reports to plan raids, and conducting a census of the peninsula's population to ferret out insurgents were reasonable tactics. These approaches had their limits, however, especially given their slow pace and the pressure growing in the United States to end the war, regardless of the terms. The Marines needed local help, quickly, and their meeting with Sheikh Aifan Sadoun Aifan al-Issawi, "Dark," in late December offered a fresh opportunity to generate such support.

Whisnant and his military intelligence sergeant, Saint One, wanted a quick follow-up to their first meeting with Dark.[1] Together the two men drafted a report summarizing their initial impressions of the sheikh, whom they referred to as "Abu Sadoon":

> Abu Sadoon is a confident individual who claims he is tired of talking about accomplishing something for the [Albu Issa] tribe and is ready for actually doing something. He talked for approximately 30 minutes about previous meetings in Jordan and his contacts that he supposedly has with [other U.S. governmental agencies]. He stated that he came back to Iraq because it is in his heart to come back.
>
> The main points of discussion centered on the following items:
>
> —Abu Sadoon doesn't believe [paramount sheikh] Khamis [Hasnawi Aifan al-Issawi] has the moral will to take on the cur-

rent fight for his tribal area even with help from coalition forces. Sheikh Khamis is afraid and would rather just sit in his house and hope for self-preservation. He's concerned that current [U.S.] contacts are just concerned in creating a relationship with the sheikhs and nothing further than that. Abu Sadoon related that he's not interested in just eating kabob, dates and nuts with [Americans], he wants to accomplish security and safety in his area.

—Abu Sadoon offered to assist in any way possible in the intel fight of identifying the insurgents. Several insurgents were mentioned during this discussion[. . . .] He then went on for approximately 10 minutes on how the insurgents use "nicknames" to fool [coalition forces]. [Whisnant] stated that his Marines were aware of this tactic and needed assistance in identifying the real insurgents because of . . . fake [ID cards] that have the incorrect name. Abu Sadoon said he would be willing personally or some of his trusted people would go along on . . . raids to [identify] residences of the real insurgents in the area. [He] turned the discussion to how a 3–6 month detainment undermines the entire process and doesn't provide any hope or incentive for the average Iraqi to provide information on the insurgents.

Abu Sadoon has solid placement and access to the information provided by virtue of his family and social connections in the area. He is actively seeking [American] assistance in security matters because of the situation with his extended family and tribal members. He is also motivated by money and ego. He states that working "underground" is the best thing and it would make him proud to see his area secure and safe again.[2]

Before sending the report up the chain of command, Whisnant and Saint One sought the blessing of CWO-5 Jim Roussell. Nicknamed "the Wizard," because of his status as the battalion's resident counterinsurgency expert, Roussell had an unusual pedigree.[3] The fifty-five-year-old had been mandatorily retired from the Corps in 2002 after thirty-seven years as an active duty and reserve Marine. Roussell had also been a cop for thirty-one years and held the rank of lieutenant in the Chicago Police Department. In 2004, the commander of 2nd Battalion, 24th Marine Regiment approached

Roussell for advice on how to defeat an insurgency, before 2/24's deployment to Mahmudiyah, Iraq.[4] Roussell's background in Marine infantry and intelligence, and his work in the Chicago Police Department's gang unit, gave him an ideal skill set for tackling the Iraqi rebellion.

Many of Iraq's insurgent cells resembled criminal enterprises as much as they did radically religious enemies. The sixteen- to thirty-year-old toughs at the core of the insurgency had a great deal in common with the Windy City's gangbangers. Many viewed the pursuit of money and power as a goal accompanied by or merely cloaked in the stated ambition of achieving religious purity and the humiliating expulsion of the American infidels. Robbery, extortion, and kidnapping were tools of their trade.[5] The indoctrination of insurgent recruits also shared striking parallels with U.S. gang initiations.

Common criminals, casual insurgents for hire, as well as some genuinely innocent men had been swept up in the mass detentions conducted by the U.S. military during the early stages of the war. Moderate Muslims and insurgent neophytes were both dumped into the general prisoner population, where they mixed with hardened criminals and hard-core Islamists preaching jihad. Much like in U.S. prisons, many of the newcomers in Iraq's facilities joined one of these groups to survive, and once a member, death became the only easy way out. In addition, U.S.- and some Iraqi-run facilities tended to release individuals incarcerated for lesser crimes after only a few months. This created a destructive cycle of incarceration, (radical) ideological indoctrination, and then release. American detention facilities like Camp Bucca became incubators that unwittingly but continually refreshed the insurgency by churning out foot soldiers for violent jihad.[6]

Roussell's experience on Chicago's streets gave him perspective on how to take a run at the gangs in Iraq. He started working with the men of 2/24 by delivering pre-deployment briefings on developing sources and analyzing intelligence. He soon concluded that he had more to contribute, however, and actually joined the battalion on its deployment, as well as 1/24's subsequent tour on Fallujah's peninsula.[7] Most men his age didn't make plans that involved coming out of retirement from the Marines to bounce around insurgent strongholds in Iraq's Triangle of Death, with its bomb-laden roads and angry fighters wielding rocket-propelled grenades. To have done that once and then volunteered for a subsequent tour to go back and "finish the job" earned the old cop unusual respect from the men with whom he served.[8]

Roussell's contributions were wide-ranging. He discovered a weekly meeting held by the "real sheikhs" of Fallujah, as opposed to the "fake sheikhs" who'd posed as powerbrokers to claim U.S. business contracts. He had caught wind of the gathering while shooting the breeze with locals as he traveled a beat in and around the city. On a late December day, the bespectacled police officer simply showed up at the meeting and introduced himself; afterward he became a regular fixture at the gatherings. His age was an asset in his interactions with these men, who considered experience a prerequisite for respect. The relationships he developed with the sheikhs would prove crucial later, when he served as an intermediary in contentious exchanges between tribal leaders and Iraqi government politicians and security personnel.[9]

Roussell also instructed young Marines, many of whom routinely grumbled about restrictive rules of engagement (ROE) and pined for more straightforward ass-kicking. During the Second Battle of Fallujah in 2004, after the city had been mostly evacuated of noncombatants, the ROE were liberal enough to be enthusiastically described by one Marine as "like setting a bunch of fat kids loose in a candy store." The current fight, however, had been severely restrained to avoid counterproductive civilian casualties. It wasn't so easy for the Americans to get shot at or blown up every day without wanting to "get some" in return. Most lusted after a stand-up fight, and Roussell understood where they were coming from. After all, he had been a young Marine once, with all the institutionally focused but prodigious aggression that entails. Many would never embrace counterinsurgency (COIN), but Roussell found that a history lesson could assuage some of the young men's frustration and cynicism about the gentler aspects of the doctrine.

The older Marine explained that the Corps boasted a proud tradition of counterinsurgency. From pioneering combat action patrols with locals in Haiti and Nicaragua during the early part of the Banana Wars to the successful model of living among the population in Vietnam's A Shau Valley, Marines had done COIN well; the mobility of the expeditionary service branch made them a natural fit for such operations. When he framed the patiently nuanced tactics as essential to earning the young Marines' rightful place in hallowed Marine Corps history, he thought that a few of them took to their responsibilities with greater enthusiasm, even if their trigger fingers still itched.[10]

Roussell's counsel also paid dividends with higher-ranking officers. Even experienced, senior personnel needed reminders to walk them back from aggressive doctrine that could be counterproductive if it inflamed local sentiment. The warrant officer's influence was, however, finite. There were plenty of times he wanted to "yank [his] hair out of [his] head" as Marine leadership attempted to make counterinsurgency progress while pulling American forces back to large bases and prematurely handing over security responsibilities to unready Iraqi soldiers and cops in late 2006. He felt that American troops needed to stop kicking doors, start listening, and "play the game, not the clock" to cultivate the intelligence necessary to beat the rebellion.[11]

Roussell's ability to analyze local Iraqis was a resource that Whisnant and Saint One needed as they assessed Dark. The cop divided Iraqi partners into categories of "*good* bad guys" (GBGs) and "*bad* bad guys" (BBGs) to educate his fellow Americans, some of whom had trouble wrapping their heads around the idea of working with former insurgents and other questionable characters. BBGs were irreconcilable. They were wholly out for themselves and to kill Americans in their quest for religious purity, power, or both; they would eliminate anyone who got in their way. GBGs were also out for themselves, and they might never come to work hand-in-hand with the nascent Iraqi government or water any seeds of democracy, but they had interests that could align with U.S. interests. Their motivations and cultural sensibilities were a far cry from the idealized values of the Marine Corps, and many had even tried to kill Americans at some point in the war. But one could work with *good* bad guys. The hard truth was that the Americans *needed* to work with them. That was the nature of COIN.[12]

Roussell doubted the existence of straight up "good good guys." It was his practical cop mentality. Every player, including every American, had an angle. You had to ascertain everyone's motivation and match his or her interests with yours. One of the Wizard's mantras was "something for something, nothing for nothing." Another, less serious philosophy was "if their lips are moving, they're lying."[13]

Whisnant and Saint One's meeting with Dark had intrigued Roussell. He wanted to see more such engagements. He told the two Marines that it was essential they leave no doubt about what they wanted and what they were willing to give in return. Roussell stressed, "We have to be careful to compare what we say, with what he *thinks* we mean. We have to be very clear."[14]

On New Year's Day 2007, Saint One and Whisnant met again with Dark, as well as with Sheikh Khamis Hasnawi Aifan al-Issawi. The elder, paramount sheikh's presence conferred authority for Dark to work with the Americans on the tribe's behalf. The encounter yielded more information, including a list of insurgents' names and insight into growing splits among the Albu Issa subtribes. Dark also indicated that recent fighting had apparently ratcheted up after members of the Abu Hatim subtribe kidnapped two prominent leaders of al Qaeda in Iraq as part of the ongoing power struggle for the peninsula. Various sheikhs were bargaining for the release of the men in an attempt to douse the growing conflict, but Dark thought that the negotiations would backfire because the al Qaeda leadership would violate any settlement that secured the captives' release and immediately retaliate with abandon. In addition to providing perspective on his tribe's civil war, Dark repeated his offer of guides to accompany the Americans on night raids against high-value targets. Khamis was more hesitant about offering cooperation and observed the meeting coolly. He voiced skepticism about the Americans' ability to protect his subtribe if he made an overt pledge of support.[15]

Roussell was consulted after the first two meetings, on December 26 and on New Year's Day, but he wanted an opportunity to assess the sheikhs for himself. On January 6, Alpha Company conducted a helicopter-borne assault into the village of Abu Yousseff that would take them near Dark's house in neighboring Albu Aifan. Roussell accompanied Saint One and Whisnant on the operation so he could visit both sheikhs afterward. It had rained on the day of the raids, which netted seventeen of twenty-seven targeted insurgents and several weapons caches. That night, Saint One, Whisnant, Roussell, an interpreter nicknamed "B. J.," and Maj. Jim Hayes left the platoon's ad hoc patrol base for the meeting. An alert march down a main road, followed by a slog through fields covered in thigh-high mud, delivered the Americans to Dark's house.[16]

The men entered the residence, except Hayes, who remained outside to keep nervous watch. He did not trust these Iraqis, and he was a little alarmed by the small size of the American party. They were exposed. The Marine air officer was responsible for approving and vectoring requests for airstrikes from Marines in the field, so he had tagged along on the mission to get a firsthand look at the local topography. As the others were filtering into the house, Hayes called in his current coordinates to air controllers back at Camp Fallujah. If the worst looked likely—he'd seen videos of what happened to captured Americans—he would be able to call in a 500-pound bomb on their position. There was no way he was getting taken alive.[17]

The men who entered the house were welcomed with friendly greetings from Dark, who referred to both Whisnant and Saint One as "my brother" and to the elder Roussell as "my father." The Marines didn't explain Roussell's presence or identity, but the young sheikh was perceptive.[18] "I want to know why you are here," Dark mused in English. "I think my brother [Whisnant] brought you to figure out who I am."[19] Sheikh Khamis' greetings to the Americans were more restrained. The elderly man projected a regal aloofness that bespoke his position.

In the course of the two-hour meeting, the business facade projected by Dark and the Americans fell—a little. It was easy to like the talkative young sheikh, and the carefully crafted intrigue and formality of their initial meeting in December gave way to a few friendly jokes and more specific offers of cooperation. First, Saint One further assessed Aifan's willingness to help and his knowledge of local insurgents by listing the names of high-value targets on whom the Americans had reliable information. Dark passed the test, verifying the identities of known BBGs. The Marines then showed the young sheikh pictures of the men they had caught on raids during the assault that day, and Dark expressed pleasure. He told them their targeting was accurate. He also chastised the Americans, however, for letting three others slip their cordon and escape. The Marines pressed for additional names and locations of insurgents, and Dark complied—with a few.

Khamis remained cordial but unsmiling, saying little as he sat and chain-smoked cigarettes. His quiet calm was characteristic foremost of his age as well as a paramount sheikh's noble persona. But it was also a reflection of his refusal to enthusiastically choose sides in the war flaring between his Albu Aifan subtribe and members of subtribes affiliated with al Qaeda. His presence enabled him to observe, and it continued to show his hesitant endorsement of Dark's leadership of a militia. But Khamis' passivity seemed designed to preserve plausible deniability of direct involvement, should the younger sheikh's campaign go poorly.[20]

"I am not a politician," he told the Marines through the interpreter. "I am not part of the army. I want no part of the government, in any way. I am just a sheikh."[21] In fact, the old sheikh agreed to accept emissaries from al Qaeda for months after this meeting; he stressed his neutrality to the insurgent representatives until a later event forced his hand.[22]

Despite continuing to play both sides of the fence, Khamis had made a few small steps toward an alliance with the Americans by virtue of his vague promises and his appearances at meetings. Many in Fallujah had heard of the rise of Sheikh Abdul Sattar Abu Risha and his battles with al Qaeda near the provincial capital of Ramadi, and knew about the young sheikh's beneficial alliance with U.S. forces.[23] Competitive pride, coupled with the reality that Fallujah's sheikhs could not hide out in exile forever, eventually drew them back home from Jordan and into a search for options to reestablish basic security and restore the traditional tribal order. The Americans represented one of the options that had grown more attractive as the "Persian Shia" (Iranians) solidified their political power in Baghdad through Shia Iraqi proxies, and al Qaeda in Iraq and other radical insurgent groups violently wore out their welcome in Sunni Anbar. Khamis legitimately disliked the *takfiri* insurgents, even if not with the outward intensity of his nephew Dark. He thought the radicals' actions were "wrong," and he resented them for forcing a violently conservative ideology on the "good Muslims" of his tribe.[24]

Another political twist complicated the Americans' hope to deal with Khamis as the ultimate authority of the tribe: Although the elder sheikh held titular and some de facto power as paramount sheikh, some Marines concluded that he was also something of a figurehead. In fact, Americans believed that Khamis' uncle Sheikh Khaled Hasnawi and his older brother, Sheikh Taleb Hasnawi, were more significant leaders and ran the Albu Issa from behind the scenes. Sheikh Barakat Sadoun Aifan al-Issawi, an older brother of Dark's who remained in exile, also held sway and had been a well-known insurgent earlier in the war. The Americans speculated that all of these men had passed on any claim to be paramount sheikh because the mantle came with a target on the wearer's back. They were content to exert influence while holding a lesser title, making Khamis the most attractive target for assassination.[25]

Though Dark showed deference toward the paramount sheikh during the meeting, he also aggressively prodded Khamis to cooperate with the Americans and support his development of the tribe's militia. Khamis remained hesitant. He told the Americans that he feared his family members would find out about his meetings with them, and he continued to withhold his open cooperation. He and his nephew argued about the degree to which his tribe should be seen as a public ally of the Marines.[26] "We need to do this," Dark said. "Let's do this, it is the only way."[27] The younger sheikh only bought his uncle's tolerance by portraying initial efforts as "underground," defensive in nature, and necessary to blunt al Qaeda and competing sheikhs' power grab for control of the peninsula.[28]

In turn, Dark demanded concrete promises of support from the Americans and asked them to set up a permanent base near his village. His people would require protection as they openly organized and declared war on the insurgents. Only with security sufficient to undermine the *takfiris'* brutally effective intimidation campaigns could he build confidence in his small band of fighters and rally the men of his tribe.[29]

"How long will you stay?" asked Dark.[30] It was an important question. The tactics and force dispositions of American units sometimes changed with the decisions of rotating commanders. Roussell considered this "playing the clock"—that is, based on a Marine unit's six- or seven-month deployment—rather than "playing the game." One unit's forward operating base might be shuttered by the next at the discretion of a commander on the ground or direction from senior officers.[31]

In early January, just prior to President George W. Bush's announcement of the "surge," U.S. forces were still playing out a strategy of pulling back to let Iraqi security forces take the lead. In Fallujah's case, as in many other areas, the effort was premature. Besides the fact that the Iraqi Army and police were operationally unready, the peninsula's tribes considered the Iraqi security forces untrustworthy competitors. To many of the Sunnis of Anbar, the Iraqi Army units were Shia outsiders from Baghdad and the south of the country; the police were variously suspected of being sellouts, tools of the Iraqi government, the Americans, or competing tribes.[32]

Khamis' and Dark's tribesmen did not yet have the manpower, weapons, or official permission to openly arm and defend themselves against any inevitable revenge for cooperating with Americans.[33] Retribution from al Qaeda was one of Dark's and Khamis' repeatedly expressed worries about an alliance. Dark knew that if he was going to stand up to the insurgency, he needed both license to fight and for Americans to agree to stay nearby and help protect his people.[34]

Roussell was impressed with Dark's enthusiasm for action, which was a rarity among sheikhs in the area. He also viewed the young sheikh as an opportunist who craved advancement and aggressively projected the image of a brave fighter, as epitomized by his frequent choice to wear a dark blue ammunition-carrying vest draped over "combat casual" clothes. In truth, Roussell judged Dark to be more of an organizer than a gunfighter, but organization was something the Albu Issa needed to marshal their forces against the radicals dedicated to insurgency. Organizers also lived longer; many day-to-day combatants, including two of the young toughs who made up the core of Dark's security forces in those early days, wound up maimed or killed. It was a common price paid by the gunfighters of Iraq.[35]

Dark had also formed equally perceptive opinions of the Americans. In a later interview with U.S. researchers, he summarized them in words that perfectly mirrored Roussell's working philosophy: "We have a theory," explained Dark. "The Americans don't have continuous friendships. They always have their interests. Their relationships with people are based on how much benefit they can get from a person."[36] In essence, he and his American counterparts varied little in their perception of the utilitarian nature of their new "friendship" with one another. Dark asked for the release of fellow tribesmen being held by the Americans, as well as for some cars, radios, and construction contracts to create jobs for his tribe. One of his requests continued to stand out in terms of repetition and forceful expression: his men needed weapons and the license to carry them.[37]

Having received permission from their superiors prior to the meeting, Saint One and Whisnant were finally able to offer Dark something concrete. They asked him for a list of thirty trusted fighters who would be vetted for permits to openly carry weapons. In addition, other men in his village were granted the right to brandish rifles only, and only at checkpoints or while stationed on the rooftops of their houses. This would enable them to defend their homes while still differentiating them from insurgent fighters traveling through the area. After the meeting, Whisnant made a recommendation to higher command to fulfill most of Dark's latest requests for cars, contracts, weapons, and ammunition. The major also agreed to stick around and protect his new allies: he directed his men to establish a new, permanent patrol base in an abandoned mansion near the village of Albu Aifan. Some of the Marines nicknamed it FOB [Forward Operating Base] Dark.

Saint One, Whisnant, and Roussell now dared to be optimistic. They thought they could "make this work." If locals identified the bad guys and took ownership of the fight against insurgents, the bleak war for the peninsula could swing in favor of the Americans and their new Iraqi allies. The agreements of the two preceding weeks marked the start of a genuine working relationship.[38] Like many relationships, however, this one would be tested—severely and soon.

❖ THE *DIYA* ❖

On the morning of January 9, 2007, 1st Lt. Jerome Greco and the interpreter "C. J." Wadhah Sahib were greeted by Sheikh Khalid Hasnawi at the doorway of his house in Albu Aifan village. The residence was situated in the toniest neighborhood within arguably the most important village of the eighteen Albu Issa hamlets dotting Fallujah's peninsula. The paramount sheikh, Khamis Hasnawi Aifan al-Issawi, Sheikh Aifan Sadoun Aifan al-Issawi (Dark), and many other leaders of the tribe lived in Albu Aifan. The relative affluence was obvious to Greco, as he appraised the home's nicer furniture and unusually spacious rooms. The lieutenant, his interpreter, and a radio operator removed their helmets as they entered the house. Greco exchanged pleasantries with the sheikh, each man waiting patiently for C. J.'s English and Arabic translations.[1]

The platoon commander was meeting with the influential Iraqi to try and gather information on an insurgent the Marines had been tracking. The lieutenant also wanted to test the waters with other tribal leaders after the Americans' three recent meetings with Khamis and Dark, and to discuss new rules of engagement and the disposition of the village's young militia. The war had gotten a lot more confusing in the past week, and Greco didn't want a misunderstanding to get someone killed.[2] Almost immediately after Maj. Dan Whisnant had allowed the Albu Aifan subtribe to legally brandish thirty weapons, the number of openly armed fighters exploded to nearly three hundred. Dark had loosely interpreted the agreement, later claiming he was given permission to arm 250 men.[3] The young sheikh took a wily initiative, moving forward with his plan to build a militia faster than either the reticent Khamis or the Americans had expected or agreed to. Quite predictably, the intensity of the tribal civil war increased quickly as well.[4]

Opposing al Qaeda–affiliated tribesmen stepped up retaliatory attacks against the village, including drive-by shootings and attempted kidnappings of tribal leaders and their relatives. Two days before Greco walked into Sheikh Khaled's house, the men in the Marine's first squad under Cpl. Matthew Zofchak had stumbled across a heavy nighttime firefight between two groups of Iraqis several kilometers outside of the village. Nothing about the combatants indicated their respective allegiances, so without means to communicate, the Americans had no choice but to sit by and powerlessly observe colored tracers zip back and forth through the darkness as the battle raged in front of them.[5] The day after the mysterious gunfight, Greco ordered Sgt. Christopher Dockter's second squad to travel to Albu Aifan and introduce his Marines to their new allies. Dockter's mission was to build a rapport, carry out a census, and map the positions of the militia's checkpoints and defensive observation posts (OPs). Greco was now accompanying his men on a follow-up visit, to meet the local leaders for himself.[6]

The Marine officer and the sheikh had barely exchanged greetings when, about two minutes into the visit, a long burst of machine-gun fire roared in the distance. Greco glanced at the door. Upon entering the house, the lieutenant had left his corpsman and two Marines in the front courtyard, while the rest of the squad spread out in a defensive arrangement within the village. Two teams of Marines were about a hundred meters closer to the source of the gunfire. Greco had C. J. tell the sheikh to stay behind as he abruptly stood up, strapped on his helmet, and moved toward the front door with the interpreter and his radio operator trailing behind. As they left the house, more shots banged in the distance. A few seconds later, the lieutenant's radio crackled.

"I've just shot an Iraqi," came Dockter's disembodied voice. "The crowd is going crazy." Though the statement was ambiguous and cloaked in static, the sergeant's implication was clear: he had just shot the *wrong* Iraqi.[7]

Split into three teams of three Marines each, Dockter's squad had been spread over a hundred-meter triangle in the center of the village. The area served as a sort of town square, marking the epicenter of tribal wealth and power. The men had entered Albu Aifan a half hour before, moving from the cover of a deep irrigation ditch splitting an open field to approach the village.[8] The crisp, predawn air was covered with a thick fog that limited visibility to no more than fifty meters. As the Marines closed in on the village, the orange flame of a lone fire cut through the mist, and the Americans saw silhouettes of armed men casually guarding one of the main roads that bisected the village.[9] The checkpoint was manned by Iraqis brandishing AK-47s and RPK light machine guns.

LCpl. Tyler Williams, a thin twenty-year-old with bushy brown hair and a thick South Carolina accent, was taken aback by the sight of the militiamen. When the polite southerner thought of insurgents, he had always pictured Iraqis wearing black hoods or ski masks, with chests draped in ammunition vests or long bandoliers of threaded heavy machine-gun rounds. This essentially described the armed individuals staring at him from the checkpoint. It "was all a little strange" for Williams, whose schoolwork and socializing at Clemson University had been interrupted by deployment to Fallujah. He later recalled wondering, "How am I supposed to tell the difference" between friend and foe?[10]

As they walked into the village, Sergeant Dockter and Lieutenant Greco had waved at the Iraqis. Other than a few mapped locations of checkpoints and outposts, it was the initial litmus test of their new allies. If the Iraqis maintained a nonaggressive posture and waved back, they were good guys. If they shot back, they were insurgents. The militiamen waved.[11] After speaking with the men at the checkpoint, the squad moved into the outer perimeter of Albu Aifan, and saw widely spread, light-brown brick and stucco huts with thatched roofs and dirt floors. Chickens and goats wandered around in ramshackle pens. As the squad continued to advance, the residences—now modest homes made of lightly colored concrete block or brick, with an occasional courtyard wall—became denser. Clotheslines and hastily rigged tangles of power lines began to dot the yards. The Marines finally reached the village center, where the houses on each side of the street were four- to six-room "mansions" with spacious courtyards surrounded by high brick walls and sturdy metal gates.[12]

Paramount sheikh Khamis' walled compound was fifty meters north of the house Greco entered, near what served as an informal town square; the wide intersection Americans referred to as Mosque and Main Streets. About two dozen men and children of varying ages were outside. The men, ranging from about twenty to fifty years old, casually sat or lolled against courtyard walls, some smoking cigarettes, while the children played on and around the road. Nearly all of them stopped to watch the column of Marines as it passed; their faces varied from distantly friendly or curious to pointedly unconcerned with the visitors' presence. As was common in Iraq, a small train of excited kids followed the Americans wherever they moved.[13]

Dockter deployed one team on a corner outside Greco's position, while the two other teams ranged about one hundred meters north, each guarding the opposite east-west approaches of a road that split Main Street. HM2 Ruben "Doc" Muñoz joined the team that was posted outside the house hosting Greco's meeting. Things seemed pretty safe to the corpsman, if unusual. He spotted an armed and masked Iraqi moving along one of the rooftops. About a week earlier, the rules of engagement would have directed him to shoot the man.[14] Dockter joined one of the northern teams, composed of Williams and Ernan Paredes, both lance corporals, and Cpl. Andrew Johnson, the team's leader. The atmosphere was relaxed and friendly. The Marines kept an eye down Mosque and Main streets while alternately clowning with kids or attempting stilted communication with the local men who had smiled or bothered to engage them out of curiosity.

The unbroken rattle of machine-gun fire punctured the peaceful atmosphere.[15] The stream of booming thunks from what might have been an RPK light machine gun echoed from about five hundred or six hundred meters somewhere to the northeast of Dockter's position. The Marines' comfort evaporated. Their hands instinctively tightened on their weapons as they raised muzzles to a low ready position.

Dockter issued orders over his PRR (personal role radio). He instructed the southern team to stay with Greco, directed his second team to deploy east to an "overwatch" position on the roof of a house, and took his third team along the sloping northeastern curve of Main Street.[16] Dockter's team spread out in a loosely inverted V and briskly moved toward the shooting with readied rifles. They heard more scattered bangs from a lighter weapon, and thought it might have been return fire.[17] Paredes, following Dockter, sprinted toward the gunfire. He struggled to keep up with the sergeant, wondering, "How does a big guy like that move that fast?"[18]

As the team of Marines crested the curve of Main Street, a dark blue BMW whipped around a curved road roughly one hundred meters in front of them, kicking up a plume of dust as it set itself on a sloping, half-circular path toward the dismounted Americans. The driver accelerated to perhaps forty miles an hour as he banged on the horn. A man gripping an AK-47 sat in the passenger side window, his behind planted on the edge of the door frame—"Dukes of Hazzard style," recalled Dockter. The Marines scattered to the sides of the road and tensed as the car closed toward their position.

At the head of the small column, Dockter snapped his rifle to his shoulder and ripped off a semi-automatic stream of about five shots into the side of the passenger as the car drew near. The driver slammed on the brakes and the sedan screeched to a halt, kicking up a thick wave of dirt.[19] Dockter's stomach dropped. "Oh shit," he thought. "This isn't good." As quickly as the car had appeared, and faster than Dockter had decided to shoot, he now realized what was happening. If the driver had been an insurgent, he would have accelerated after the shooting, not stopped.[20] A young male got out of the driver's seat of the car with an AK-47. Dockter barked at him to put down his weapon, and he complied. The Iraqi was yelling, and tears streamed down his face. A pale dishdasha billowed around him as he moved around the hood to the other side of the vehicle. The distraught Iraqi opened the passenger door and his compatriot fell out, along with a wash of blood that soaked into the powdery dirt street. Dockter had shot a very young man. The Iraqi's face was pale. His eyes were rolled back in his head, and his light robes were rapidly turning red. He was limp, with his limbs askew. When the sergeant saw the Iraqi slump from the car, he immediately recognized the implications for the Marines' new alliance with the tribe. In his words, he "hoped this deal [wasn't] screwed."[21]

Pandemonium quickly ensued. Time sped up. A second car of armed Iraqi men stopped a few meters behind the first car. The occupants, some in trousers and shirts, others in bland-colored robes, jumped from the vehicle, rushed toward their injured friend, and screamed at the Marines. Anger and grief twisted their faces. Dockter and his men pointed their M-16s at the men, aggressively motioning and yelling in stilted Arabic and English, telling them to stop: "Oh-khef! Oh-khef! Drop the weapons, now!"[22] The grief-stricken Iraqis complied, putting their rifles on the ground while continuing to lob a steady barrage of angry Arabic at the Americans. Dockter radioed for Greco and his other teams to join them. According to platoon sergeant Michael Gillitzer, who communicated with Dockter via radio from a nearby position, he "could tell" the situation was dire from the unusual edge in the typically laconic squad leader's voice.[23]

Men and women of all ages quickly streamed from nooks and crannies in the village—from courtyard gates, houses, and around corners of side streets and alleys. In what seemed like less than a minute, the mostly barren street had filled with more than a hundred people. Most tried to crowd around the fallen man, crying or screaming at the Americans; some of the women began to wail a characteristically Arabic lament while slapping themselves in the face. A few of the civilians started to throw small stones at the four Marines, who moved closer to one another and were surrounded on all sides.[24] Dockter was having trouble taking it all in, so he didn't. Instead, he focused on disarming each new group of armed men that materialized. The Iraqis were carrying everything from AK-47s and light machine guns to rocket-propelled grenades (RPGs) and Vietnam-era M-14 rifles. "Good God," thought the sergeant. "This is going to be a bloodbath."

Dockter barked at his men, "Take all their weapons!"[25] Paredes focused on clearing the area to the right of the car. Four or five Iraqi men suddenly sprinted around the corner of a house, three of them armed with rifles. Paredes pointed his M-16 at them and screamed, "Put the guns down. *Put the fucking guns down!*" The men yelled back at him in Arabic, but complied with the Marine's instruction when Williams and Johnson arrived to back him up.[26]

As armed group after armed group arrived, the Marines pointed their guns at them and commanded the Iraqis to drop their weapons. Though outnumbered and having just shot a "good guy," Dockter's instinct and training told him not to be apologetic and meek. He consciously tried to project authority and dominance, barking at the militiamen to disarm themselves. The sergeant lasered in on each new Iraqi with a gun. He recalled that more than three dozen men with weapons arrived at the scene in "something like two minutes." Wailing and curses became superfluous, background noise. The Marines ignored the smattering of small rocks flying at them.

"Don't shoot! Don't shoot!" Corporal Johnson yelled several times at the Marines, according to Paredes. Johnson, the team leader, was a stocky Marine in his late twenties from Michigan who was described as mature and serious. Dockter thought he could probably rely on him the most to keep his head.[27] The younger lance corporals, Williams and Paredes, held their firearms rigidly and followed the lead of their sergeant and the corporal. Williams was a good-natured Marine who spoke in a very deliberate, southern drawl. His buddies constantly ragged on him, calling him "a hick" or "a hillbilly dumbass" because of his slow affectations. Williams would just laugh. It was all in good fun, and he was the type of guy who Marines could talk shit to all day long without letting it get to him. His sweet nature was now probably an asset as the confrontation with the locals escalated.[28] Paredes was a twenty-one-year-old Chilean American with sharp features and a thin, dark mustache. The slim, five-foot-nine Marine was usually "a chatterbox" who "asked a million questions and never shut the fuck up," joked Dockter. Paredes was now gravely quiet and focused. "Holy shit," he thought, as he watched armed Iraqis taking up positions on the rooftops above. "This is going to be [our] last stand, like Custer. . . . I'm probably going to die."[29]

The four men moved in concert as they followed Dockter's cues to disarm the militiamen. The cliché that training takes over in an emergency materialized for the grateful squad leader, who was relieved, impressed, and more than a little amazed that none of the surrounded Marines had panicked and squeezed off a round.[30] His ears awash in noise, Williams was "very ready to shoot someone." Men were yelling, car horns honking, women still screaming. It seemed like there was no end to the stream of upset, cursing men wearing masks and toting guns. It was "getting ready to get bad. So many of them had guns," Williams recalled.[31]

The scene bore scaled-down parallels to an infamous incident in 2003, when members of the U.S. Army's 82nd Airborne killed seventeen Fallujans at a protest in the city. The soldiers had started firing after hearing gunfire that they had assumed was directed at their position from within the angry crowd. The city's more strident imams quickly capitalized on the tragedy as what they would likely call one of the "most grievous injustices perpetrated by the infidel occupiers." Many of the locals and an American intelligence specialist thought that it was one of the sparks that had accelerated the Fallujan insurgency into widespread, popular rebellion.[32]

Dockter's Marines continued to hold their fire as they waited for backup, keeping an eye on the distressed civilians and the growing stack of confiscated weapons lying at their feet. Within minutes, the squad leader's second team, led by Cpl. Jack Blevins, joined them after abandoning an overwatch position on a nearby roof.[33] Several members of the crowd picked up the wounded young man and dragged him up and down the street in a frantic scrum, while a thick cordon of followers wailed and wove a grieving chorus around them. Many of the young tribesmen stood a few feet from the Marines and yelled in their faces. The Americans didn't know exactly what the Iraqis were saying, but they got the message.[34]

———————— ❖ ————————

Tha'er Khalid Aifan al-Issawi yelled at the Marines. The thirty-year-old couldn't recall ever being so angry at them. After the 2003 invasion, many members of his immediate family had dealt cordially with the U.S. military, as had he. As a boy, he left middle school to go to work in his father's construction company, and his family had eagerly solicited contracts from the newly arrived Americans. Though some members of his extended family had proudly fought against the Americans, others saw the invaders as just another temporary power with whom the tribe would have to bargain. Tha'er viewed this willingness by some of his subtribe to deal with the "infidels" as one of the main reasons they were now engaged in a civil war against their "ideologically pure" fellow tribesmen who had allied with al Qaeda and other mujahidin. As a brother of Ma'an Khalid Aifan al-Issawi, one of Dark's lieutenants, Tha'er had been an early recruit to the sheikh's new militia.

On January 9, Tha'er had been commanding a checkpoint when the first shots broke the midmorning peace. Soon after, a familiar dark blue BMW had sped to his position and stopped. A wildly upset Shafi Hamid Shafi was brandishing an AK-47 and leaning out of the passenger window of the vehicle. The twenty-two-year-old beckoned Tha'er and his men to follow his car and bring their heavier PK general purpose machine guns and RPG-7 launchers. He told them that his relatives who lived in a house on the outskirts of Albu Aifan were being attacked by al Qaeda–affiliated tribesmen from a village to the south. The young man's uncle had called him on his cell phone and begged for help.

After shouting his hurried request for reinforcements, Shafi's dark BMW took off, as Tha'er and his three militiamen grabbed their weapons and rushed to another vehicle. The second sedan peeled out less than a minute later and chased the lead car toward Main Street. Tha'er heard another short burst of gunfire and soon came upon the BMW ground to a halt in the middle of the road. The Iraqis jumped out of their chase car and ran toward four "angry" Marines and the prone form of Shafi, splayed in blood and dirt below the open passenger door.

"We are good to you and you want to kill us!" an enraged Tha'er shouted at the Americans, who pointed their M-16s at him, yelling and motioning for him to drop his weapon. He complied, but continued cursing them. "Why are you doing this? All you do is cause problems when you come around!" screamed another man. "All you ever do is kill people!" said a third militiaman. "Why do you want to help al Qaeda?" shouted another.[35]

If they had understood Arabic, the Marines would have been mystified at the suggestion that they were intentionally helping al Qaeda. But the accusation sometimes circulated in local gossip circles due to American missteps, civilian casualties, and Iraqi suspicions. In one instance several days earlier, unbeknownst to Dockter, his platoon had enabled the escape of two al Qaeda operatives—Barakat Hussein Abdel Majid and Jabar Salma—who had been kidnapped and held by members of another subtribe, who were loosely allied with Dark and his militia against the radical insurgents and their allied tribesmen.

The Abu Hatim tribesmen had nabbed the men to interrogate them and strike a blow against the leadership of the *takfiri* insurgency. They were holding the pair hostage in a residence in the village that bore the name of the subtribe. Sheikhs from various peninsula subtribes had been attempting to mediate negotiations for a peaceful settlement to the conflict and the release of the hostages. Meanwhile, the captors had roughly questioned the insurgents, who had proceeded to divulge lots of valuable information on relationships between the competing sheikhs and their foreign insurgent allies.[36] By coincidence, Lieutenant Greco had chosen to use the house where the pair were being held as his platoon's patrol base on a long op into Abu Hatim. When the Americans arrived unexpectedly and knocked on the door, the tribesmen panicked.

The sheikhs of this subtribe had not yet formed an alliance with the Marines, and in any case, they knew they would be detained immediately if U.S. forces found two thoroughly beaten men tied up in one of their houses. The quick solution was to throw their prisoners out a back door and into a shallow canal. Despite being handcuffed, the two insurgents escaped from the area, slipping their jailors and their unwitting American saviors.[37] Word of the costly blunder had spread among those at odds with the *takfiris*. Now, days later, the Marines had shot one of their fighters, who was only trying to save his family from attackers. The Iraqis were frustrated and furious with American missteps.

Greco grabbed Doc Muñoz and the southern team and led them toward Dockter's position, marked by the thickest press of upset locals. The village center was in chaos. More than a hundred Iraqis, some of them still armed, were going crazy. Here and there, Greco saw his Marines mixed in with the throng. He could see that his teams had instinctively deployed in a loose pattern near any available cover. All were tense and grim, and a couple of the young men looked alarmed. All of the Marines except for those disarming Iraqis had their weapons "in the ready position" and heads on a swivel keeping watch down the avenues of approach to the scene.[38] Along the way, villagers screamed at the lieutenant, C. J., and Muñoz. Greco saw a few tribesmen throw small stones.

"What are they saying?" he asked his interpreter.

"They're saying 'Why you come around here? All you do is cause problems and kill people,'" replied C. J.

Greco told the Iraqi to ask the crowd "to please calm down."[39] C. J. did his best, authoritatively raising his voice over the shouts of the crowd, but this only drew ire toward him. The angry villagers called him a traitor and cursed him for working with the Americans, who were described as incompetent, conspiratorially malicious, or both. "Sons of Dogs! God will take revenge on you!" one yelled. "Mercenary!" added another.

Iraqi accusations of betrayal never wounded C. J., mostly because the young, middle-class Shia from Baghdad loved Americans. His family had been frightened when the United States invaded Iraq, but also excited. His father, a diplomat with the Ministry of Foreign Affairs at the time, regarded Saddam Hussein as an "unjust ruler" and celebrated the dictator's removal. A lot of people in their neighborhood felt that way, until al Qaeda started wreaking havoc in the capital, killing people en masse, and the Shia militias retaliated in kind.

C. J.'s father had taught him and his sister some English, and the fifteen-year-old boy honed this skill by hanging around a U.S. Army outpost in his neighborhood of Adamiyah. The American soldiers "were really friendly and cool." They were impressed by his English, started paying him for simple translations, and finally encouraged C. J. to become a full-time interpreter. When he turned eighteen, he submitted his application and was then sent to Fallujah to help the Marines. It was a dangerous assignment, but C. J.'s family supported his decision. They wanted him to be "on the good side" of the war and thought it might provide them more options for protecting the family as civil order disintegrated around them.[40]

C. J. was a valued interpreter, with above-average English skills, but his tour with Alpha 1/24 was not always smooth. He would sometimes get cranky about keeping up the brutal pace demanded by the company's officers. Several times Whisnant or Greco had to yell at the young man to pry him off the FOB and onto patrol. For his part, he sometimes bragged to the enlisted Marines that he knew better than the officers, saying, "If I was in command, we'd win things tomorrow." C. J. was good at his job, brave, occasionally lazy, still immature, popular with the Marines, and ultimately irrepressible. One sergeant benevolently described him as "just a kid out there, having a good time."[41]

The young interpreter was a little worried now, however. He had never seen local tribesmen "so pissed off." C. J. took the current insults in stride, but they surprised him. Usually Fallujans spoke to him with fearful respect, conscious of the power he had to twist their words to the Americans. At that moment, however, they had lost all sense of discretion. One screaming man was even trying to lunge at the Marines to fight them, but was being held back by his friends who said, "They'll kill you." The linguist continued to appeal to the crowd for calm.

"Sir, they are talking lots of shit," C. J. told Greco. "It's gonna get bad. We should take a position or get the fuck out of here."[42] As Greco, Muñoz, and C. J. worked their way through the press toward Dockter with other Marines in tow, they saw a group of distraught men carrying the bloody body of the young Iraqi. Muñoz focused his sight on the injured man and thought that he was moving slightly, and therefore still alive. The corpsman instinctively started to rush forward, but Greco grabbed his arm. "Stay back for a second," said the lieutenant, as he tried to assess what they were getting into.

The Americans watched as the hysterically yelling men dragged the body dozens of feet toward them and then abruptly reversed course, carrying him dozens of feet back toward the car. Muñoz saw some of the militiamen they had met at the checkpoints hollering at the Marines or seemingly at no one at all. Many of the children had scattered. The situation was looking worse by the second, thought the corpsman.

"Maybe I can help," Muñoz said to the platoon leader.[43]

"Go," said Greco, following with C. J. as the Puma plunged into the crowd and toward the injured man, who was still being hauled around like a ragdoll by the careening huddle of tribesmen. Muñoz grabbed some bandages out of his bag and now waved them at the Iraqis while shouting, "I'm a doctor! Doctor! Doctor!" Meanwhile, Greco moved to Sergeant Dockter's side and forcefully encouraged his squad leader to relax and to make sure the men were pointing their weapons at the ground.

When Muñoz arrived near the patient, the Iraqis had already set the injured man on the ground. One tribesman was gently slapping Shafi's pale face, while another sprinkled drops of water over his lips.[44] The crowd parted when they realized Muñoz was a medic. The corpsman dropped to his knees in front of the still figure, and the newly distracted locals pressed in on all sides to observe. The men immediately surrounding him continued pushing, but the panicked shouting quieted to a worried murmur as they watched the Puma work. Muñoz saw Greco's and Dockter's (comforting) tan combat boots immediately next to him on his right. He looked down at his patient.

One quick glance was all it took to determine the young man was now dead. Blood was all over the place. The militiaman's robes were soaked and caked in reddish dirt, and large streams of blood were turning the ground into a sloppy mess under his knees. The Iraqi was unmoving and pale. Muñoz checked brachial and carotid pulses, each for several seconds. Nothing.

"Hey, this guy is done," he said in a low voice to Greco, at his side. Muñoz moved to get up, but balked. The Iraqis around the corpsman had stopped screaming and were intently watching him. He thought he had to try to "do something" to continue to hold the crowd's attention. "Lieutenant, I'm going to do something, because these guys are pretty pissed off," he murmured to Greco, who did not hear him. First Muñoz ran a hand over Shafi's vacant eyes to close them. Then he lifted Shafi's robe to reveal a femoral leg wound and a series of seeping holes in his abdomen. The medic quickly removed a tight elastic pressure bandage from his bag and cinched it around the tattered leg. Then he grabbed a bigger dressing and loosely wrapped it around the Iraqi's stomach, asking one of the tribesmen to help him roll the man on his side as he applied the bandage.

He heard Greco behind him, talking to someone. The Iraqis had lowered their volume even more and now resembled a crowd jostling for position before a rock concert. Muñoz quickly glanced up as he shifted his weight to one knee. The men directly in front of him looked on expectantly, seeming to buy the ruse. They thought the tribesman still had a chance at survival or at least gave no indication that they knew he was dead.

"He needs to go to a hospital, right away!" Muñoz said loudly. C. J. shouted his translation. The corpsman held the wounded leg aloft as three Iraqis picked up the other limbs of the body and carried it to the bullet-pocked car. A tribesman opened the door, and the Iraqis recoiled, raising their voices and shouting anew when they saw the broken glass, blood, and viscera on the front seat of the sedan.

Someone ran to get an undamaged vehicle, and soon thereafter another BMW arrived and parked in front of the first car. Muñoz and the militiamen loaded Shafi into the back seat. Two of the Fallujans climbed into the front seat. The driver turned the engine over and hit the gas. The militiaman's feet dangled from the dark sedan's rear passenger window as the car spun up dust and sped off toward the local hospital.[45]

Soon after Muñoz had begun to treat Shafi, Dark had arrived with Ma'an and two other lieutenants. The agitated sheikh shouted at the crowd to calm down as he tried to ascertain what was going on. Seeing the Marines, he made a beeline for Dockter.

"It is okay. I am Dark," said the sheikh, wearing a black ski mask and a dark blue ammunition-carrying vest over a shirt and pants. "That's great, buddy. Whatever," thought Dockter, paying little mind to one more unknown, hooded Iraqi.[46] Dark then moved toward Paredes, who fellow Marines had joked bore a resemblance to Major Whisnant.

"Major Dan!" said the sheikh. Paredes ignored him.[47] LCpl. Dickie Prince recalls a grief-stricken Dark, tears in his eyes, yelling at him, "Mister, no more mistakes!"[48]

Dark moved on toward Greco. There was no time to waste; an Albu Aifan family was under attack by members of al Qaeda in Iraq at a house six hundred meters away. He needed the Marines to come with him—now. Greco had heard of Dark, but had never met him, until a "frazzled" Iraqi wearing a ski mask approached him amid the residual commotion. The man lifted the mask, revealing his relatively youthful, full face, and said, "I am Dark. I know Major Dan!"[49]

The sheikh was clearly upset. The dead young man was a close cousin of the sheikh's, but it was more than just grief, assumed Greco. With the recent alliance, he recognized that Dark's fate was tied to the Americans' actions. Everything the sheikh had worked for—the endorsement of Khamis, the right to carry weapons and form a militia, and the confidence of his tribe— was in peril. More than anything, Dark was intently focused on getting the Marines moving to save his besieged tribesmen. As he stood up to al Qaeda, he had sworn to protect his people. He now needed to unambiguously and publicly deliver on that promise, and so did the Americans.[50]

Greco recognized the sheikh's nickname. The Marine started to explain what had happened and apologized for the misunderstanding. "It's okay. It's okay," replied Dark. "I need you to come with me right now. We have a serious problem." He then instructed the Americans to follow the road for fifty meters and enter an unfinished two-story building on the opposite side of Main Street. Greco wanted more information, but he also had no desire to further push the Marines' luck with the village. He told Dockter to gather his squad and get on the move immediately.[51] Dark turned back to the crowd. Ma'an and Tha'er listened as he spoke.

"Calm down," the sheikh said in Arabic, raising his voice. "I just talked to them and they apologized. Calm down. It was an accident. If this man is dead, it is God's will."[52] The Americans were relieved and impressed as they witnessed, with great curiosity, the *wasta* (influence) of a sheikh in action. The crowd stopped yelling, gave Dark its attention, and then began to disperse at his direction.[53] There was something a little different about Dark's mannerisms compared to other sheikhs, according to Greco. The platoon commander had met a few sheikhs and seen some in operation. Most moved with a noble aloofness that set them apart from the average tribesmen. Dark's interaction with the men and women of the village seemed less formal. He commanded respect, but was almost casual with them. Greco thought he might be something akin to a populist politician in the United States, a "man of the people."[54] To the Marines' amazement, the road had almost emptied. Much of the crowd had dispersed almost as quickly as it had appeared.

C. J. had a different assessment of Dark. He knew the tribesmen had respect for him as a man of wealth and noble lineage, and some genuinely liked him, for sure. The interpreter also thought, however, that others resented the brash young sheikh, regarding him as "a crazy person looking for power." And a greater number feared him, though that was not remarkable. C. J. knew that to be any kind of leader in Iraq, people had to be afraid of you. Fear was the one motivation that all Iraqis understood. Not all of his American employers seemed to fathom this simple truth.[55]

The Marines, the interpreter, and the corpsman formed up into a staggered column and conducted the short march toward the residence down the street. They entered the unpainted, concrete-block building, which was missing two of its walls. There was a gravel floor and a long spiral staircase that led to a second floor and the roof, which bore the standard three-foot wall along its edges. Dockter assigned one team to pull security on the ground floor and a second team to overwatch up top. The third team joined him and Greco on the middle floor.[56] Dark met up with them less than a minute later, along with Ma'an and another lieutenant. He turned to the task at hand: across an open field from their position, al Qaeda fighters were surrounding a family member's house, "and they were going to kill them. We need you to save them."[57] Dockter, Greco, and the three Iraqis moved to the roof.

Visible several hundred meters away, across a big field, was an isolated two-story house surrounded on all sides by large hedges and trees. A main road ran in a north-south direction just behind the home. The Marines heard scattered gunfire, but saw no muzzle flashes.[58] Through their scopes, Dockter and Greco thought that they could make out the slightest movement around the residence.[59] Others saw nothing.[60] An excited Dark entreated the Americans to fire at the house. Greco was reluctant; he faced a dilemma. The Americans had no positive identification (PID) on an enemy combatant, which was required to open fire under the rules of engagement. Legalities aside, they didn't want to unleash the directed fire of a Marine squad into a building known to contain civilians. Nonetheless, the sheikh and his men were looking to his Marines to do something. It struck him as a test of the Americans' willingness to help after the day's tragedy, and to back up their new alliance not only with words but with deeds. On top of everything, the radios had gone out (again), so Greco had lost contact with Whisnant, whom he had been gradually updating on developments throughout the day.

The lieutenant made a decision. He arrayed a second team of Marines on the roof and instructed them to shoot to the sides of the residence, focusing on the trees and bushes bordering the house. Dark had said the home was surrounded by al Qaeda fighters; any civilians probably would be within the structure itself. Greco ordered his Marines to fire initially at a "rapid rate" for about five seconds, followed by a "sustained rate" of controlled bursts. He hoped the bullets would kill or flush out any insurgents without hitting innocents.

A steady burst from one of his Marine's M-249 SAWs erupted next to Greco for several seconds and briefly deafened him. It was quickly joined by the beat of M-16s and a few AK-47s fired by Dark's militiamen. The sound tapered to a sporadic cacophony of bursts and bangs that lasted another fifteen or twenty seconds. Greco instructed his men to "cease fire." The acrid aftermath of gunfire hung in the air.[61] Dockter heard more distant banging and thought he recognized the dull thump of rounds hitting one of the finished walls of the house they were in. Some of the men on the roof heard the snap of return bullets over their heads.[62] Others did not remember return fire at all.[63]

Within seconds, some of the Marines saw movement around the yard of the target house. A white pickup truck burst out of the tree line and "hauled ass" westward along the road that ran parallel to the Marines' position. Dark, who was receiving intelligence on his cell phone from someone in the besieged house, shouted that the car belonged to the enemy. Greco decided to trust the sheikh, and gave his men the green light. He was pushing the limits of PID, but decided that the fragile alliance was worth it. With a profile shot on a target cleared hot, everyone opened up. A furious fifteen-second wave of bullets hit the fleeing truck, which smoked, slowed, and rolled to a stop.[64]

One of the Americans shouted that he had seen a gunman somewhere within the large field directly in front of them. A shooter or shooters might be taking pot shots from one of the deep, reed-filled irrigation ditches crossing it. The Marines fired back at their discretion where they thought they saw movement. The radio was still dead; Greco had started using Dark's cell phone to communicate with Whisnant.[65] He tried to update the major in quick, vague terms that suited the unencrypted line, while Dockter sent one of his teams back to the platoon's observation posts to get another radio. By the time the team returned, the firing had stopped. The exchange had only lasted a few minutes.[66] Dockter sent the newly returned team five hundred meters up the road to check the smoking, bullet-riddled truck. The Marines found no sign of the insurgents, who had evidently escaped through the canals. The next day, one of the Albu Aifan tribesmen told the sergeant that an insurgent had been wounded.[67] Dark later claimed that some of the attackers had been killed.[68]

With the engagement over, Dark sent some of his militiamen to rescue the family in the house and escort them to safety. All of them had survived the attack, and they were immediately moved out of the isolated residence and into temporary lodgings within the well-defended perimeter of the village.[69] A smiling and grateful Dark passed out cigarettes to the young Marines in a gesture of gratitude.[70] As if bestowing a reward, the sheikh gave the Americans information on two IEDs buried on Main Street. Greco quickly readied his squad to go and search for the bombs. The Americans appreciated the information, but made note of the complicated local politics: There was always the possibility that Dark knew the locations because some of his tribesmen had placed the bombs.[71]

CWO-5 Jim Roussell frequently admonished the Marines, "Don't fall in love with your sources."[72] Greco developed a healthy skepticism of his new allies and tried to view his interactions with them as discrete business deals in support of a larger, ongoing negotiation. Although they had just met, Greco realized that mentally keeping Dark at arm's length might prove difficult. The sheikh was "one of the most charismatic people" he had ever met. He spoke excellent English, was warm and cheerful, and his boundless energy and talkative nature were infectious. Further, his passionate motivation stood in stark contrast to the laconic fatalism of many Iraqis.

Dark was a man of action and seemed like a natural leader. An intensely competitive self-starter himself, Greco wanted to like the guy. As their relationship continued to develop over the following weeks, Dark asserted to Greco that he was also a veteran of the Second Battle of Fallujah. During a meeting at his house, the sheikh beckoned the lieutenant closer and pulled down his trousers to show off a jagged ribbon of dark, raised flesh along the side of his leg. He claimed to have been wounded by an American bullet during difficult fighting.[73] The Marine briefly admired the scar, looked at the Iraqi, smiled, and said, "I'm probably the guy who shot you." They laughed.[74] At other times to other people, the sheikh claimed to have been shot by Americans under more innocent circumstances.[75] Whatever the true story, it was now not so bizarre to imagine that former adversaries on a battlefield renowned in Arab and Marine Corps lore had cooperated in rescuing a nascent alliance from the brink of disaster. This was the new way forward in Anbar province.

Dockter was relieved. He never felt guilty for killing Shafi, the well-intentioned young tribesman rushing to rescue his family. Insurgents had been conducting drive-by attacks in the area, and the Iraqi had sped toward the Americans while brandishing a firearm. Dockter considered it a righteous shoot; he would not hesitate to fire again in the same circumstances. The sergeant did, however, carry the weight of almost killing the Marines' new alliance with the locals before it got off the ground. Thankfully, now that things had calmed down, he could breathe a bit easier.

Several months later, while pulling security as Major Whisnant visited another leading sheikh of the tribe, Dockter met the man's son, a sixteen-year-old who spoke good English and "loved shooting the shit with Marines." As the young Iraqi and the Americans chatted and told stories late that night, the boy asked Dockter if he knew the Marine who had killed his cousin. He described the circumstances of Shafi's death. Dockter discreetly said no, he did not know the Marine.[76]

In the end, Ma'an had been pleased with the day. His tribesmen had been furious, perhaps angrier than he could ever recall seeing them. Shafi's death had been a tragic mistake, however, and the Americans had apologized. In addition, their willingness to allow his militia to have weapons and fight with them when Dark asked for help showed him that their arrangement was different from past relationships, when Americans merely offered jobs or dictated terms to his tribe. This was collaborative.[77]

Tha'er had screamed himself hoarse at the men who had shot Shafi, but forgave the Marines. The Americans had apologized, and the doctor Marine had tried to save his fellow tribesman, who unfortunately "died in the car on the way to the hospital." Dark explained the mistake, and the Marines stayed to protect the village, opening a permanent base at the highest building in the area. Tha'er's new allies manned checkpoints with more professionalism than the militiamen under his command. These overtures restored his opinion of Americans.[78]

Dark recalls asking his angry tribesmen to have "patience" with their new allies. He later explained how he had contextualized the accidental shooting. "Why are [the Marines] here?" he asked them rhetorically. "They are here to protect us. The deal is, I talked to the Americans, and it was one mistake. But how many people do al Qaeda kill every day?" The sheikh's argument was bolstered by the fact that the Americans and his Iraqi militiamen "saved" the family under attack and "killed some of the people" who had attacked them.[79]

Beyond the accidental nature of the shooting, two elements of local culture might also help explain the tribe's willingness to forgive the tragedy. The first, stressed in Dark's entreaties to the justifiably angry mob, is the concept of fatalism symbolized by the Arabic expression *insh'allah*—"It is as Allah wills" or "God willing."

Islamic cultures are suffused with this sentiment. Sometimes the term is used to indicate a desired future event, such as, "We will defeat al Qaeda, insh'allah" (God willing). At other times, it is used as a rhetorical shrug, which could frustrate the disciplined sensibilities of American military personnel who worked with Iraqis. "I was late to our meeting. Insh'allah" (it was as God wills, so no sense being upset about it). But the concept can also serve as an antidote to powerlessness in the face of harsh reckonings, such as a cruel natural environment, brutal dictatorship, or uncontrollable violence. This element of Islamic identity helped Iraq shoulder the misery of war. The Iraqis suffered greatly and grieved to be sure, but they appeared to handle the hardships in a way that often surprised the Americans who came to know them. Insh'allah: "I must be strong and move on. Events are as God wills."[80]

The other cultural touchstone that might have worked in the Marines' favor was the concept of tribal blood debt. For thousands of years, tribes in the region had operated according to their own customary criminal and civil codes to settle disputes, prior to or outside of the reach of any central government's legal system. If a tribesman killed someone, revenge for the killing was typically required, lest the victim's relatives permanently lose honor and incur shame.[81] Endless cycles of revenge killings, however, could spiral into perpetual war and threaten the survival of entire tribes. Thus the option of the *diya* (blood price) arose, whereby the offending (killing) tribesman or his family could pay an agreed sum of money or compensatory goods to the aggrieved family. With the debt negotiated and settled, everyone could move on without further bloodshed.

Although the U.S. military eventually adopted condolence payments as a routine practice in Iraq and Afghanistan, the American "tribe" paid no money to the family of Shafi Hamed Shafi. It did, however, act immediately to help Dark rescue the family members that the young man had been rushing to save. And the Marines would soon establish a base nearby to watch over the tribe's village. The actions of the Americans that day, along with subsequent measures, showed faith in collaboration and the will to protect Shafi's tribe. This could be interpreted as repayment of any blood debt. After all, as Tha'er put it, "We needed the Americans' help to fight al Qaeda more than we needed their money."[82]

6

❖ PULLING THREADS ❖

Just as the Albu Issa needed the Marines, the Americans needed the tribe's help, which they got in the form of an unprecedented intelligence bonanza. The trickle of actionable firsthand information about the peninsula's insurgency quickly surged into a flood. Maj. Dan Whisnant, the military intelligence Marine Saint One, and CWO-5 Jim Roussell were pleased with the new alliance, and the "Hobbits" of Alpha Company's intelligence cell became busier than they had thought possible. Fellow Marines had saddled the clique of analysts with the Tolkienesque nickname because of their small stature; none of the men stood much over five-foot-six. Their responsibilities, however, were expansive. The Hobbits managed the breadth of the "intelligence cycle," cataloguing and analyzing the information that orchestrated the company's war against the insurgency.[1]

Prior to deployment, Whisnant had established the company-level intelligence cell by picking "smart Marines" who had useful backgrounds, skills, or mindsets for intelligence work. At the top of his list was Sgt. Jeremiah Howe, who was charged with leading the team. Howe was a Transportation Security Administration officer in his civilian life, as well as a "common-sense grunt" who Whisnant believed would "intuitively grasp the capabilities of both Alpha Company and [their] enemy."[2] The sergeant wasn't enthused about being chosen for the job, but acquiesced to the position after receiving assurances from Whisnant that he wouldn't be stuck inside the wire for six months.[3] Howe was put in charge of a team of five: the lance corporals Matt Robinson, Curtis Mejeur, Ryan Brown, and Josh Clayton and Cpl. Andrew Tyink. Only Clayton and Mejeur had any training specific to the task. A few had sufficient analytical skills and aptitude, and all of them were proficient with computers, but Clayton stood out as an asset.[4]

A computer programmer by trade, the young lance corporal was unhappy when he was pulled from his platoon during pre-deployment drills and shuffled to headquarters to "do computer stuff." Clayton had seen enough war movies to worry that his transfer might have been the result of higher-ranking Marines thinking that he "couldn't hack it."[5] As it turned out, his commanders had allocated resources wisely. During his first combat deployment, the computer specialist wound up developing and maintaining the Marines' singularly important asset for counterinsurgency: the intelligence database.

The most basic qualifications for the job were patience and possession of a strong work ethic. Mapping the massive spider web of the peninsula's tribes and insurgent cells was a complicated, time-consuming task, and the Hobbits' company commander worked them, in his words, "like galley slaves." Often pulling interminably long shifts, seven days a week for much of the deployment, the intel Marines executed a lengthy list of functions. They catalogued local tips, gathered information from "human intelligence exploitation teams," verified intelligence, designed "targeting packages" to snatch suspected insurgents on raids, sometimes accompanied the platoons on raids, briefed missions, debriefed missions, tracked insurgent activity, and handled detainees.

The alliance with Dark, Sheikh Aifan Sadoun Aifan al-Issawi, both increased and changed the nature of their work. Building a basic census of the peninsula to isolate insurgents and reviewing old intelligence reports were augmented by verifying and applying the bounty of information from newly allied tribesmen. The tips quickly paid dividends.[6] Amazingly, roadside bombs became scarce in some areas. Tips about where the IEDs were placed had been hard to come by for the first half of Alpha Company's deployment; whether fearing insurgent retribution or simply lacking sympathy for the occupiers, tight-lipped locals refused to divulge widely known hiding places for the booby traps, which were far and away the deadliest threat to American forces. The newly acquired blessings from Dark and the paramount sheikh, Khamis Hasnawi Aifan al-Issawi, combined with promises of American and militia protection, made a difference. Tips on the location of buried bombs within the Albu Aifan sphere of influence quickly accrued. Within weeks, modest sections of the peninsula's highway morphed from routinely explosive "red routes" into mostly secure "green routes" after explosive ordnance disposal (EOD) teams moved in to scoop up and safely detonate the bombs.[7]

A major coup occurred in late January 2007 when some Albu Aifan sheikhs brought in two informants who knew the location of a factory manufacturing vehicle-borne improvised explosive devices (VBIEDs) within the city of Fallujah. Marines with Charlie Company 1/24 raided the location, destroying its lethal capacity and capturing some of the bomb makers. Given the unique role of truck bombs in al Qaeda in Iraq's ongoing campaign of spectacular attacks, which killed scores of people per operation, this lone tip saved many lives.[8]

Aside from the fresh influx of information, some of the men affiliated with the Albu Aifan subtribe and other subtribes of the Albu Issa undoubtedly stopped hiding the explosives themselves. Though plenty of bombs and people willing to plant them remained on the peninsula, the alliance with influential leaders of one of the area's subtribes drained a fraction of the insurgency's more casual labor pool, including many attackers for hire.[9] Progress in this area delivered a modest but tangible boost against the number one killer of American military personnel.

Dark, his lieutenants, and their extended family members comprised the vanguard of informants. The familial and tribal connectedness of the Albu Issa and the ubiquity of cheap cell phones meant that sheikhs had spies throughout the peninsula's villages and subtribes. This widespread network of relatives tracked insurgent activity and fed information to the Albu Aifan militia, which now began to pass it on to the Hobbits, Saint One, or Whisnant directly. A typical tip arrived via a hurried phone call: "A white car is moving from [this house] to [this house]." If the Marines were lucky, the Iraqis specifically identified the location with a prearranged system of grid coordinates. Failing that, tipsters referred to local landmarks.[10] Once in possession of the information, the Americans attempted to verify it by scrambling or vectoring circling air assets. When they achieved "eyes on" a suspected insurgent, Whisnant, Maj. Jim Hayes, or one of the other air officers chose between two courses of action: an immediate attack or surveillance.

Sometimes, when a particularly opportune or high-value target presented itself, the Marines opted for a summary strafing run or devastating drop of guided munitions from a Cobra attack helicopter, F-18 Hornet, or Harrier jump jet. Often, it proved more valuable to simply wait and watch,

tracking the insurgents' movements from location to location via helicopter, fixed-wing fighter, or unmanned drone. In combination with the census
and database, this tactic allowed the Marines to map new nodes of the rebel
network. Casual visits to the newly discovered locations or subsequent raids
sometimes led to the capture of insurgents, many of whom quickly gave up
other insurgents to interrogators, revealing more tendrils of their organization.[11] In the first eighty-four days of Alpha Company's deployment, the
Marines detained 172 suspected insurgents; many were soon freed due to
lack of evidence. In the subsequent eighty-six days—after the alliance with
the Albu Issa—the number of detainees doubled, to 347.[12] The improved
evidence gathered to indict suspects meant that fewer of them would be
released in a short time to wreak vengeance on suspected informants.[13]

Bit by bit, the Albu Issa and their American allies began to unravel
the insurgency on the peninsula. For the Marines, the effort involved classic
police work, spy craft, and counterinsurgency doctrine greatly accelerated
by the infusion of a wide network of cooperative local sources. The effect
was akin to pulling multiple threads on a sweater at once.

The relationship between the Americans and allied members of the
Albu Issa was not without its difficulties. Though quickly coming to rely
on each other, both parties constantly maneuvered for position and sometimes butted heads during intelligence-sharing sessions. In one instance,
Whisnant pointed to a large map and randomly asked who lived in a specific
house near the paramount sheikh's village.

"I know why you ask about that house," Dark answered before attempting to change the subject. His reticence naturally triggered Whisnant's curiosity, and the sheikh grudgingly elaborated under pressure. "Yes, yes, he
fought against Americans. But he is a good guy now," said Dark irritably.
Whisnant let the issue go but made a mental note to later check out the
house.[14] Their conflict was sometimes more overt. Dark yelled at Whisnant
on several occasions, including whenever a U.S. Joint Special Operations
Command anti-terrorism cell independently detained some of his relatives.
American units shared some intelligence but not all information with each
other. Given the energetic campaign by special operations units targeting
high-value targets, it was not unheard of for them to pick up some of Alpha
Company's new allies in the confusing hunt for insurgents and former
insurgents.[15] At other times, the sheikh aggressively chastised the Americans
for helping business competitors within his own tribe.

In one significant respect—getting information out of detained al Qaeda suspects or sympathizers—the Marines' new tribal allies could be overly enthusiastic. Dark frequently asked Whisnant to release some of the men Alpha Company had detained into tribal custody. The requests were accompanied by an ominous promise: "Give them over to us. We can find the information out."[16] Earlier in the war, U.S. interrogators had utilized "counter-resistance techniques" considered by some to constitute torture. These methods included sleep deprivation, withholding food, and isolation.[17] The 2004 revelations of prisoner abuse by U.S. soldiers at the Abu Ghraib detention facility, however, had led to a systematic softening of the way detainees were routinely held and questioned by Americans.

Paradoxically, while the Abu Ghraib scandal severely damaged the U.S. military's reputation among many Iraqis, the Fallujans also tended to sneer at the comparatively soft interrogation methods of their new Western partners.[18] Threats, beatings, and sometimes crueler methods of torture were locally understood ways of obtaining information under tribal and vigilante justice. The cold reality was that they sometimes worked. In addition, incarceration and interrogation in official Iraqi jails run by the police were often nightmarish environments of overcrowded squalor and fear, especially by American standards.[19]

Whisnant repeatedly declined Dark's entreaties, sternly shooting down some of his more aggressive designs against suspected insurgent operatives. The garrulous sheikh broached a series of schemes to kidnap, roughly interrogate, or assassinate his enemies. In response, Whisnant simply admonished him, reminding his Iraqi ally, "Dark, we can't do that. Anything you tell me [that violates human rights], I am obligated to report."[20] Whisnant committed his company to operate within the law, relying on a shaky U.S. and Iraqi detention and judicial system. Many allied members of the tribe therefore learned to refrain from revealing some of their ethically dubious operations to the Americans. Dark liked to talk, however, and he was less circumspect with younger enlisted Marines. He sometimes happily told them about killing this or that insurgent enemy, and bragged about "leaving their bodies by the side of the road" as an example to others.[21] The tribe's sometimes dirty war against al Qaeda was carried out in open secrecy and was probably more effective than any gains in U.S. intelligence gathering. In 2009, Dark told American military historians, "On the ground, under your eyes, we destroyed al-Qaeda."[22]

Whisnant knew his limits. He could largely control the actions of his men and, to a lesser extent, the actions of Iraqis when they were in the presence of his men. Although he lacked specific awareness, the local reality required acceptance of the moral ambiguity of his allies' practices. The Americans could nudge the militiamen toward the rule of law, but most remained intractably reliant on the rougher tenets of tribal justice. In the chaos of Fallujah, the Marines reaped benefits from this uncomfortable accommodation.[23]

One example included the December capture of two al Qaeda operatives by some of Dark's cousins from the Abu Hatim subtribe. Iraqi interrogators questioned the insurgents for some time before the two made an escape. Obtaining a videotape of the interrogation represented an intelligence coup for the Americans. The clip had numerous gaps in recording, however, each undoubtedly marking a portion of the interview where the captors had turned off the camera to beat the insurgents. Whatever the methods used in the interrogations, they were effective. Before their getaway, the two prisoners divulged the names of dozens of insurgents, information that later proved to be invaluable as the Marines mapped the network of al Qaeda in Iraq operatives and other mujahidin.[24]

As American intelligence personnel began to successfully assemble pieces of the puzzle, they were routinely surprised by the crafty methods of some of their enemies, the brazen stupidity of others, and the number of their early assumptions that proved to be incorrect. Most interesting of all, however, was the way individual families turned out to be riddled and rent by choosing sides in the peninsula's civil war. As the Marines uncovered insurgent name after insurgent name and mapped location after location, they were shocked to learn how many close relatives of their new tribal allies had forsaken their families to make common cause with the radical *takfiris*. One insurgent cell, composed of cousins and brothers of some of Dark's top lieutenants, was discovered hiding out in a house five hundred meters south of the paramount sheikh's compound. The Marines also came to learn that Talib Ajami Aifan, al Qaeda in Iraq's executive officer who had been killed in a gunfight over the fall, was a close cousin of Khamis'. In addition, various grandsons of the second and fourth wives of Aifan, the deceased patriarch of the Albu Issa tribe, remained dedicated insurgents.[25] Some sons and nephews of the Albu Issa's leading sheikhs had renounced traditional tribal loyalties for perceived religious purity, the romantic glory promised by insurgency, or cash. As time passed and the tide shifted, some of these men were allowed to reconcile with the tribe. Those who refused, or had committed unforgivable atrocities, drew an enduring verdict of exile, jail, or death.[26]

In addition, Alpha Company ramped up large "cordon and sweep" operations after forming the alliance with Dark. Villages were blocked off, one at a time, and all military-aged men were casually questioned. This time Dark, Ma'an Khalid Aifan al-Issawi, and another militia lieutenant, Uthman Majid Aifan al-Issawi, or one of the other charter members of the Albu Aifan militia would accompany the Americans. With their faces covered and dressed as Marines, the militiamen identified insurgents they recognized, whom the Americans subsequently investigated more closely or detained. The Marines' acquisition of local "guides" degraded the most important advantage held by insurgents: the ability to hide in plain sight. On one occasion, Uthman and Ma'an donned their ski masks and Marine uniforms and joined some of the Hobbits and Capt. Jeremy Hoffmann's Weapons Platoon for a visit to a local mosque thought to headquarter insurgents. Once there, the Marines gathered all of the men and paraded them in front of their Humvees parked in the adjacent quarry. The Albu Aifan tribesmen sat in the front seat of the vehicles and gave each suspect a thumbs-up or a thumbs-down. Two men were detained, and enough corroborating evidence was amassed to subsequently prosecute them as insurgents.[27]

The information gleaned from their new tribal allies was plentiful and valuable, but never completely trusted. The Americans were well aware that the Fallujans held back from identifying certain insurgents who were close family members or friends, or those who had potential as recruits for the tribe's nascent militia. This had to be tolerated. As illustrated in Roussell's lectures on the distinction between "good bad guys" and "bad bad guys," the Marines learned to accept the idea of letting less committed, less dangerous insurgents reform or walk free. Given how many men on the peninsula had directly fought Americans or supported rebellion in some fashion, it was unavoidable, especially if the Marines were going to gain the critical mass of allies necessary to defeat the insurgency.

The "poison pen" was also rampant in Iraq. There was the omnipresent possibility that some tribesmen would use their relationship with the Marines to settle scores or eliminate financial competitors by turning them in as terrorists. To mitigate this risk, interviewers on the ground and the Hobbits cross-checked the name of each suspect with databases at the company and battalion levels in an attempt to verify whether he was an insurgent. If nothing matched or if the evidence against a suspect was insufficient, the Marines would let him go, at least until further information came in. Other times, they would let "human intelligence exploitation team" interrogators attempt to sort it out. If the Hobbits had a strong enough case—usually two corresponding reports plus two witness statements—they would put together a "detention package" and forward it to the personnel at the regimental detention facility, or to the Iraqi police and the barely functioning Iraqi court system.[28]

In earlier years, these detention packages had been thinly sourced. As a result, many suspected insurgents were quickly released from prison due to insufficient evidence—after making new insurgent contacts in detention facilities. This situation bred more dangerous terrorists and reinforced the wildly successful intimidation campaign of the radicals: locals refused to inform on an individual because of the distinct possibility he might soon return to wreak bloody vengeance.[29]

The tribal leaders' overt support of the Americans and the Marines' pledge to protect their new allies incrementally thawed this climate of fear. Men and women of the tribe began tentatively writing and signing statements indicting insurgents on the peninsula. This evidence was "like gold" to U.S. legal personnel, giving them the ability to incarcerate insurgents for longer periods. As local faith in the detention system grew, even more civilians began to cooperate, exposing and imprisoning radicals or violent criminals in their midst.[30]

The rapid snowballing of evidence was so unprecedented that within a month, the Hobbits received suspicious pushback from regimental legal personnel. The officers of the Judge Advocate General's Corps had never seen so many public witnesses stand up near Fallujah and therefore speculated that "the statements could have easily been coerced" by the Marines of Alpha Company. The surprised lawyers were eventually convinced of the testimonies' veracity and enthusiastically put the new evidence to work.[31] The lawyers' skepticism was understandable. Despite the newfound tribal support, informing on radical insurgents remained a dangerous gamble.

❖ ADILAH ❖

On a crisp, clear day in late November 2006, Cpl. Alex Albrecht and his men were looking for an overwatch house in a small village about a kilometer south of Albu Aifan. The twenty-year-old team leader in Weapons Platoon's 2nd Squad had directed his three Marines toward a cluster of modest cinder block residences along Main Street. They needed to find a building with elevated views and sufficient cover on the roof; from there, they would watch over the squad's other two teams as they conducted a census of the neighborhood.[1]

The endless patrols and interviews had become a little boring for Albrecht, and were not at all what he had expected of a deployment to Fallujah. Training, briefings, and his imagination had made him anticipate daily firefights and up to 25 percent casualties for the company. They had gotten shot at and blown up, and they had shot back, to be sure, but "90 percent" of their activity consisted of "just walking around, talking to people." Some of the young Marines had started referring to census ops as "senseless ops."[2]

Capt. Jeremy Hoffmann, commander of Weapons Platoon, ran his squads ragged. The difficult workload began before deployment. While other platoons were relaxing and goofing off, Hoffmann had them hiking, studying Arabic, learning to fix radios, or conducting weapons drills. When they got to Iraq, the pace became positively brutal. They walked, walked, and then walked some more, covering the breadth of the peninsula on foot.[3] The hardship wasn't the unexpected part for Albrecht; he had joined the Marines for exactly that. As a senior in high school, he had carefully toured the military recruiters in his hometown of Grand Rapids, Michigan, before making a choice. An Army sergeant had tried to entice the seventeen-year-old by stressing that it was "easier to get promoted." In contrast, the Marine recruiter told Albrecht that "nothing comes easy" and "you gotta' earn it."

The latter sales pitch appealed to the competitive cross-country and track athlete. He left for Marine boot camp two days after high school graduation.[4]

Once in Fallujah, it was the amount of talking, as opposed to shooting, that surprised Albrecht about war, although Hoffmann had tried to prepare the Marines. The tough platoon commander conducted endless drills and never hesitated to bark his displeasure when someone screwed up. But above all, he hammered two goals into his men's heads: they would keep pressure on the enemy, even if they had to walk twenty clicks a day to do it. And they would get to know the people and treat them with respect. "One way I will be able to judge our success is if at the end of the deployment, we can look at a picture of anyone from the area and tell a story about where he lives, what he does for a living, who his family was, and what were our interactions with him," Hoffmann lectured. "If we can do that, I'll know that we knew the people well enough that security and stabilization must be a side benefit of that relationship."[5] So they walked and talked, and walked and talked some more.

On that crisp November day, Albrecht's Team 2 was walking toward a potential overwatch site. The modest house only had one story, but it was surrounded on three sides by a thick line of trees, and it had the characteristic low wall bordering its roof. They decided to see who was home. LCpl. Jared Kimmey and Albrecht knocked at the door and announced themselves, while LCpl. Chris Jongsma kept eyes toward the neighborhood. No one answered, and the door was locked. This was unusual. In fact, it was the first time Albrecht had come across a locked house.

The Marines moved around the perimeter of the home and noticed a smaller cinder block structure in the backyard. They approached the second building and knocked on a wooden door. After a moment, a thin woman in her late twenties or early thirties opened the door and shyly greeted them. Though covered head to toe in a dark scarf and robes, her face was exposed; the three Americans noted that she was pretty. Two boys, roughly three and five years old, curiously peeked at the Marines from behind their mother.[6]

The Americans introduced themselves and, with a combination of stilted Arabic and methodical hand gestures, communicated that they would like to ask her some questions and have a look around her house. The woman told them her name was Adilah and beckoned them to follow her to the main building.[7] The Marines searched the smaller structure first; it didn't take long to look over its two tiny rooms. One 8 x 8 foot space was used for cooking on a little propane stove. The other, similarly sized room served as the family's living room and sleeping quarters and contained blankets, two plastic lawn chairs, and a small television set on a tray.

As the group escorted the small family to the main house, they were joined by a heavyset, curious neighbor in her fifties. Once inside, the Americans conducted another brief search. The residence's four rooms were nearly barren. Aside from a few rugs covering portions of the concrete floors, the only furniture present was a shelf in the main room stocked with stacks of multicolored blankets.[8]

The two women spoke to Kimmey while Jongsma and Albrecht cleared the house before inspecting the roof as a potential overwatch position. Kimmey quickly got down to business, asking his stock census questions. How many people are in the family? What are their names? Most important, he asked, "Shlone mantaka?" (How is the area).

"Zien, zien" (Good, good), answered the middle-aged neighbor assertively as Adilah remained quiet.

"Wayn Ali Baba?" (Where are the bad guys) continued the lance corporal.

"Laa Ali Baba" (No bad guys), responded the elder woman. "Laa, laa, laa Ali Baba!" she added for effect.[9]

Kimmey noticed that Adilah was hesitant. Her body language was tense, and he thought he heard her quietly whisper under her breath: "Naam" (Yes). The younger woman glanced at him. Her eyes seemed to motion him toward the other room. "Hey Al, I think she's trying to tell us where the bad guys are," Kimmey told Albrecht in a low voice as the team leader was about to climb the stairs to the roof.[10] Albrecht had not picked up on the woman's body language or Arabic, but he had learned to trust his lance corporal's instincts where Iraqis were concerned. Kimmey possessed a knack for the language and had quickly become the platoon's best nonnative linguist, eclipsing even Captain Hoffmann in skill. Combined with his amiable, curious nature, the lance corporal was great at reading the locals, making him a highly valued member of the team. This had not always been the case.

In garrison, the native of Lansing, Michigan, had started out as something of a screw-up who flirted with outcast status. About a year out of high school, after working a series of "crappy jobs," he was adrift and wanted to make his parents proud. Kimmey's late grandfather had been a Marine, so he joined up. It seemed like a good way to "make something" of himself.

Once in the Corps, the nineteen-year-old quickly discovered that he had some "issues" with the way the Marines did things. Some of the rules—especially the rigid grooming and greeting regulations—seemed silly. Kimmey didn't pay close attention to saluting, how short his hair was, or which hat he was allowed to wear, when. In addition, he was out of shape and stood out like a sore thumb among the extremely fit athletes on his team. Of most significance, he had a fundamental problem grasping the importance of rank and seniority. As a newcomer to Alpha Company, the lance corporal resisted paying his dues as low man on the totem pole by adopting a humble attitude and a strong work ethic. He was immature, seemed disinterested, and consistently pushed his luck with superiors.[11] Kimmey just didn't get what all the fuss was about: "We're supposed to prepare for war and they're worried about whether my shirt's tucked in?" he thought. "What's the point?"

Kimmey also quickly came to hate his team leader. The tall, square-jawed Albrecht was "a stereotypical Marine" who achieved perfect scores on his physical fitness tests in between chewing out Kimmey for doing something wrong. "Fuck this guy," thought Kimmey at the time. "I don't give a shit about this guy." When Albrecht was promoted to corporal before they deployed, Kimmey rolled his eyes and thought, "Oh great, now he's going to be an even bigger dick."[12] A few weeks before their flight to Fallujah, a frustrated Albrecht had finally had enough of Kimmey's insouciance. He was just "a lazy goof-off who [lost] gear and [acted] like he didn't want to be [there]," recalled the team leader.[13] Albrecht sat the rebellious lance corporal down for a talk.

"Listen," he said sternly. "I don't know what you've got going on in your life. But this, *this* is what's going on now. You need to focus. Do you think you're ready to go to Iraq? Do you really think you're ready for combat?"

"Yeah, of course I do," responded Kimmey without hesitation.

"Well, a lot of guys don't think you are," said Albrecht. "A lot of guys are nervous about serving with you. And if you're not serious about this and make a mistake, it can get someone killed."[14]

Albrecht's words were like a punch to Kimmey's gut. The message finally cut through a lot of the bullshit that came along with being a Marine. It was one thing to think the rules were stupid, but it was an entirely different matter to go to war with guys who did not trust his commitment or judgment and thought he might get them killed.[15] Albrecht's talk began to do the trick: Kimmey started applying himself and taking things a little more seriously. Albrecht noticed a difference, but the real change occurred weeks later, during their first firefight. When those bullets started snapping, Kimmey changed into a totally different Marine. From then on, he was "Johnny-on-the-spot with the radio," effectively calling in reports or casualty evacuations in between laying down rounds against the enemy.

He also threw himself into his language studies, honing his natural aptitude by illicitly conversing with detainees. The good-natured Kimmey treated captured Iraqis like they were innocent until proven otherwise, and practiced his Arabic by asking about their homes and families. After a couple of months of long marches, he even got into shape. To Albrecht's surprise, Kimmey morphed into an "amazing combat Marine," and the two men wound up being friends.[16]

By November, Albrecht knew to trust that the lance corporal's interpersonal and language skills had spotted something worth investigating about Adilah. The two Marines ushered her into another room under the pretext of searching for something. Albrecht instructed Jongsma to distract the older woman with more census questions while they spoke with the younger woman. Once they were alone, Adilah became more talkative, though she remained stern and was clearly nervous. She cautioned the Americans that she had to be quiet so the other woman, a relative, would not hear her.

Adilah told the Marines that there were indeed bad people in the area. A few months ago strangers had come to her house to recruit her husband into the jihad against the occupiers. When he refused, they shot and killed him. The insurgents then threatened her husband's brother with the same fate, and the man fled. She now lived alone with her two children and had no income. The small family stayed in the tiny building in the backyard because she could not afford to heat the main house during Fallujah's freezing winter nights.

Adilah drew the Marines toward a window and pointed toward some nearby houses. Earlier that morning, Weapons Platoon had detained some suspected insurgents in those residences. Through his functional Arabic and her hand gestures, Kimmey came to understand that the insurgents would regularly transit through the area and stay in the houses for a night or two, a pattern roughly analogous to Marine patrols and census ops. Since they could not understand everything she was trying to tell them, the Americans asked her to write down the names of insurgents and details about their activities. Adilah complied, but with difficulty. Albrecht could tell that she didn't write much by the way she struggled to remember certain words.

After a few minutes, Adilah worriedly asked them to leave. If the Marines stayed too long, she explained, it would be noticed, and if the *takfiris* caught wind of their visit and suspected her of helping the infidels, they might kill her, or worse, her children. Albrecht instructed Kimmey to tell her that they would leave and search all of the other houses in the neighborhood for the same amount of time so that their visit with her would not stand out. She was glad for the discretion. The Americans thanked her and left the house. The intelligence she provided, if correct, would prove valuable.[17]

Kimmey had a feeling that she was telling the truth. Adilah wasn't exactly friendly with the Americans, but she seemed sincere about wanting someone to establish security and capture or kill the men who had ravaged her family. As he learned more about her situation, he felt sympathy for her and realized that "she was caught between a rock and a hard place": if she helped the Americans, al Qaeda might kill her and her family; if she didn't help the Americans, al Qaeda would continue to terrorize her neighborhood and kill men like her husband and brother-in-law. Either path was perilous. In the end, she decided she might as well assume the risk of stepping forward to provide information. Kimmey respected her for it.[18]

Later that night, some of the Americans briefly returned with Captain Hoffmann and "Joe," an interpreter, to show Adilah pictures of the men the Marines had detained that morning. Without the Americans coaching her on who they were or what they were suspected to have done, she positively identified them as insurgents and wrote a statement detailing their offenses. Over the next three months, the Americans would speak with her several more times, but not all the visits would go so smoothly.

Several weeks later, 1/24's Charlie Company, which typically operated within the city, ran a joint operation with Alpha Company in Adilah's neighborhood. Major Whisnant had issued specific orders for the visiting Marines to avoid the young widow's house; he wanted to ensure that she was consistently treated in a way that maximized her intelligence value and respected her security concerns. Unfortunately, someone in Charlie Company failed to get the message, and a large contingent of Marines, including human intelligence exploitation team (HET) personnel, wound up stopping at her residence and aggressively questioning her for almost two hours. Jongsma and LCpl. Kelly Carlson tried to persuade a captain with the HET team to leave, but the two enlisted men were brushed aside: "We have experience questioning people. We know what we're doing."[19]

Albrecht's team returned for another visit shortly thereafter, again bringing Captain Hoffmann and Joe the interpreter to ensure that they didn't miss any details. Adilah was nervous and uncooperative. She was angry at the way the HET and Charlie Company Marines had treated her and also scared about how long they had stayed in her house. Kimmey thought that she regretted having ever talked to the Americans. The Marines apologized profusely for Charlie Company's visit and promised her that it would never happen again.[20] Adilah remained reluctant to help them. In the end, it took Joe—and the Quran—to convince her.

A Sunni from Baghdad, Joe was liked and appreciated by the Marines for being the hardest-working interpreter in the company. The serious-minded, approximately thirty-year-old man never complained, and he was remarkably reliable. He never quite opened up to his American employers like some of the other linguists did, with at least one exception. If there was one aspect of Joe's personality that shone through to the Marines, it was his disgust for the terrorists he felt were destroying Iraq. Joe may not have loved the Americans like his fellow interpreter "C. J." did, but he absolutely hated what criminals and the radicals were doing to his country.[21]

Adilah's refusal to help raised Joe's passion. He picked up a copy of the Quran sitting on a shelf in the woman's house, after which his Arabic became too fast for Kimmey to completely follow. The lance corporal understood enough, however, to later paraphrase the exchange, in which Joe said to Adilah, "As Muslims, *this* is what the Quran compels us to do. Even if it is dangerous, we're called to help the good people and fight those who are bad." His entreaty to Adilah's Islamic piety apparently worked. Her attitude softened and she agreed to continue helping them.[22]

The Americans had brought a camera with pictures of a number of men who had been detained based on intelligence provided by Dark and his lieutenants. Hoffmann was hoping that Adilah could verify whether some or all of the suspects were legitimate insurgents to rule out the possibility that the young sheikh was using the Marines to eliminate competitors. They showed Adilah the series of photos and asked whether any of them were criminals or terrorists. She recognized some of the men and agreed to sign witness statements that would be used to detain and indict them. Much of Dark's intelligence checked out. Not wanting to overstay their welcome, the Americans thanked her again and left in less than fifteen minutes. They made a show of searching every neighbor's house for a period equal to or greater than the time they had spent in her home.

On Team 2's final visit to Adilah's house several weeks later, the Marines bore modest gifts. Adilah had never asked for anything, but the Americans gave her two $20 bills, and they presented her more significantly with a well-oiled AK-47 and several magazines of ammunition, along with a note in English stipulating that the weapon was a gift from Alpha Company 1/24.[23] The Americans recall that Adilah was grateful and had by now even warmed to the Marines a little. Where she was once stern and nervous, her attitude was now more comfortable, within the strict bounds of Muslim reserve proper for a woman speaking with strange men.

That visit was the last time Albrecht and Kimmey saw her. Before they left, they told her that some of Lt. Jerome Greco's men from 3rd Platoon would soon visit her and also ask for information. The Marines promised her that these men would treat her with similar respect. Greco and his men indeed visited her in March 2007. During their interview, Adilah corroborated a tip provided by Dark about two men in the area who had been bragging about having placed explosives that killed Americans. She was cooperative, but also frustrated; she continually steered the conversation toward nudging the Americans to find and capture the men who had killed her husband.[24]

The Marines acted on the information and detained the suspects. Dark's tip, and Adilah's corroboration, turned out to be legitimate. When all was said and done, the Marines caught some insurgents they suspected of running the IED cell that killed LCpl. Jonathan Thornsberry and Sgt. Tommy Gilbert in October. To the Americans' knowledge, they never caught the men who had killed Adilah's husband.

8

❖ CIVIL AFFAIRS ❖

Successful counterinsurgency relies on more than killing insurgents. Properly executed doctrine combines judicious efforts to kill the *right* people, while implementing humanitarian, reconstruction, and economic development projects aimed at building local support and legitimizing allied governance. In the Marine Corps, this "softer side" of war is officially spearheaded by the Civil Affairs Group, otherwise known as the CAG units.

By late 2006, both civil affairs and reconstruction work in and around Fallujah had developed troubled histories. These efforts had become ineffectual—failing to adjust to realities on the ground—and then impossible when the city fell under the control of insurgent and jihadist organizations. And when the Marines and the U.S. and Iraqi armies took back the area during the Second Battle of Fallujah, in November 2004, they also damaged or destroyed a large portion of the city's buildings and infrastructure.[1] In a pointed bid to contrast the iron fist with a velvet glove, the U.S. government quickly poured huge resources into rebuilding the area. Driven by the U.S. Army Corps of Engineers, the ambitious effort included new schools, clinics, residential damage reimbursements, electrical substations, water treatment plants, and other new infrastructure replacements or enhancements. Many of the projects carried price tags from $4 million to $28.6 million apiece, and some utilized local contractors in order to stimulate the post-invasion economy.[2]

Unfortunately, many of these idealistic efforts failed to account for security and were plagued by two fundamental problems. First, almost every project utilizing locals was heavily "taxed" by insurgent groups. Soon after starting work, a civilian contractor would be approached by whatever criminal element held sway in the area. He was then offered a choice: give up a large portion of his fee or be killed, often in a tortuous fashion. Faced with this decision, most contractors fled or gave in to the extortion, and large sums of well-intentioned American money consequently wound up funding an insurgency in the business of killing Iraqi civilians and Americans.[3] The second problem was more directly tied to Fallujah's persistent insecurity: the insurgents tended to blow things up. From bombing cell phone towers, power lines, and TV broadcast towers to sniping security contractors guarding water system maintenance workers, the more radical strains of the insurgency had little compunction about destroying anything that challenged their authority or legitimized the local government or the Americans, as long as the action didn't upset their revenue streams.[4]

Thus, until American and Iraqi security forces could provide a minimally secure environment aided by intelligence from civilians—everyday Iraqis with both a stake in reconstruction and a chance at surviving if they cooperated—many civil affairs and reconstruction projects were wasted efforts.[5] Worse yet, many actually fueled the insurgency. Fallujah's newly installed district police chief, Colonel Faisal Ismail Hussein al-Zobaie, summed up the dire situation in January 2007: "From Fallujah to the city of Abu Ghraib, the radicals control everything. Gas stations, power, contracts and, believe it or not, contracts with the Americans themselves. The Americans give a contract to someone and the insurgents extort their share. This is how they finance their operations. An oil distribution facility in al-Anbar, believe it or not, half of its production goes to those radicals and to finance insurgency activities."[6] This was the conundrum confronting the mishmash of American engineers and CAG personnel deployed to the province in autumn 2006. Capt. Jodie Sweezey, a civil affairs team leader who had recently returned to the Fallujah area after serving a 2004–2005 tour, recalled how disappointed she was to find that things had "sort of fallen apart" in the interim.

The Marine Corps had no primary military occupation specialty (MOS) categorized as "civil affairs" in 2006. Instead, CAG was a "secondary MOS," and units were assembled via volunteers from a wide spectrum of occupations who rapidly trained in civil affairs theory and practices before deployment. In Area of Operations (AO) Raleigh, which spanned the cities of Habbaniyah, Karma, Ameriyah, Fallujah, and others, the entire regimental combat team was assigned a CAG detachment of only four teams consisting of five to seven Marines. Of these small groups, Team 3, also known as Team Yankee, was charged with supporting the entire 1st Battalion of the 24th Marine Regiment and with them the large and diverse area comprising the Fallujah peninsula and the city of Fallujah itself. Sweezey's Team 1, The Regulators, primarily supported the regimental combat team and the Marine 3rd Reconnaissance Battalion, but sometimes helped out 1/24 on the peninsula as well.[7]

Team Yankee was a tight-knit group of five men, led by Capt. Jason Brezler. Dubbed the "Ultimate American" by one of his men, the twenty-eight-year-old Reservist's resume read like a set of paint-by-numbers instructions for patriotic service: Naval Academy graduate, New York City firefighter, and Marine Corps officer. Brezler's leadership philosophy was described by his subordinates as energetic and, by military standards, occasionally unconventional. He drastically informalized the chain of command within his small group, and he encouraged consensus rather than decree in determining which projects were most important. In all but a few circumstances, pulling rank on others was verboten, and each member was granted latitude to act as the authority within his assigned role.

Team Yankee's independence had one major string attached: Brezler dictated at the start of the deployment that the group's operations would be "high tempo"—military jargon for "aggressive" and consequently dangerous. Roughly speaking, while all American units in Anbar province had a mission to accomplish, some took this self-evident directive to heart more than others. Some leaders chose to "get after it," while others quickly concluded that bringing everyone home safely was the highest, and occasionally only, priority. After being confronted with the area's morale-sapping nexus of extreme violence and vicious local politics, for some leaders the latter was arguably the more rational approach.

None of Team Yankee's members described their outfit as reckless, but Brezler emphasized the mission over playing it safe. And to accomplish a civil affairs mission in Fallujah required constant convoys along the area's bomb-laden roads. Every original member of his team initially agreed to assume the risk, but two men soon dropped out or were nudged out by the team after being hit and severely spooked by roadside bombs. (Team Yankee's convoys would be hit by five during the deployment, in addition to being targeted by a grenade and numerous small arms and indirect fire incidents.)[8] The core of the CAG team held true to its compact and stuck out the high tempo of the next six months.

SSgt. Tylor Belshe was a laid-back twenty-nine-year-old with an obscure military pedigree as an "embarkation specialist." On his previous deployment to Iraq, Belshe had escorted equipment transiting back to the States but craved more direct involvement in the war. He had volunteered for the CAG because he thought he had "something more to offer." In civilian life he had run a couple of retail stores in Colorado that sold "Scandinavian metalwork," so his business acumen qualified him as the team's contracting official and project manager.

Gy Sgt. Michael Abragan was "a cook who loved to shoot, move, and communicate," according to Belshe. Abragan's aptitude for tactics wound up getting him reassigned from the kitchen to an infantry platoon prior to joining the CAG. Abragan subsequently became Team Yankee's security chief. In this role, he was responsible for managing the route and tactics of convoys and maintaining security once on site. Much of the twenty-nine-year-old Filipino American's job also consisted of begging other units for bodies to accompany the team on its missions so it could meet the minimum number of personnel required to set foot outside the wire. At first this task was easy; many of the mechanics, administrators, and other non-infantry personnel jumped at the chance to get off base and maybe see some action. As the deployment progressed, and the number of dead and wounded Americans skyrocketed, however, it became more difficult for Abragan to find volunteers.

Cpl. Edward Przybylski was a thin Polish American from a tough neighborhood in Aurora, Colorado. "Ski" was a not-uncommon example of a Marine who had problems in barracks because of his penchant for speaking his mind to superiors (often in barely comprehensible hip-hop slang). Some "problem kids" in garrison became happily competent in war, as the "chickenshit" priorities of saluting were replaced by more serious duties. In Przybylski's case, this consisted of keeping the vehicles running and pulling security.

In stark contrast to Przybylski stood Corporal Bill Cahir, who was something of an oddity in the Marine Corps. The Pennsylvanian boasted a Brahmin education and culturally elite series of occupations prior to military service. His former career as a journalist had been punctuated by stints on Capitol Hill as an aide to liberal senators Harris Wofford (D-Pa.) and Ted Kennedy (D-Mass.). After the al Qaeda attacks of September 11, 2001, Cahir enlisted in the Marines at the ripe old age of thirty-four. Cahir's age, education, and leftist politics surely made him one of the few corporals in the Marine Corps who read *Mother Jones* and the *New York Times* before breakfast, and certainly the only one who had taken heat for writing a scathing newspaper article about his boot camp experience. Cahir served as Team Yankee's navigator and lead turret gunner. His energy for the job led him to learn the city's twists and back alleys like some of the locals.

Team Yankee's core was rounded out by its interpreter, Omar al-Sady. The linguist was born in Baghdad and had lived in the United States, the Netherlands, and Canada before returning to post-invasion Iraq as a translator. His grandparents were Fallujans. Sady's local knowledge and ability to read people was invaluable. He was also assessed as fearless and unwilling to "take any shit" from the locals, the latter trait being particularly cherished by his American employers.

Brezler, true to his promise, threw the group into trying to influence Fallujah. In Team Yankee's civil affairs wheelhouse, this meant pursuing development and aid projects that had the potential to improve the "kinetic atmospherics" of the most violent areas of the city and peninsula.[9] At a superficial level, these projects embodied the cliché of "trying to win hearts and minds" by helping the local population. But from a practical perspective, the more successful efforts represented quid pro quo arrangements between the Americans and Iraqis, echoing CWO-5 Jim Roussell's mantra of "something for something, nothing for nothing."

Brezler was also after something called "combined effects." A worthwhile project needed to have impacts beyond meeting, greeting, and giving to locals. For example, a simple CAG visit to deliver supplies to Fallujah General Hospital had several goals. First, the effort was aimed at bolstering goodwill and cooperation with the Americans. The much-needed supplies increased the facility's capacity, and U.S. medical personnel tagging along could liaise and establish relationships with Iraqi doctors. Second, also accompanying the CAG team would be "human intelligence exploitation" personnel, who would use the friendly civil affairs auspices as an opportunity to develop Iraqi spies and learn about insurgents using the hospital. Psychological operations personnel would tag along to case the facility for signs of enemy propaganda. The snipers who sat in overwatch positions as security for the team conducted reconnaissance of the area and mapped out future sniper hides. The civil affairs missions provided these units access under a casual aegis that was good for gathering intelligence.

During its seven-month rotation, Team Yankee executed more than forty projects, ranging from delivering medical and school supplies to a "toys for weapons" program. Objectives included engaging key city leaders and improving infrastructure and economic development. A few of these projects succeeded in influencing local leaders and perhaps reducing violence in particularly dangerous areas. Of note, providing generators to a local cement factory turned out to be popular for practical reasons, whereas the unit's reconstruction of a revered cemetery wall in the city's Jolan district had cultural resonance and succeeded in softening the attitude of the neighborhood toward the Americans. Intelligence reports indicated that some less radical insurgents even came to hold their fire when they saw CAG Humvees with characteristic blue coolers strapped to the roof, because they carried what were considered to be "good," or at least helpful, Marines. Of course, other reports hinted that insurgent sniper teams were specifically looking to kill the civil affairs Marines, so it was a mixed bag.[10]

Despite some successes, the majority of projects utterly failed in their overt goals of making inroads with the local population and improving their lives. Because of the violence and murderous intimidation of contractors, Team Yankee quickly learned some hard lessons about the types of civil affairs activities that accomplished little except spending money and generating PowerPoint presentations for their superiors.

"I think if somebody comes into this area with a civil affairs group to build schools and they measure their progress by how much money they spent, they've done worse for the community than if they never would have spent a dollar," explained Belshe. "I think if a civil affairs group or whatever group comes in here—whether it be USAID, Army Corps of Engineers—if you come in here and every project has a purpose, it's a something-for-something project: if you're building a school and [you say] 'we're not just gonna build you a school; [rather,]the school's going to come because we [also] want you to employ teachers. If it's a something-for-something, then it's a very effective program. But if you're just coming in here and spending money, then it's not effective at all."[11]

Some Americans also worked hard at preventing self-inflicted errors by aggressive Marines up the chain of command.[12] "The biggest thing we [civil affairs] were able to do was make [the chain of command] realize the impact that some of their missions had on the people," explained Sweezey. "Because we were dealing directly with a lot of the [local] people, and they were frustrated."[13] In one example, Team Yankee caught wind of the new regimental combat team's orders to take over a multiunit apartment building as a command post. The CAG had put in a lot of effort to (successfully) build rapport with the locals in the area, which was imperiled by American plans to unceremoniously evict five families of about seventy people from their homes with little notice. The civil affairs Marines convinced the regimental combat team to give them time to ease the transition by moving the residents into better housing with the aid of local contractors, the Iraqi police, and three tractor trailers.[14] In another example, Sweezey convinced the recon battalion she worked for to refrain from switching off the water to the city of Ferris, located at the southern edge of the peninsula. Those who had broached the scheme wanted to teach the locals a lesson after a spate of attacks, but the civil affairs captain talked them out of it after pointing out that it would cause a humanitarian crisis.

The nature of civil affairs work—meeting and greeting a wide variety of Iraqis—necessarily made the small teams of Marines some of the most well-traveled units in the area. This mobility, coupled with frequent stops, also made the work dangerous. Driving around more meant increased exposure to ubiquitous roadside bombs. Stopping at any location for more than twenty or thirty minutes attracted mortars; staying a little longer brought out the snipers and small-arms fire.

Team Yankee's aggressive mobility sometimes put the team at odds with superiors. According to various CAG Marines, before deployment, the head of the civil affairs teams in Anbar province delivered a speech to Marines and their families promising to "bring everyone home." Given the efforts by AO Raleigh's civil affairs leadership to restrict some of the team's more ambitious travels and projects, Belshe assumed that their chain of command had taken this unrealistic directive to heart. Several civil affairs personnel came to refer to their overprotective commander in AO Raleigh by the nickname "Daddy." And as children tend to do, they often circumvented one parent's authority with that of another. Brezler and his men soon came to rely on Col. Richard Simcock, who headed the regimental combat team, and Lt. Col. Harold Van Opdorp, 1/24's commander, as supplemental bosses. These two senior officers were far more comfortable with and supportive of attempts to "get after it."[15]

Team Yankee had one last, crucial function: it became Chief Warrant Officer Roussell's taxi service. The CAG's unique mobility gave the old cop access to the people and places he needed to visit in order to develop sources and intelligence in and around the dangerous city. By the midpoint of their rotation, Roussell had become a regular fixture in the small civil affairs convoys and was considered an adjunct member of the team. Brezler welcomed the company, and Belshe enjoyed listening to Brezler and Roussell banter about the ins and outs of how to fight an insurgency during the endless road trips. The jokes weren't half bad, either. During one trip in late January 2007, Brezler, Belshe, and Roussell heard the distant boom of a large explosion, followed by a series of extended bursts from automatic weapons. The sounds were unremarkable background noise to the team's trips around the streets of Fallujah, but the familiar beat was soon oddly augmented by an awful, Chicago-accented rendition of a John Lennon classic. "All we are saying, is give peace a chance," sang Roussell.[16]

Despite the violence and the difficulties of navigating local politics and the U.S. chain of command, many of the civil affairs personnel plugged away at the frustrating mission until the end of deployment. Belshe even managed to maintain some optimism about the area. "There [are] great people here. It has all the ingredients. They just need to come together," said the civil affairs project manager in January 2007. He continued:

> It has all the ingredients to become a success, but they just need to stand up. That's what I say in my mind: they just need to stand up. Just reading history in our own country—and I know [Iraq] is not the U.S.—but at one point, there were a bunch of people in the . . . United States that said, "We're standing up. This is what we want." And they put it in a document and they lived behind it. So, these people need to decide as a people "this is what we want" and stand up and just go forward and commit to that.[17]

9

❖ WASTA ❖

The cooperation by some members of the Albu Issa opened American eyes. At the beginning of their deployment to the Fallujah peninsula, the Marines had groped for progress in the dark: painstakingly building a census and hunting for opportunities to engage their enemies in stand-up gunfights. Now they had what amounted to a guided tour of the ethereal insurgency, gaining a fresh set of tangible targets and a foothold in the struggle against al Qaeda.[1] Maj. Dan Whisnant hoped to build the momentum of his valuable new alliance with incentives aimed at empowering his Iraqi partners in the eyes of their people. The idea was to consolidate local respect and political support for coalition-friendly sheikhs. Capt. Jason Brezler's civil affairs team would serve as the linchpin for this support.[2]

The measure of a sheikh lies in his "ability to keep and attract followers" and build consensus among fractious subtribes and extended family members.[3] Anyone who is the son of a sheikh qualifies as a sheikh. From there, the system becomes more egalitarian: it is up to the individual to impress his fellow tribesmen in order to acquire and maintain stature. A great deal of this authority stems from the security as well as the largess he can provide for his tribe. Accumulation of personal and tribal wealth through private business, strictly legal or otherwise, is an essential part of the path to *wasta*, or influence.[4]

Over the centuries, Anbari tribes were alternately left alone by, at war with, or grudging partners with a foreign occupier or an Iraqi central government. Conflict followed by wary patronage or cooperative détente with the Ottomans was replaced by roughly analogous relationships with the British and the Baath Party led by Saddam Hussein, the latter of whom aggressively manipulated the tribal system. Saddam feared the Sunni tribes as competitors, but he also needed them to maintain his grip on Iraq's Shia and Kurdish populations and to man the barricades against the Persian (Iranian) threat. To simultaneously co-opt and dilute their power, he created an Office of Tribal Affairs, which registered and "graded" sheikhs using a government-run caste system.

In a sense, Saddam's actions and approach elevated the stature of the tribes. They had always operated on the edges of central government authority, but the new initiative granted them unprecedented official recognition as political players in Iraq. Of significance, however, it also prevented the province's tribal confederations from posing a cohesive threat to the regime. Saddam effectively played the tribes against one another, sometimes creating "fake sheikhs" from outside tribal bloodlines or traditional selection criteria and by selectively distributing resources to his favorites.[5] When Baathist influence evaporated after the 2003 invasion, well-funded foreign insurgents and the Americans moved to create their own versions of this historical role. The Americans had difficulty partnering with the tribes. A combination of aggressive military and cultural missteps, naively well-intentioned insistence on forcing democratic reform, and the rebellious character of Anbar's citizenry doomed early overtures to abject failure. Only Anbari fatigue after three years of bloody conflict and the rise of a more dangerous, common enemy held the keys to *rapprochement*.[6]

Among the spectrum of insurgent groups, the foreign jihadists, including those affiliated with al Qaeda, began their relationship with Anbari tribes as a visiting ally against what many Sunnis considered the infidel occupiers and the Shia "Persians" in Baghdad. Their hesitant accord was quickly soured and soaked in blood, as the *takfiris* moved to dominate the tribes with shadow governments, like the Islamic State of Iraq.[7] The radicals were also greedy. As part of their consolidation of power, al Qaeda's so-called emirs and other insurgents aggressively encroached on the tribal revenue streams that remained in the post-invasion chaos. By 2007, government work, smuggling, agriculture, and the construction and service businesses that had formed the basis of tribal wealth in Anbar province had either been impeded, destroyed, or taxed by radical insurgents.[8] Anbar was insecure and its economy was in shambles. Sheikhs could no longer provide for their tribes or keep their people safe. Basic necessities—jobs, food, power, and clothing—had become much harder to come by for average tribesmen, and this did not reflect well on their leaders.

On Fallujah's peninsula, paramount sheikh Khamis Hasnawi Aifan al-Issawi's traditional authority over the twelve Albu Issa subtribes dramatically weakened, and continuation of the war now threatened the tribal system itself. Caught between the Americans and their radical enemies, the leaders of the Albu Issa found themselves profoundly vulnerable and eventually decided to turn to the coalition for relief. The Americans were not particularly liked, but they were rational. They would make a deal; al Qaeda in Iraq and other Salafist mujahidin would simply subjugate or kill.[9]

After the recent accord with tribal leaders, Whisnant's Marines had begun to more effectively assist allied members of the Albu Issa with security. The major knew, however, that he also needed to help jump-start the *wasta* of his favored sheikhs—Khamis Hasnawi, Aifan Sadoun (Dark), Khalid Hasnawi, and Shalaan (Mishael Abdullah Owdeh), among others—to enhance their leadership and personal stake in a lasting alliance. There was also a tangential hope that new projects would stimulate "honest" employment, replacing some of the dangerous yet popular jobs of planting roadside bombs for the insurgency.

For starters, Whisnant needed to prove to his chain of command that the allied Iraqis could complete any proposed work. The Americans had become understandably cynical about throwing money at local contractors, who tended to half do a job or abandon a project after insurgent threats. With allied subtribes providing militia security for a project improving their own area and employing their own people, Whisnant believed the Albu Issa contractors could get things done. If the reconstruction partnership started small and showed initial success, he figured that his superiors would free up more money for more substantial efforts.[10] For resources and expertise, Whisnant turned to the Civil Affairs Group (CAG). Brezler's Team Yankee had already quickly injected tangible incentives into the new relationship. Some of the confiscated vehicles and weapons that were distributed to members of Dark's militia had been routed through the CAG.[11]

Reconstruction projects got under way after being individually approved by the chain of command. An enthusiastic Cpl. Bill Cahir took charge of contracting the efforts slated for the peninsula while the CAG team's overall project manager, SSgt. Tylor Belshe, continued to focus on the city itself.[12] The Marines started modestly, acquiring a $19,000 generator for Sheikh Shalaan, who used it to get a local water pumping station back online.

Soon after, a $90,000 road-paving job was awarded to Shalaan's construction company. Eventually, Dark received a $250,000 contract to refurbish a severely damaged school. Of course, the markup for the work was steep; a large portion of these funds padded the sheikhs' pockets after employees were paid and materials purchased. The initial burst of CAG projects totaled slightly less than $500,000 during the remaining three months of Alpha Company's deployment.[13]

Some critics of the tribal Awakening described this patronage of Anbari sheikhs as bribery, something akin to Americans paying their enemies not to attack them while empowering a new, yet established, class of gangster.[14] This perspective, however, ignored a few genuine relationships forged between Iraqis and Americans, and the critique significantly downplayed the growing hatred and widespread fear of al Qaeda in the province. Given the proper resources, many sheikhs and civilians wanted to rid themselves of the *takfiris* much more so than they did the Americans.[15] Everyday tribesmen, in addition to wanting security, simply wanted an honest day's pay.[16]

Whisnant, Brezler, CWO-5 Jim Roussell, and other Americans were and remain unfazed by any cynical assessments and consider their investment in the sheikhs to have been a bargain. The price tag of contracts awarded to tribal allies over several months paled in comparison to the daily cost of Alpha Company's combat and support operations while providing comparatively spectacular results. The sum was also eclipsed by the literal and emotional cost of every additional American who might have been killed; each life insurance and compensation package paid $500,000 to surviving family members. And the difficulty of losing friends and comrades was impossible to calculate.[17]

Conducting business with the sheikhs presented a number of challenges. The Americans quickly found themselves tiptoeing through a minefield of intratribal politics. In addition to taking sides in what essentially had become a tribal civil war for control of the peninsula, they also became enmeshed in the fiercely competitive family dynamics of their allies. Infighting among sheikhs complicated decisions about the distribution of contracts.[18] For example, when Corporal Cahir awarded a paving contract to Sheikh Shalaan's construction company, which had experience working with coalition forces, Dark fumed.[19] "Why do you give it to him?" Dark asked. The young upstart expected immediate rewards for the steep risk he was running in leading a tribal militia. Whisnant sternly but cordially replied that Shalaan was the best man for the job and counseled his new partner to have patience; there would be other projects.[20]

Such complaints would be repeated from many quarters of the Albu Issa subtribes. As a growing number of sheikhs overtly joined the alliance and formed militias or flirted with American partnership, the Marines arbitrated more requests, more jealous demands, and more sharp elbows as the Iraqis jostled for contracts along with the wealth and position they afforded.[21] The role of besieged patron became routinely frustrating work, but Chief Warrant Officer Roussell's pragmatic advice injected clarity into the decision making: "Who cares what they want?" the old cop said again and again. "The more important question is, 'What do *we* want to get out of this?'"[22]

To that end, the Americans established the following criteria in assigning contracts: Who had the capability to actually complete it? Who, at the time, was closest to Khamis, as paramount sheikh, and other influential leaders? And primarily, who was making the biggest intelligence and security gains?[23] Regarding this last criterion, Dark's ambitiously risky stratagem was paying off. The lesser sheikh was sometimes at odds with Khamis, but his aggressive efforts to form and use his militia paid huge security dividends and correspondingly earned him a significant share of the contracts. This soon translated into significant influence in the peninsula's shattered economy. As Dark had accurately calculated, a willingness to go after the *takfiris* and deal with the Americans increased his prestige. His *wasta* was ascendant.[24]

10

❖ A MACY'S THANKSGIVING DAY PARADE ❖

The leaders of Alpha Company 1/24 attempted to strengthen their relationship with the Albu Issa by conducting a "medical/veterinary civil action program" (MEDCAP/VETCAP) mission organized by Capt. Jason Brezler's civil affairs team. The two-day event was designed to bring medical care, veterinary services, food, and other supplies directly to the members of the tribe.[1]

Iraqis living in the city and on Fallujah's peninsula weren't starving, but food had become more difficult to obtain in recent years, because of the war's disruption of traditional government rationing implemented by the defunct Baathist regime. Every family in Iraq had cards that entitled them to certain allotments of basic necessities, including food. The prewar list of items included supplies like rice, flour, oil, sugar, tea, infant formula, lentils, salt, a children's nutritional supplement, and cards to purchase fuel and heating oil. That old system still functioned to an extent, but mainstays regularly went missing from the deliveries; the ration of beans might go unseen for a month or more, followed by chai and sugar. By 2007, distributions that once consisted of fifteen elements sometimes had as few as three.[2]

Supplies meant for Fallujah were directed from national government ministries in Baghdad to Anbar's capital, Ramadi. From there, the provincial government was responsible for distribution to individual cities, including Fallujah. The lengthy administrative and logistical chain afforded plenty of opportunities for skimming by government officials, black market sales of goods by delivery drivers, and wholesale theft of shipments by bandits. In the first few months of 2007, the entire supply chain ground to a halt as insurgents repeatedly hit food convoys after they had left Ramadi.[3] The residents of the peninsula made do with the disruption better than most city

dwellers because many could supplement their rations with personal livestock and crops from local farms.

The war had made food, like so many things, more expensive and
harder to come by.[4] While Fallujans cinched their belts a notch tighter,
Brezler's civil affairs unit focused on finding alternate supplies for the
citizenry. SSgt. Tylor Belshe had discovered a contractor willing and able
to purchase supplies with American money and run a risky convoy from
Baghdad to Fallujah. The shipment miraculously arrived intact, after which
the Marines distributed it to residents of the city. The staff sergeant, however, held in reserve several twenty-foot-long containers of rice, flour, beans
and tea. "Could they use this on the peninsula?" Belshe asked Brezler.[5]

Brezler and Cpl. Bill Cahir, Team Yankee's project manager for Civil
Affairs Group (CAG) efforts on the peninsula, offered the shipment to Maj.
Dan Whisnant and Dark. The major and the sheikh jumped at the offer.
The Americans then began planning an infusion of aid in the village of Albu
Aifan that included not only food, but also medical supplies and aid ren-
dered by Navy doctors and corpsmen; veterinary aid provided by an Army
vet; and clothing, school supplies, books, and toys to be handed out by the
Marines. Rounding out the list would be the choicest goodies from the end-
less stream of care packages sent from well-wishing civilians back home.[6]
A simple handful of candy, travel-size toothpaste, soap, and shampoo were
prized items among poorer Iraqis.[7]

Cahir and Belshe organized a convoy of two Humvee gun trucks, three
highback Humvees, and a seven-ton truck packed with medical personnel
and supplies. At 0800 on February 28, 2007, the CAG team launched from
Camp Baharia, picked up the medical personnel at Camp Fallujah, and met
Weapons Platoon from Alpha Company 1/24 at a small schoolhouse in Albu
Aifan.[8] The tan, flat structure had a deceptively nice exterior, with stylized,
split columns flanking the front entrance and carefully painted, dark blue
horizontal trim along the top third of the roof. Inside, however, the building's barren concrete floors were dusted with powdery dirt, and its rough
walls were split by metal doors covered in peeling yellow paint and rust.
Stripped of desks and educational decorations, most of the bleak building
resembled a Western storage facility or a prison as much as it did a schoolhouse. The Marines unpacked the supplies and set up individual rooms for
the various tasks.[9]

One large room held long rows of eighty-pound sacks of flour, fifty-pound sacks of beans, and other foodstuffs. Another room had a neat stack of Arabic-language children's books, toys, school supplies, and care packages. In a third room, JAG attorneys sat behind folding tables, ready to adjudicate property damage claims against the coalition. A final room contained more folding tables, chairs, and what came to be the main event: four corpsmen, two doctors, and one dentist providing medical care for anyone who showed up and was willing to wait.

By 10:00 a.m., several hundred Iraqis of both sexes and all ages and social classes stood in a line stretching out the schoolhouse door. The men wore everything from traditional dishdashas to carefully pressed suits or casual Western clothes. Many of the women and teenage girls had covered themselves with dark robes from head to toe, except for their faces, while others' housedresses peeked from underneath. A number of women wore burkhas, which covered everything except their eyes.[10] Capt. Jodie Sweezey was struck by how many of them dressed in the latter fashion compared to the style during her 2005 tour in the area. The revival of conservative clothing was undoubtedly a survival mechanism in response to punishments handed out by radical religious insurgents to those they considered immodest and impure. Little girls milled among the adults in brightly colored jumpers or dresses, whereas boys knee-high to military age favored Western trousers and shirts or multicolored track suits. The generational contrast in styles was typified by a small boy in a purple FUBU jumpsuit standing next to a man wearing traditional white robes.

The rooms housing the food and school supplies were dirty, rectangular spaces with boarded-up white window frames, high ceilings, and tan walls. In each room, one of the longer walls was lined by small, square windows that let in a little light, although not enough to combat the oppressive atmosphere of the dusty tan cement. Belshe, Sweezey, Cpl. Edward "Ski" Przybylski, and other Marines stood around folding tables covered with food. Large empty sandbags made of green plastic had been stacked near the doorway. As each Iraqi family entered, its members were issued five sandbags, which they then carried through an assembly line of Marines manning large scoopers. The Americans filled each bag with several helpings of different foodstuffs. Roughly, the rations were enough to feed a family of six for a couple of weeks. The atmosphere was friendly, though restrained. The

Iraqi men and women, many of whom had had little firsthand interaction with Americans, projected quiet curiosity. Some were hesitant; most were patient and polite.

An adult man or woman heading a small family shuffled by each station and tentatively waited for direction. Some asked for the food in quickly translated Arabic or merely issued a look that asked, "Can I have that?" The Americans would often smile, answer affirmatively, and enthusiastically start scooping. Most, though not all, of the Iraqis would smile back. Some offered a "Shukran" (Thank you) while others didn't, perhaps out of nervousness or because the Americans had taken great care in stressing that the food was a gift from the sheikhs of the tribe.[11] Some Iraqis were so reserved that the Americans had to proactively entice them, asking, "Want some of this?" "Want some of that?" "How about this?" The usual response roughly translated to "Heck yeah!" accompanied by wide grins. As the day went on, the Americans recalled, the Iraqis seemed to become more comfortable. Easy smiles supplanted looks of wary curiosity, and here and there members of the tribe approached the Marines, striking up conversations in broken English or aided by an interpreter.

Most of the Americans reciprocated the Iraqis' curiosity and friendliness. While some Marines found civil affairs work boring, and others would never like the locals after the violence of the preceding few months, some reveled in the chance for friendly interaction. The simple pleasure of helping genuinely appreciative people with basic needs tended to register with all but a few intractable cynics, especially those who stopped to consider how needy some of the Iraqis were. Besides, near the end of a kinetic deployment, for most Marines it beat being blown up or shot at.[12]

The Americans trotted out a large box filled with candy scavenged from care packages. After opening the top of it, an interpreter naively instructed those in the room to "take as much as you want." Excited men, women, and kids gathered and crouched around the box, grabbed a few handfuls, and then melted back into the press. Fortunately, there were plenty of Tootsie Rolls, lollipops, and small bags of Skittles to satisfy the local sweet tooth. Candy was an item sufficiently luxurious that it was capable of spurring a small, good-natured riot.[13]

During the height of the food distribution, Belshe noticed a subtle yet discernible vibe ripple through the crowd. All of the Iraqis seemed to briefly pause before continuing what they were doing. Belshe looked around and saw that Dark had entered the room, flanked by his small security entourage. The sheikh was resplendent in a red-and-white checkered headdress and a gleaming white outfit that blended the lapels of a Western suit with the unbroken hem of traditional tribal robes. Belshe nudged Przybylski: "Look, it's the R. Kelly of the group." The two Marines had recently watched a music video featuring the American R&B singer wearing an all-white suit.[14]

Dark glided through the room, inspecting the food and supply stations with a satisfied air. He periodically stopped to speak with members of the tribe, asking them how they were doing and if they had everything they needed. All seemed familiar with and respectful of him.[15] Belshe and Przybylski asked Dark if they could pose for a picture with him, and he obliged. Dark's natural affinity for cameras aside, it enhanced the young sheikh's prestige to have the Americans ask him for his photograph.[16]

The Americans had also brought along a veterinarian to check up on the tribe's livestock. Local farmers prized their sheep, chicken, goats, and cows, and the animals had gained even greater importance as the government's food rationing sputtered in the postwar chaos. For poorer families within the Albu Issa, an animal or two might represent significant personal wealth and a source of income. The Iraqis bred the livestock, milked the cows, sheared the sheep for their wool, and periodically slaughtered various animals for meals. Modest ranching was one of the few somewhat intact elements of the peninsula's prewar economy.[17]

Ken Baum was Alpha Company's first sergeant. As the senior non-commissioned officer (NCO), the forty-three-year-old's responsibilities typically included overseeing all of the platoon sergeants and ensuring that Whisnant's intent was carried out among the enlisted ranks. On this day, however, Baum was assigned as the Marine Corps' designated cow wrangler. He had the qualifications. At roughly 215 pounds and six-foot-one, the muscular American sometimes worked out by dragging huge tires fixed to a chain in a circuitous route around Forward Operating Base (FOB) Black. He was widely known for having once been viciously kicked by an angry horse back in the States and hitting it back. Baum's formative years in Arkansas had left him with a deep, southern drawl and an enduring love for animals. The Marine Reservist had worked as a farrier in Michigan for more than a decade before volunteering for a series of active rotations with the Corps.

He jumped at the chance to bring these skills to bear in Fallujah and volunteered for the veterinary aid portion of the mission.[18]

The team was led by a stout, redheaded Army veterinarian who was "down-to-earth and really loved his work," according to Baum. Sgt. Gabe Foerster and his 2nd Squad from Weapons Platoon escorted the men as the security element. A roughly fifteen-year-old Iraqi boy arrived at the schoolhouse and introduced himself to the Americans, volunteering to guide them to the village's livestock. The retinue visited several dozen homes over the course of a day. A few of the nicer residences vaguely resembled modest ranches in the United States, each with a number of well-kept animals in sturdy, simple pens. Some farms had one large makeshift enclosure of bound palm fronds or loosely arranged concertina wire. The majority of owners kept one or two cows in a field adjacent to their house. A chain attached to a ring in the animal's nose was staked to the ground, and the grazing livestock were moved from area to area after they had eaten all of the grass within reach.[19]

The veterinarian and Baum approached each residence, introduced themselves to the man or woman of the house, and explained that they were available to examine, inoculate, and possibly treat the animals. The reactions of the Iraqis were positive, varying from pleasantly surprised to extremely grateful. Most of the homeowners offered the visitors tea and food; one man tried to give them a baby goat. Arab culture emphasizes hospitality, but some of the enthusiastic displays stood out to Baum, and seemed to underscore both the value of the animals and the rarity of good veterinary care.

Baum believes he figured out why the women were especially happy to see them. As he traveled from farm to farm, he noticed that sometimes if the man of the house showed the Americans to the livestock, he would sidle up to the larger animals hesitantly. When the animal moved, he would nervously jump back. If an older female was present, she would clomp up to the animal, grab its chain, and lead it to the vet. In some cases, the elder women took the lead. They would nonchalantly slap on well-worn rubber boots and gloves before trudging into the field to handle the animals. Baum quickly learned that a great deal of the ranching—and a large proportion of the overall field work—was done by them. The farrier developed respect for the tough, weather-beaten old women who ran some of the farms.[20]

As their patrol progressed, the Americans were joined by one of Baum's local acquaintances, a schoolteacher who sported a silver mustache, a red kaffiyeh, and black robes. Whenever the first sergeant came through the area on a patrol, the good-natured Fallujan greeted him and struck up enjoyable conversations spanning nearly every topic except one: He refused to talk politics. Baum enjoyed the articulate educator's company and was happy to have him along to observe their veterinary work.[21]

The Americans inoculated the larger animals for common parasites: The cattle were sprayed with a chemical that they absorbed through their skin, whereas the sheep had their hides yanked up for a syringe injection to the neck. Baum and the vet also examined livestock for injuries, sores, and infections and administered and handed out supplies of ointment or antibiotics as necessary. Some animals were sick and required extra attention. With the cows, Baum would wrestle the beast to the ground while the vet examined it and administered medication. In most cases, this went well. Baum made his approach, grabbed an ear or horn with one hand, put his fingers up a nostril to trigger a pressure point, and smoothly roll the animal down and onto its side. Occasionally there was a fight.[22]

The owner of one small, ramshackle residence led the Americans to an ornery old cow staked at the edge of a field. The beast was ill-tempered and sickly. Its black and white coat hung loosely over an emaciated frame. Every time the first sergeant approached the animal, it kicked dirt and wagged its head, snorting strings of snot to-and-fro. When Baum got too close, it moved to charge, and the Marine sidestepped or backed off to try again. Baum's Iraqi escorts became concerned. "They say that cow is crazy," explained the Marines' interpreter, who also told them not to worry about it.[23] Baum kept at it anyway.

"First Sergeant . . . Muzien!" ([The cow is] no good!), the schoolteacher insisted, waving the American off. The Marine persisted for another minute or so before finally admitting defeat. The animal's owner and the schoolteacher patted the big American on his shoulder in a way that communicated, "Don't worry, don't worry." The interpreter elaborated that the Iraqis didn't want him getting hurt over a "crazy cow."

At another residence, the Americans tracked down and treated a fugitive animal afflicted with "gastro bloat." The cow's stomach had filled with air, putting pressure on internal organs and cutting circulation. The distressed beast had pulled its stake from the ground and fled. When the owner and the trailing Americans found the animal in the middle of a large, grassy field, its left side was grossly distended. Treatment called for running medical tubing down its throat to relieve the pressure. The vet didn't have any tubing on hand, so he made do with a long section of old garden hose provided by the owner.

The cow snorted as Baum and the veterinarian approached. The Marine gradually edged close enough to swiftly grab a nostril and an ear. The animal wanted no part of this. The fight was on. The cow bucked and shook while Baum held his arms around its neck in a death grip and a set of fingers up the animal's nose. The wrestling match lasted less than a minute, abruptly ending when the big American wrangled enough leverage to spin and roll the animal's side into a small tree. He pinned the struggling cow against the sapling and wrapped his arms around both the tree trunk and the animal's head and neck. The veterinarian moved in to finish the job, quickly prying its mouth open before threading the orange hose down its throat. The improvised equipment began to do the trick, gradually relieving trapped air from the animal's swollen stomach.[24] At some point during the mission, a pair of mortars landed in the distance. Baum and the vet continued to treat the animals, chuckling as they continued their work.[25]

"Where else . . . in the world?" Baum later recalled thinking.[25]

—————— ❖ ——————

Back at the schoolhouse, the food and supply distribution was winding down, but the medical services were still going on. Some of the Iraqis would have to be turned away after having waited in line. Hundreds of men, women, and children had come through the supply line in four hours, and the Americans fortunately had enough candy, food, and goods to send everyone home with something.[26]

As the crowd thinned, a group of older Iraqi boys and young men continued to hang around the rooms distributing food and supplies. At one point during the day, candy had been eclipsed by an even bigger draw: two American women wearing tan Marine flight suits. Captain Sweezey and Capt. Christine Hauser, an F-18 "backseater" (weapons systems officer) who had volunteered to run a women's engagement program for CAG had come to assist Team Yankee with their mission. As was often the case, the Iraqi men on this particular day were especially intrigued. Being "a woman in combat gear," Sweezey knew that female Marines were "just a novelty" to the Iraqis.

The two officers had earlier posed for pictures with some of the children who came through the line with their families. Sensing opportunity, several enterprising young men quickly found small children, approached the women, and offered up the kids (and themselves) for pictures. In at least one case, Belshe thought he witnessed a child give one of the teenagers a puzzled look that translated, "Who are you and why do you want me for a picture?"

The young men's ploy achieved its culturally transcendent aim: a foot in the door for friendly chitchat and posed photos with the opposite sex. Sweezey and Hauser gamely complied, and Przybylski served as photographer for a series of digital pictures the Iraqis seemed to cherish, even though they would never actually possess a copy.[27]

After the excited photo session, a young tribesman wearing a light gray denim jacket and a sparse mustache spotted a pair of sunglasses in Belshe's hand. The boy, who looked about seventeen years old, asked if he could have them. Belshe considered it. He pointed at Przybylski and motioned: "If you beat him at arm wrestling, you can have them." "OK!" the Iraqi answered, and it was on. A crowd of youngsters pressed into a semicircle to watch the showdown, while a few older men shook their heads and chuckled on the sidelines.[28]

Little did the Iraqis know, theirs was a sucker's bet. Przybylski hid bizarre reserves of strength in his thin frame and routinely won arm wrestling contests against much bigger Marines. His Iraqi opponent looked young and healthy, but Belshe was confident about wagering his sunglasses. True to form, the American won handily. This failed to settle the matter, however. The young tribesmen insisted on an impromptu arm wrestling tournament. First prize: bragging rights and plastic shades. After the first loss, the Iraqis combed the schoolhouse for older and bigger tribesmen to take on the Americans.

The corporal soon tagged out for Belshe, who faced off against a bigger Iraqi who looked to be in his twenties. The match turned out to be a struggle, but the sergeant wasn't going to let himself lose in front of the other Americans. Belshe eked out a hard-fought victory and retained the U.S. crown. During the next contest, a left-handed Przybylski resumed the tournament and agreed to wrestle a right-handed Iraqi. To heady cheers and vigorous backslapping, he lost. The Americans gave the eventual victor an aluminum flashlight, and Belshe handed his original challenger the sunglasses he had hoped for. The Iraqi tried to refuse, pointing out that he had lost, but the Marine insisted.[29] "Thank you," said the young man in English, before quickly leaving the schoolhouse.

A few minutes later, the teen returned and handed Belshe a ring. Its small band of silver was set with a square, beveled onyx. It was a modest piece of jewelry, but had obviously been professionally set. Belshe tried to refuse the present, handing it back to the boy, but the smiling teen also insisted. The American relented and thanked him. The gift remains a treasured memento from his civil affairs work in Fallujah.[30]

The exchange with the teenager stood in stark contrast to some of the other interactions between Marines and the peninsula's young men. When Alpha Company 1/24 arrived at FOB Black to replace Alpha Company 1/25 in October 2006, Capt. Jeremy Hoffmann noticed a sign posted on the wall of its predecessor's command post: "We are no longer destroying bicycles." He came to learn that there had been a report of insurgents using bicycles to smuggle weapons and IEDs. For a time, Alpha 1/25 had responded to this information by destroying every bicycle it came across, failing to determine whether the property belonged to insurgents or peaceful citizens.[31]

Less than a week in country, one of the men from 1/24 accompanied a platoon from 1/25 on a tour of the area of operations. While conducting a large convoy down Main Street, the newly arrived Marine heard a ping against the side of the Humvee. An NCO in the front seat told the driver to stop and quickly dismounted the vehicle. The Marine walked over to a group of young men, one of whom had apparently thrown a rock. After a contentious exchange, he punched an Iraqi in the face, knocking him to the ground. The American turned and strode back to the Humvee. "If you're not careful, next time, it'll be a grenade," he explained to the surprised Marine from 1/24. The man who had hit the Iraqi failed to appreciate that his own aggression might further inspire the escalation he feared.[32]

Some Marines in Alpha 1/24 criticized the tactics and perceived tenor of their predecessors' deployment and believed that alienation of the peninsula's citizenry by more than one previous unit had made their job much more difficult by setting back intelligence gathering by months. According to some of their replacements and some local residents, instead of getting out of the vehicles in small teams and engaging with locals, preceding units tended to run large, mounted security patrols along the area's main roads. They would roll through the trouble spots of Fuhaylat and Hasa in big convoys, get in gunfights, and return to base. There was neither extended engagement with the people nor constant pressure on insurgents, who simply regrouped to fight another day while intimidating the rest of the population after the Americans left.

Alpha 1/25, however, also had its proponents among its replacements in Alpha 1/24. Some note that all of 1/25's men came back alive from a dangerous deployment. In addition, holistic counterinsurgency was not an official, widely promulgated doctrine of the U.S. military at the time, so each company commander independently navigated his path through a confusing, dangerous environment. Turnover from short Marine deployments exacerbated the steepness of this learning curve.[33] "Each rotation presented challenges," offered Whisnant. "The enemy exploited transition periods. Often lessons learned were lost, and 'seams' exploited."

Some Marines also empathized with rough reactions to frustrating attacks and almost universal noncooperation from locals. Earlier trends shaped each unit's approach. And after 1/24 arrived, the dynamics of the peninsula did not miraculously change because one unit replaced bad tactics with good ones.[34] For one thing, some previous units had also (unsuccessfully) attempted to partner with the tribes, and some had even started census patrols during earlier tours on the peninsula.[35] In addition, Alpha Company 1/24's execution of counterinsurgency doctrine in 2006 and 2007 wasn't perfect.

The Marines got out of their vehicles and engaged the people, often with professionalism, but not everyone took to the softer aspects of the counterinsurgency mission. A number of them candidly assessed that some of their fellow Marines were callous with the civilians, typically directing their ire at those who were suspected as insurgents. The most common examples of bad behavior included passive or active mistreatment of detainees—usually consisting of verbal abuse or not giving them enough food or water while being held in ad hoc patrol bases on long ops—or rough searches when the Americans cased the home of a suspected insurgent. One enlisted Marine believed that there were a few guys in his squad who harmed the mission with this attitude, adding "it would have been better if they weren't there at all." Another Marine, cited by others as being really kind to local kids, later reflected, "We were probably a little hard on them." He was specifically referring to the destructive handling of some homes during searches.[36]

Most officers and NCOs in Alpha 1/24 energetically asserted that any abuse of local citizens or their property was the exception, rather than the rule; they claimed success in instructing their Marines down to the lance corporals and privates first class to treat Iraqis with respect. As is the case in any unit, the overall tenor reflects the leadership. The company officers, including a majority of the platoon commanders, explicitly attempted to set this precedent from above.

Complicating matters was the fact that by 2006 the relationship between coalition forces and Fallujans had become remarkably dysfunctional. After the 2003 invasion, the U.S. military had initiated contact with a combination of well-intentioned attempts at local outreach, heavy-handed detention tactics, and a series of tragic, mistaken shootings of civilians. In 2007, one intelligence official ruefully shook his head at all of the mistakes and missed opportunities, asserting that "things didn't have to be as bad as they'd become." He was not alone in his opinion.[37]

Some aspects of Fallujah seemed to destine it for violent conflict, however. The sheikhs had run a double game on the Americans during the invaders' early attempts at outreach, superficially engaging the westerners while also supporting the insurgency or simply looking the other way. The famously rebellious history of the area and the relatively conservative religiousness of its citizens were dry tinder. The spark for widespread insurgency came from opportunistic local imams and foreign jihadists, who effectively stoked outrage at infidel occupiers "trying to steal Iraq's oil."[38]

After the two large battles in 2004, a complete evacuation of the city, and years of guerrilla war, the U.S. military and Fallujans had by 2006 come to eye each other with weary distrust. One can never know if the insurgency and the enmity that characterized American-Fallujan relations could have been avoided—and if so, to what degree—but in early 2007, specific circumstances and doctrine changed things for the better. Alpha Company 1/24 and the Marines of the Civil Affairs Group seized a new opportunity to turn things around, finally establishing a beachhead in the long struggle for a genuine working relationship with the tribes.

At Dark's request, a special event was organized to help local widows. The number of men who had been slain during the war was staggering; those who weren't killed by Americans had been killed by their rivals, criminals, or *takfiri* insurgents. Several hundred women of all ages queued outside a room in the schoolhouse where Dark, resplendent in his finest traditional white regalia, Brezler, Whisnant, and several other Americans sat and waited behind folding tables.

As each woman entered the room, she respectfully approached the table to speak with Dark. He would then explain to the Americans, "This is the wife of [so-and-so]. He died [in this location]" or "Terrorists captured her husband in [name of area] and then killed him." After the brief greeting and explanation, the sheikh would hand each woman a crisp $20 bill. The modest amount was happily received. In the peninsula's shattered economy, it would go far. The event fulfilled Brezler's attempts at "combined effects" to a tee. The money helped generate goodwill among the widows in addition to boosting Dark's stature within the tribe. At the same time, the recitation of how and where the men were killed was an information bonanza that helped map out the history and nature of the peninsula's insurgency. A good gesture was also great intelligence gathering.[39]

❖

At the end of the day, Dark invited Whisnant and Brezler, along with Cahir, Roussell, the military intelligence Marine Saint One, Sweezey, Lt. Cdr. Andrew Zwolski, the battalion medical officer, and another Navy physician back to his house for a celebratory dinner. Joining them were several of the sheikh's lieutenants, including Ma'an Khalid Aifan al-Issawi, Uthman Majid Aifan al-Issawi, and Mushtaq Khalid Aifan al Issawi. The Americans and Iraqis settled on lavish pillows arranged in a white tent outside of Dark's courtyard and feasted on a spread of goat, lamb, dates, vegetables, olives, and bread. The atmosphere was jovial and the conversation light, although the Iraqis inevitably steered the friendly chatter toward contracts, while the Americans attempted to gather more intelligence.[40]

The Marines had become accustomed to learning of close family ties between combatants on opposite sides of the peninsula's tribal civil war, but they were fascinated nonetheless by several revelations by their host. Dark began to speak at length about his family tree, detailing the personalities and careers of his close relatives. The sheikh was raised in Iraq and Saudi Arabia, and a few of his brothers had chosen radically different paths. His older brother Barakat, then residing in Jordan, had been an insurgent leader who actively led in the rebellion against U.S. forces earlier in the war.[41] Another brother had long ago emigrated to the United States, obtained an education in computer science, and become an information technology professional.

A third brother was alleged to be somewhere in Afghanistan or Pakistan, waging jihad against NATO forces with Osama bin Laden and al Qaeda. Dark shook his head ruefully and remarked that he was "a bad guy."[42] Dark's penchant for tall tales was legend, so the Marines took some of his stories with large grains of salt, but the idea of one of the sheikh's brothers waging holy war against the United States and another working in America's computer industry still had the power to surprise.

The Americans spent the night in the sheikh's house at his invitation, staying in his "secret room," the entrance to which was hidden behind a wardrobe. It was a massive space, with two king-sized beds, two dressers with mirrors, and four wardrobes lining a far wall. The next morning, most people were up and about for the sheikh's serving of an "American breakfast" of boiled eggs when Brezler made his move.[43] The tall, lanky captain quietly opened one of the closets, chose a set of traditional white robes, and slipped them on. He quickly completed the ensemble by wrapping a red and white kaffiyeh around his head and donning a pair of dark sunglasses. He then stepped into the courtyard.

Uthman and another of Dark's lieutenants jumped to their feet and looked around for their weapons when they saw the tall stranger in white robes striding toward them, wondering how this man had gotten into the house. When they realized it was Brezler from his Cheshire grin and blonde mustache, the Iraqis howled in laughter. Dark, Whisnant, and the rest of the visitors got a kick out of it too, when they saw what all the commotion was about.[44]

With the mission complete, the visiting members of Alpha 1/24 and the civil affairs teams packed up their supplies and personnel for a midmorning departure from Albu Aifan. The Marines turned over the engines of their staged vehicles and pulled onto "Main Street" for the careful convoy home through rainy weather. They were greeted by a surprising sight: The muddy streets at the village center were lined with men, women, and children of the Albu Aifan subtribe. Many of the adults smiled and waved, a few cheered or clapped. Some of the kids ran alongside the Humvees, waving and asking for candy. Even some of the more jaded Marines couldn't help but smile at the friendly send-off. To Whisnant, it was "like a Macy's Thanksgiving Day Parade." He also picked up on a tentative vibe that he described as a sense of "gratitude" tempered with "caution . . . as to what the next day would hold for them."[45]

For Sgt. Gabe Foerster, "it was kind of a weird feeling. It was a happy time for me, because we had some bad days in Iraq, and then you had a day like this where you were like, 'Wow, we did some good in the village. I think these people have opened up to us a little bit.'" Foerster thought it was maybe "the first time anyone tried to help them in a long time."

After arriving back at FOB Black, Whisnant gathered his platoon commanders and squad leaders for a talk. "You need to remember this day for the rest of your lives," he recalled saying to his Marines. "Dark didn't tell those people to cheer us. They did that of their own free will, because they feel like normal people again, because they feel safer. You need to remember today because it's so important. Down to the PFC level, you need to make your men understand that what they are doing is extremely important. We're actually accomplishing something, not just ticking time away on a calendar."[46]

Whisnant's message was delivered and received in a low-key manner, but it quietly resonated. The Marines were proud of what they had accomplished. Gains are difficult to make in a counterinsurgency and even more difficult to gauge. An unexpected and kind send-off from Iraqis once deemed intractable—and who only months before had avoided any meaningful interaction with them—was a rare, tangible measure of progress for the Americans.

11

❖ DOWN BY THE RIVER ❖

One afternoon in late February 2007, Maj. Dan Whisnant, the military intelligence Marine Saint One, LCpl. Joshua Clayton, and Sgt. Jeremy Howe visited Dark, Sheikh Aifan Sadoun Aifan al-Issawi, at his home in Albu Aifan. Three of the sheikh's lieutenants—Ma'an Khalid Aifan al-Issawi, Uthman Majid Aifan al-Issawi, and Mushtaq Khalid Aifan al-Issawi—joined them in a sitting room to play something the Americans dubbed "the Zien-Muzien Game." Clayton had brought along his laptop, which was stocked with the company's massive database of detainees, everyday citizens, and suspected insurgents. The Americans flipped through a seemingly endless series of pictures while the Iraqis scrutinized and judged each as *zien* ("good" guy) or *muzien* ("bad" guy). The repetitive quiz lasted hours. The Americans had also brought along a map and had Dark place dots outlining his new militia checkpoints, each of which the Americans and Iraqis assigned a number for ease of communication when the militiamen called in reports.[1]

Late in the afternoon, Dark's face lit up as he answered a call on one of his many cell phones. He hung up after a few minutes and excitedly proclaimed that a man "who was kidnapped [by insurgents] is coming over right now. . . . He's got some very good information!"[2] At around 7:00 p.m., the kidnapping victim arrived at the sheikh's house. He was from a subtribe and village south of Albu Aifan; the Americans had never seen him before. His lined face and salt-and-pepper mustache and hair placed him somewhere around his forties, and he wore scruffy clothing and a dirty workman's jacket not untypical of peninsula residents. From the moment he was ushered into the house, a stream of Arabic poured excitedly from his mouth. Dark quickly translated what he could to the Americans.

The night before, he and about four other men had been kidnapped by insurgents. Howe recalled that the captors suspected the men of providing information to the Americans or Dark's militia. The kidnappers blindfolded their prisoner before throwing him in a car for a long, suspenseful ride. Eventually, the man was pulled from the car and shoved into a pitchblack, approximately 11 x 11 foot space with the other captives.[3] The room was so dark and deathly quiet that he assumed they were being held underground. This setting roughly matches the description of the partially buried crates sometimes used by farmers as a break room or equipment shed insulated from the midday sun.[4] The following day, the insurgents inexplicably released the man, but several fellow captives remained imprisoned; at least two of them were the freed man's relatives. If the Iraqi's story was legitimate, his family members were possibly suffering beatings or torture. Given local precedent, they could be slated for executions.

It was common knowledge that Dark was leading a militia against al Qaeda and other radical mujahidin, so after his release, the man rushed to make contact with the sheikh's people. The Iraqi was "in a hurry" to communicate what he knew and "[spat] out information almost faster than" the Americans and Albu Aifan militiamen could absorb it, recalled Howe. Saint One, Howe, and Dark took over the questioning. The Marines and the sheikh asked the man for details: Where had he been kidnapped? How long was he in the car? Did the car make many turns? Did he recognize any of the voices? Could he point to a location on this map? Why was he released?[5] The man became frustrated because he couldn't read a map or remember much except that the ride had been a long one, and he could tell that he'd been near the river. After about thirty minutes of questioning, the witness had given them all the information he could.[6]

Once the interview was finished and the visitor had left, the sheikh offered an enigmatic assessment to the Americans. "I trust the man's information," said Dark. "But I do not completely trust the man." Howe speculated that the Iraqi was now going through the same vetting issues that plagued the Marines. Dark also wasn't always sure that the information provided by local informants was completely legitimate. It was always possible that tips were being planted to send the Marines or their militia allies against personal enemies or business competitors.[7]

Saint One had a similar, though more nuanced take: the man's demeanor didn't perfectly match his story, but that didn't mean it wasn't true. Iraqi sources tended to embellish events. The Americans would joke about "Iraqi math" ("Make sure you divide the number they give you by 10."), and Arabic speakers famously lend themselves to poetic allusions and flourishes. Plus, local culture, like every other, has its tellers of "tall tales" and "fish stories." Thus, Saint One believed that the man could have indeed been kidnapped by hardcore *takfiri* insurgents, or he could've been involved in a personal dispute that led to his being asked or taken somewhere to hash it out. The experienced intelligence analyst tended not to take incidents like this one at face value, but rather collected them as pieces that might fill in a larger puzzle.[8]

The Americans and Iraqis pondered their large map of the peninsula in an attempt to figure out where the captives had been taken. Wide areas locked down by American or militia checkpoints were removed from the analysis. This factor, the amount of time the captive rode in the car, and the sparse number of turns meant his prison had to have been somewhere south of Albu Aifan. Along with proximity to the Euphrates River, the clues pointed to the village of Hawa.

In the hierarchy of trouble spots on the peninsula, Hawa was on the Americans' short list; it definitely made the top five, but lagged well behind the villages of Abu Hasa and Fuhaylat as known insurgent strongholds where Marines invariably encountered gunfights or roadside bombs. Earlier that month, on February 7, Capt. Jeremy Hoffmann's Weapons Platoon and a recon platoon had run an operation near Hawa that stirred up a gunfight.[9] One Marine had even received a tip from a local elder that the main road running toward the village had been nicknamed the Mujahidin (holy warriors) Highway.[10]

Marine units were attacked all over the peninsula, but would most assuredly come under fire when they ventured near the southwestern villages of Hasa and Fuhaylat. After staging a quick ambush, the insurgents often retreated to the north. Howe and the Marines of the intelligence cell had speculated that their enemies might be running toward the city or to hideouts within the series of villages that runs along the northeastern corridor toward Dark's village of Albu Aifan. As the Americans pondered the maps, things started to click. If moving northwest on the main thoroughfare dubbed Route Iron, a couple of turns eastward along less-traveled roads would put their attackers on a straight shot to Hawa.[11]

Despite the Americans' attempts to consistently project force, Hawa remained one of their least traveled areas. It was just outside of Alpha 1/24's area of operations. The company simply didn't have the manpower to establish a presence in the village, and the fifteen-kilometer-plus routes from Forward Operating Base Black or FOB Gold were littered with roadside bombs.[12]

Given the previous fight stirred up near Hawa, the pattern of attacks, and the lack of a U.S. presence, the man's testimony added one more data point implicating the village as an unmolested staging area for radical insurgents.[13] This assessment was endorsed by Dark, who claimed he knew the names of a couple of "bad guys" who were hiding out in Hawa. In the following days, the sheikh made a series of phone calls to his network of family members and informants to verify that insurgents were still operating from the village. He enthusiastically told the Americans that his suspicions had been confirmed and that they needed to move decisively.[14] "If you go down there with many men, you will find [insurgents] and weapons," Dark told his American allies. "If you can do this and catch them by surprise, you will only have to do it once."[15]

Hawa was a focal point, a big catch, he claimed. The sheikh emphasized that if the Marines took the village quickly and in force, the insurgents wouldn't have many places left to rest and refit with any degree of comfort. The Americans took Dark's assessment under advisement, but also considered that he was prone to enthusiasm and exaggeration, especially whenever he attempted to spur the Americans into action. They would have to check it out for themselves.[16]

When Howe had been pressed into serving as Whisnant's intelligence cell leader prior to deployment, the major had tried to prepare him for the task ahead. "For the first few months, you're going to have no idea what you're doing," Whisnant told him. "By month four or five, you're going to begin to figure it out. And by the sixth month, just as you really get a handle on things, it's going to be time to go home." The admonition had come to eerie fruition. Nearing their last month in country, the puzzle pieces were coming together. Dark's information, the mapped pattern of attacks, and other local sources seemed to point to a key insurgent stronghold.[17] The Americans began planning their first and only operation that used three of Alpha Company's four platoons at once. They were going down to Hawa in force.

❖ HAWA ❖

A mission to flush out and kill or capture insurgents in Hawa kicked off in the early morning hours of March 3, 2007. The largest operation of Alpha 1/24's deployment aimed for surprise: three of the company's four platoons would surround and sweep through the isolated village in a swift maneuver designed to cut off any chance of escape for their targets.

Maj. Dan Whisnant and his platoon commanders needed to move their Marines to the destination quietly. Humvees were ruled out; their approach would be too obvious, and besides, the main road to Hawa remained a "red route," littered with pressure-plate improvised explosive devices (IEDs). To maintain stealth and avoid the bombs, the Marines would have to walk up to 16 kilometers through the peninsula's countryside of burgeoning spring crops, widely spaced farmhouses, and irrigation canals. Individual squads would begin their long marches just after midnight so they could take up positions around the village before daybreak.[1]

First Lt. Robert Lehner's 1st Platoon left from Forward Operating Base Black to take up blocking and overwatch positions looking west to east across the width of the village. First Lt. Jerome Greco set up his three squads from 3rd Platoon in positions north and northeast of Hawa and established a patrol base that would serve as a detainee collection point. Two of Capt. Jeremy Hoffmann's squads from Weapons Platoon looped into positions to the south and southwest of their target and from there cut north through the village, house by house. If their movement flushed out any insurgents, the escapees would run into the Marine blocking positions watching the main roads and canals exiting the area.[2]

Fortunately for the Americans, insurgents tended to be creatures of habit. They were typically asleep before sunrise, and almost never bothered to assign overnight lookouts for Marine patrols. Once the Americans stabbed into the village, they would have to move fast to maintain any advantage offered by their early morning surprise.[3]

By 5:00 a.m., about an hour and a half before sunrise, all the platoons had moved into position. Captain Hoffmann was accompanying Weapons Platoon's 3rd Squad, led by Cpl. Ron Jansen, for its sweep into Hawa. The thirteen men had walked about ten miles through fields and palm groves lit in the claustrophobic green relief of night vision goggles before stopping at their staging area southwest of the village. The Marines now stood, sat, knelt, or laid behind a tall berm that screened them from view, waiting for the command to move out.[4]

Jansen's men had been down here only once before in their deployment, about a month earlier. His squad—like now, accompanied by Captain Hoffmann—had been moving through the area with elements from Weapons Platoon's 2nd Squad when the other Marines had taken "a huge amount of fire" from insurgent machine gunners and snipers near the village. On that day, Hoffmann had immediately moved the men into a blocking position to back up their sister squad. As Jansen's men laid in and around a palm grove, waiting for a fleeing target or the order to assault, an insurgent drove a white sedan straight into their lines while rushing to back up his compatriots attacking the other group of Americans. The Iraqi belatedly realized his error and backed up furiously before grabbing an AK-47, bailing out of the vehicle, and shooting most of a magazine at the Marines. He never had a chance. He went down in a hail of bullets, and Sgt. Brandon Osborne lobbed a grenade behind the car to finish him.[5]

After his platoon's contact with the enemy, the aggressive Hoffmann repeatedly radioed back to the combat operations center at FOB Black to request an assault toward the village, but the officers further up the chain at battalion headquarters were cautious. They ordered Whisnant to deny Hoffmann's appeal. It was too risky in their estimation. The Marines were too few and far away from backup to press the fight, and Hawa was beyond the outer edge of Alpha Company's area of operations. Hoffmann was furious at the timidity of his superiors. "What is the point of fighting a war," he thought, "when officers are too afraid of casualties to close with the enemy?"

Some of the platoon commander's men shared his frustration, and were eager to escalate the gunfight against their attackers. They smelled blood, knew the insurgents were close, and wanted to "get some." Others agreed with the officers up the chain of command. "We were exposed," said one lance corporal. "Our radios weren't working well, we had no air support, and QRF [quick reaction forces] were a long ways away. If we would have gone in, I think something bad could have happened." In the end, the Marines were pulled back from Hawa.[6] Now they had returned, with plenty of back-up, and were waiting to move in.

Jansen knew it was a tough area, so their leaders had prepared them for a strong possibility of contact. The twenty-five-year-old squad leader was pumped, but held on to reserves of cynicism bred from experience; most of the time when you expected something big to happen, nothing happened at all. This might wind up as just another long march capped by a day-long meet and greet with barely cooperative locals.[7]

The 3rd Squad had been relaxing only five minutes before Hoffmann issued the order to move out. Jansen's men marched toward a house at the southern tip of the village in a "V" formation. The plan was simple: one team, consisting of four Marines and Captain Hoffmann, would take an overwatch position on top of a suitable house. Sergeant Osborne would lead a second team of lance corporals, Mike Panasuk and Jessie Wortman, to establish security at each house they visited. Jansen and the lance corporals Joel Zavalavargas and Guadalupe Ponce would interview the occupants.[8]

The first house they came to was a modest two-bedroom with one story and no courtyard wall. The Marines swiftly opened the door and announced themselves to a family of four who had been sleeping on mats in one of the bedrooms. The interviews and a cursory search took barely five minutes. The groggy residents gave their names, but not much else. Their hesitance reminded Lance Corporal Ponce of difficult interviews from earlier in the deployment. Ponce had trained as a machine gunner, but he was now the squad's scribe, responsible for recording all names, tips, and grid coordinates, as well as taking pictures of all military-age males. The twenty-one-year-old Mexican American had been born in Texas and then bounced around the East Coast as a kid before finally settling in Michigan. His family had moved to the Midwest to escape gang-related trouble plaguing their neighborhood in Arlington, Virginia.

His older brother eventually joined the Marines. Ponce followed him a couple of years later "on a whim" and to challenge himself. He chose the Reserves so he could be the first member of his family to attend college.

Ponce had been pursuing a criminal justice degree at Grand Valley State University, in Michigan, when he was called up for deployment to Fallujah.

The lance corporal initially found his job as a scribe frustrating, but eventually it became rewarding. Iraqis offered up little information during the first few months of the deployment, and they always balked at having their picture taken. The alliance with the paramount sheikh, Khamis Hasnawi Aifan al-Issawi, and Sheikh Aifan Sadoun Aifan al-Issawi (Dark) over the past two months seemed to break the ice. He had finally gained traction during his interviews, and it had been remarkable to see the Iraqis finally stand up and take responsibility for their own security.[9] His newfound optimism was tested, however, by the first interview in Hawa. The questioning went nowhere. The house's sleepy occupants had no weapons, said little more than their names, and claimed there were no insurgents in the area. Their demeanor was wary and odd.[10]

Jansen quickly ordered his second team guarding the perimeter to move on to the next house and establish security while his team finished the interviews in the first house. The village's residences had cement walls and were spaced thirty to fifty meters apart. This gave the Marines the advantage of surprise as they bounced from house to house, as long as no explosions or gunfire broke the predawn calm.[11] Sergeant Osborne led the security team toward the second home. He had been a little disappointed when their first target ended up being a dry hole. "Shit, this mission's going to be another tease," Osborne thought at the time. "We're not gonna find anything."[12]

Their new destination was an odd, U-shaped residence with six rooms on a single story. Five of the rooms opened onto the cup of the "U," which formed a small courtyard with a solitary palm tree shooting from the center of its dirt floor. The Marines quickly flooded into the home, announcing themselves as they woke the sleeping occupants to gather them outside. The first room the Americans entered was a bedroom where a middle-aged man, his wife, and two small kids were sleeping. When the man was woken and asked if he had any weapons, he responded, "Laa" (No), but the Marines quickly found a loaded AK-47 stashed on the top shelf of a closet. Civilians were allowed to keep a single rifle in their home, but they also couldn't lie when American or Iraqi government forces asked them about it.

"No weapon, huh?" Osborne angrily flexi-cuffed the man and separated him from the rest of his family. "OK . . . something's going on here," he thought. The sergeant had barely moved into a second bedroom, filled with women and children, when someone beckoned him to come outside. Lance Corporal Wortman had spotted something when he looked into a room that comprised one side of the house's U-shape. It was the only room that didn't connect to the rest of the house from the inside or open directly onto the courtyard. Inside, he saw three groggy men and something that looked like the stock of a rifle peeking out from below one of the Iraqis' sleeping mats. "I think they are sitting on AKs," Wortman said in a low voice.[13]

After Osborne had emerged from the room where the women slept, he saw Wortman standing off a few feet from a doorway. When the lance corporal informed Osborne that he thought he could see AK-47s, it got the sergeant's attention. Although the Iraqis could legally possess one firearm for protection, who would sleep with a rifle under his pillow? Osborne clicked the switch on his radio and said, "Hey Jansen, get over here now."[14] Jansen had already begun walking toward the second house but could see the pair of Marines standing near a doorway.

Osborne was higher in rank, but he was Jansen's subordinate for the squad. Osborne was the leader of the company's mortar section, and was periodically pulled out of Weapons Platoon to back up other platoons that required the services of mobile artillery. This situation in his "home" unit led to unusual (but not unheard of) instances of a sergeant taking orders from a corporal who is a squad leader. Although the two men occasionally butted heads—an invariably blunt Osborne was always the first to tell Jansen when he thought he was doing something wrong—they usually worked well together. Jansen had basic faith in the sergeant's instincts and tactics. If Osborne thought something was fishy, he was probably right. Osborne quickly briefed him on the three men inside the small room. Jansen and Osborne immediately moved inside with their weapons raised. Wortman positioned himself in the doorway behind them.[15]

Jansen had a blinding SureFire flashlight attached to the front of his M-16, which he waved around the room. Osborne had detached his flashlight and held it in his left hand as he steadied the muzzle of his M-16 on his left forearm. Along with the stability offered by a three-point rifle harness, this gave him the ability to point his weapon at a target while flicking his wrist to shine the flashlight in any direction.

There were three points of interest in the 12 x 14 foot room. Two men had been sleeping among mats and blankets lining a long left wall, while a third lay along the far wall. The space lacked furniture or decorations, except for a large red and white patterned area rug that covered most of the dusty cement floor. The pair of men on the left wall had by now sat up among a swaddle of cloth blankets surrounding them. Confusion suffused their faces as they rubbed their eyes. The third man continued to lay by another wall, moving slightly under a blanket.

The Marines pointed their weapons at the men while Jansen screamed at them in Arabic to stand up and show him their hands: "Shufuni idak! Shufuni idak!" The two men on the left hesitated. Their confusion was quickly supplanted by another emotion, as they looked askance toward the third man, who remained squirming beneath his blanket. Usually people stand up and show their hands pretty quickly when someone puts a gun in their face, but these two men weren't complying, and the third was rustling around under cover. Alarm bells were clanging in Jansen's head.

He again yelled, "Shufuni idak!" His instincts were screaming at him to shoot, but he didn't have legal or moral authority for doing so. Osborne's adrenaline surged as well. Every fiber in his body told him that something was wrong, but he couldn't disregard the possibility of a language or cultural gap; they couldn't simply take the chance of killing a roomful of people because sleeping Iraqis didn't wake up and comply fast enough. The two men on the left continued to steal glances at the third man as they slowly rose to comply with the Marines' instructions. Their expressions seemed resigned as they stood up and finally showed their hands. Jansen continued screaming at the man rustling under the blanket. His instincts were now on fire. He was beginning to dismiss concerns about the legality of pulling the trigger. "Shufuni idak!"

The third man finally sat up and then began to stand. The Arab was lightly bearded and young, maybe in his twenties, and he wore a light grey dishdasha. As he rose, the blanket fell from his body and he seemed to drop something. He quickly dipped down to pick up a small object. Beams of white light flashed across a smooth metal grenade in the Iraqi's right hand. His left hand moved toward it. Jansen fired first. Osborne joined him a millisecond later. Six or seven deafening bangs boomed and echoed through the tiny cement room as the Marines pulled their triggers in rapid succession. The Iraqi's body jerked about in the bright glow of their flashlights. Two parallel rows of small bullet holes looked like pencils pricking a pillow as they leap-frogged up both sides of the man's chest. The firing lasted barely more than a second. The insurgent's body immediately went limp, crumpling against the wall and then sliding to the ground like a marionette whose strings had been cut. A small red smear of blood stained the tan wall behind him.

Jansen's adrenaline overpowered any memory of the next few seconds. Osborne recalls that his mind switched to training and instinct. "Remove the two remaining threats," the sergeant thought immediately. The other two Iraqis had surged toward the doorway as soon as the shooting started. "They wanted no part of it [the grenade]," recalled Wortman, who briefly considered whether he should "shoot them, or take them?" while blocking the door. In the end, he yelled and stepped out of their way, shoving at least one of the men out the door. Several Marines tackled the two Iraqis, grabbing firm handfuls of clothing and roughly pinning them.[16]

Ponce had been walking toward the doorway of the room when he heard shouts and then loud bangs accompanied by bright flashes. Almost immediately, he saw Marines grappling with a pair of Iraqis. Ponce moved to assist Wortman with one of the captured insurgents. The Marines quickly dragged the men apart, separating the prisoners according to detainee-handling procedures. Wortman and Ponce pushed one man to the left of the room and shoved him against a wall while Osborne and Jansen threw the other Iraqi to the ground near the palm tree in the middle of the courtyard. Both insurgents were pinned, flexi-cuffed, searched, and blindfolded.

Jansen screamed at the Iraqi he was handling while pressing his knee into the man's back. More than half of what he said was in English, about half of which seemed to consist of expletives.[17] "What the fuck are you doing!" yelled the squad leader. "Who is that guy!" he screamed, referring to the dead man. Ponce had never seen his squad leader so angry. Jansen was typically amiable and could even be a bit of a goofball when he was relaxing in barracks. Once outside the wire and on the job, he was all business and ran his squad calmly but seriously. A number of Marines described Jansen as a good leader who was exceptionally professional. But something had happened in the room to make the corporal more furious than Ponce had ever seen him.[18]

As Wortman and Ponce held on to their detainee, the Iraqi seemed to be shouting instructions in Arabic to someone other than the Marines. "Ahras!" (Shut up!), Ponce yelled. "Ohkef!" (Stop!).[19] The man kept yelling. Wortman finally emphasized the command with a knock on the head from a barrel of his rifle, and the insurgent shut up. To Ponce, this also seemed like unusual behavior. Wortman was a quiet, gentle fellow whose youthful looks and demeanor sometimes earned him a ribbing as the "squad mascot." Clearly though, something had really set these guys off. And the area was still insecure. The Marines couldn't tell if the screaming Iraqi had merely been plotting a cover story with his friend or yelling instructions to other insurgents hiding in the area.[20]

After the two men were secured, Jansen reentered the room. Adrenaline still coursed through his body as he aimed his weapon and stepped toward the man they had shot. The insurgent looked dead, and in his chest was a grouping of six or seven bloody holes a little larger than a paper plate. Jansen couldn't, however, account for the grenade. He carefully sighted his M-16 and shot the man in the head to make sure the insurgent couldn't pull a pin. A spray of bone fragments or plaster clattered against the wall, causing Jansen to register that the Marines had been shooting bullets in a small cement room. They had been fortunate that no one caught a ricochet.[21]

Osborne then entered the room and told his squad leader and another Marine to back up as he looked for the grenade. He rolled the dead insurgent to the side and found the small metal sphere atop the mat under the man's body, its pin still intact.[22] The room secure, Jansen dragged the two captured Iraqis back into it one at a time and angrily shoved their faces inches from the corpse. "Who is it!" he yelled in Arabic. The detainees refused to speak.[23]

The Marines radioed a report to Hoffmann at his position on the roof of a nearby house. They continued their "sensitive site exploitation" of the scene while Marines from the other squads swept through the village. Ponce took pictures of the dead man, the detainees, and the room. Other Americans gathered weapons and suspected bomb-making materials, taking additional pictures of them, and interviewed the other residents of the house. All of the proof would be used to form one of the "evidence packages" that JAG attorneys used in trying to obtain convictions in Iraqi court. It was important to be thorough, as the American attorneys upheld a frustratingly strict standard for conviction, in the opinion of most of the grunts on the ground. In addition to the grenade, the Marines found three AK-47s, three "chest rigs" holding four magazines of ammunition apiece, and three black masks in the room with the dead insurgent. The Iraqis in the rest of the house, including four military-age males, were universally noncooperative, each claiming not to know the identities of the men with the guns and a grenade.[24]

The Marines had a long day ahead of them and couldn't carry the confiscated weapons and ammunition, so Hoffmann sent over an explosive ordnance disposal (EOD) team shortly after the shooting. The EOD guys placed all of the contraband in the trunk of a car parked in front of the house before blowing it up. Jansen felt satisfied. Some of the men in this house who refused to talk might wind up going free due to insufficient evidence, but at least they had lost their vehicle.[25]

Though he managed to calm himself significantly in the aftermath of the incident, Jansen remained angry. Later, he puzzled through his unusually furious reaction. He had come within a hair's breadth of being killed—if the man had been smart enough to pull the pin under the blanket, they could have all been dead or wounded—but there was more to it. It was almost like the incident had uncapped a massive well of suppressed anger and frustration.

Hoffmann drilled it into their heads leading up to and during deployment that the Marines had to be respectful and patient with the locals and stick to highly restrictive rules of engagement. As a result, the Americans tolerated all kinds of shady behavior and typically held their fire when they didn't have explicit "positive identification" of an insurgent with a weapon. This could be frustrating, especially when someone had just shot at you or blown up some of your fellow Marines.[26] Jansen felt like he'd spent so much energy practicing restraint with the locals over the prior six months that it was natural to explode in rage when he found a couple of no shit, honest-to-goodness bad guys. They'd tried to kill him, and undoubtedly had tried to kill other Marines. Yelling at these two assholes felt right. It was cathartic.[27]

Third Squad's careful exploitation of the scene was soon interrupted by excited radio traffic from the men at the overwatch position, who reported spotting a blue bongo truck fleeing from a nearby house. The vehicle had tried to head out of town quickly before running into a Marine blocking position. In addition to the truck being on the road before first light, when a vehicle curfew was still in effect, the driver drew more suspicion when he turned around as the Marines motioned for him to stop. He might have been a farmer headed to work before sunrise, or an insurgent scrambling from the village after hearing gunshots and realizing that Hawa was crawling with Americans. Several teams quickly joined the hunt for the blue bongo.

Jansen immediately deployed his men in a cordon of widely separated two-man teams. The sun had risen. As the Marines walked further into the village, a huge plume of inky black smoke from the destroyed weapons cache and car curled into the early morning air behind them.[28] Within a few minutes of walking, Ponce and Cpl. Tyler Kenny spotted the vehicle moving toward their position. It was closing on them fast. When the driver saw the two Marines, he slowed to a stop about sixty meters in front of them. Kenny pointed his M203 grenade launcher at the idling vehicle, clicked his radio, and eagerly asked Jansen for permission to shoot.

"No," broke in the voice of Captain Hoffmann.

"Negative," added Jansen. "We don't know who's in that vehicle. Stop it and approach them to search it." [29]

Kenny and Ponce waved at the vehicle to stay put, but the driver quickly executed a three-point turn into a nearby driveway and sped off in the other direction. Soon after, Cpl. Elijah Villanueva and LCpl. Christopher Benedict from Weapons Platoon's 1st Squad watched as a truck approached their blocking position, in a local shop. Villanueva fired a warning shot. The bongo turned around and sped away down a decline; the two Marines chased after the vehicle on foot. They saw two men bail out and run toward a set of houses. [30]

When the pair of Marines reached the abandoned blue bongo, they found an astounding cargo: several AK-47s, a Czechoslovakian Mauser rifle, some South African 82-mm mortar rounds, a chest harness filled with magazines, rocket-propelled grenade warheads with added fuel accelerant, a heavy machine gun tripod, a recoilless rifle, a Soviet 14.5-mm heavy machine gun, and tons of ammunition. The drivers had clearly heard the shots at the nearby house, figured the Marines had come in force, and loaded up the truck with everything they could before trying to escape. [31]

The hunt for the bongo now morphed into a search for the drivers, one of whom might be wearing "white pants," according to someone in over-watch. The Marines had established a tight ring around the area where the Iraqis had last been seen, and small teams of two or three began to bounce in and out of the handful of residences within the cordon. Jansen moved the six members of his squad who were on the hunt toward a pair of modest one-story houses. The squad leader and Lance Corporal Panasuk entered one of the residences with raised weapons. [32]

Inside the nearly empty home, the Marines found two Iraqis, a scruffy-looking pair of men in their twenties. One wore a purple and blue short sleeve polo with black trousers, the other wore a blue soccer jersey and white pants. Two robed women also stood quietly in the house; the Americans assumed they were their wives. The men were cooperative and told the

Americans that they were brothers who owned the residence. The pair fit the description of the men Jansen was looking for, but Panasuk wasn't certain. He took their ID cards and recorded their names: Adnan Mahal Hussein Abbas and Lateef Mahal Hussein Abbas.

Other Marines kept an eye on the building, while Jansen and Panasuk moved to search a nearby house. They were greeted by a small family. Jansen asked an elderly male if anyone in the neighborhood owned a blue bongo truck. The wrinkled Iraqi was unusually gregarious; Jansen suspected he might be slightly senile. The man happily divulged the information, offering up two names—"Adnan Mahal Hussein Abbas . . . Lateef Mahal Hussein Abbas." "Bingo," thought Jansen.[33]

When the Americans asked where the brothers lived, the old man pointed toward a third house about a hundred meters away. Jansen and Panasuk moved back to the first house to detain the men. They found them crouching on the barren concrete floor, their heads hung low. It was as if they knew the game was over and were simply waiting for the Marines to come back and detain them.[34] Sure enough, a search of the brothers' actual home turned up another weapons and equipment cache. An AK-47 and a belt of 14.5-mm ammunition that fit the weapon found in the truck were hidden behind a bed. A grenade, three ammunition chest harnesses full of AK-47 magazines, and a black ski mask were discovered under a brush pile in their yard. And the definitive items were more ID cards for both men and a rack that they found inside the house that fit the blue bongo. The "Blue Bongo Brothers," as the Marines dubbed them, were now buried under a mountain of evidence.

Within the first hour of the operation, two Marines had almost been killed, an insurgent attacker had been shot dead, and the Americans had detained nine suspects and found three weapons caches. Alpha Company continued to sweep from house to house through the village. Their tally grew over several more hours. Two additional insurgents attempted to evade the Americans before being captured, but many others were detained without a struggle. All told, the Marines wrapped up twenty-four detainees who would be presented to JAG attorneys for potential prosecution.[35]

Back at their patrol base in Albu Aifan, Whisnant and Sgt. Jeremiah Howe monitored radio traffic detailing the initial resistance and a growing roll call of detainees. Howe nodded in satisfaction at the intelligence provided by Dark. "Yep, this is it," he said to Whisnant. "Dark was right, this is gonna be a good one."[36] By the end of the day, it was almost *too* good. Alpha Company ran the entire operation on foot, but had to transport a wealth of captured weapons and detainees back to the FOB. Whisnant charged Howe with organizing a convoy of Humvees to drive down and help ferry the captured insurgents and crucial evidence. Any prisoners who couldn't fit in the vehicles would be walked out with the platoons when they marched home.

Howe's small convoy of four Humvees was led by Sgt. Michael Moose. The Alpha Company Marines were glad to be accompanied by a Pathfinder EOD unit driving three massive mine-resistant ambush protected (MRAP) behemoths nicknamed Cougars. The EOD engineers had specialized equipment to detect and disable any bombs they came across on the dangerous red route to Hawa. They needed it. The convoy encountered and disabled about a dozen roadside bombs on its slow, roughly fifteen-kilometer crawl toward the village. It was late afternoon by the time Howe, Moose, and their EOD escorts arrived in Hawa. The waiting Marines had long since cleared the entire village and rounded up their two dozen detainees at a collection point set up by Lieutenant Greco near a large tan mosque.[37]

"Let's try to load up as many as possible into the Humvees," Howe briefed Sgt. Christopher Dockter, who was charged with corralling the detainees. "We can walk the rest of them out."[38] Before their departure, Howe took pictures of each man and the evidence arrayed against him for LCpl. Josh Clayton's database detailing the insurgency. He then considered ways to get the weapons, ammunition, and other evidence back to the FOB. Leaving it was not a good option; the material was important to satisfy skeptical JAG attorneys. Howe and Moose finally decided to load much of the evidence into another captured blue bongo and have someone drive it out of the village. The creaky, unarmored truck, however, wasn't the safest vehicle for a trip along roads littered with bombs.

A group of Marines from 1st Platoon had mustered near the vehicle. "Hey, any of you guys know how to drive a stick?" asked Howe. No one raised a hand, although it was doubtful that not one of a dozen Marines knew how to work a manual transmission. "You motherfuckers," Howe muttered, shaking his head.[39] Howe and Moose decided that one of them would have to drive the evidence out himself. Neither man wanted to do it, so they played a game of "rock, paper, scissors" to decide the unlucky driver. Howe won—paper covered rock—but he eventually volunteered to drive the bongo anyway, so Moose could stay with his men.[40]

When he apprised his EOD escort of the ad hoc plan, a gunnery sergeant lectured him on the dangers of driving an unarmored vehicle.[41] Howe
responded that he would "tuck in between the Cougars," which would turn
on their chameleons (electronic countermeasures) and have turret gunners
look for pressure plates. He would "be fine," he said. The Gunny relented,
and Howe slipped the dumpy blue bongo in between the third and fourth
Cougar as part of the tense convoy home. The ride was slow. They never
broke ten miles per hour and repeatedly stopped to examine pieces of trash
or disturbed earth that might hide a bomb. If he hit anything, he was a
dead man. He dwelled on this fact for about the first ten minutes or so,
but eventually took a page from the Iraqis and handed over his fear to fate.
"Insh'allah, I guess," thought Howe.[42]

A little more than an hour later, the relieved sergeant pulled the rolling
evidence locker into the safety of the FOB's gravel parking area. The rest
of the company's squads had hours left on their long march walking the
remaining detainees back to base. Later that night, Sergeant Dockter asked
Howe what route he'd taken on his ill-advised ride home. Howe told him.
"You're a crazy motherfucker," responded Dockter. "We walked out that way
and found an IED. You drove right past it."[43]

About a month later, on April 10, Osborne, Jansen, Villanueva, and another
Marine traveled to Baghdad to testify against some of the captured insurgents in court.[44] In the Iraqi legal system, when a suspect is detained, a package that includes witness statements, photographs, and other evidence is
compiled by Iraqi police—and for a time American legal officers—who
forward it to an investigative judge. The judge acts akin to a combination
of a U.S. district attorney and a judge, reviewing the strength of the assembled evidence before deciding on one of three courses of action: the case is
immediately moved to criminal court if the evidence is strong; the detainee
is ordered held for an additional period of time pending accumulation of
additional evidence; or the detainee is immediately released due to insufficient evidence.[45]

A lot of the detainees wrapped up in Hawa were released. For example,
all the military-age men who were in the U-shaped house, but not in the
room where Jansen and Osborne's shooting took place, wound up being let
go. Other than a solitary AK-47, there were no weapons in the residence's

contiguous rooms, and no evidence tied them to the three men who had rifles, ammunition, and a grenade. It was a frustrating way to fight a war for the Marines on the ground, but it was the law. In addition, to be fair, there was a very real possibility the released Iraqis were merely intimidated homeowners who had been forced to provide a room for the night. There was no way to be sure.[46]

Kasim Shuker Alawi and Hesam Sada Hamed were the two men who had been in the room with weapons of their own when their ill-fated compatriot tried to kill the Marines with a grenade. Their case, along with that of the Blue Bongo Brothers, Adnan and Lateef, easily qualified for trials.[47] Sergeant Howe's dangerous drive with the brothers' weapons paid off in court. The insurgents' staggering armory resulted in swift and harsh verdicts of thirty years each in prison.[48]

Jansen and Osborne sat patiently with their legal officer and an interpreter while waiting to testify against Kasim and Hesam. Earlier, the Marines had been led to a holding cell and asked to identify the two defendants. There were about twenty men wearing identical yellow jumpsuits in the cell, "but it was easy to pick those two out," according to Jansen. The Iraqis briefly made eye contact with their accusers before looking away, and studiously avoided glancing at the Americans for the rest of the day. When Jansen and Osborne were called to testify, they were led down a grubby hallway to a small office. The judge sat behind a modest wooden desk as he motioned for the Marines, the JAG attorney, a defense attorney, and an interpreter to take a seat. The two defendants were then ushered in and seated. First, the Americans gave their testimony. Jansen and Osborne simply recited what had happened without any cross-examination, frequently pausing to allow for translation. The remainder of the trial carried on in Arabic they didn't understand, though the interpreter occasionally bothered to clue the Marines in on small details.

Despite having weeks to sort out a strategy in jail, Kasim and Hesam failed to mount a compelling defense. One man argued that he was merely a fisherman and had been sleeping before going to work.[49] The other defendant said he'd stopped at the house for a night while on his way to a relative's birthday party. Both suspects claimed not to know the man who'd tried to kill the Americans, and neither had an explanation for the rifle, four magazines of ammunition, and the ski mask stuffed under their pillows.[50] The judge wasn't having any of it. He quickly sentenced each man to fifteen years in prison. As the verdict was delivered, the two defendants hung their heads low in resignation. The judge then asked the interpreter to give the Marines a message. "You should have just killed [the accused] there" and saved them all the trouble.[51] In retrospect, Osborne and Jansen agreed.

Jansen is certain they acted ethically, and is grateful that "things turned out OK, in the end." No Marines were injured; one insurgent was killed, and two others were successfully sent away to prison. But after returning to the United States and having time to ponder events, he asked himself a question: "Thinking about it now, would I step into a small room with three guys who I knew, at the very least, had loaded AK-47s under their pillows? No, no I wouldn't. I'd probably stand off and lob grenades. At the time, we were so used to [searching rooms], I guess the thought was, 'They have guns, we have guns, we'll sort it out.'" Osborne feels lucky to be alive, and also thinks the Marines would have been within their rights to immediately kill the other two men upon spotting the grenade. After all, they might have had grenades as well.

Neither man has any regret or second thoughts about killing anyone in Fallujah. Whether because of the restrictive rules of engagement, good fortune, or both, Jansen's conscience is crystal clear. Every time he shot at another human being, he believes that it was the only thing to do. Osborne has suffered symptoms of post-traumatic stress and has had some moments of doubt. He isn't bothered by anyone he killed, but instead dwells on those he could have killed but didn't. In particular, he thinks about men he was confident were bad guys but let get away because of restrictive rules of engagement. He sometimes feels guilty when he considers the possibility that those men might have later killed Americans.[52]

❖

The operation in Hawa was a success. Alpha Company netted about two dozen detainees, caches of weapons, and sent a message to the insurgency: one less spot was safe for them on Fallujah's peninsula. Dark's assurances had come to fruition, and the Albu Aifan militiamen were pleased with the results of the U.S. operation. In later months, their militia and the Iraqi security forces would follow up with more operations into the village. In the meantime, the Americans tried to keep up the pressure.[53]

(*left to right*) Maj. Dan Whisnant, Dark (Sheikh Aifan Sadoun Aifan al-Issawi), and Capt. Jason Brezler in early 2007. *Photo courtesy of Tylor Belshe*

LCpl. Mitchel Greer, LCpl. Jason Dirks, and Cpl. Rick Szymanski are medevaced after walking over a buried, shape-charged IED near the intersection of Water Tower Road and Main Street on October 28, 2006. The directional explosive blew straight upward. All three suffered grade three concussions. *Photo courtesy of Joshua Price*

Sgt. Matthew Hunt being evacuated after a sniper shot him through both legs as he conducted a battle damage assessment following a mortar strike on IED emplacers on November 11, 2006. Hunt soon returned to duty, only to be injured again in an IED blast that hit his convoy on January 19, 2007. Cpl. Jacob Neal was killed in the latter attack. *Photo courtesy of Matthew Hunt*

Marines sleeping on the floor of a commandeered local home while conducting "long ops," multiple-day patrols far from the forward operating base. *Photo courtesy of Chad McHugh*

An insurgent overwatch position near the intersection of Main Street and Route Boston. A triggerman would sit and wait until an American convoy approached, at which time he would detonate a roadside IED. After Marines demolished the post, the number of IEDs in the area decreased. *Photo courtesy of Alex Albrecht*

Sgt. Christopher Dockter (*left*) and HM2 Ruben "Doc" Muñoz in front of the permanent patrol base at the intersection of Water Tower Road and Main Street near Albu Aifan. The patrol base's proximity to Dark's house prompted some Marines to nickname it FOB (Forward Operating Base) Dark. This was also the site of the second ambush of Sgt. David Kopera's squad in November 2006. *Photo courtesy of Christopher Dockter*

Cpl. Alan Webster mugs for the camera—prior to morphine administration—after being shot by a sniper and dragged inside a house by fellow Marines while conducting a foot patrol. *Photo courtesy of Alan Webster*

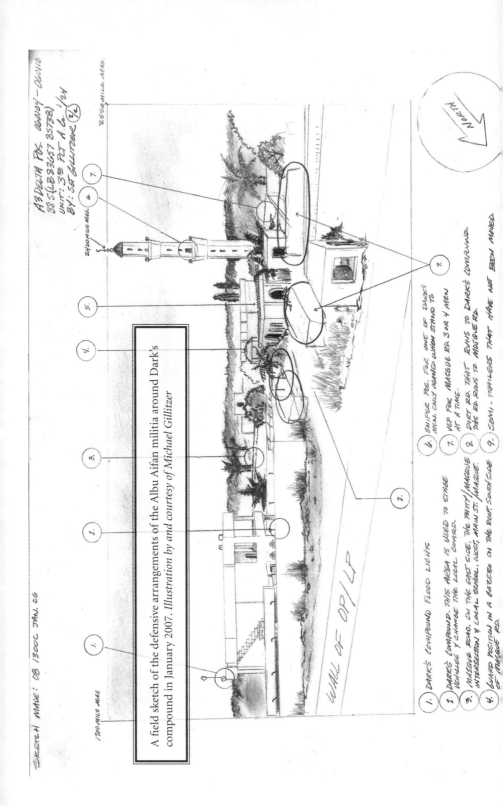

A field sketch of the defensive arrangements of the Albu Aifan militia around Dark's compound in January 2007. Illustration by and courtesy of Michael Gillitzer

SKETCH MADE: 08 1300C JAN. 06

AZ DEATH POS. 000104-000110
38 S(LB 83657 85738)
UNIT: 3RD PLT A.C. 1/24
BY: SGT GILLITZER (½)

255OMILS MAG

240OMILS MAG

1700 MILS MAG

NORTH

WALL OF OP/LP

1. DARK'S COMPOUND FLOOD LIGHTS.

2. DARK'S COMPOUND. THIS AREA IS USED TO STAGE VEHICLES & CHANGE THE LOCAL GUARD.

3. MASQUE ROAD. ON THE EAST SIDE, THE PHTY/MASQUE INTERSECTION & LOCAL SCHOOL. WEST, MAIN ST./MASQUE.

4. GUARD POSITION IN A GAZEBO ON THE ROOF. SOUTH SIDE OF MASQUE RD.

5. SNIPER POS. FOR ONE OF DARK'S MEN. ONLY MANNED WHEN STAND TO.

6. [untitled]

7. VEP FOR MASQUE RD. 3 OR 4 MEN AT A TIME.

8. DIRT RD. THAT RUNS TO DARK'S COMPOUND. THIS RD. RUNS TO MASQUE RD.

9. SEMI-TRAILERS THAT HAVE NOT BEEN MOVED.

The view from a temporary patrol base established during a long op on the Fallujah peninsula. *Photo courtesy of Ernan Paredes*

Capt. Jodie Sweezey of the Civil Affairs Group poses with children during the Medical Civil Action Program (MEDCAP) mission to Albu Aifan that commenced on February 28, 2007. *Photo courtesy of Jodie Sweezey*

Capt. Christine Hauser, an F-18 Hornet weapons system officer who volunteered to help with civil affairs in Fallujah, poses with kids during the MEDCAP mission to Albu Aifan that commenced on February 28, 2007. *Photo courtesy of Jodie Sweezey*

First Lt. Jerome Greco and Cpl. Jack Blevins (*kneeling*) conduct census operations in Fallujah peninsula. *Photo courtesy of Christopher Dockter*

(*left to right*) LCpl. Jared Kimmey, Sgt. Gabe Foerster, LCpl. Kelly Carlson, Dark (Sheikh Aifan Sadoun Aifan al-Issawi), the paramount sheikh, Khamis Hasnawi Aifan al-Issawi, Cpl. Alex Albrecht, and LCpl. Chris Jongsma. *Photo courtesy of Alex Albrecht*

Capt. Jason Brezler, wearing borrowed robes, poses with Sheikh Aifan Sadoun Aifan al-Issawi (Dark) in the sheikh's home after the MEDCAP mission to deliver supplies and medical care near Albu Aifan. *Photo courtesy of Jason Brezler*

The "Blue Bongo Brothers" in front of a mosque with weapons captured from their vehicle and home during a raid on Hawa on March 3, 2007. *Photo courtesy of Jeremiah Howe*

Marines itemize material found in a car counter-ambushed by Cpl. Alex Albrecht's team on March 11, 2007. LCpl. Kelly Carlson killed a sniper sitting in the left rear seat of the car before he could fire a scoped rifle at Americans down the street. Shown here are rifles, ammunition, and a GPS mapped with the coordinates of U.S. patrol bases on the Fallujah peninsula. *Photo courtesy of Alex Albrecht*

1st Sgt. Ken Baum and a U.S. soldier hold down and treat an ornery cow during the Veterinary Civic Action Program (VETCAP) mission near Albu Aifan from February 28 to March 1, 2007. The veterinarian is running a length of hose down the animal's throat to treat it for "gastro bloat." *Photo courtesy of Alex Albrecht*

CWO-5 Jim Roussell and Capt. Jason Brezler stand in the crater left by a chlorine truck bomb that detonated the previous day, March 16, 2007, in Albu Aifan. *Photo courtesy of Jason Brezler*

LCpl. Dickie Prince loads a detainee into a Humvee after the man had tried to escape a Marine raid in Hasa by dressing as a woman. Prince spotted a group of women leaving the village and told Sgt. Christopher Dockter that one set of feet "were way too big." *Photo courtesy of Christopher Dockter*

A seriously injured militiaman from Albu Aifan is treated by Navy doctors, corpsmen, and Marines in the dining area at FOB Black after a chlorine truck bomb detonated on March 16, 2007. *Photo courtesy of Lee Kyle*

Marines and Navy corpsmen treat civilians sickened after a chlorine gas attack on Albu Aifan on March 16, 2007. *Photo by and courtesy of Joshua Robert de Bruin*

The aftermath of an antitank mine that detonated under a Humvee during one of 3rd Platoon's last missions of its deployment, near Hasa. Cpl. Andrew Music and the lance corporals Steve Auton, Justin Norman, and Luke Reames were knocked unconscious and suffered intermediate to severe concussions. *Photo courtesy of Ernan Paredes*

Sheikh Mishael Abdullah Owdeh (Sheikh Shalaan) attends the 2009 U.S. Marine Corps Ball in Chicago as a guest of Maj. Dan Whisnant. *Photo courtesy of Dan Whisnant*

❖ SCORE ❖

It was happening, again. A call came over the radio. A sheikh had been shot, and a team of four Marines from Weapons Platoon's 2nd Squad was calling for backup from the middle of a burgeoning riot. Scores of angry, grieving Iraqis had streamed into the street of a small village along Route Boston after he was killed in the crossfire of a firefight.[1]

Based on tips from Dark's militia, the Americans knew that a number of insurgents, including several high-ranking members of al Qaeda in Iraq, were still operating in a group of villages northeast of Albu Aifan. The intelligence was quickly verified—every time Marines set foot in the area, they were engaged by snipers, improvised explosive devices, or small-arms fire.[2] Most of the attacks were characteristically frustrating "shoot and scoots." In these operations, Iraqi gunmen would fire on an American foot patrol from an automobile three hundred to four hundred meters away from their position. After the car's occupants loosed some carefully aimed sniper shots or a few long bursts of machine-gun fire, the driver would peel out to escape retribution, making a getaway through a network of narrow back roads. The retreat sometimes included ditching the vehicles to move on foot through deep irrigation ditches. To counter the threat, the Marines tweaked their tactics.

Capt. Jeremy Hoffmann had always run each of his platoon's twelve-man squads as two or three dismounted, widely dispersed fire teams, with at least one group providing overwatch from the roof of a nearby house. Now, they attempted to gain the element of surprise by secretly inserting the overwatch teams onto a roof at night. One or two other teams would then walk into the village in daylight to draw out attackers. When the insurgents inevitably took their pop shots and ran, the theory went that the hidden team would have a field of fire along their path, cutting off the attempted escape in a hail of bullets. It almost never worked. Whether because the armored Marines made too much noise when they snuck in at night or neighbors informed on their position in the morning, the insurgents always seemed to know where the overwatch was located. They either attacked it directly or hit the teams on the ground and positioned their escape route away from the trap. The plan had failed again this morning, and a civilian had paid the price.[3]

On the early morning of March 11, 2007, under cover of darkness, Sgt. Steve Morris had quietly led his team, the lance corporals Corey Steimel, Dave Bigger, and Gabe Manis, into the overwatch house. Around 7:00 a.m., just as the sun broke the horizon and the squad's other Marines prepared to move toward the village on foot, a fusillade of forty to fifty rounds fired from a light machine gun ripped into Morris' position. One stray bullet struck a village elder known as Sheikh Halal, who was caught out on the street, killing him instantly. The Americans returned a few rounds down-range, but the insurgents made a quick getaway. Minutes later, distraught family members poured into the road. Much of their ire was directed at fate and the insurgent gunmen, but plenty of it flew toward the Americans. The angle of the shot made it clear this time that the elder had been killed by an insurgent's bullet, but some of the Iraqis argued that it wouldn't have happened if the Marines hadn't been there.[4]

After receiving Morris' call for backup at Forward Operating Base (FOB) Gold, Captain Hoffmann and Sgt. Gabe Foerster directed the squad's remaining men on a hurried march to the village. Cpl. Alex Albrecht took point on the roughly three-mile trip; he was the head of a loose column of men fast walking through palm groves, fields, and irrigation canals. On the way, they heard a couple of distant explosions. Radios crackled to life. The platoon's 1st Squad had been hit by two roadside bombs on its way to al-Taqaddum airbase to pick up the platoon's mail. No one was injured, but nerves amped up a notch.[5]

"The insurgents are active today," Albrecht remembered thinking as he and the others hurried toward the sheikh's village. "We've got to back these guys up quickly."[6] By the time they arrived, perhaps forty-five minutes later, the protest had started to die down. The mood was mournful and upset but not violent. About a dozen women dressed in long, dark robes still clustered outside the dead man's house, softly wailing at the loss of their sheikh. Hoffmann and LCpl. Jared Kimmey spoke to several villagers, expressing condolences.

Hoffmann soon ordered his men to continue the day's planned patrol of the area, so the squad split up into two new fire teams. Sergeant Foerster and Captain Hoffmann led Sergeant Morris, Sgt. Josh Siekman, and the lance corporals Steimel, Bigger, and Manis northeast along Route Boston on foot. A smaller team, consisting of Albrecht, Kimmey, and the lance corporals Michael Beemer and Kelly Carlson, moved into a new overwatch position to provide security for the patrol.[7] Albrecht's team was down a man. Two weeks before, LCpl. Chris Jongsma had been shot in the neck while setting up an ambush from a house near the patrol base at Water Tower Road and Main Street. Jongsma fell like a stone after bursts of PK machine-gun fire and well-aimed sniper rounds had poured onto their position. Albrecht dropped to his knees and quickly wrapped Jongsma's neck wound—luckily, the bullet didn't hit anything vital—and then immediately popped back up to let off several long bursts from his M-240 medium machine gun.[8]

The Marines gave better than they got that day. The suppressed insurgents fled after a few minutes, and the Americans found proof of Albrecht's accuracy when they searched the building the Iraqis had been shooting from. A discarded head wrap coated with pieces of skull and brain lay among a pile of spent cartridges, and a long smear of blood marked the path to a getaway car that must have been parked outside. Jongsma, apart from acquiring a wicked scar, was not seriously wounded. The lance corporal walked under his own power onto the medevac helicopter and for the next two weeks harassed his doctors to let him get back to his Marines. He had just been released at the time of the sheikh's death, but hadn't yet rejoined the squad.[9]

For their new overwatch position Albrecht's small team picked a two-story cement house about 150 meters northwest of the dead sheikh's residence. The Marines had used it several times before. It was a spacious, secure structure that boasted one particularly great reconnaissance feature: the centers of its low, tan parapets were inlaid with dark reddish-brown grates instead of solid cinder blocks. When the Marines crouched behind the barriers on the roof, they could see through the square holes in the decorative metal work, but people on the street couldn't see them.

The Americans knocked on the door and notified the owner that they would be using his house. The man's family of about fifteen people briefly greeted them before going about their business as the four Marines made their way through the residence's great room and up the stairs to the roof. The Iraqis had hosted Marines from 2nd Squad before, and for whatever reason, they tended to be friendly, even though they were nervous about having the Americans in their house. Kimmey always felt comfortable setting up in this residence. It had good fields of fire and great hiding spots, and his instincts told him that the accommodating owners wouldn't rat them out to insurgents. "They were just good people," he explained.

The roof of the house had two levels. A wide, second-floor balcony faced Route Boston, which crossed directly in front of the residence. From there, a set of doors led into a couple of bedrooms filled with blankets and pillows. A stairwell on the lower balcony provided access to an upper roof offering 360-degree views of the village. Each of the four men deployed to watch a sector. Carlson and Beemer set up to look west and south from the lower balcony. Kimmey and Albrecht took their places on the upper level, watching east and north, respectively.[10]

Anbar's warm spring had arrived. The sun rose across a clear azure sky. The four Marines sat against the inside of the parapets and absorbed the midmorning's growing heat, watching their sectors while keeping an eye on the team making its way down the street.[11] Hoffmann and Foerster inched their men further and further northeast, stopping at houses to conduct interviews. An hour passed, then two. When the Marines on foot had moved roughly 500 meters from Albrecht's house, they split into two more teams. One group set up a second overwatch position, while Hoffmann, Foerster, and another Marine conducted a "snap vehicle control point" to stop and search cars traveling Route Boston.[12]

Another hour passed. Kimmey started to zone out a little. It was easy to do while conducting hours of overwatch in the midday heat, plus they'd been up since 6:00 a.m. The only sounds came from the whoosh of a passing vehicle, the rustle of one of the Marines shifting his position on the wall, or the muffled voices of the family who lived in the house. The Iraqis went about their day as if the Marines weren't there. The smell of cooking food drifted to the roof from the kitchen downstairs.

Despite the monotony, Albrecht's men tended to stay relatively sharp on watch. None of them smoked, dozed, or otherwise goofed off. They rarely even spoke, and as usual, Carlson was particularly vigilant. The quiet twenty-four-year-old was appreciated as a classically great combat Marine by his peers. Carlson was workmanlike, was a great marksman, and had a love for guns that was exceptional even for the Marine Corps. He was brave and composed in combat, once running through incoming fire to man a .50 caliber machine gun that he used to suppress an ambush. Of most value, the lance corporal had "eagle eyes" and a spooky ability to quickly figure out where bullets were coming from when they were attacked. If war were a sport, talent scouts might say that Carlson had great "field vision."[13]

At about 3:15, Carlson saw a black, four-door Opel sedan with four Iraqis inside pull into the dirt parking lot of an automotive shop about sixty to seventy meters west of his balcony. A few days earlier, their squad had been attacked by insurgents driving a similar vehicle. Taken on its own, that didn't mean much; the streets of Anbar were littered with dark Opels, along with omnipresent Toyota pick-ups and old, beat-up Bongo trucks.

As Carlson watched through the square gaps in the metal grates, two men dressed like mechanics left the shop to greet the visitors. They approached the driver's-side door with casual familiarity, smiling and joking with the men in the car. The mechanics conversed briefly before leaning forward to look at something displayed by a passenger in the rear seat. Whatever it was, it made the men grin and nod. Their smirks and the fact that the car's occupants didn't get out of the vehicle to greet the others further raised Carlson's suspicions.

The two mechanics started pointing northeast down Route Boston, in the direction of the Marine checkpoint. They then swiftly backed away from the car, their wide grins still in place. The driver of the Opel revved its engine slightly, backed up a few feet and stopped, then backed up a few inches more, lining up the car's profile with the road. Carlson wasn't alarmed, but he was increasingly wary. Suddenly a long, black barrel crept out of the rear right side window. It was pointed toward the Americans down the street.

"Sniper!" yelled Carlson, clicking the switch on his radio with his left hand as he began to aim in on the Iraqi with his right. He snapped his left hand to the rifle, sighted the shooter through his ACOG scope, and pulled the trigger.[14] Two methodical bangs split the silence. The Iraqi sniper's body jerked when the rounds shattered holes in the rear windshield. Carlson then started aiming rounds through the rear of the vehicle toward the driver, who almost immediately realized they were being shot, but may have assumed the fire was coming from the Marines at the checkpoint to his right. He drove the car down a muddy embankment on the left side of the automotive shop. The insurgents were now screened from the patrol on foot, but not the Marines above them.

Carlson kept shooting. Beemer soon joined him. Albrecht and Kimmey were sitting forty to fifty feet away from Carlson on opposite sections of the upper roof. After they heard "Sniper!" and the steady sound of an M-16, Albrecht was the first to the western edge of the roof. He glanced at Carlson and followed his line of sight to the fleeing sedan.[15]

"Sniper!" Albrecht repeated as he steadied his .240 Bravo medium machine gun on the lip of the wall, sighted the vehicle, and ripped off a ten-round burst at the target.[16] An instant later, Kimmey joined him on the western edge of the roof. Once the .240 roared to life, positive identification of the target was obvious. Kimmey saw a stream of red tracers track the car on its flight toward a deep irrigation ditch and immediately joined the turkey shoot. His M-249 Squad Automatic Weapon joined Albrecht's machine gun for a second chattering stream of automatic fire.

The bullet-riddled Opel continued down the slope to the left of the shop, crested a small ditch, and settled in wet dirt with a rocking bounce. The vehicle's undercarriage had bottomed out in a patch of sinking mud at the edge of the irrigation canal. Much of the length of the driver's side was profiled to the Marines, who continued to pour bullets into the target. Two insurgents were, remarkably, still alive. They stumbled out of the passenger side toward the canal as bullets popped the metal and thumped the mud around them. The Marines saw the men successfully make it from the car to the cover afforded by the deep ditch. Carlson had stopped firing and was excitedly calling in a situation report to Captain Hoffmann up the street.[17] While Carlson worked the radio, Albrecht intently scanned the edge of the canal. The fleeing insurgents had to have been hit, and he thought they'd probably just drop and bleed out in the ditch. Perhaps twenty seconds passed. Nothing. Maybe ten or twenty more seconds. Suddenly, Albrecht saw a figure burst from the opposite bank of the canal, about 200 meters southwest of the car.

"Holy shit, this guy is still alive?" he thought. "And running!"[18] The man was sprinting toward a loosely spaced neighborhood of cement houses bordered by an eight-foot-high brick wall with gaps in it. "There's the guy, right there!" Albrecht yelled at Kimmey. The two machine guns again roared to life in a pair of bursts. But the man made it to cover again. Carlson was still on the radio with Foerster's team down the street. "Get off the fucking radio and wait for this guy!" yelled Albrecht, but Carlson's view on the lower roof was by then obscured by dust.[19]

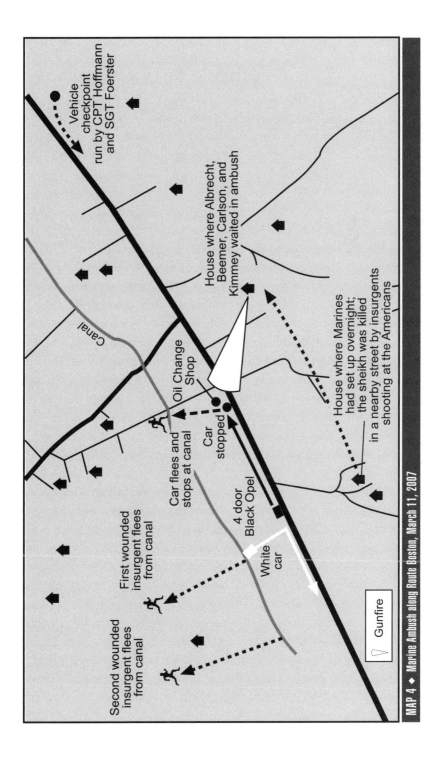

Vehicle checkpoint run by CPT Hoffmann and SGT Foerster

House where Albrecht, Beemer, Carlson, and Kimmey waited in ambush

Canal

Oil Change Shop

Car flees and stops at canal

Car stopped

House where Marines had set up overnight; the sheikh was killed in a nearby street by insurgents shooting at the Americans

First wounded insurgent flees from canal

4 door Black Opel

White car

Second wounded insurgent flees from canal

▽ Gunfire

MAP 4 ◆ Marine Ambush along Route Boston, March 11, 2007

Albrecht and Kimmey next sighted their weapons on a small gap in the wall about fifty meters further along the fleeing insurgent's path. Sure enough, their target briefly popped from cover, and the Americans ripped off another burst to meet him, but the man kept going, making it to next section of the wall. Then he was gone. Albrecht was disappointed, but he was sure he'd hit the man.[20] A few seconds later, they saw the second insurgent who had made it to the ditch run into the neighborhood about five hundred meters to the southwest of their position. No one had a shot.

Carlson continued updating Hoffmann on the radio as everyone else continued scanning for the fleeing insurgents. The Marines were pumped.[21] "Finally, it worked!" thought Kimmey. They'd set up so many unsuccessful ambushes that he had begun to suspect the tactics were pointless. Suddenly, things had gone perfectly. It was an awesome feeling. A few minutes later, the Marines saw a white sedan peel out and drive erratically on a road west of their position. All they could make out was an elderly driver with no visible weapons and at least two men in the backseat who were frantically moving around, perhaps treating someone with an injury. All of Albrecht and Kimmey's instincts told them that this was the getaway car for one or both of the insurgents. "Carlson, shoot some pyro (flares) and get it to stop!" said Albrecht, but Carlson was still handling the radio and couldn't fire warning shots fast enough. Albrecht and Kimmey couldn't shoot flares from their automatic weapons, and without positive ID on an insurgent with a weapon, they decided to let it go. The car turned away on Route Boston and sped off unmolested.

Hoffmann and Foerster quickly maneuvered their teams back toward Albrecht's position to set up security and conduct "sensitive site exploitation" of the engagement. The Marines needed to scan the area for evidence, intelligence, and bodies. As Albrecht's team kept watch from the house, the two mechanics who had pointed out the American checkpoint gingerly walked from the automotive shop while waving white t-shirts in surrender. Albrecht guided Hoffmann and Foerster to the mechanics, who were quickly detained.

Once the area was secured, the Marines combed the scene for evidence. Carlson's bullets had killed the sniper before he could pull the trigger. Hazim Ahmed Abd's body was found slumped in the backseat of the car. His youthful, clean-shaven face was peaceful, and his long-sleeve shirt and trousers looked untouched. Were it not for the tan FAL assault rifle and the shattered glass that lay around him, he might have been mistaken for someone settled in for a nap. Closer examination revealed a neat hole drilled through the top of his head. On the slope of the canal just below the passenger side of the car, the Marines found a second body. Ghazi Jarala Fayad had taken several bullets as he crawled into the ditch and had died in the mud. When the Americans rolled him over to check for weapons and ID, they discovered a bloody mess. What may have been one of Albrecht's 7.62 rounds had caught him in his right cheek and blown out the lower right side of his face.[22]

The Marines on the ground also found two AK-47s, one scoped M-16, a PK medium machine gun, two chest rigs filled with ammunition, a GPS marked with the positions of all the American patrol bases, and a discarded ID card identifying a third man, Ayad Khalaf Abd. Local sources later verified that Ayad was the second insurgent who had escaped into the neighborhood through the canal. American intelligence reports later held that he had been shot through the testicles but somehow managed the dramatic, sprinting getaway. Ayad was eventually picked up by the Iraqi police, though subsequent rumor implied that corrupt cops had been bribed or threatened to let him go.

Kimmey interrogated the two mechanics, who both claimed to recognize but not personally know the insurgents who had pulled up in the Opel. Carlson was sure they were lying through their teeth. He had seen their easy familiarity with the car's occupants and watched them laugh and enthusiastically point out the Marines up the road.[23] As the investigation continued, a call from the combat operations center at FOB Black revealed that Marines at one of the entry control points (ECP) leading toward the city had detained five men in a car matching the description of the vehicle that had fled from the village. One of the men had a gunshot wound in his stomach, and the car was apparently headed toward Fallujah General Hospital before the Americans stopped it.

Despite a Navy corpsman rendering aid, the wounded insurgent died at the checkpoint. Hoffmann immediately ordered his platoon's 1st Squad to travel back from al-Taqaddum to pick up him and the Iraqi mechanics for transport to the ECP.[24] Once there, the two witnesses were isolated from each other before being shown a picture of the dead insurgent. Both men verified that he had been an occupant of the vehicle that had pulled up to their gas station. They also identified him as Amr Jassim Nezham, one of the Marines' high-value targets. Amr Jassim was a known associate of Mullah Fallah Hamadi, al Qaeda's so-called emir on the peninsula.

Back at FOB Gold later that evening, Maj. Dan Whisnant called Captain Hoffmann with the news that the successful kills had been identified. Hoffmann told his men. Albrecht, Kimmey, Carlson, and Beemer were pleased when they learned of Amr Jassim's identity, but they were even happier to have such a clean shot on a carload of bad guys. Given the insurgents' stubborn refusal to stick around during firefights, it was a rare, gratifying opportunity to "get some." It had also validated their tactics, as well as Albrecht and Carlson's instincts; the pair had advocated staying in the overwatch position longer than the Marines' standard operating procedure, and Hoffmann had let them make the call.[25] Later, after the adrenaline had worn off, the Marines gratefully considered the fact that they'd stopped the sniper from getting off a scoped shot at one of their squad mates standing in the middle of the road.[26]

"It was a good day," recalled Carlson matter-of-factly.

14

"BECAUSE THE LANGUAGE THEY USE IS KILLING"

AL QAEDA AND THE SUNNI INSURGENCY

By March 2007, the insurgency around Fallujah faced serious threats. Its American enemy had become more effective, having been empowered by new local intelligence sources. More significant, the insurgents now also had to contend with organized opposition from the area's tribes, and the Iraqi police and the Iraqi Army were becoming capable after being reinvigorated with new, competent leadership. The Islamist insurgency needed to formulate a response to these challenges. But who among the insurgency's leaders would formulate a counterattack? For that matter, who were the insurgents? What motivated them?

Many of the young Marines didn't know exactly against whom they were fighting. Most had notions that they were battling al Qaeda, or disaffected Baathists from Saddam Hussein's defunct regime. Some linked their foes to the global, radical Islamist ideology that had brought down the Twin Towers in Lower Manhattan on September 11, 2001. Officers, intelligence officials, and other specialists in the U.S. military had a better handle on the identities of the enemy, although even experts sometimes got lost in the kaleidoscope of organizations attacking Americans and Iraqis.

The population of Fallujah and the rest of Anbar province was almost uniformly comprised of adherents of the Sunni branch of Islam. Thus, the insurgency in the western part of Iraq was by definition the "Sunni insurgency," unadulterated by the additional complexity of Shia militias, which fought the Americans in Baghdad and other sections of the country. By the time Alpha Company 1/24 arrived on Fallujah's peninsula, U.S. military spokespersons had long singled out al Qaeda in Iraq (AQI) as the number one enemy in their public pronouncements on the Sunni insurgency. Much of the rationale for this focus was reality. Although responsible for only a portion of attacks, AQI was the most ruthless and dangerous element of the insurgency. There were also reasons related to messaging, however: the brand name "al Qaeda" was easily understood by Iraqi and American media consumers as shorthand for "villain." And more important, Americans wanted to exacerbate natural divisions among their enemies. Most members of al Qaeda would never come to terms with U.S. or Iraqi government forces, and they had angered many Sunnis by casually murdering competitors as well as noncombatants. By emphasizing AQI as the enemy, the Americans left the door open for negotiation with other Sunni insurgent groups.[1]

For their part, Fallujans had varied knowledge of the insurgency and the criminal patronage networks vying to consolidate power in the chaos of war. Many of the sheikhs of the Albu Issa tribe were familiar with the rebel hierarchy, either through familial relations to insurgent leaders within their tribe or the receipt of threats and contacts with emissaries representing the militant organizations.[2] At the same time, many ordinary Iraqis remained bewildered by the confusing mix of groups that threatened them, hired them, claimed to protect them, or otherwise jockeyed for influence in the post-invasion power vacuum. Some civilians also used the U.S. military's shorthand of "al Qaeda" or "mujahidin" (holy warriors), but many others avoided the labels for fear of giving offense to anyone who might be listening.[3]

Some Iraqis called the radical insurgents *takfiris* (those who judge other Muslims as apostates), a derisive term critical of the intolerant religious radicalism of a portion of the insurgents.[4] But most locals who came to view the insurgents in a dim light defaulted to using the all-purpose *irhabiyin* (terrorists). The word had the benefit of being both descriptive yet vague enough to avoid offending members of any specific militant group who might overhear its use; after all, few of the holy warriors or gangsters in the insurgency considered themselves "terrorists."[5]

The overall Sunni insurgency consisted of armed, angry men touting membership in a long list of romantically named organizations: the Shield of Islam Brigade, the Resistance Brigade, the Iraqi Jihad Union, the Iraqi Islamic Resistance Front, to name just a few. It was a confusing mix, and the simplest way that Americans came to make sense of the Sunni and Fallujan insurgencies was to compartmentalize their motivations for fighting. These included nationalism, a desire for political influence, criminal activity, and religiousness.

The core of the Sunni insurgency had been composed of proud nationalists who resented having foreign occupiers on Iraqi soil; it included a large number of former Iraqi military personnel who had resolved to continue their fight against the invading Americans. The nationalist insurgency's ranks had been swollen by the decision of the Coalition Provisional Authority to disband the Iraqi military and intelligence services on May 23, 2003.[6]

The insurgency was also strongly motivated by a desire to reestablish Sunni political influence, which it sought to achieve by violently destabilizing Iraq's new Shia-led government. The removal of Saddam Hussein and his Baathist regime and the attempted installation of democracy threatened to reverse historical Sunni dominance of Iraq, as the long-repressed Shia majority—almost two-thirds of the country's population—asserted itself through representative government to lead the Iraqi state.

Mafia-like gangs and syndicates also played an underappreciated but pervasive role in the Sunni (and overall Iraqi) insurgency by fomenting chaos in their efforts to achieve status and wealth. On Fallujah's peninsula and across the rest of Iraq, second- and third-tier tribal leaders, outcasts, and violent entrepreneurs viewed the dissolution of the country's social order as a once-in-a-lifetime opportunity to prosper through the power of the gun.

The last major motivation for insurgency was religious purity. Broadly speaking, it was intolerable for non-Muslim infidels to invade and occupy a Muslim land, killing members of the *ummah* (the Muslim community, the faithful) and dictating terms to them. Religion would eventually become more of a divisive element within the Sunni insurgency than a unifying rallying cry, as more radical groups sought to impose their strident religious standards on those Iraqis who held less conservative views of Islam.

Some insurgent groups straddled all four categories to varying degrees. For example, while many of the organizations made up of former Iraqi military officers were strongly nationalistic, many of their members were also devoutly conservative Muslims who resented the presence of foreign infidels on Iraqi soil. Much of this religiosity is ascribed to Saddam Hussein's "faith campaign," a promotion of Islamic values begun in 1993. The government printed and distributed five million copies of the Quran, built new mosques, and officially added elements of sharia, Islamic law, to the Iraqi penal code in 1994. This government-sponsored religious revival served to distract and unify Iraqis, especially the Sunnis, against any threat (real or concocted) from the country's historical enemy and neighbor, Shia Iran, after Iraq had been weakened by Western sanctions as a consequence of the Persian Gulf War in the early 1990s. Some also speculated that Hussein's religious campaign was an attempt to deter religious extremist groups that might be tempted to target his regime as running a secular state. Whatever the dictator's exact intent, the public relations project wound up effectively increasing the piety of many Iraqis, including military officers who lived in and around historically religious Fallujah, long known as the "City of Mosques."[7]

In addition to their Islamic or Iraqi pride, many homegrown militants gravitated toward the Sunni insurgency after the U.S.-led invasion because of the opportunities afforded by the loss of civil order. Former members of the Baathist regime's Fedayeen Saddam (Saddam's Men of Sacrifice) played a significant role in both criminal activity and the insurgency.[8] During Hussein's tenure, these paramilitary enforcers murdered and intimidated Iraqi citizens into obedience at his behest, and after the fall of the Baathists many of these same individuals melted into the population and embraced both mafia tactics and violent rebellion.

In January 2007, one Fallujan police officer described the motivations for rebellion in simple terms. The insurgents, he said, were in it for "money and to be famous. And I think the first reason is to fight the American troops." He also equated the former regime elements with the radical religious insurgents in methodology, if not theology, on some level contradicting the perception in the Western media that the secular nature of the Baathists made the two groups irreconcilable: "[S]ome people here actually like killing and they liked Saddam Hussein as well," explained the police officer. "I think the al Qaeda organization and Saddam Hussein are the same face . . . because the language they use is killing."[9]

Most of the Sunni insurgent groups loudly touted both Iraqi nationalism as well as Islamic values, often indicated by their names, like the Iraqi Resistance Islamic Front and the Islamic Army in Iraq (IAI). But there were differences: The 1920 Revolution Brigades, perhaps the most significant Sunni nationalist insurgent group, had a large contingent of former Iraqi military officers and proclaimed devotion to Islamic principles; but it also had significant secular elements, including a few former Baathists who were thought to be closet atheists. The organization, named after the rebellion against British occupiers in 1920, had a religious character, but it was primarily nationalist and Sunni supremacist in nature.[10]

In contrast, although the Islamic Army in Iraq also comprised many former Iraqi military officers and proclaimed to have nationalist motivations, it was primarily a religious resistance group. The IAI was considered to be a major player in Iraq's radical Islamist insurgency, seeking to establish a pure Islamic state that would spread throughout the world from seeds planted in Anbar province. This goal, shared with other radical groups, including al Qaeda, was at odds with the more moderate, nationalist vision that groups like the 1920 Revolution Brigades had for Iraq.

Most reasonably well-informed Americans serving in Iraq viewed the Sunni insurgency as a hodge-podge of groups—mostly consisting of locals, but with a few foreign leaders and foot soldiers—vying for power as all tried to assert Sunni supremacy, nationalism, or conservative Islam according to their individual priorities; also, all of them wanted to kick the Americans out of Iraq and put the Shia Iraqis back in their (subordinate) place. There was a clear and brutal trajectory to the Sunni insurgency that the insurgents and Iraqi tribal leaders understood much earlier and more clearly than the Americans. This arc—the brutal rise of the radical Islamists and the existential threat they posed to the nationalists—would prove crucial to American fortunes in Iraq.

When the U.S. military invaded in 2003, it achieved a quick victory against the Iraqi military. The rapid dissolution of civil order and the security forces, however, pointed to the Americans' failure to stabilize the country and decisively defeat their enemies. The invading forces had won a conventional war, but left intact the core of a resistance to their presence. Thus, the first phase of Iraq's insurgency was dominated by holdovers from the Baathist regime, including its former military officers, who were determined to continue resistance. When the Americans captured Saddam Hussein hiding out on a farm near his hometown of Tikrit on December 13, 2003, however, any hope of reviving the Baathist regime ended.

In 2004, a new category of Sunni Iraqi insurgent—Sunni nationalists with strong religious identities—rose to prominence around Fallujah. Their most high-profile leader was Harith al-Dhari, the chair of the Association of Muslim Scholars, the most influential Sunni religious organization in Iraq. Dhari was a member of the fiercely independent al-Zobaie tribe, based southeast of Fallujah. His family had been involved in a legendary event in the previous century. British and local lore differ on the exact details, but Dhari's grandfather shot and killed a British military officer, Brevet Lieutenant-Colonel Gerard Evelyn Leachman, over a disagreement in 1920. The killing sparked Iraqi resistance against the British governorship that year, and the assassin is remembered as a national hero and a patriot to this day. Generations later, the killing continued to reverberate, motivating the Sunni insurgents with the 1920 Revolution Brigades as they fought a new foreign enemy—the Americans. Harith al-Dhari denied direct involvement in the Brigades—a denial believed by few Iraq observers—but his nephew was known to be the leader of the insurgent group named after the famous rebellion.[11]

Dhari was influential, vocal, and adamantly anti-American, insisting that Iraq's Sunnis rise up and resist the occupation. As the insurgency began to coalesce in and around Fallujah in 2004, it morphed from being comprised of mostly former Baathist military personnel to a conglomeration of groups led by one of Iraq's most prominent nationalist and Sunni religious figures. In addition, a new component began to insert itself into Iraq: the foreign mujahidin. Dhari and other Sunni insurgents welcomed or tolerated these foreign fighters, including al Qaeda–affiliated radicals, as visiting allies. The resulting loose conglomeration of former Baathists and foreigners, all fighting under the banner of Iraq's Sunni nationalists, were determined to make a stand against the occupiers in the City of Mosques.

In spring 2004, a spark set fire to the insurgency. On March 31, insurgents killed and mutilated four American contractors who had been tasked by the Blackwater Worldwide security firm with escorting a convoy sent through Fallujah to pick up kitchen equipment. Gruesome images of their charred corpses hanging from the city's Old Bridge across the Euphrates River were broadcast on cable news stations around the world.[12] Many in the West were shocked and outraged at the spasm of violence, and the administration of George W. Bush and the higher levels of the U.S. military leadership insisted on a massive response. The broad scope of any operation was at odds with the recommendation of the Marine Corps leaders around Fallujah, who favored a targeted reaction to specifically kill or detain the insurgents responsible for the atrocity.[13] They were overruled, and the resulting U.S. offensive became the ironically named Operation Vigilant Resolve, which later came to be known as the First Battle of Fallujah. The massive U.S. Marine incursion to clear the city of insurgents kicked off on April 4, 2004.

The battle was hard fought, and initially successful for the Marines, but ultimately short-lived. Al Jazeera and other Arab media outlets began to highlight and, according to many western analysts and military personnel, to exaggerate civilian casualties, and regional outrage against the American operation began to spiral.[14] Facing widespread condemnation from the Arab community and even allies in the Iraqi government, the U.S. pulled up short of the invasion's goal of securing the city, declaring a cease-fire on April 19, 2004.[15] Initiating, but not finishing, a large-scale incursion into the insurgent stronghold was regarded by many strategists as the worst possible scenario. The homegrown and foreign Sunni insurgency predictably viewed the pause as a sign of weakness, and the insurgents crowed about their victory over the Americans in Fallujah.

Later that year, Lt. Gen. James T. Conway, the outgoing Marine general in charge of western Iraq, would criticize the decision to pull up the Marines short of accomplishing their mission. "When you order elements of a Marine division to attack a city, you really need to understand what the consequences of that are going to be and not perhaps vacillate in the middle of something like that," he said. "Once you commit, you got to stay committed."[16]

The large American incursion, followed by claims of extensive civilian casualties and a quick pullback, had the dramatic impact of cementing the City of Mosques as a potent symbol of the Iraqi resistance. "When the fight started in Fallujah . . . the insurgency, whatever you call them, the resistance against the American occupation in Iraq, it was here, everything started here," explained Colonel Faisal Ismail Hussein al-Zobaie, a former nationalist insurgent with the 1920 Revolution Brigades who later switched sides to head the Fallujan District Police Department in early 2007. "It was one of the first cities to fight against the Americans, and since that history it has had that name, that reputation that this city is the best, with the most heroes who fought the Americans. And even if you ask the insurgents which city they would prefer to be fighting from, Fallujah or Baghdad, they choose here. Now everybody knows Fallujah in Iraq, that it is the capital of the heroes who fought the Americans."[17]

After the cease-fire, the insurgency grew in and around the city, as more and more fighters journeyed to the fabled battleground. Among these pilgrims were more foreign jihadists determined to expel the infidels from Iraq. As the resistance grew stronger and civil order within the city disintegrated, the Americans decided to invade Fallujah again in a bid to cripple the insurgency. Thus the Second Battle of Fallujah—officially known as Operation Phantom Fury and later as al-Fajr (the Dawn)—was a full-scale invasion of the city by the U.S. military and Iraqi Army that began on November 7, 2004. Although a lot of insurgents slipped out of the area when the coalition allowed civilians to evacuate prior to the battle, perhaps 3,000 to 4,500 militants stayed behind to fight. In more than a month of hard combat, the U.S. and Iraqi militaries retook the city, killing or wounding about 1,200 to 1,350 fighters and capturing roughly 1,500 insurgents.[18] Coalition casualties consisted of 95 Americans killed and 560 wounded, with 8 Iraqi soldiers killed and 43 wounded.[19]

In conventional terms, the battle was an utter defeat for the confederation of Iraqi militants. It was not, however, a decisive victory for the United States and the Iraqi government. Harith al-Dhari and other insurgent leaders either hadn't been in the city or were able to escape; their organizations, though wounded, scattered and regrouped to fight another day.[20] The invasion served only to disrupt the insurgency, not destroy it. Indeed, the confrontation prefaced the movement's evolution into a new, even more violent phase. The brutal rise of the radical Islamic insurgent groups, especially al Qaeda in Iraq, would define 2005.

Although a large number of mujahidin had been killed in Phantom Fury, al Qaeda in Iraq and other insurgent organizations began benefitting from a steady stream of recruits from abroad and from within Iraq's disaffected and unemployed Sunni population. Al Qaeda had established itself as a well-known and feared brand name during the early Sunni resistance, and it had plenty of foreign funding. It launched a brutal recruiting and consolidation campaign as it attempted to fight the Americans as well as dominate the Sunni population. Tribal and religious leaders were given an option: join al Qaeda or die. Those who refused were either killed outright or their subordinates were poached from them with the lure of glorious jihad and cash. The story of 2005 and 2006 became the blood-soaked rise of al Qaeda as the dominant force in the Sunni insurgency.[21]

From its inception, al Qaeda in Iraq had attempted to have a strong hand in all the categories of Sunni resistance. Despite being led by foreigners, the organization trumpeted Iraqi nationalism in its press releases exhorting locals to fight the occupiers. AQI also portrayed itself as a champion of Iraq's Sunni population. Its suicide bombers embarked on a concerted strategy to stoke sectarian war by killing Iraqi Shia en masse and destroying their shrines in a series of high-profile bombings in Baghdad and other parts of Iraq. In addition to receiving operational funding from foreign donors, many of al Qaeda's foot soldiers were street thugs who embraced criminality to acquire money and other resources. Their fundraising methods included committing robbery, shaking down contractors, skimming from oil refineries, and kidnapping for ransom.[22]

But first and foremost, al Qaeda in Iraq promulgated a form of religious radicalism considered extreme even by conservative Fallujan standards. Al Qaeda's global ideology is generally associated with Salafism, which calls for a strict, puritanical interpretation of Islam based on originalist interpretations of the Quran. Two examples of the Salafist influence on al Qaeda are Wahhabism, a branch of Islam that originated in Saudi Arabia, and Deobandi Islam, a strict form of Islam prominent in South Asia.

Salafists advocate the eventual worldwide dominance of "pure" Islam, but there is a spectrum of disagreement on how to achieve this end. Some members of mainstream Salafist organizations, like the Muslim Brotherhood, support or sympathize with violent entities like al Qaeda, at least passively. Other Muslim Brothers, however, emphasize the spread of the faith through persuasion, rather than violent conquest. Insurgent cells associated with the Brotherhood indeed fought in Iraq, but many did so under the principle of "defensive jihad," arguing that U.S. encroachment on a Muslim land was an infidel offensive that must be repelled.[23]

Al Qaeda's true believers, in contrast, explicitly embrace the concept of spreading their version of Islamic values and dominance through the exportation of violence and terrorism. This doctrine of "offensive jihad" fueled the attacks of September 11, 2001, the bombing of the USS *Cole* in 2000, and the 1998 bombing of U.S. embassies in Nairobi and Dar es Salaam. This aggressive philosophy is why al Qaeda and its ideological fellow travelers are sometimes referred to as Salafist-jihadists or Qutbists, after the Muslim theologian Sayyid Qutb.[24]

Qutbists (or Qutbiyyun) are followers of the ideology advocated by Qutb and several of his like-minded contemporaries and descendants. The Egyptian educator was a prominent spokesman and theorist in the Muslim Brotherhood prior to his execution in 1966 by the regime of President Gamal Abdel Nasser. Qutbist philosophy diverges from the mainstream and even conservative Salafist Muslim theology in two significant ways. First, it maintains that Islam *must* be spread by the sword; offensive jihad to expand the faith was an obligation of all true Muslims. Second, al Qaeda and other Salafist-jihadists practice *takfir,* declaring other Muslims to be apostates and sinners. Qutb had "argued that the entire world, including the Muslim, was in a state of *jahliyah,* or ignorance where man's way had replaced God's way."[25] Fellow Muslims who did not follow a pure interpretation of the Quran were not really considered Muslims at all.[26]

This Qutbist idea of *takfir* provided al Qaeda and fellow Salafist-jihadists the "legal loophole" they needed to justify murdering anyone they wanted to kill. Islamic verses are equivocal about whether non-Muslim infidels should be put to the sword, but members of al Qaeda believe they have plenty of scriptural justification from violent suras that supercede those calling for tolerance of nonbelievers. The Quran's strong prohibitions against killing fellow Muslims, however, made killing believers a trickier issue. But the concept of *takfir* meant they could kill those who *claimed* to be Muslim, but weren't *sufficiently* Muslim, at least according to the judgment of a *takfiri*. This malignant stew of factors—hatred of the perceived decadence of the West and the modern Muslim world, belief in offensive jihad, and the concept of *takfir*—gave al Qaeda the ideological framework to attack both the "external enemy"—the United States and the West—and the "internal enemy"—fellow Muslims who were insufficiently religious.[27]

In Iraq, the external enemy, sometimes described by al Qaeda leaders as "the head of the snake," had invaded and was within convenient striking distance. The internal enemy included both Iraq's Shia, who were considered apostates and polytheists for venerating saints, and any Sunnis who either failed to interpret the Quran according to al Qaeda's views or simply got in the organization's way.

These last targets included Sunni sheikhs, like the Albu Issa's paramount sheikh, Khamis Hasnawi Aifan al-Issawi, and Dark, Aifan Sadoun Aifan al-Issawi, who refused to bow to the insurgent group's authority. By 2006 and 2007, members of al Qaeda in Iraq had even started executing imams in Fallujah who had refused to read the organization's prepared statements during Friday prayers. Many of the religious leaders *had* been exhorting fellow Iraqis to resist the Americans, but their pronouncements somehow weren't extreme enough, according to the standards of AQI. Some paid for it with their lives.[28]

Iraq's al Qaeda franchise was consolidated after the 2003 U.S. invasion under the leadership of Abu Musab al-Zarqawi. A Jordanian who had run al Qaeda–affiliated training camps in Afghanistan "specializing in producing deadly poisons" in the 1990s, Zarqawi had been "a bully and a thug, a bootlegger and a heavy drinker" prior to undergoing a religious conversion at twenty-three, when he traveled to Afghanistan for the first time in 1989.[29]

In subsequent years, he founded Jama'at al-Tawhid wal-Jihad (Group of Monotheism and Jihad), a Salafist-jihadist outfit that cooperated with al Qaeda and was dedicated to overthrowing the Jordanian monarchy, which it had deemed an "internal enemy." The group operated from the Kurdish region of Iraq prior to the U.S. invasion in 2003, and formally swore allegiance to Osama bin Laden and the al Qaeda organization in October 2004.

Zarqawi claimed responsibility for a number of high-profile kidnappings and attacks, including the bombing of the UN headquarters in Baghdad on August 19, 2003, and the videotaped beheading of American contractor Nicholas Berg on May 7, 2004. After the 2003 invasion, Zarqawi had made his way to Fallujah, the birthplace of the Sunni resistance, where he allied with a local man named Omar Hadid, a former electrician and longtime Salafist-jihadist. Long before the United States invaded, Hadid and a mentor had killed members of the Baath Party and waged a violent campaign against all of Fallujah's "sins." They threatened beauty parlor and music store owners and blew up the city's only movie theater in the mid-1990s.[30] Along with a third man, Abdullah Janabi, a local imam who railed against the occupiers in "inflammatory sermons," as well as Harith al-Dhari of the Association of Muslim Scholars, the two al Qaeda leaders were among the highest-profile members of Fallujah's insurgency circa the famous battles of 2004.[31]

Zarqawi and Hadid ran their operations, including a hidden torture chamber and video studio, from a safe house in the Jolan Park area of Fallujah, until just prior to the coalition invasion of the city in November 2004.[32] Hadid stayed to fight the Americans and was killed in their assault, whereas Zarqawi fled. From a series of locations in Iraq's Anbar and Diyala provinces, he continued al Qaeda's fight against the Americans, the Iraqi government and Shia community, and eventually his Sunni competitors. AQI's hallmark became a campaign of horrific bombings of markets and shrines in Baghdad that were designed to stoke sectarian war between the Sunni population and besieged Shia "apostates."[33] On June 7, 2006, Zarqawi was killed in a U.S. airstrike on a house near the city of Baqubah, in Diyala province. By that time, he had succeeded in his effort to start a bloody sectarian war between Iraq's Shia and Sunnis.[34]

Al Qaeda in Iraq was arguably at the zenith of its power when Zarqawi was killed, but it had also begun to weather challenges to its authority from Anbari sheikhs and other Sunni insurgent groups. Many of the Sunni nationalist and religious insurgents resented the murderous tactics of a foreign-led organization that had proclaimed itself the leader of Iraq's insurgency.

In January 2006, AQI's media wing had announced the formation of the Mujahidin Shura Council, an umbrella organization of insurgent groups spearheaded by al Qaeda. The leader of the council was said to be a man named Abdullah Rashid al-Baghdadi, who was actually a fictional Iraqi invented to put a local face on the organization. Zarqawi, the council's "military commander" and al Qaeda's emir for Iraq, remained the real leader. Although the new organization achieved some minor success in consolidating the Sunni insurgency, several major insurgent groups and tribes continued to resist its authority.[35]

After Zarqawi's death, the Mujahidin Shura Council morphed into a new political front, the Islamic State of Iraq, on October 15, 2006. Like its predecessor, the so-called state was another attempt by al Qaeda to consolidate local insurgent support by putting an Iraqi face on the organization. It announced a cabinet that was supposedly filled with Iraqis, but the true leader was its Egyptian "minister of war," Abu Ayyub al-Masri. As with the Mujahidin Shura Council, some major Sunni insurgent groups saw through the ruse, and refused to swear fealty to an organization with an anonymous, possibly fictional emir named "Abu Omar al-Baghdadi." Indeed, the supposed leader's name was a clumsy attempt to make him sound quintessentially Iraqi; an equivalent American name might be "John Smith the Washingtonian." Many of the insurgent groups, including the nationalistic 1920 Revolution Brigades as well as the religiously radical Islamic Army in Iraq, again refused to bow before al Qaeda's expansion and in fact directly competed with it for influence within the Sunni insurgency.[36]

The killing of Sunni insurgents by members of opposing Sunni insurgent groups had become increasingly common by 2007, as the various organizations vied for primacy. In a particularly high-profile operation, the head of the 1920 Revolution Brigades—Harith Dhahir Khamis al-Dhari, the famed Harith al-Dhari's nephew—was assassinated in an al Qaeda ambush on March 27, 2007, after refusing to pledge allegiance to the Islamic State of Iraq.[37] According to a Fallujan police officer, bands of vigilantes affiliated with the police also had begun killing radical insurgents and then spreading rumors that the attacks had been waged by other mujahidin. This deceptive, "false flag" campaign was part of a concerted effort to weaken the radical insurgency by causing its elements to fight among themselves.[38]

Thus, by early 2007, the Sunni insurgency had transformed once again. It was no longer dominated by former Baathists as in 2003, or a confederation of groups making an organized stand under a nationalist and religious banner, like they had against the Americans in the First and Second Battles of Fallujah in 2004. And although al Qaeda had risen in stature and still maintained the fearsome reputation it had built in 2005 and 2006, it now had to deal with concerted challenges to its authority. The insurgency had developed into a conglomeration of sometimes cooperative, but often competitive organizations consisting of small cells sniping targets of opportunity, planting roadside bombs, and conducting suicide attacks. By 2007, many of these groups had either joined with al Qaeda or were struggling to survive a decision to defy al Qaeda's authority.

The insurgency's smallest organizational level was a "cell," typically a group of five to seven men, often close family members. It might specialize in manufacturing and planting IEDs, often paying unemployed Iraqis modest sums to place the bombs on roads transited by U.S. forces. Another cell might serve as an insurgent mortar team, driving to preset coordinates, firing one to three rounds at a target, such as the Fallujah Government Center or an American patrol base, and then running away before the Americans' counter-battery technology could fix the attackers' location and respond in kind. Still other cells served as snipers. One particularly adept marksman with night vision technology terrorized U.S. and Iraqi forces around Fallujah in early 2007, and was referred to as the "Chechen sniper" (as intelligence assessments reported he had honed his unusual skill during the jihad against the Russians in Chechnya). Some cells worked to smuggle weapons and fighters from other countries, or to finance the insurgency through crime. Most of the cells engaged in multiple activities but were particularly proficient at a few of them.[39]

It was impossible for members of the U.S. and Iraqi security forces to estimate with certainty the size of the dedicated insurgency in the Fallujah district in 2007. Some judged it to be as low as two hundred men, while others thought rebels to number around five hundred. In late 2006, members of the Islamic Iraq Party, a Sunni political organization, had posted around Fallujah a list of 120 "wanted" insurgents. Most analysts agreed that at the time the number of insurgents was in the hundreds, and certainly less than 1,000, down from a peak of around 3,000 to 4,500 during the Second Battle of Fallujah. Whatever the specific number, hundreds of men with bad intentions, irregular tactics, explosives, weapons, and the ability to hide in plain sight could kill a lot of people and sow a climate of terror.[40]

In 2007, Iraqis comprised the vast majority, upwards of 90 percent, of Anbar province's insurgency. Locals were in leadership positions, but almost uniformly comprised the foot soldiers and middle management. Foreigners were represented in the senior leadership of al Qaeda in Iraq and some of its affiliated Salafist-jihadist cells, and they dominated the ranks of AQI's suicide bombers.

An analysis of al Qaeda personnel records captured in a U.S. raid near Sinjar, a town along the northern border with Syria, revealed that a steady stream of seven hundred foreign fighters were funneled into Iraq between August 2006 and October 2007. The jihadists traveled through Syrian rat-lines from Saudi Arabia (41 percent), Libya (18.8 percent), Syria (8.2 percent), Yemen (8.1 percent), Algeria (7.2 percent), Morocco (6.1 percent), and Jordan (1.1 percent), plus a handful from Tunisia, Egypt, and other places. The average foreign insurgent was around twenty-four or twenty-five years old and had been a student prior to leaving home for jihad in Iraq. Of the individuals who had listed their intended "work" for the insurgency, 56.3 percent classified themselves as "martyrs" or "suicide bombers." Saudis made up the majority of those volunteering to blow themselves up for Islam, a tangible indicator of the influence of radical Wahhabist ideology in their home country.[41]

During the 2006–2007 tour, members of Alpha Company 1/24 had targeted, captured, or killed a wide range of foreigners, among them Somalis, Sudanese, Syrians, and even an Iranian on Fallujah's peninsula. The Iranian was captured when Uthman Majid Aifan al-Issawi, one of Dark's lieutenants, had started "going crazy" when telling the Marines with whom he was riding that they should stop a particular car. "It's a bad car! He's an Iranian!" Sure enough, Uthman was correct. The Americans detained the insurgent, who was confirmed to be on their regiment's high-value target list. The militant had $10,000 in $100 bills in his possession.[42]

The man's identity hinted at the bewildering complexity of Iraq's insurgency: a Shia Iranian, likely an operative sent with the blessing of the Iranian Revolutionary Guards, was helping Sunni insurgent groups fight Americans in western Iraq. This cooperation took place despite widespread Sunni distaste for Shia Iran; the slaughters of Shia, as alleged apostates, by radical Sunni insurgent groups in Baghdad; and Iranian-backed Shia militias responding in kind with attacks on Sunnis. Fighting Americans and destabilizing the Iraqi government made for strange bedfellows at higher levels of the insurgency.

Sometime in 2006, al Qaeda in Iraq had appointed "Mullah" Fallah Hamadi as its so-called emir of Fallujah's peninsula. Fallah was a local man, a member of the Albu Issa's Abu Hatim subtribe who based his operations near the troublesome southern village of Hasa. Some members of subtribes on the southern portion of the peninsula had been the historical "have-nots" in the tribal hierarchy of the Albu Issa, as opposed to the wealthier "haves," represented by Dark and Khamis. Now Fallah was directing his network of at least eight semi-independent insurgent cells to fight the Americans while he also attempted to consolidate his power over tribal rivals.[43] In addition, his role as an al Qaeda emir induced him to pursue the goal of a Salafist Islamic state in Anbar province. His tools were violent intimidation and the principle of *takfir*, which, in his eyes, gave him license to kill any Muslim who defied him.

Fallah was something of a ghost to the Marines and his tribal enemies. Prior to becoming an insurgent leader, he had been a smuggler, an experience that gave him an uncanny ability to escape capture and airstrikes, often using a series of aliases to fool his enemies. Dark and Sheikh Shalaan (Mishael Abdullah Owdeh) told the Marines in early 2007 that Fallah had been stopped at one of their vehicle checkpoints at least twice, but he had gotten away via a combination of smooth talking and a good fake ID.[44] Despite his cunning escapes, Fallah's campaign around Fallujah and al Qaeda's broader campaign in Iraq faced a worrisome situation by March 2007.

The Americans and a confederation of tribes, famously led by Sheikh Abdul Sattar Abu Risha, had already pushed the seat of al Qaeda's declared "Islamic caliphate" out of the former insurgent stronghold of Ramadi, Anbar's provincial capital. In addition, instead of accelerating a withdrawal as popular support for the war waned in the United States, President George W. Bush had announced a looming "surge" of military forces in January that was just beginning to enter Iraq. Moreover, al Qaeda and its Islamic State of Iraq had failed to consolidate the Sunni insurgency and continued to fight with other insurgent organizations. And most critically, Fallah was being directly challenged on the peninsula by the leading sheikhs of his own Albu Issa tribe and their new militia.

The surge of American forces might be problematic for the insurgents, but al Qaeda had been able thus far to evade its enemies or regenerate after other U.S. offensives. The challenge from Khamis, Dark, and others, however, was a much bigger deal. It was an existential threat. If local Iraqi leaders regained the initiative by successfully organizing a militia and rebuilding the police with the support of the Americans and the Iraqi government, they could deny *takfiri* insurgents unmolested staging areas, freedom of movement, and their crucial ability to hide in plain sight.[45]

Fallah and others fighting under the banner of the Islamic State of Iraq knew that their number one priority was eliminating the biggest threat; they had to strike back at those who dared to ally with the Americans. The response would also have to be dramatic, something that killed local leaders *and* attracted enough attention to frighten others back into exile or servitude. Only then could the *takfiris* reestablish their hold on Fallujah and Anbar province as a whole. Defiant Iraqis, including paramount sheikh Khamis and Dark, had to die.

❖ GAS ❖

Cpl. Steven Levasseur had to relieve himself before he left the patrol base. His squad, led by Sgt. Kendrick Doezema and accompanied by 1st Lt. Jerome Greco, had pushed out to "FOB Dark" earlier that day to support Weapons Platoon in the area south of Albu Aifan village. After conducting an hours-long foot patrol, capturing a detainee, and encountering a fierce firefight between Iraqi combatants, the Marines had returned to the large abandoned house and staged their vehicles to leave for home; warm meals and beds awaited them at Forward Operating Base (FOB) Black.[1]

Levasseur was sitting in the front passenger seat of his Humvee, which also held the lance corporals Jacob Dennert, Robert Bishop, and on the turret, Matt Hough. The squad had been waiting in and around their vehicles for about ten minutes while Greco conferred with their replacements. As soon as the lieutenant was finished, they would move out. If Levasseur was going to go to the bathroom, he had to do it now, so he opened the front passenger door and stepped into the dusty courtyard. It was about 6:00 p.m. on March 16, 2007. A pre-dusk gloom had started to settle over the peninsula, and the dry air had cooled to a relatively comfortable temperature. The corporal walked about ten paces to the inside wall of the courtyard.[2]

He soon heard the low rumble of an approaching vehicle. Levasseur glanced to his right and back. A dump truck with a blue cab and yellow trailer was moving slowly down the street that ran alongside the patrol base. It was a little unusual to see a civilian on these roads around sunset, and the truck was crawling at an oddly slow ten miles per hour. "Could that be a truck bomb?" he thought. Vehicle-borne bombs were a constant threat, an omnipresent specter in the mind of every Marine when a nonmilitary vehicle approached his position. Levasseur held on to his opened trousers with his left hand and raised his M-16/203 with his right. He "chickenwinged" the rifle for support, sandwiching the butt against the medical pack attached to the side of his flak vest, and then steadied his finger over the trigger and tracked the driver with the weapon's muzzle.

The truck turned left at the corner of the base, moving north on the road that ran directly in front of him and the parked Humvees behind him. Its elevated cab drew within a few meters of Levasseur, and he got a clear look at the driver over the curved stone wall that separated them. An Arab with long black hair stiffly gripped an oversized steering wheel. The man's eyes were wide and the color had drained from underneath his dark brown complexion. He looked "scared shitless," recalled the young Marine, who suspected "something wasn't right." He knew that "if that guy has a bomb and turns into our compound . . . we're fucked."

As the driver passed the Marine, he furtively glanced left at the wary American before returning his gaze to the road. The vehicle moved beyond the entrance to the patrol base and continued north. Relieved, Levasseur lowered his weapon and fixed his trousers. The Iraqi had driven slowly and acted strangely, but oddness itself wasn't necessarily odd around Fallujah. Harmless locals often acted nervously around Marines. Iraqis recycled well-worn tales of trigger-happy Americans, and some feared being shot for making any kind of potentially provocative move, especially while driving. And in this case, Levasseur had been pointing his weapon at the truck. The corporal climbed back into his team's idling Humvee. The tired Marines waited for Greco. They were "pissed" that they had been forced to conduct an unexpected mission that day, so the men sat in silence.[3] A few minutes later, the ground shook with the rumble of a huge explosion.

Through the windshield, Levasseur saw a flash of light and a massive cloud of smoke shoot straight and high into the air less than a mile away. The column of dirt morphed into a multi-story mushroom cloud, a light gray stem with a dark cap. In a neighborhood sometimes rocked by several detonations a day, this one stood out as massive. Waiting in an adjacent Humvee, Doezema, the squad leader, marveled at the size of the blast. "That was ridiculous," he thought. The Iraqi detainee they had captured earlier that day was sitting in the vehicle with him. When the explosion shook the ground, the blindfolded, flex-cuffed prisoner began shaking in fear.

"Oh my God, did you see that shit?" yelled Lance Corporal Hough from his vantage in the turret of Levasseur's Humvee.

"Yes," replied Levasseur. "Get in the house, *right now*."[4] Fearing they might be the target of an attack, the Marines poured from the staged vehicles and ran for the superior cover afforded by the fortified patrol base.

The loud explosion resembled the thunderous boom of 155-mm Marine artillery rather than a garden-variety roadside bomb. Some of the Marines suspected it was a 120-mm mortar lobbed at the patrol base and that more might be headed their way. Someone had heard a gunshot right before the explosion.

"It's an IED, someone hit an IED," was one assessment.

"No, no. That was *not* an IED," said Levasseur.[5]

—————— ❖ ——————

Tha'er Khalid Aifan al-Issawi commanded a team of militiamen at the southernmost checkpoint guarding an entrance to the village of Albu Aifan. The sun had begun to slip below the horizon, and the haunting, electric chant of the muezzins broadcast from speakers atop the area's mosques had called the faithful to prayer. As Tha'er manned the checkpoint, most of the eight militiamen under his command knelt in worship inside the courtyard of a house next to their roadblock, which consisted of a series of large stones set in the center of the dusty street. Though the way was partially blocked, the largest boulder was not in place; the militiamen had planned only on light traffic in the hours prior to sunset, and each movement of the heavy stone required the strained effort of four men.

In the distance, Tha'er saw a twinkling set of headlights approaching his checkpoint. He squinted toward the road in the gathering gloom. At first he thought it was the Americans, but he quickly discarded that idea. There was only one vehicle, and the Americans traveled in groups. The headlights floated several feet above the road, so he realized it had to be a truck. Only minutes before, civilian traffic had almost ceased; the prayer was under way, and the peninsula's widely enforced nighttime curfew was near. Tha'er gripped his rifle and jogged south, toward the oncoming headlights. Sa'ad Salah, his twenty-two-year-old nephew, scooped up his Kalashnikov and followed. Tha'er began to make out a large yellow dump truck. No one from his village or the villages of allied subtribes owned anything like it. He and his fellow militiamen usually prepared for an attack if they didn't recognize a vehicle.

The truck moved slowly but steadily forward, seemingly weighted down by heavy cargo. The militiamen continued on to meet the vehicle until it drew within a few dozen meters. Tha'er motioned and yelled at the truck to stop. The driver paid no heed to the militiaman's commands and signals. Instead of stopping, he hit the gas. As the truck strained to accelerate under its heavy load, Tha'er and Sa'ad barely had time to scramble off the road to avoid being hit. Tha'er glimpsed the driver's face in the fading light. He recalls dark features and a "hateful expression." Purpose replaced the militiaman's scrutiny. He now knew that it was a bomb, and "if it reached the center of the village it [was] going to kill a lot of my friends and family." He had to stop the attack.

Tha'er flipped the selector switch on his AK-47 downward to fully automatic, braced the rifle, and aimed at the back of the dump truck. The trailer was where the explosives would be, and it was the only clear shot he had. The militiaman pressed and held the trigger, ripping off a seven-to-ten-round burst at the vehicle, now only about ten meters from breaching the pervious roadblock. Sa'ad's rifle barked to life beside him.[6] "The truck is so close, I am going to die when this explodes," he later recalled thinking.[7] Suddenly, the clatter of the two Kalashnikovs was obliterated by a massive explosion.[8] The truck disappeared in a soaring burst of flame, which itself was snuffed quickly and replaced by billowing clouds of dust. A wave of overpressure seemed to douse the fire as a column of smoke towered several stories into the darkening sky and began to mushroom.[9]

Tha'er doesn't recall being knocked down. He examined himself for injuries, but his probing fingertips couldn't find any major wounds to his legs or torso. He then looked around for Sa'ad, who was lying several meters away. On unsteady legs, Tha'er slowly moved toward the young man. He saw a wash of blood covering his nephew's youthful face; a piece of shrapnel had left a small gash on the top of his head. He was in a great deal of pain. Tha'er pulled him farther from the truck's mangled ruins, until the strength drained from his limbs and he had to sit down to rest.

The light had faded, and a thick, chalky haze descended around him. The air smelled odd, vaguely like chemicals or building materials burning in a house fire. Tha'er couldn't see more than three or four meters in any direction. He began to cough. His lungs burned. A row of lights danced up and down through the darkness and smoke. There were no distinguishable sounds, as if his ears were packed with cotton. He began to make out the dim outlines of his tribesmen holding flashlights. They had run to the site of the explosion and were picking through the ashy metal wreckage of the dump truck looking for bodies.

For some reason, Tha'er recalls methodically running his hand along the side of his rifle, still slung around his neck, and conscientiously flipping the selector switch up to "safe." Someone spotted him, and about a half dozen men ran over with flashlights. He couldn't hear them although they were yelling questions at him. It was irritating. Tha'er's rescuers helped him back toward the village. The chemical odor became stronger and stranger. He had never smelled anything quite like it; he felt as if he might throw up. He looked back and saw that Sa'ad was in distress. An asthmatic, his bleeding nephew was panicking and choking as tribesmen helped him toward the village. The Iraqis' lungs were on fire, but they didn't know exactly why.[10]

A few kilometers away, Maj. Dan Whisnant had been sitting in the front passenger seat of a Humvee crossing the New Bridge, north of the peninsula, when he heard a distant explosion. His convoy from Camp Baharia to FOB Black included Lt. Cdr. Andrew Zwolski, the battalion medical officer, and Cdr. (Select) Edwin Taylor, the regimental combat team surgeon. The two doctors had hitched a ride on the resupply mission for the first leg of their trip to a local hospital, where they hoped to advise civilian medical personnel and investigate the facility. Whisnant wondered if the blast was within his area of operations and if any Marines had been injured. He started monitoring radio traffic for clues.[11]

First Lt. Robert Lehner was the watch officer on duty at FOB Black when the bomb detonated. The walls of the combat operations center shook as the massive explosion boomed in the distance. He looked around at the radio operators sitting in the company's communications hub.

"Whatever that was, it was big," he said.

The Marines set to work with their computers and olive-green radio equipment, broadcasting requests for information from units in the field.[12]

Back at the southern patrol base, Greco's Marines had immediately braced for an attack on their position after the explosion. When no indirect fire or complex assault materialized within a few minutes, the lieutenant issued orders to move out. The Marines quickly determined that the explosion had come from the general direction of the house of Sheikh Khamis Hasnawi Aifan al-Issawi. Their route back to FOB Black went through the blast area, offering them a chance to investigate on the way home. Doezema ordered his squad members into their vehicles.

The four Humvees growled to life and turned onto Main Street in a cautious convoy moving at a snail's pace. The sun had almost set; the narrow dirt road could be lined with IEDs that were tough to spot in the gathering darkness. Heads swiveled and eyes narrowed to spot freshly churned earth, odd rubble, the glint of a command wire, or any of the other subtle cues that might betray a roadside bomb.

After a few minutes passing houses, dirt lots edged with palm trees, or lush fields of burgeoning spring crops, the small train of vehicles was forced to stop. A rusted red tractor, probably a relic of the 1950s, had been left in the middle of the road. A few Marines dismounted, while the turret gunners swiveled to keep watch in 360 degrees around the convoy. Doezema and Levasseur strode to the tractor to investigate.[13]

"No way, you won't know how to start that thing," Levasseur cracked, rolling his eyes. Doezema ignored him. He mounted the vintage equipment, but found no keys or simple ignition. Doezema and Levasseur then began searching the neighborhood for a local who could move the vehicle. The two men had a complicated relationship. Sergeant Doezema was the squad leader, and Corporal Levasseur was one of his three subordinate fire team leaders. The corporal had previously helmed the squad, however, briefly taking over in early December after Doezema was shot in the leg by a sniper.

Doezema had grown up wanting to be a Marine, and once he'd achieved that dream, became one of the most stereotypically "moto" (motivated) men in the Corps. He loved to drill, talked tactics to the exclusion of other topics, and pined for action prior to and at the beginning of the deployment. Some of the Marines in Alpha Company wryly expressed doubts about whether Doezema owned a piece of clothing without a USMC logo, and nicknamed the sergeant the Moto Dragon to canonize his gung-ho attitude. Many of the men used the moniker with chuckling benevolence, while a few infused it with derision.

Doezema's defining characteristic was considered a double-edged sword. He was an energetic and physically brave leader, but one of his critics contended that he was "the type of guy who would [unwisely] charge Hell with a water pistol." He also tended to volunteer his squad for assignments. Some resented the extra work and grumbled that Doezema was only trying to impress their platoon leader.[14] Another Marine assessed this trait positively: "He just wanted to be a notch above . . . and he wanted us to be better Marines all the time."[15]

That same energy willed the sergeant to recover from his wound faster than his doctors at the U.S. hospital in Germany predicted, and spurred him to hitch rides on planes, helicopters, and Humvees back to Fallujah after less than two months of convalescence. Though he had lost much of his desire for combat after being shot, the Moto Dragon refused to let a sniper's bullet through his thigh stop him from finishing his tour.[16] When Doezema returned to his squad's hooch unannounced, gingerly walking through the door with a slight limp and a grin, Levasseur looked up from reading a magazine and experienced a mix of feelings: "Holy shit, he's back! Good on 'im, he's back. Oh shit, he's back."[17]

The complexity that hallmarked Doezema's relationship with Levasseur also typified a number of other relationships between officers or non-commissioned officers and their subordinates. Not everybody got along, but almost all nevertheless did their jobs, with Marine indoctrination and the chain of command performing their time-tested function of thinly restraining, if not extinguishing, personality conflicts.

Several Marines jumped out of the vehicles to find a way to move the tractor. Levasseur and Doezema walked down a road perpendicular to Main Street, took a corner on another side road near a residence, and ran into two Iraqi men in their late twenties. Both wore light-colored dishdashas and sandals. At the sudden appearance of the Marines, the pair muttered in surprise and started to run away.

"Ta'ala hina!" (Come here!), yelled Levasseur. The Iraqis stopped, looked at each other, and furtively glanced back at the bristling silhouettes of the Americans walking toward them. "No, it's OK," continued Levasseur. He held his hand out in front of him, fingertips downward, and limp-wristedly wagged it toward his body, beckoning them with local body language that he always found peculiar. The men reversed course and approached the Americans, who then walked them to the tractor. The Marines pointed and made steering motions indicating that it needed to be moved. The Iraqis quickly understood and one of them ran into a nearby house, returned with a set of keys, and drove the vehicle out of the way.[18] Just then, Lance Corporal Hough reported something strange from his perch in the turret of the lead Humvee. His voice was edged with alarm.

"My nose is burning," said Hough. "Something's wrong, something is burning my nose bad." In another vehicle, LCpl. Luke Reames saw a nearby cloud of gray smoke, and his nose started burning. Levasseur and Doezema took deep breaths.

"Do you smell that?" said a surprised Levasseur.[19]

"What the hell *is* that?" said Doezema.

"It smells like chlorine," offered Levasseur, who immediately recognized the odor from helping his dad clean their pool when he was a kid. They shared a surprised look. It quickly dawned on them that the insurgents had detonated some sort of chemical bomb. They ran to their trucks.[20] From his seat in the convoy's second Humvee, Greco saw his men scramble to their vehicles in the deepening dusk. "That was odd," he thought.

Doezema's disembodied voice then squawked through his headset: "We smell gas, like a chlorine gas."[21] For a moment, the lieutenant didn't believe them.

"I don't smell anything," said Greco.

"Sir, Hough's complaining his nose is burning," Levasseur chimed in over the net. Both Doezema and Levasseur insisted to their platoon leader that it was chlorine gas and that they "had to go."[22] The Marines in Reames' vehicle were "kind of freaked out." They had concluded that "this is burning us, we need to get the fuck out of here."[23] Greco noted the edge in their voices and soon smelled chlorine himself.

"I think you're right," he said, ordering them to turn the vehicles around and drive several hundred meters along the route they had come.[24] The Marines were unprepared for an unconventional attack, having left their chemical weapons suits and gas masks at the FOB. While standard operating procedure dictated that Marine units keep specialized equipment on hand at all times, no one followed this seemingly impractical directive. The threat of chemical weapons had come to be considered somewhere between highly unlikely and impossible, and food, ammunition, and water received priority for space on patrols.

As the Marines beat a quick retreat, a memory jogged the lieutenant's mind. While sifting through the battalion's intelligence archive a couple of months prior, Greco had read a report discussing the possibility and effects of insurgents making "a poor man's chemical weapon"—bombs packed with chlorine. He recalled the author concluding that the resulting gas could severely burn lung tissue if inhaled, but that it tended to disperse quickly.[25]

The explosion sounded like it had probably come from somewhere on Main Street near the village of Albu Aifan. Greco had been trying to raise Dark, Sheikh Aifan Sadoun Aifan al-Issawi, via the predetermined frequency on the handheld radios they shared. As was often the case, local interference was blocking the signal. The lieutenant spotted a tan, two-story farmhouse and ordered the convoy to stop. He dismounted the vehicles with Doezema and two other Marines. The Americans knocked on the door, told a surprised middle-aged man that they needed to use his roof, and attempted to contact the sheikh from the elevated position.[26] A strange-sounding Dark finally answered.

"We've been attacked! We can't breathe!" said Dark. He had clearly been affected by the gas. He was coughing, and his voice sounded sleepy, despite his obvious distress. "We need help!"[27]

"Hold on, Dark," replied Greco. He radioed the combat operations center (COC) at FOB Black on a secure channel, but Whisnant wasn't at the base. Instead, the platoon commander communicated the situation to Lehner. Greco advised him that his Marines did not have gas masks and requested that the battalion's nuclear, biological, and chemical officer confirm whether a chlorine gas attack would quickly dissipate.[28] As the request was passed up to battalion, the lieutenant returned to the walkie-talkie.

"Dark, we don't have gas masks," said Greco, who then explained that the Marines had to "wait a few minutes" for the gas to dissipate before approaching the village. He told Dark to get his people out of there.

"People are very sick," insisted the coughing sheikh. "We need your help."[29]

A frustrated Doezema and Greco conferred. They felt helpless and guilty listening to the sheikh's pained calls for help. The naturally aggressive pair of Marines might have been personally willing to risk a move up to the village to investigate, and they briefly considered asking their Marines for volunteers to travel as close as possible to it.[30] They didn't want to split up, however, and risk the lives of the squad in the unknown of a chemical attack.

Greco decided it wouldn't do their allies any good if they became ill as well.[31] He considered the options.

They couldn't charge into gas without protective gear, but they also couldn't simply abandon their new allies by waiting until the situation was entirely safe. He split the difference with a new plan: his men would wait another ten minutes, until the gas had somewhat cleared, and then move to ground zero.[32] The platoon leader's squawking radio validated his assumptions. Lehner told him the battalion's nuclear, biological, and chemical officer had confirmed that chlorine gas should dissipate quickly. The lieutenant told his Marines to get ready to move out.[33]

--------- ❖ ---------

Capt. Bill Ghilarducci, Alpha Company's executive officer, had been standing outside the COC smoking a cigar when he heard and felt the bomb. It had been big, but he otherwise didn't think much more about it until about twenty minutes later, when one of the Hobbits burst from the COC with a radio in his hand.

"Hey sir, Dark is talking. Dark is talking!"

Ghilarducci heard the Iraqi's low voice crackle from the equipment. Dark was mumbling in English to the Americans at FOB Black. He was "choking a little bit."

"We are coming to you," said the distressed sheikh. Ghilarducci didn't have a lot of experience dealing with Dark; tribal engagement was what he termed "Dad's project." As executive officer, his job was usually to serve as the "asshole" who put his boot in people's behinds to make sure the will of Whisnant, the company commander, was done. Nevertheless, he was aware that a handful of Albu Aifan militiamen had previously come to FOB Black for medical treatment after battles with al Qaeda, so a request to help a few of the sheikh's men was casually accepted.[34]

As Whisnant's convoy arrived back at the FOB, he'd gathered from radio traffic that something large had exploded in the peninsula on Main Street. Saint One, the military intelligence Marine, explained that a bomb had detonated in Albu Aifan, adding that Dark had called and wanted help. "They've got lots of injured civilians, and he wants to bring his people here." The sheikh was already on his way.

"OK, bring them in," said Whisnant. A quick reaction force was also ordered to muster and push out to help evacuate the wounded villagers.

Whisnant didn't know how many people were injured, and bringing a large number of hurt civilians onto an American FOB around Fallujah was unheard of. But in addition to the moral impulse to help innocents, the major's calculation was practical: the Albu Aifan were the key to winning the peninsula. The Americans needed the Iraqis, and right now the Iraqis needed American support.[35]

Ghilarducci waited outside the COC for the arrival of Dark and Whisnant. The sheikh had pulled into the base's parking area first, in a black BMW carrying two militiamen who had been close to the truck bomb when it exploded. One of the fighters had suffered blast-related blunt trauma to his chest, while the other's shoulder had been filleted by a piece of shrapnel. The Marines helped them from the vehicle, placing the more seriously injured militiaman on a stretcher before carrying him to a makeshift treatment room in the mess hall.

Dark wore his characteristic "combat casual" Western trousers and shirt accessorized with a dark blue ammunition vest. He bore a pained look and coughed as he strode up to Ghilarducci, put his hand on the taller man's shoulder, turned his head, and launched a stream of vomit into the dirt. Ghilarducci leaned in to support the sheikh and smelled the strong odor of "bleach." A watery-eyed Dark righted himself and hurriedly tried to explain what had happened. His efforts to maintain composure and communicate were obviously hampered by waves of nausea, but the request to bring the injured of his village to the Americans for treatment was clear.[36] A minute later, the newly arrived Whisnant and Saint One approached both men, and Dark repeated his entreaty to bring the wounded to the base.

Between the sheikh's gasped report and the radio calls from Greco to the COC, the picture was growing clearer: Some sort of chemical bomb had exploded in Albu Aifan, injuring militiamen and civilians. In response, one of Greco's squads was moving north to the village. GySgt. Brian Ivers' 2nd Platoon was pushing south from the FOB with Humvees and seven-ton trucks to help transport the wounded back to the base. In addition, some of the injured villagers were headed toward the FOB in their private vehicles.[37]

The civilians of Albu Aifan were scared and confused. Many of them had never smelled chlorine, so they couldn't identify what was poisoning them. Others recognized it as "Clorox" (bleach).[38] They needed assistance, but they didn't trust the doctors and nurses at Fallujah General Hospital, which was within walking distance from FOB Black. There was a strong possibility that insurgents had operatives within the facility, or might violently coerce the staff to let them in to kill patients. In addition, the standard of care at the hospital during the war was rudimentary, at best.[39] The leaders of the subtribe had quickly concluded that their best chance lay with their new American allies.[40]

As Greco and Doezema's convoy renewed its trip toward the village, the sun had completely set. The smell of chlorine still hung in the air, but it wasn't burning the nostrils of the exposed turret gunners as it had twenty minutes earlier. The men gradually began to see more houses among the palm trees, barren lots, and farmland lining the narrow dirt road. As the convoy drew closer to the village center, the street became solidly flanked by fancier stucco homes surrounded by sturdy courtyard walls. The smell of chlorine grew stronger, but it never became overpowering.[41]

The Americans knew they were close when they saw scattered trash and debris and came upon an ad hoc checkpoint of armed militiamen. Greco and Doezema jumped from the Humvees to briefly confer with the men. The guards pointed the Marines a few meters up the street toward a smoking wreck in the middle of the road.[42] The Americans remounted and moved to the site of the blast. A huge crater spanned most of the road. All that remained of the dump truck that carried the bomb was the burnt front end of the cab and the twisted half-skeleton of the chassis. All that remained of the driver were a far-flung foot, its toes blackened but intact, a few ashy bone fragments, and a portion of the man's skull and teeth.[43]

Angry men with covered faces and weapons surrounded the smoking metal. Several palm trees and a small cinder block wall near the crater had been toppled, with pieces of wood and concrete cast outward in an unfinished mosaic depicting the blast wave. Doezema saw two dead cats with dark fur lying side by side on the road near the wreckage. The animals looked like they were sleeping, but red foam poured from their mouths. Part of the courtyard wall of a nearby house had been knocked over, and the windows had been blown from the residence. On a concrete wall that remained, oily black streaks marked where the truck's tires had melted and splattered.[44]

The Marines pressed on to Sheikh Khamis' compound at the center of the village, where they parked their vehicles and dismounted into an atmosphere of panic and disarray. The dark street was "sort of a mob scene."[45]

Ghostly figures of militiamen with flashlights and AK-47s materialized in and out of the hazy darkness, their faces covered with checkered *shemaghs* of red and white or black and white. Fearing the gas and a second attack, few of the village's women and children were about, many apparently having moved indoors for protection.

Doezema had never witnessed so many armed Iraqis; there were perhaps "50 or 60" of them. Most of the men's eyes raged with anger and some with fear, and all were breathing heavily. Some yelled and seemed to mill about aimlessly, but most remained stoic and moved with a purpose. "Well, I guess they're used to this type of violence," thought the squad leader.[46] Greco ordered Doezema to position his Humvees and the squad's three teams in a protective arrangement to surround the village center and block all avenues of approach. The lieutenant then moved inside the large residence to look for the paramount sheikh or any other authority figure he could find.[47]

On the way in, Greco had radioed to and received updates from FOB Black. He was told that the only thing that would help those seriously injured by the gas was administering oxygen, and he was tasked with helping triage and evacuate wounded civilians to the American base for more advanced medical care. Gunnery Sergeant Ivers' 2nd Platoon was on its way with Humvees and seven-ton trucks to help with transport.[48]

Greco and Doezema found Khamis in a sitting room of the large house. He was surrounded by angry old sheikhs and tense young guards. The paramount sheikh maintained most of his characteristic regal aloofness, which stood in stark contrast to the chaos swirling around him. Greco asked about the Iraqi's welfare and what his men could do to help. Khamis cordially greeted them and requested that the Americans check on a sheikh who had become very ill from the gas. The Marines and a corpsman were ushered into an adjoining room, where a semiconscious elderly man in light-colored robes lay on a couch. Greco and Doezema recognized the man as someone they'd suspected of working with al Qaeda and who had in fact been one of their targets only weeks earlier. The Americans checked his vitals, but thought they could do little except make him comfortable. It seemed likely that the man was going to die. "Wow. [The insurgents] got one of their own guys," thought Doezema. The sergeant shook his head in wonderment at the family relationships and rivalries that characterized the peninsula's tribal civil war.[49] Greco passed word to his Marines, Khamis, and the other sheikhs to gather the injured at the paramount sheikh's compound for triage and transport to the American base.

At FOB Black, Lehner set to work managing the barrage of communications in and out of the command center. Calls from battalion staff requested updates over computer "mIRC chat" (Microsoft Internet Relay Chat): "What is the situation?" Calls to and from elements of Greco's 3rd Platoon, pushing north to the village, provided partial answers over encrypted Green Gear radios: "We are moving to round up the injured; most of them have problems breathing." Calls to and from elements of 1st and 2nd Platoon, on their way south to the village, also provided information, along with requests: "We're going to need more stretchers."

The chaos was intensified by cell phone and walkie-talkie calls from Dark and other leading militiamen, who had started shepherding small convoys of civilian vehicles carrying the injured to the American base. Lehner and his Marines struggled to understand the heavily accented English. "Look for a four-door black car. I'm going to be in it. . . . There are going to be two vehicles behind me" was a typical instruction.[50] The lieutenant had to make sure the Iraqis' communiqués were relayed carefully to the network of Americans guarding the roads to and gates of the base. Civilian vehicles charging a military installation normally would be greeted with warning gunshots and then quickly destroyed if they failed to stop. In addition, some of the speeding cars would be carrying armed men. The young Marines needed specific information if they were to hold their fire as the makeshift convoys bore down on the FOB. This restraint would make the Marines vulnerable if al Qaeda had another vehicle bomb ready, but it was a risk that needed to be run to get the injured onto the base.

The battalion's nuclear, biological, and chemical officer stationed at Camp Fallujah repeatedly called for updates. When he was told that Greco's unit was first on the scene but lacked their chemical weapons gear, the chief warrant officer demanded answers.

"How come these guys don't have gas masks?" he asked.

"I don't know," replied Lehner. The NBC officer persisted in criticizing Greco for not having the equipment and lectured on the specifics of standard operating procedure. "Roger, I'll let him know that," said Lehner, allowing sarcasm to suffuse his voice. The conversation briefly disrupted the flow of communication, and Lehner was not happy about it. "I'm dealing with a mass casualty incident . . . and this asshole is asking me questions about gas masks," he thought at the time. "Not the time, nor the place. How about you ask what you can do for me?"[51]

Members of 2nd Platoon rolled into the center of Albu Aifan from the northern approach along Main Street about fifteen minutes after Greco's men had arrived.[52] Gunny Ivers' convoy included two large seven-ton trucks capable of holding about a dozen people and two "highbacks" resembling a cross between a Humvee and a pickup truck. Each could safely carry perhaps seven or eight patients in the back. The vehicles were directed toward the large courtyard of Khamis' compound. The newly arrived Marines dismounted wearing dark green chemical suits and black gas masks. Their "alien stormtrooper" appearance added to the sureality of the dark, confusing atmosphere.

"Did you bring us gas masks, at least?" Levasseur asked Sgt. Steven Ophoff. The newly arrived Marine was nearly unidentifiable in his bug-eyed, black mask.

"No," came the muffled response.[53] Levasseur knew from his dad's warnings while cleaning their pool that concentrated chlorine can burn the lungs and eat away exposed skin if left there long enough. Most of the Marines in the village were worried when they first smelled the gas; some gulped pockets of air they thought to be uncontaminated and held their breath. Minutes after their arrival at the village, some of the Marines' throats burned slightly and their eyes watered, but no one was incapacitated or severely affected. Others smelled the chlorine but suffered no symptoms at all. After Greco issued orders to help round up civilians and load them into the vehicles, many of the Marines became too busy to be worried about the gas.[54]

Militiamen ran into residences to fetch their families, and nearly fifty of the village's women, children, and elderly began to stream out of houses. Some of the women and children were crying. A few of the mothers with covered faces were wailing a lament; most dragged or carried terrified or listless children toward the vehicles. A few old men and women were walking as though they were drunk, unsteadily weaving as coughs shuddered through their frames. Marines and militiamen rushed to help them.[55]

Many of the Iraqis kept their faces covered, but the Americans glimpsed pale skin and eyes that shone with fear and confusion. Some paused to spit as they walked to the trucks. The more seriously injured were carried to the courtyard and laid out. HM2 Tony Zermeno assessed and triaged them, but there was little he could do for inhalation injuries beyond checking their vital signs and categorizing the injuries. Zermeno identified "about 14 to 16" people as "reds"—critical patients who "definitely needed oxygen or even needed intubation."[56]

The Marines began loading the injured women, children, and elderly into the seven-tons. While standing on the back steps of one of the large vehicles, Doezema's heart sank when he saw a middle-aged father carrying the limp body of a toddler wearing a colorful dress. Tears streamed down the man's face as he rapidly murmured Arabic and held up her small form like a supplication to the American. Doezema reached down from his perch on the truck's steps and gently took her limp body from the man, passing her up to another Marine in the back of the truck. Her eyes were closed and her face was a deathly blue. The memory would stay with him.[57]

After all of the villagers who could fit were loaded onto the trucks, the yelling or crying diminished to occasional moans, coughs, and retching. Levasseur thought they'd calmed down because they knew they were going to get help. He took one last look inside one of the seven-tons before shutting the back door. The bench seats and bed were packed with the elderly, women, children, and a few men. The Iraqis quietly looked at him. About a dozen sets of mournful eyes seemed to entreat the corporal, "Are we going to be OK?" It was a depressing sight. Levasseur shut the doors, jumped down from the truck and smacked the side of the vehicle to indicate that they were ready to move.[58]

16

❖ MassCas ❖

After their convoy made it to Forward Operating Base (FOB) Black, Cdr. (Select) Edwin Taylor and Lt. Cdr. Andrew Zwolski, the two visiting physicians, took charge of treating the wounded. By the time the officers arrived, Dark's most seriously injured militiamen and a small number of civilians had already started to "trickle into the compound," and Alpha Company's Marines and corpsmen had hastily prepared a triage area. The two doctors gathered all of the base's medical personnel, conducted a quick briefing, and issued orders to forage whatever supplies they had on hand. The physicians were augmented by six Navy corpsmen and a handful of Marines with civilian experience as paramedics and firefighters.[1]

The initial casualties were moved into the compound's dining hall, a roughly 20 x 20 foot space in an abandoned house. Deferring to modesty and local custom, six women from the first wave of casualties were separated from the men and evaluated in the company aid station. One woman was about twenty weeks pregnant, and there were "approximately twelve [sick] children, half under the age of five." In the confusion, no one had communicated to the doctors that the explosive was laden with chemicals, but they soon figured it out when they assessed patients who reeked of chlorine.[2]

Chlorine gas was weaponized nearly a century before, during World War I. German forces first unleashed toxic clouds on French troops during the Second Battle of Ypres on April 22, 1915. The gas makes an effective weapon because it is quite poisonous and heavier than air. With favorable winds, its relative weight allowed it to waft across battlefields, where it would settle into trenches and blanket personnel. When inhaled, chlorine reacts with the moisture in the lungs and becomes hydrochloric acid. As the acid burns its way through tissue, alveoli, the small sacs normally responsible for absorbing oxygen, seal themselves to keep out the poison, and the lungs begin to fill with water, exacerbating the deadly cycle. At minimum, inhaled chlorine will cause labored breathing as mildly burned tissue struggles to get enough oxygen. At worst, the chemical causes sufficient irritation to trigger severe spasms in the bronchi, the air passages to the lungs. The smooth muscles surrounding the bronchi seize and constrict the airway to the point that victims suffocate or drown in their own fluids.[3]

Zwolski was worried. At his emergency room back in the United States, he had an impressive array of equipment that could help patients breathe. Here on FOB Black, the physicians had almost nothing up to the task: one oxygen tank and four albuterol inhalers commonly used by asthmatics to relax muscles in the airway. The two doctors "nebulized" (medicated) the albuterol with the oxygen before sparingly administering it with a facemask to the victims with the most severe symptoms. Some of the most violently ill Iraqis who were vomiting were also injected with Promethazine, an anti-nausea drug.[4]

Within a few minutes, a handful of the Marines and a corpsman began to cough or vomit, and some of the mildly affected Iraqis worsened. Besides the chlorine, some individuals smelled like hydrocarbons. "Oh my God, there's another [chemical] agent here," thought Taylor. The doctors soon surmised that staying indoors was amplifying the effect of any gas trapped in the patients' clothing. In addition, some of the men closest to the blast reeked of the propane accelerant used in the bomb. The inhaled hydrocarbons started to sicken both nearby patients and those who were treating them. Despite inferior lighting and potential exposure to indirect fire, the Americans moved everyone outdoors to let the fresh air do its work.

The corpsmen and Marines organized a triage area at the chow hall from which the wounded would be diverted to two possible destinations: the least injured would go to the company's outdoor weight room and an empty building normally used as an overflow barracks for guests, while the more serious patients would go to the covered patio outside the main barracks.

Lighting, bandages, blankets, buckets, food, and water were quickly staged within each zone. Chem lights and white engineer's tape marked paths from area to area, and nonmedical personnel stood by as guards, guides, or gophers, ferrying information, patients, and supplies. Taylor and Zwolski marveled at the Marines' proactive efficiency as they designed and executed an ad hoc system for managing the MassCas—mass casualty incident. The doctors thought the breadth of civilian law enforcement and first responder experience among the Reservists must have made the difference.[5]

Cpl. Matthew Zofchak's 1st Squad of 3rd Platoon had been running base security when the bomb exploded. As the FOB began admitting wounded locals, he ran to the barracks to request additional Marines.[6] LCpl. Eddie O'Connor had been playing poker for cigarettes in the barracks when he heard the sound of a distant explosion. Zofchak soon entered and told O'Connor, "You need to get one of your guys to go out and do security for [Dark's] BMW, just keep an eye on it." As the lance corporal grabbed his gear and his rifle, Zofchak added, "Oh yeah, bring your gas mask too." At first, O'Connor thought he was joking.[7]

As more civilian vehicles started arriving, Zofchak requested that Sgt. Christopher Dockter bring his entire 2nd Squad to assist. A combination of the two squads guarded the southern entrance to the FOB, even after the original Marines' guard shift had ended. The situation required "all hands on deck."[8] Dockter ran back and forth between two security posts, making sure the men had sufficient ammunition, batteries for their night vision goggles, and of equal importance, instructions not to shoot every civilian vehicle that approached their position at a high rate of speed.

The wind had carried the sickening chemical smell of oil and chlorine, and Dockter was worried about what might follow. A wave of civilians bore down on his position, some in Marine seven-ton trucks, many more in personal vehicles. Insurgents might take advantage of the chaos and slip another bomb in with the traffic. As a precaution, he instructed his men to stop the incoming vehicles several dozen meters away from the gates of the base and conservatively apply "escalation of force" if drivers failed to slow down.

At first, the locals arrived one at a time. A white Toyota pickup truck or a dark-colored Opel sedan bearing coughing civilians hurtled out of the darkness every five minutes or so. Soon, small convoys of two and three vehicles began to arrive, some escorted by Dark's militiamen in Land Rovers or Mercedes. Once the vehicles stopped, the Marines took a quick look for wires and weapons. The searches varied in intensity relative to the medical condition of the passengers. The Americans looked more closely at cars and trucks riding unusually low to the ground. The searches were far more casual than the sergeant would have liked, but it was a calculated risk deemed necessary to help their new allies.

When the Americans stopped them, many of the Iraqis were coughing. Some were vomiting, others spit phlegm from the windows. A number of them were convulsing with dry heaves, and a few were almost unconscious. Many of them seemed disoriented, "almost like they'd seen a ghost." Most reeked of chlorine.[9] "These guys don't have a clue what's happened to them," Dockter later recalled thinking.

After a car was searched and waved through, a Marine guided it into the parking lot, where other Marines and corpsmen helped the wounded to the triage area. Weapons were confiscated from the fighters and stacked in a growing pile in the corner of the parking area. Each group was assigned an American escort to make sure insurgents hadn't slipped in with the crowd, and to ensure that the Iraqis didn't touch anything they shouldn't on the typically secure military installation.[10] As Sgt. Dave Ogden helped coordinate the company's response, 1st Platoon's platoon sergeant "floated around between, making sure nobody was going anywhere they weren't supposed to be, assisting people to see the doctors," and making sure the patients were comfortable with blankets, food, and water. Many other Marines joined him.[11]

———————— ❖ ————————

Sheikh Shalaan (Mishael Abdullah Owdeh) ran carloads of civilians back and forth between Albu Aifan and the U.S. base. As one of the leaders of the Albu Issa and a close cousin of the paramount sheikh, Khamis Hasnawi Aifan al-Issawi, the wealthy fifty-eight-year-old had dedicated his pickup truck, his BMW, and his Land Rover to the effort. Shalaan and his sons alternatively drove or navigated one of the three vehicles during the convoys he participated in. Shalaan had seen and endured many acts of violence in his life, a flurry of them in the previous few years. Three of his nephews had been killed by Marines—"accidentally" or in crossfire—since the U.S-led invasion. Prior to that, members of Saddam Hussein's secret intelligence service had murdered his son in 2001; he, consequently, had not mourned the downfall of the Baathists.

Sheikh Shalaan recalled that Sheikh Khamis and some other leading sheikhs of the tribe had declared a truce with the Americans in 2003, hoping the occupiers would keep their promises to be economic benefactors and shape Iraq into something resembling post–World War II Japan and

Germany. But many others, including angry imams and impetuous tribes-men, some of them close blood relatives of Shalaan's subtribe, had refused to abide by the truce. They declared Shalaan and some other elder sheikhs "traitors" to Iraq and Islam for failing to fight the "infidels."

Early in the war, the Albu Issa had split into two camps. Many men initially opted to indirectly support the insurgency or to actively fight the Americans. Their decision stemmed variously from nationalistic or theolog-ical passion and a youthful quest for fame and heroism; some were drawn to the money paid by foreign jihadists in a chaotic postwar environment with negligible employment prospects. Only recently, as more and more Albu Issa became tired of the bloodthirsty tactics of al Qaeda in Iraq and the Americans worked effectively with the tribe, had the balance of loyalty and action tipped away from the *takfiris*.

After prominent members of the Albu Issa organized a militia and began openly fighting the radical insurgents, Sheikh Shalaan had expected the enemy to come after his people. But he did not expect their decision to try and murder the innocent women and children of his tribe with chemi-cals. "They want to kill everyone, not just the men who fight them," Shalaan recalled thinking. "Women, children . . . anyone." After the chlorine attack, anger and disbelief coalesced into resolve. He wanted revenge, but it was also something more cold and practical than that. "Anyone who could do this must be killed," he concluded. "We must rid them from our area."[12]

While Taylor and Zwolski evaluated the wounded, both soon concluded that they could merely stabilize the few patients with serious blast injuries and triage for transport those severely affected by the gas. The patients in criti-cal condition required more complex treatment, including ventilators and "advanced cardiac life support." Some of the victims needed better facilities available at Camp Fallujah—a larger American base to the northwest—if they were to have a shot at survival.[13]

Commander Taylor had quickly deemed Dark's two wounded militia-men stable enough for transport to Camp Fallujah Surgical. Taylor called and briefed the camp's medical personnel, while Sgt. Matt Stout organized a small four-vehicle convoy to pick its way along the often bomb-laden route to the well-stocked "surgical resuscitation site."[14] Zwolski assigned one of the most trusted senior corpsmen, HM3 Raymond Shirkey, to take charge of the two patients, whom he would monitor during the trip in the bed of a highback Humvee.[15] "Pick up as much oxygen and albuterol as you can" and bring it back, he told Shirkey before the convoy left, adding that they would "need it."[16]

First Sgt. Ken Baum helped with the wounded, carrying men, women, and children of various ages from the parking lot to the triage area. Baum was struck by how far his Marines had come during their deployment. He suspected that the Albu Aifan tribesmen were coming to them because the Marines of Alpha Company were now "their people" more so than some of the Fallujans who worked at the local hospital.

On one trip to the parking lot, he spied a man in his thirties who was coughing, moaning, and slightly rolling back-and-forth in the bed of a civilian truck. When the Iraqi saw the big American, he clutched at his chest, held an arm out and said, "Mister!" Baum squinted and wrinkled his nose when he noticed that "the gentleman had thrown up all over himself." Dried vomit clung to the front of his tan robes. The 215-pound Marine didn't want to get vomit smeared on himself, so he moved behind the Iraqi, slipped his arms under the slightly built man's armpits, and picked him up. Baum held the tribesmen straight out in front of him and walked toward the triage area, the Iraqi's feet dangling above the ground. In the midst of the rush, some of the Marines couldn't help but pause and chuckle at the sight.[17]

SSgt. Ken Fall was a seven-year veteran of the Marine Corps who thought he'd become desensitized to the violence common to Fallujah, but had to admit that he'd never seen anything like this. As the platoon sergeant for 2nd Platoon, Fall had deployed his men to help with security, supply, and transporting the wounded from the village and on to Camp Fallujah.

He was waiting with some of his Marines when several cars pulled into the parking lot. Iraqi men jumped out of the vehicles to help women and kids. A few cradled small children in their arms. Others supported them by the shoulders, "half dragging" them toward the Marines. Many had bloodshot eyes and "were hacking their lungs out." Looking back, Fall recalls that the image made him angry and sick to his stomach: "This guy [the suicide bomber] could have attacked Marines, but decided to kill a bunch of women and little kids."[18]

Cpl. Trevor Pickel and a couple of other Marines went to the parking lot to briefly assess and move patients to the triage area. Most, but not all, of the men in his platoon had enthusiastically taken to helping the tribesmen. A couple of the Marines who disliked the locals or considered them "dirty" had loudly carped about helping out. One American told the others not to "fucking touch [them], it is not your job to fucking help them. Get the fuck away, go back in the hooch. That's a corpsman's job." Pickel shook his head and ignored the man. While a few Marines shared this attitude, Pickel regarded them as exceptions to the rule. He was impressed at how quickly almost everyone pitched in to help.

Being an EMT (emergency medical technician) and firefighter from Tennessee who had been one semester short of qualifying as a paramedic when he was deployed, the corporal found his civilian qualifications now in demand. The Iraqis weren't much different from many of his patients back in Knoxville. He threw himself into the work, telling both the doctors and "Docs" (corpsmen) to grab him for whatever they needed, and "guys upon guys" in turn asked him what they could do to help.

When members of 2nd Platoon pulled into the parking lot with a full load of patients, he moved to the back of one of the seven tons. Someone opened the gate of the truck, and Tony "Doc" Zermeno started offloading the injured. Pickel saw a sobbing little girl who was "maybe three or four years old." The light brown skin on her face had a small cut, and she had abrasions on her arms. Her injuries were minor, but she seemed lost and was "scared to death." When she cried and held out her arms, Pickel thought of all his nieces and nephews. He picked her up and carried her around for about the next half hour as he and other Marines rounded up other children who had been transported to the FOB. Most had trouble breathing and were terrified, but otherwise looked like they'd be OK. Pickel and a corpsman focused on a small group of five kids "ranging from four to seven" years old. The pair took turns cleaning them off, administering oxygen, and giving them food and water. He eventually handed off the little girl he'd been carrying to a group of women who had gathered near the weight room. About forty minutes later, on one of his trips back to the parking lot, Pickel saw the Marine who'd yelled at others not to touch the Iraqis helping two injured tribesman to the picnic area.[19]

❖

Ruben "Doc" Muñoz shuttled back and forth between the treatment zones, handing out water, cleaning and bandaging cuts and burns, and checking vital signs. There were a couple of serious trauma patients who had been transported to Camp Fallujah by then, but the vast majority of the injured simply suffered from nausea and labored breathing. After the bomb blast, the women, children, and elderly had naturally moved inside for safety. Muñoz soon realized that their clothes had been saturated by the chlorine released in the massive gas cloud, and the lack of fresh air exacerbated their exposure to the poisonous chemical while they stewed indoors. The corpsmen were removing what clothes they could and handing out blankets.[20] This was tricky when dealing with the women, but Muslim propriety had dampened as most tribesmen let the medical personnel do their jobs.[21]

Muñoz tried to get those who had trouble breathing into fresh air and moved around with an albuterol inhaler and an interpreter, helping administer preciously rationed puffs to those having the most difficulty.[22] A group of children seemed to be the worst off; the corpsmen focused on washing their skin with bottles of water and bags of saline.[23] Eventually a corpsman and four Marines became significantly ill from inhaling the chemicals in the Iraqis' clothes. The corpsman became so violently sick that he was medevaced along with his patients for advanced care.[24]

Many of the Americans didn't know what exactly had sickened the villagers as they treated them, only that they'd been victims of some sort of chemical attack, and everyone smelled like "bleach."[25] Through interpreters, some of the Iraqis said that it was "Clorox."[26] Most of the Americans were so busy that they didn't give it much thought until things calmed down or their compatriots started getting sick.

Within a few minutes of treating the initial wave of about forty-five casualties, Doctors Taylor and Zwolski realized that they would need to transport additional patients, beyond the first two injured fighters, to a better standard of care.[27] Taylor rushed to the combat operations center to get on the radio with Camp Fallujah Surgical. While the notification to transport a couple of militia fighters was casually accepted, the request to start transporting more civilians from a mass casualty event encountered "pushback." The resistance from U.S. personnel at Camp Fallujah wasn't cruel or necessarily uncaring; rather, they prioritized the mission of treating American casualties. If too many resources were devoted to saving civilians hurt by other Iraqis, the small facility could be overwhelmed and unable to handle injured Americans if a spate of insurgent attacks sent them more wounded. Given the violence in the area, this was a realistic concern. Taylor, however, passionately pressed his case for permission to transport.[28] In the end, the fact that kids were in trouble probably made the difference. "I'm not going to sit here and let these kids die," he told them.[29] The Camp Fallujah personnel acquiesced, giving the doctor and the Marines permission to send more injured civilians.[30] A second convoy was hastily assembled to leave the wire.[31]

In and around the fluorescent-lit overflow barracks, which held the less severely injured, Iraqis stood or sat in circles, quietly huddling in colorful blankets. Close to one hundred civilians had arrived on the FOB. Many asked for food. Pickel and others handed out bottles of water, Otis Spunkmeyer muffins, and the more palatable portions of their MREs.[32] The interpreters "C. J." and "Joe" trailed the corpsmen, doctors, and Marines, translating instructions, medical complaints, and requests from the villagers.[33] During a lull in their duties, the younger linguist, C. J., spotted three teenage girls sitting in a circle, blankets drawn around their shoulders. They looked about seventeen or so, and C. J. marveled to Joe that they were "hot." The young interpreter was surprised that he'd never seen such good-looking girls on their endless census patrols through the villages. The older interpreter dared C. J. to say it to them.

The nineteen-year-old Iraqi had spent nearly four of his teenage years in the middle of a war, almost two of them working for the U.S. military. He'd experienced plenty of fear and seen a lot of death, but he'd never had a girlfriend. C. J. was nervous when he saw the girls, and excited when he recognized his unique opportunity to speak to them. "Oh my God, what luck, I'm a translator," he recalls thinking.

Some of the fighters from Dark's militia were keeping an eye on several groups of women, probably including the group that caught the young interpreter's eye.[34] Nevertheless, the scene was chaotic, and the members of the tribe had relaxed their standards of propriety to receive medical assistance. C. J. sidled up to the girls and attempted conversation. He offered them water and extra blankets, and asked if they needed anything. The flirtation was brief. In addition to being shy, the would-be suitor from Baghdad didn't want to get in trouble with Major Dan Whisnant or anyone else for hitting on young women after a bomb attack. He returned to his linguistic duties and his amused friend Joe.[35]

———————— ❖ ————————

Pickel had noticed an approximately eighteen-month-old boy who "was having a tough time breathing and was getting tired." The corporal propped the child up to open his airway and watched him closely. The boy started "going in and out of consciousness," and Pickel began roughly rubbing his knuckles along the toddler's sternum to keep him awake. About five minutes later, he heard that a third and final convoy, comprised of members of GySgt. Brian Ivers' 2nd Platoon, was heading out to Fallujah Surgical. The corporal picked the boy up, ran to a seven-ton truck about to leave the wire, and handed the child to Zermeno.[36]

The forty-four-year-old corpsman, from Oglesby, Illinois, had an unusual amount of experience. Zermeno had been in the Navy for fifteen years, and he'd spent twenty-two years as a civilian firefighter and paramedic. Despite this track record, he had been "fired" from Weapons Company prior to deployment, because he "didn't see eye to eye" with its commander. When officers with Alpha Company learned that there was an open "green side" (infantry) corpsman, they snatched up Zermeno and assigned him to Gunny Ivers' 2nd Platoon. As the deployment progressed, he wound up being regarded as one of the best corpsmen attached to the company. "I'd want him anytime I deployed to combat again," recalled Major Whisnant.[37]

Though much older than most of the Marines he served, Zermeno was "in pretty good shape." He recalled that he "couldn't run up front with the young chickens anymore, but [he] could still keep up with the core of the group." Stamina was a necessity. While Ivers' platoon didn't quite work the punishing schedule of some of the other platoons, they worked hard, and there were fewer corpsmen than there were squads in a platoon. Consequently, the medical specialists often wound up doubling up on patrols to ensure care was always available to the Marines.

The aftermath of the chlorine bomb wasn't the first time Zermeno had dealt with a mass casualty incident. He'd responded to vehicle pileups on highways back in the States, as well as treated a number of wounded Iraqi police, soldiers, militia, and civilians who had been brought in to the Americans' entry control point bordering the city after being shot or blown up. In one case, he recalled running so low on supplies that he'd been forced to prepare ammunition bandoliers to use as tourniquets. But the aftermath of the chlorine attack, involving about one hundred patients, was the largest of his career.

Marine drivers started the engines of the seven ton and three escort Humvees, and the convoy left FOB Black. In the back of the seven ton, the "reds"—critical patients Zermeno was treating—had respiratory rates that were either "way too high" as they struggled to catch their breath or "way too low" as their systems started to shut down altogether. Of no more than a half dozen patients, three—the eighteen-month-old, an approximately six-year-old boy, and an elderly woman—were worse off than the others. The toddler was unconscious and discolored, looking "really pale" and having "cyanotic" (blue) lips indicative of oxygen deprivation.

The vehicle was cramped, so Zermeno had to crawl over people to assess the injured; he turned his weapon over to a young Marine because it hampered his movement. It was pitch black. As the corpsman moved from patient to patient, he pressed on a tiny plastic LED light clipped to the front of his flak jacket to guide his way around the tangle of bodies and benches in the truck bed. Emotion had mostly left the equation for the corpsman. Years of experience as a first responder helped him turn "into a machine" when he began treating patients. That said, medical professionals who regularly deal with trauma are not emotionally immune when confronted with injured children. "When we see kids, it's automatic, you turn it up another notch," he explained. "Adrenaline gets pumping a little bit. Just like at the firehouse, when you hear 'five-year-old hit by a car,' all of a sudden your foot presses down on the accelerator a little more. You step it up when you see kids."

Zermeno placed the smaller child in a position where his airway was open. He didn't have oxygen, so he simply moved from patient to patient, checking pulses and respiratory rates. He also checked their capillary refill rates, pushing on fingernail beds or earlobes to see how quickly blood returned to the tissue. Less than a two-second delay was good, more was bad. This would tell the corpsman if their tissues were still exchanging oxygen for carbon dioxide, though there wasn't much he could do about it without an oxygen tank. The smallest child's capillary refill rate was bad.

The convoy was moving fast, but as Zermeno worked, it seemed like it was moving too slowly for his patients. The top was unarmored, but the sides of the seven tons were covered with thick metal that would protect the occupants from small-arms fire. More worrisome was the fact that the route through the city was routinely studded with improvised explosive devices. The corpsman didn't spend time worrying about it. He had a lot of faith in the units from 1/24's Weapons Company that patrolled the roads. Zermeno figured that if his superiors had gotten the word out that a convoy was headed to Fallujah Surgical, there was a good chance that the Marines were staged along the road to get them through in a hurry. This didn't change the fact that the insurgents had a lot of success planting roadside bombs under the Americans' noses, and the convoy was traveling faster than usual as it rushed the patients to the hospital. With Marines carefully scanning for bombs, convoys from the upper peninsula typically took more than half an hour to get to Camp Fallujah, but on this night, the three medevac convoys would make it through the city in less than twenty minutes.[38] The Marines would sacrifice a bit of caution to give the patients a better shot at survival.

As Zermeno monitored the Iraqis, the older woman in the front of the truck bed, by the bulkhead, had started going downhill. She had immense difficulty breathing and would clearly soon require rescue breaths, pure oxygen, or intubation. Shortly after he checked on her, he saw that the six-year-old boy's breathing had slowed to the point that it was "going to stop any second now." Zermeno immediately started giving the child breaths, forming a seal over the boy's mouth with his own and breathing into his small lungs. Every five seconds or so, he supplied another breath, watching the boy's chest rise and fall. The corpsman soon checked on the nearby eighteen-month-old and saw that the toddler had also stopped breathing. Zermeno moved to the smaller child and began breathing for him as well. After a bit, he moved back to the six-year-old and applied breaths.

The corpsman was forced to make a difficult decision. The elderly woman at the front of the truck was deteriorating. "Her respiratory rate was less than ten" breaths per minute, which is "bad for an adult, but not as critical" as it is for children. He couldn't maintain the airways of three patients. At least two other patients lying on the two benches in the middle of the truck bed were coughing and gasping for air, but they were conscious and breathing on their own. Zermeno decided to focus on the two small children, and moved them side-by-side near the truck's tailgate. He was certain the elderly patient was going to stop breathing before the convoy arrived at Fallujah Surgical. He assumed he would have to "let . . . the old lady die." It was a quick, coldly professional calculus. "It's two for one. I can save these two but I can't save all three," he surmised. "I'm going to work on the kids."

Thankfully, both children still had a pulse. As he gave them breaths, he wondered how much good it was doing. The corpsman had sucked in a lot of chlorine by that point, and he wondered how much of the poison gas versus oxygen he was delivering into their lungs. He worried he was exchanging bad air for bad air. After a few minutes of switching back and forth between the kids, the older child started breathing again on his own. The boy's respiration remained slow and shallow, but "it was enough to sustain life." Zermeno returned to the eighteen-month-old and kept breathing for him for the remainder of the trip to Fallujah Surgical.

When the convoy arrived, Zermeno picked up the toddler, jumped down from the truck, and handed the child off to a chief hospital corpsman at the emergency entrance while quickly briefing him. He helped unload the six-year-old next, followed by the rest of the patients. He quickly assessed the stricken elderly woman when he finally made it to the front of the truck bed. She didn't seem to be breathing, and he couldn't find a pulse.[39]

———————— ❖ ————————

Back at FOB Black, the initial burst of furious activity calmed quickly to a waiting game. Over the span of about three hours, the majority of less seriously injured patients quietly sat and improved with fresh air, water, and the removal of chlorine-saturated clothing. The first Iraqis had arrived on the base at about 7:00 p.m., less than an hour after the chlorine bomb had exploded in their village, and the last wave of wounded—those with the mildest inhalation injuries—had arrived at approximately 9:30 p.m. Confident they would be OK, the Iraqis who had not been transported to Fallujah Surgical began to filter back to their vehicles or American trucks in the following two hours. The FOB had cleared of civilians by approximately midnight.[40]

Pickel reflected on the job his fellow Marines had done that night. He considered how quickly many of them had made the transition from aggressive "warfighters" who jawed about killing terrorists to "humanitarians" tending to injured locals, some of whom many thought had supported attacks on Marines. But along with most of the guys he spoke to, Pickel didn't give it a ton of thought. "Orders were orders, and somebody needs help, they need help," he later summarized.

As the emergency seemed to pass, random Iraqi men stopped and shook his hand or hugged him, while repeating "Shukran!" (Thank you). At one point, a middle-aged woman patted his shoulder and said "Shukran" as he administered oxygen to a child.

"Afwan" (You're welcome), he replied.

"If they didn't know we were trying to help them before [that event], they definitely knew after," Pickel reflected a little more than two years later. Many others, including some of the Iraqis, agreed.[41]

Sheikh Shalaan settled on two lessons from the evening: The bond between his tribe and their new American allies had solidified, along with their resolve to exterminate al Qaeda on the peninsula.

According to the sheikh, "Major Dan" [Whisnant] had come to Fallujah during one of the toughest and most violent periods of the war to offer his help. The American quickly fulfilled his promise with guns, licenses, and financial support for the tribal militia and by stationing his Marines near the village as guards. Helping the wounded men, women, and children after the chlorine bomb was more proof that the American was "a man of honor." In late 2009, Shalaan asserted that the young people of Albu Aifan still knew of "Major Dan from 2006 or 2007."

People of his tribe were "crying, they were pretty amazed" by the way the Marines rushed to their aid and brought them into their home for treatment. Word of the Americans' help and of al Qaeda's depravity rapidly spread to the other subtribes. The assistance rendered by Alpha Company finally elbowed its way into local lore along with the crowded field of unflattering stories about Marines.[42]

According to Shalaan, the impact was significant: "People's opinions started changing," and in addition to members of his subtribe, even many of those who lived within the city of Fallujah reevaluated some of their basic assumptions about the occupiers. Those who continually griped about "Americans being worthless" or "hating Iraqis" were told of how "they helped us." Some Fallujans even began to warily suspect that the current rotation of Americans might be *zien* (good) or at least not entirely *muzien* (bad).

In contrast, al Qaeda further condemned itself to pariah status with the desperate bombing.[43] Members of subtribes that had been on the fence about joining the Awakening and fighting the *takfiris* and *irhabiyin* were spurred into action by the utter viciousness of a chemical attack on civilians. Like dominos, leaders and members of other subtribes began to fall in line against the Fallujans and foreign terrorists who made up al Qaeda and the panoply of Islamist groups that comprised the shadow Islamic State of Iraq. Increasing numbers of subtribes began contributing militias and recruits to the area's police force.

Dark's campaign against his enemies had been energized with new informants and allies, but this came with a steep and tragically familiar price. The morning of the chlorine attack, Turkiyah, Dark's mother—who was also Sheikh Shalaan's mother-in-law—had refused evacuation and had died. The following day, insurgents attacked her funeral with mortars, killing Dark's sister. Sheikh Shalaan said he suffered minor shrapnel wounds.[44]

In the immediate aftermath of the chlorine bomb, ninety-five Iraqis had been welcomed onto FOB Black for treatment. Ten seriously ill patients had been medevaced to Fallujah Surgical in three convoys. Seven of the ten—including five children—were subsequently transported to a hospital in Baghdad to receive more advanced care. Of the seven, three of the youngest patients died after a few days on ventilator support: an adolescent, a three-year-old girl, and the eighteen-month-old boy Zermeno had tried to save in the back of the seven-ton truck.[45]

The day after the attack, Taylor asked Dark what had become of the suicide bomber. The sheikh replied that "He is feeding the dogs."[46] The Iraqi was speaking literally: some of his men had gathered the attacker's meager remains—a hand, a foot, a section of the man's jaw, and some bones. In lieu of a traditional Muslim burial, Dark said he gave most of it to some dogs, but kept the man's teeth in a plastic container in one of his trucks. He claimed that every so often, he would have a one-way conversation with the bomber's ghost in front of his passengers: "How are things? Look at you now."[47]

❖ ENDGAME ❖

The chemical attack against Albu Aifan civilians represented the beginning of the end of widespread insurgency around Fallujah. March 2007 marked the peak of overall attacks in Area of Operations (AO) Raleigh; by August, they had dropped by 86 percent.[1] Nevertheless, al Qaeda–affiliated insurgents executed more than a dozen poison gas attacks—a flurry of them between late January and June 2007—primarily in Anbar but also in Baghdad and Diyala province. A second chlorine bomb was detonated on the southern edge of Fallujah's peninsula on the evening of March 16, near a housing complex in Ameriyah, and another one was deployed against the Iraqi police and Iraqi Army based in the Fallujah Government Center on March 28.[2]

The tactic and targets underscored the *takfiris'* desperation. In lieu of specifically going after Americans, the insurgents now focused particularly vicious, spectacular attacks on Iraqis who had dared to defy them and ally with the occupiers. The reason was simple: The locals who stood against the insurgency were by far the biggest threat. The tribal militias and empowered Iraqi cops had begun waging their own brutal and effective war against al Qaeda and the other intransigent insurgent groups, and their natural network of informants finally enabled the Americans to focus their vaunted firepower with accuracy.[3]

Success by local security forces bred additional success. Acquiring local, reliable informants led to military and intelligence gains, which prefaced more local informants and more progress. Most Fallujans had long soured on the religious radicals and ruthless criminals terrorizing their communities, but dislike of the Americans, desire for money, and a climate of fear had kept most of them cooperative toward the extremists, or at the least quiescent. The reinvigoration of strong local leadership and the increased effectiveness of U.S. forces punctured the bubble of intimidation that gripped the area and made insurgency for hire expensive and risky. As fear subsided, the network of local spies assisting local security forces and the coalition grew rapidly. Targeting and detentions improved. Increasing numbers of insurgents were captured and convicted, or simply killed when they tried to resist. And local tribesmen and police continued their extrajudicial campaign against their insurgent enemies.[4] Thus the *takfiris'* bet on the depraved gambit of using chemical weapons to halt their downward spiral.

Chlorine gas wasn't the most effective weapon, but it was terrifying and certain to attract media attention. The latter had become difficult in a climate where bombings and assassinations were as routine as weather reports. It was a novel tactic in a wider, concerted assassination campaign against all of the sheikhs and Iraqi leaders in Anbar who openly opposed them or refused to swear fealty to the Islamic State of Iraq.[5] If the insurgents could make a sufficient splash and cow the sheikhs back into cooperation or exile, all that remained would be to wait out the loss of political will by the Americans and the eventual departure of their forces from Iraq. The tactic backfired. This time, the sheikhs had enough resolve and momentum to stand fast. This time, they gained new allies as more and more fed-up Fallujans sensed al Qaeda's weakness and stood up to oppose it. Average Iraqis finally had enough support from their leaders, backed by the Americans, to publicly reject the insurgents' religious radicalism and savagery. Enough was enough.[6]

The war, however, was far from over. There was still hard fighting to be done, and the Albu Issa sheikhs and their Fallujan and American allies were to endure more bombings, battles, kidnappings, and assassination attempts during the rest of 2007. Alpha Company 1/24 executed a large, moderately successful operation to capture detainees and obtain intelligence in the insurgent stronghold of Hasa before it left in April. Two pivotal battles would be fought by the Iraqis in 2007, with only combat support (reconnaissance, air coverage, and so on) from the Marines: an alliance of the Albu Issa militia and the Iraqi police clashed with insurgents in significant firefights one American intelligence official dubbed the First and Second Battles of Ameriyah.[7] Two close lieutenants of Sheikh Aifan Sadoun Aifan al-Issawi (Dark), including Uthman Majid Aifan al-Issawi, were maimed in a roadside bomb attack on May 5, 2007.[8] Dark himself escaped numerous attempts on his life over the next few years.[9] Insurgents attempted to kill

Khamis Hasnawi Aifan al-Issawi, the paramount sheikh, with a roadside bomb that exploded in the midst of his motorcade as late as 2009.[10] Sheikh Abdul Sattar Abu Risha—Dark's compatriot, competitor, role model, and the man often lionized as the leader of Anbar's tribal Awakening—was assassinated by an improvised explosive device outside his compound near Ramadi on September 13, 2007.

Besides al Qaeda, there were other insurgent and political groups on the confusing landscape of Iraq's insurgency that had held their fire against the tribes or actively turned on the Islamic State of Iraq, but would later seek revenge on the tribesmen. Some religious supremacists who had competed with al Qaeda after refusing to swear fealty to its shadow government would also never forgive Awakening forces for daring to work with the infidel Americans, even in the face of the mutual, existential threat from AQI. A desire for vengeance by the enemies of the Albu Issa sheikhs still smoldered, and more Iraqis and Americans would be seriously injured or pay the ultimate price as Fallujah's insurgency gasped for relevance.

Nonetheless, a decline in violence had begun, and most of the remaining religious and tribal civil war was fought with good intelligence and in the dead of night. Kidnappings, extrajudicial killings, negotiated surrenders, peaceful detentions, and the eventual flight of insurgents characterized the struggle's twilight.[11] Insurgencies don't die in a climactic battle. They diminish, but rage on for years as a series of small brush fires, each snuffed out by security forces who have won the cooperation of the people.

Many insurgents, especially those from the peninsula's southern subtribes and villages, attempted to make peace with tribal leaders. Most of them claimed that they had been intimidated by the foreign radicals, although some had fought the Albu Issa's traditionally powerful sheikhs to gain money or status. The tribe reconciled with a portion of these individuals, allowing them to rejoin the tribal order; the leading sheikhs of the Albu Issa had had informants operating throughout most of the peninsula during the height of the war, and therefore believed they had a good idea of who acted in bad faith. Those with too much blood on their hands were denied reconciliation and killed or imprisoned.[12]

No longer able to hide in plain sight, many die-hard insurgents, especially the foreign *takfiris* and well-known Iraqi leaders incapable of rapprochement with the tribal hierarchy, fled to areas north and east of the city of Fallujah.[13] Dark, Sheikh Shalaan (Mishael Abdullah Owdeh), Sheikh Taleb Hasnawi, and other tribal leaders told the Marines that the insurgents had been forced to "sleep in the fields" after losing their safe havens among the populace.[14]

As the tribal militia gained strength on the peninsula, so did the security forces of the Iraqi government. Some tribesmen were merged into the Iraqi police, while others morphed into "provincial security forces," a paramilitary militia that allowed the tribesmen to maintain some autonomy while becoming an official component of the government. Local Iraqi Army units improved with the infusion of new leadership and the support of American trainers; they were eventually moved out of the city in September 2007 to provide security in rural hotspots surrounding Fallujah. The most effective force in the city, and arguably the broader district of Fallujah, was the Iraqi police. Spurred by the January 2007 arrival of an energetic, highly competent district police chief, Colonel Faisal Ismail Hussein al-Zobaie, the force began its own effective campaign to rid the City of Mosques of the *irhabiyin*.

The U.S. Marines and Iraqi cops and soldiers launched Operation Alljah, an urban counterinsurgency campaign, on May 29, 2007. Neighborhood by neighborhood, they set up new police precincts, established vehicle checkpoints, recruited security volunteers and day laborers, and began aggressive reconstruction projects in newly secured areas. The softer side of the COIN effort caused some Marines to joke that "Alljah" was "Fallujah" without any of the "F U" ("fuck you"). The operation, based on a similar campaign successfully executed in Ramadi, pushed the insurgents back on their heels. Their staging areas on the peninsula as well as in the city were under siege, and they had lost the freedom of movement required for a commuter insurgency. Such efforts incrementally choked their rebellion from Fallujah.[15]

Many of the hard-core fighters fled north, around the towns of Saqlawiyah and Karma, but were then driven from there by Iraqi soldiers, cops, Marines, and Awakening forces from tribes in those areas.[16] During 2007 and 2008, the insurgency splintered further as former allies of al Qaeda denounced them. Asaeb al-Iraq al-Jihadiya (Iraqi Jihad Union) was a mainstream Sunni insurgent cell that "claimed at least seven joint operations in conjunction with fighters from Al-Qaida's 'Islamic State of Iraq' between April and July 2007," according to journalist Evan Kohlmann.[17] In October, however, the group had issued a statement denouncing their former allies for killing its fighters, desecrating bodies, and murdering women and children.

Hamas al-Iraq also denounced al Qaeda in October. Iraqi Hamas had splintered from the nationalistic 1920 Revolution Brigades, perhaps the most significant insurgent group comprised of former Sunni military officers, because some of the group's leaders had dared to work with the Americans. Even these die-hard, religious-nationalist insurgents came to recognize the depravity of a greater enemy, however. Their public denouncement of al Qaeda was quoted at length by Kohlmann at the time:

> Every day they witnessed heads or headless bodies lying in their streets. Each one of these victims had been accused of a so-called "crime" prohibited by al Qaida fatwahs . . . then [Al Qaida] attacked Ameriyyat [al-Fallujah] with a car bomb packed with chlorine gas canisters, and they even laid siege to the area to prevent food and fuel from getting to people. Finally, they killed several men at the local market and smashed their heads against boxes of food. . . . We [have] witnessed dozens of beheaded bodies and none of them were Americans. Rather, they were all local people from the area—people who, at one point, had supported the Al Qaida network until they themselves had become disposable.

Kohlmann continued, "In fact, according to Hamas in Iraq—as a result of the various crimes al Qaida has committed against innocent Muslim civilians—'the al Qaida network has actually made people here think that the occupation forces are merciful and humane by comparison.'"[18]

Never a cohesive entity, the Sunni insurgency broke into warring factions as nationalist and less radical Islamist elements shunned the *takfiris* because of their unpopular brutality. Many former insurgents, finally convinced that the occupiers would eventually leave without stealing Iraq's resources, even accepted the idea of working with the Americans, while others merely held their fire temporarily or reduced attacks as they dealt with the bigger threat.[19]

By 2008, much of al Qaeda had wound up on the edge of the desert or the northern Iraqi city of Mosul, where remnants of the organization rebranded themselves and fight Iraqi security forces to this day.[20] As of 2012, some analysts argued that the radical Sunni insurgent group is diminished but is regaining strength, and it still executes bombings designed to undermine the Shia-dominated central Iraqi government.[21] On July 23, 2012, the

Islamic State of Iraq claimed credit for "coordinated attacks in six of Iraq's 18 provinces that killed more than one hundred Iraqis and wounded hundreds more."[22] In another high-profile attack, more than ninety al Qaeda fighters dressed as Iraqi police commandoes killed twenty-seven policemen, including two commanders, in a raid in Haditha on March 5, 2012.[23] AQI has also attempted to take advantage of unrest in several other countries, establishing influential cells in places of political upheaval, including Libya and Syria.

Despite the organization's attempt to make a comeback in Iraq, its brand name has been significantly tarnished; as in the United States, to many Iraqis, the name "al Qaeda" has become an epithet that serves as shorthand for "terrorist."[24] In counterinsurgency terms, this unpopularity signifies that the group will likely never regain its stranglehold on Anbar province, ending the 2006 Salafist-jihadist dream of establishing and exporting an Islamic caliphate from Fallujah or Ramadi.

"Mullah" Fallah Hamadi, al Qaeda's onetime "emir" for Fallujah's peninsula, was finally caught in the nearby city of Abu Ghraib in late 2011. After Dark was informed of the arrest, he visited his enemy in custody to interrogate him. The sheikh asked the *takfiri* about his attacks on civilians, including the chlorine gas bombs. "Why do you kill? Why do you do this?" According to Sheikh Aifan, Fallah expressed no remorse for his actions. He simply looked at the sheikh and said, "I do what I should do."[25]

Alpha Company 1/24 left the Fallujah peninsula on April 18, 2007. In the weeks before their departure, Maj. Dan Whisnant's Marines kept busy maintaining pressure against the insurgency and smoothing the transition to their replacements: Kilo Company of the 3rd Battalion, 6th Marine Regiment.

Inconsistent strategy caused by unit turnover often impaired the U.S. war effort. New officers sometimes arrived in Iraq with their own rigid, preconceived notions about how things needed to be done. Others had the right idea, but inherited a poorly run area of operations. If key personnel didn't "get" counterinsurgency or the local political dynamics, they could unravel hard-fought gains made by units with leaders who did "get it." Mass detentions, disrespect, and a spate of tragic friendly-fire incidents could hinder the burgeoning tribal alliance, or get in the way of the tribe's war against the insurgents. And if the Americans pulled back to their bases again, instead of projecting into the population and cutting off the insurgents' freedom of movement, the war could shift against them.

Whisnant and CWO-5 Jim Roussell weren't particularly worried as they departed Fallujah. The momentum of the Americans and their allies was strong, the young commander of Kilo 3/6 seemed competent, and the leader of U.S. Forces in AO Raleigh "got it." Col. Richard Simcock of Regimental Combat Team (RCT) 6 had rotated into theater at the end of 2006. He had allowed Whisnant remarkable latitude as the Reservist major forged the alliance with Dark and Khamis and had provided essential support. Simcock's rotation with the RCT would last until the end of 2007, and he would likely enable strategic and tactical consistency from the Marines and soldiers who followed.[26] Whisnant stressed one overriding goal to his replacement, the young commander of Kilo 3/6: "Keep Dark and Khamis alive," he said. "They have the answers. It's up to them. Now that they have confidence, build on that."[27]

In addition, the counterinsurgency methodology that certain U.S. Army and Marine commanders had selectively employed in Anbar and other pockets of the country had gained crucial endorsement from the U.S. political and military leadership. President George W. Bush had handed Gen. David Petraeus the keys to the campaign in Iraq, and the officer's recently published summation of counterinsurgency doctrine emerged as the official strategy of the U.S. effort. The application of COIN thus became much more consistent.

"Bottom up" political progress exemplified by tribal engagement in Anbar was met by "top down" counterinsurgency endorsement from the brass, marked by a fresh influx of troops as the first of the "surge" units arrived over the summer. On the peninsula, Whisnant's lone company was effectively replaced by three companies, while a U.S. Army battalion took over the region just south of the AO. The tribal militias would enjoy immense U.S. firepower at their backs as they squeezed al Qaeda from their area. Former secretary of defense Donald Rumsfeld's "light footprint" doctrine was well and truly dead, and Roussell was happy to be done with it.[28] This second time, he and Whisnant exited their Iraq tours with confidence. Things were in good hands and rapidly moving in the right direction.[29]

Whisnant marveled at what his men had accomplished. The reserve unit had set foot on the peninsula with the goals of improving security and beating an insurgency during the most violent period of the conflict, in a war and a province some analysts deemed all but lost.[30] His group of young Reservists, primarily from the Midwest and several southern states, had accomplished the first task, and the second now seemed possible. Above all, Whisnant was proud of how they'd improved the lot of "ordinary Iraqis" who just wanted to move forward with lives free of privation, terrorism, and war.

The company that had preceded Alpha 1/24 had left the peninsula without losing any men. In contrast, five of Whisnant's Marines had been killed and more than thirty injured, for a casualty rate nearing 15 percent. It was a bitter pill to swallow, but their impact on the area gave the major reassurance about his decisions. He believed that he could look the parents of the fallen in their eyes and tell them that their sons had died making a difference.

"The history of al-Anbar will include the sacrifice of Alpha 1/24," Whisnant reflected three years later. "These men will be able to tell their grandkids what they accomplished. We made people's lives safer and more secure. We gave them hope. I could not have asked for better Marines."[31]

———— ❖ ————

Dark told his "brother," "Major Dan," and his respected "father," Roussell, that he didn't want them to leave. These Americans had worked with Fallujans better than many of the commanders who had preceded them, and the young sheikh preferred not to start over with new Marines.[32] Besides, he and the other tribal leaders were a little wary of the forty-two-year-old Whisnant's replacement. The commander of Kilo Company was only a captain, and he had a boyish, clean-shaven face. Iraqis respect rank and age and conflate the latter with wisdom. The young officer would be starting from a deficit as he tried to win the tribesmen's respect.

With the support and acquiescence of the Americans, Dark and other tribal leaders effectively won back the peninsula from their enemies. Dark's ambition paid off. Much like his ill-fated mentor, Sheikh Sattar, Sheikh Aifan's name now rang out in Anbar as one of the men who had stood against al Qaeda in the darkest days of the war. For all of 2007, he ran the Albu Aifan militia and established himself as a prominent leader of the tribe and a member of Anbar's Sahwa (Awakening) movement.

The Americans believed that Khamis had agreed to let Dark form and lead the militia because of his nephew's enthusiasm, expendability if the effort failed, and rare English-speaking ability. Dark's responsibilities in turn increased his stature and gave him the inside track on U.S. contracts and other business opportunities, which benefited him and, to a lesser extent, the tribe. Already rich by peninsula standards, his personal wealth grew even more from the culturally common skimming and kickbacks sheikhs receive from all tribal business ventures.[33] But according to Roussell, despite Dark's ambition and wealth, other sheikhs retained greater status within the tribe, including Sheikh Taleb and Sheikh Khaled Hasnawi, who maintained traditional roles as the primary arbiters of tribal authority.[34]

Allowing Dark to assume the immense personal risk of publicly waging war against the *takfiris* while they kept a lower profile was a cold, calculated move by some of the other leading sheikhs and an example of their prudence, according to some Americans. Now that the existential threat to the tribe's traditional hierarchy was gone, the old guard would attempt to reassert control. In the end, Dark was still too young, his birth order too inauspicious, and his temperament too hot-headed; despite his accomplishments, the ambitious upstart would not soon succeed Khamis as the tribe's paramount sheikh.[35]

The Americans became worried that the young sheikh would be assassinated by the enemies he had acquired in his fight against the insurgency.[36] To provide him with an escape option, Colonel Simcock presented Dark with a letter of recommendation for U.S. citizenship before the Marine left Iraq at the end of 2007. Though presented in dry military vernacular, Simcock's respect for the sheikh's contribution is tangible:

> Subject: Recommendation for Aifan Sadun Aifan al Issawi and family to become U.S. Citizens
>
> 1. Sheik Aifan Sadun Aifan's participation in Coalition Force (CF) combat operations against Al Qaida during 2007 directly benefitted the Marines and Soldiers under my command and resulted in significant success for my mission. Specifically, Sheik Aifan's leadership of his indigenous tribal security forces set an example for all of Fallujah that an Iraqi could successfully oppose Al Qaida. Sheik Aifan's actions came at a time when no other Iraqi outside of the security forces would openly side with CF to oppose Al Qaida. In this matter, Sheik Aifan was essential in creating momentum and

carrying a pro-CF message to the citizens of Fallujah that ultimately resulted in Al Qaida's defeat in the area.

2. Sheik Aifan accomplished these feats at great risk to his family and to his own life. Not only did Sheik Aifan bravely lead combat missions where he confronted the enemy in battle, he was, and is still, a target for assassination. There have been numerous attempts on Sheik Aifan's life during my 13 months in Iraq. During March, 2007, a suicide truck bomb packed with chlorine and nearly 2,000 lbs net explosive weight detonated at Sheik Aifan's compound. Sheik Aifan lost his mother in this attack and suffered the death of his sister in a subsequent attack. More recently, Sheik Aifan foiled two attempts on his life in October, 2007; the second of which resulted in the capture of two explosive laden Al Qaida suicide bombers sent to murder Sheik Aifan at a local mosque during Friday prayers.

3. Sheik Aifan has undoubtedly saved numerous lives of U.S. servicemen under my charge. For this reason, I believe that Sheik Aifan and his family will continue to be targeted by extremist elements. Due to Sheik Aifan's unparalleled contribution to CF's mission in Fallujah, I believe he and his family merit special consideration for U.S. citizenship or legal resident status.

R.L. Simcock II
Colonel, U.S. Marine Corps.
Commanding Officer[37]

Despite the recommendation, Dark stayed in Iraq. For one thing, he still had considerable business interests, and could continue to reap financial benefits from both his newfound political influence and his U.S. benefactors for years.[38] In an interview with American military researchers in February 2009, he offered additional reasons:

"This is my history, my life. My people, my tribe. I can't just leave. . . . We should be honest: life won't stop if I leave, but I have a thousand people who trust me. They follow me blindly. Leave Iraq now? It would be a black point in my history if I leave them. We have to be willing to participate more in the government—the government of Iraq and Anbar—because these people's rights are my responsibility. I should take care of them."[39]

Dark might not be the paramount sheikh, but two paths to prominence remained: businessman and politician in Iraq's brand new democratic experiment. He went after both with characteristic abandon. Shunning his nickname and "combat casual" ammunition harness for his proper name and a series of silk suits, Sheikh Aifan soon parlayed his wealth and reputation as one of the men who vanquished al Qaeda into a seat on Anbar's provincial council in elections held in 2009.[40] The charismatic sheikh then joined the political list led by the brother of the famously martyred Sheikh Sattar in a bid for Iraq's national parliament in 2010. He expressed cocksure confidence to the *New York Times*: "'I'll win, sure,' he said with a touch of humor. 'People like me, and god is with me.'"[41] In fact, he lost. But Sheikh Aifan eventually became a member of Iraq's national Council of Representatives in August 2011 after a parliamentarian was assassinated, and the sheikh (who had by then switched political parties) was appointed to replace him.[42]

Americans have a complicated opinion about Sheikh Aifan. U.S. military and intelligence personnel who worked with Dark view him as a salesman, a fighter, a leader, an entrepreneur, a killer, a comedian, a brigand, and most commonly and succinctly, "a real character." In an interview with an American journalist in 2009, one Marine compared the sheikh to a boss in the Italian Mafia. Despite aspects they regard as flaws, including a fierce temper and ethics alien to Western sensibilities, many considered him heroic.[43]

Roussell has complex feelings toward his former ally, whom he referred to as "a smart kid" after their first late night meeting. The old cop is aware of Aifan's shortcomings. He used to joke to his fellow Americans that "when they make a movie about Dark, only Johnny Depp can play him, because *he is the pirate king*." But despite cynicism honed by time in Fallujah and his civilian career in law enforcement, for Roussell, one telling memory of the young sheikh stands out: "When you cut through all the bravado and bullshit, he had loyalty to his tribe and wanted to protect his people," he said. "That kid has to have an ulcer. He was always pleading for assistance for his people—with us, with the Iraqi police. Every night, he made sure that his checkpoints were up and running. And then he'd wait for an attack. That's what I remember: Him sitting in a window of his house, a loaded AK and three radios in front of him, waiting and worrying about an attack on his tribe."[44]

On January 15, 2013, the sheikh's *hadn* (luck) ran out. A suicide bomber killed Aifan when he stopped to inspect a road construction site just outside of Fallujah. Almost immediately after he exited his vehicle, a man dressed as a worker approached the sheikh, hugged him, shouted "Allahu Akbar! (God is greatest!)," and detonated a vest packed with explosives. The blast killed Aifan, three of his bodyguards, and two civilians, and wounded at least four others. Five days later, al Qaeda's Islamic State of Iraq claimed responsibility for the assassination, labeling Aifan a "dog of the Americans" and crowing that he "join[ed] the sheikhs of the awakenings of shame [assassinated] before him." The sheikh's supporters eulogized him in posters as "the lion of Anbar," bidding "farewell to the vanquisher of terrorism." One mourner added that "Even in your death you exterminated one of [al Qaeda's] dogs," a reference to the suicide bomber killed in the blast.[45]

About a year prior to his death, Aifan had reflected on the constant threats to his life after embarking on a public battle with al Qaeda in 2006. "Every day when I woke up in the morning I thought, 'maybe I won't stay alive for the [whole] day.' A lot of people around me were killed, they lost their hands, their legs, because they fought. But we were fighting because . . . al Qaeda killed any good people, they made rules, they kidnapped people, they were [earning] money from kidnapping and killing. Because of this we fight, because of this we believe. And I am happy because we fight al Qaeda."[46]

❖

Most of the young Marines of Alpha Company 1/24 and 3/24 were happy to be heading home. A few men—like Sgt. Jeremiah Howe—had mixed feelings. Howe would have liked to have seen the job finished. It had been exciting to witness their slow, painstaking intelligence work suddenly and dramatically paying off. Like his boss had predicted, the sergeant was becoming an expert on the peninsula just as he had to leave it. He'd have to have faith that his replacements would be quick learners who wouldn't squander the groundwork laid by his unit.[47]

Many other Marines were mentally and physically exhausted, and simply glad to have a break after a brutal six-plus months. They were sick of the endless missions, sick of the omnipresent danger and stress, sick of an alien culture, and sick of walking up and down the peninsula. In comparison to Fallujah, America seemed like a fantastical paradise of luxury and security. They were going home, and home was wonderful.

With hindsight, the Americans believed that they accomplished something significant in Fallujah. Although everyone could see a dramatic difference in the peninsula by the end of the deployment, many weren't so sure that the changes would stick. The war was a frustrating slog that easily bred cynicism about Iraqis and their country's future. But as reports of improved security continued to filter back to the States for months, a year, and then two years, many of the Marines became confident of their contribution.[48]

LCpl. Corey Steimel, a machine gunner with Weapons Platoon, resumed his education after returning home. He ran into a number of other Iraq War veterans while attending classes at Michigan State University, including some who had been Marines and had preceded him on one or multiple tours of Anbar province. Many of these men expressed doubt and frustration about their time in the area, and felt that the war was a wasted effort. "That place [Iraq] is fucked," was a common assessment. Steimel would argue that things around Fallujah had turned out a little better. He believed that their service wasn't in vain and assured them that he'd seen things change with his own eyes. Steimel attributes the improvement to hard work and great leadership, and feels fortunate to have had the opportunity to serve at a time and place where he believes he made a difference.[49]

Steimel's fellow Marines are almost all proud of their time in Fallujah, and many have come to forgive, understand, or unabashedly admire the platoon commanders who pushed them to their limits. Many of the enlisted Marines regard 1st Lt. Jerome Greco and Capt. Jeremy Hoffmann as the best platoon leaders they had in their careers. Despite working his men hard, Greco maintained much of this popularity during the deployment. The mercilessly hard-charging Hoffmann garnered more mixed reviews during his tenure as Weapons Platoon leader, but many of his men years later say they now understand and admire him for pushing them.

One officer who was and remains nearly immune to criticism is Whisnant. For the military, this is rare. It's almost inevitable that enlisted men can find something bad to say about an officer, whether offered seriously or in jest, but the men who served under Whisnant in Fallujah have great affection for their commanding officer. He is respected and almost idolized as a company commander. Many say that they didn't understand some of the things he had them do at the time—most notably arming Iraqi tribesmen—but they trusted him.[50]

"Oh, my goodness, he is the best officer I've ever worked with," recalled Luke Reames, a lance corporal at the time. "If he ever needs me to do anything, if I could ever help him out throughout the entire rest of my life, I'd do it. If he went [to war] again and wanted me to go with him, I'd join him in a heartbeat." Reames' and LCpl. Guadalupe Ponce's assessment of their commander and their mission were typical: "He's very smart," said Ponce. "Whisnant knew how to get the most from his men. He wasn't soft, but he was approachable, and took the time to talk to you, to explain things to you. You could tell he cared about us. He was a great CO."[51]

Upon arriving in Iraq, Ponce felt a lot of sympathy for Fallujans plagued by shocking violence and intimidation. "The poorest people in America have it a thousand times better than most of the people in Iraq, with what they had to deal with," he explained. "I was just a college kid, and the whole situation was mired in politics. Maybe the reasons weren't 100 percent clear why we were there. But it was clear they needed our help." His idealism was quickly challenged. Frustration set in as U.S. attempts to help were rebuffed by uncooperative and seemingly apathetic locals. "I couldn't believe how they lived, what their attitude was. Bombs would go off, and they would just shrug. It was like they didn't care, like they were sleepwalking through life. But in the end, I learned that we just needed to finally convince them that we were going to be there for the duration, that we were in it to win it."[52]

Ponce's assessment was eerily echoed by a volunteer for the city of Fallujah's neighborhood watch in September of 2007: "Before, we had the terrorists; they controlled the city, so they had the power to do what they wanted to do. But you can say we woke up right now, we were asleep. We woke up to move the bad guy, to push him out, to kill him or to put him in jail. We were waiting for help from the government."[53]

"Now we start to know what is right and what is wrong," said another Iraqi recruit at the time. "The picture is so clear now. When things started and the [initial U.S.] invasion came to Fallujah, we said, 'It's OK for civilians to . . . fight the invasion and throw [the Americans] out from Fallujah.' We said, 'OK, they are the enemy and that's our friend.' But things were confused, and the enemy has become the friend and the friend became the enemy."[54]

Ponce's idealism and the bravery of the Iraqi security volunteers were rewarded with improved security. "They needed to know that someone was really there to help," Ponce summarized. "When you give them that glimmer of hope, that someone is really here to work with you, people will stand side-by-side with you against the bad guys."[55]

As Ponce and many Americans and Iraqis who fought in Anbar province know, the truth is more complicated. An effective U.S.-Iraqi alliance and an improvement in security only happened after tragic missteps and miscommunication by Americans and Iraqis, and the bloody rise of a more dangerous, common enemy. Years later, some Fallujans have kind words for their U.S. allies after fighting side-by-side with them in 2006 and 2007, whereas others will always view the Americans as hated occupiers who unleashed a horrific spasm of violence on their country. About 3,000 Fallujans—out of a city of several hundred thousand—celebrated with a parade on the day the U.S. military left Iraq.[56] Whatever the circumstances, in the war's darkest days of 2006 and 2007, the young lance corporal's assessment was accurate. Iraqis stood up to take back their home from radical insurgents, and the Americans supported them. Fallujah awakened.

❖ AFTERWORD: A NOTE ON COIN ❖

Counterinsurgency doctrine has gone through some dramatic ups and downs over the past decade. Though some U.S. military commanders (including those mentioned in this book) had studied historical examples of counterinsurgency and selectively applied lessons from them in Iraq, the doctrine was not a widespread strategy before the arrival of David Petraeus as commanding general of coalition forces on February 10, 2007. Following Iraq's rapid improvement in security thereafter, COIN became both fashionable and a professional imperative. The U.S. military reoriented itself toward the doctrine as a means of maintaining progress in Iraq and redoubling its efforts in Afghanistan, accompanied by a 2009 "surge" of forces in the latter country. COIN's newfound popularity also inspired a backlash among some active duty military officers, analysts, and pundits, and their criticisms gained steam after the strategy failed to generate quick results in Afghanistan as it had in Iraq.

Both COIN's detractors and proponents have valid points. Many critics of the military's counterinsurgency focus are correct in the assertion that the doctrine is not a one-size-fits-all template for success. The conditions that enabled rapid gains in Iraq—such as relative tribal and geographic homogeneity, a more centralized population, strong nationalism, and a widely hated common enemy in the form of al Qaeda—were not as prevalent in Afghanistan. In addition, some doubters argue that the Western media's popular narrative of Petraeus and his advisors rescuing Iraq with a novel strategy was overplayed. These criticisms have merit. Local political conditions, many of them beyond U.S. control, were responsible for much of the rapid security progress seen in Iraq during 2007–2008.

Critics of COIN go too far, however, when they diminish the impact of the 2007 "surge" in Iraq and the strategy that accompanied it. The conditions for rapidly improving security may have been specific to Iraq, but they were critically supported by the U.S. military's implementation of essential components of the doctrine. Most pivotal was a reengagement by U.S. forces, which projected into the population, incrementally choked off the insurgents' freedom of movement, supported local security forces, and protected civilians. I saw it work. Of more significance, the doctrine was lauded to me by average Fallujans not ordinarily inclined to praise the Americans. Security volunteers, politicians, and day laborers alike matter-of-factly credited the effectiveness of Iraqi cops and U.S. Marines, and the civil affairs engagement of the latter, with turning around local opinion and security in their area.

Counterinsurgency doctrine does not produce miracles. Well-executed in most political environments, it is a methodology that can take years and years to yield tangible gains. But COIN made a rapid difference in Iraq, for a number of reasons. And understanding its potential and limitations will have further value if the United States finds itself embroiled in another complex fight against an insurgency.

❖ A NOTE ON RESEARCH METHODOLOGY ❖

This book tells a true story. The narrative of the events described here is based on interviews with the Americans and Iraqis who were present at them. Many of the recollections of interviewees are influenced by personal bias, time—many interviews took place between two and five years after the events occurred—and the confusion of combat. To maintain the narrative feel of the book, I have included a number of quotes. Since there were no recorders present at everyday conversations between participants, my standard was to present short quotes if they were based on a confident recollection by an interviewee. Otherwise, quotes are sometimes presented as paraphrased sentiments, and I have noted these occurrences as such.

To re-create the narrative, I typically interviewed a minimum of three people involved in or present at a given event, though usually more. When I could not verify descriptions of some of the dramatic and heroic actions and events told to me, I usually chose to omit them. Key portions of the narrative required corroboration by multiple interviewees, but this was not possible for certain, individually witnessed anecdotes. In those cases, I made a judgment call as to whether I believed the anecdote to be well recollected, self-serving, exaggerated, or dishonest. I excluded those that did not pass this litmus test. There were a small number of incidents extensively described in the book for which verification of details by multiple participants was not possible. The notable examples of this nature are based on testimony by Tha'er Khalid Aifan al-Issawi and Corpsman Tony Zermeno.

The relevant material based on Tha'er's interviews involves a small portion of chapter 5, where he describes Shafi Hamid Shafi approaching his checkpoint, and a longer excerpt recounting the explosion of a chlorine truck bomb at his checkpoint, in chapter 15. He was the only interview subject available to recount the specifics of these incidents. I chose to include these narratives because his presence at the checkpoints and credit given to him for shooting at the truck (in the second incident) were verified to me by three of his fellow tribesmen, and the nature of the automatic weapons fire that he described was verified independently by a U.S. Marine report. In addition, his demeanor during interviews was modest and seemed to lack exaggeration.

In chapter 16, certain specifics of Zermeno's testimony about treating children sickened by the chlorine bomb on March 16, 2007, were similarly impossible to verify. His presence as the corpsman on the last convoy transporting injured civilians to Camp Fallujah as well as that of the children, the final health status of the children, and Zermeno's general attempts to save them were, however, verified by multiple after-action documents and interviews with Marines and Navy medical personnel. Much like my interviews with Tha'er, Zermeno's testimony lacked the boastful elaboration occasionally noted in other interviews.

I granted anonymity to professionals in the intelligence community, Iraqi interviewees if those persons might suffer retribution for their actions or opinions, and Marines who offered off-the-record negative assessments of events or individuals. The latter condition was necessary, as some Americans were hesitant to publicly offer such observations, but it was imperative to include the negative aspects of the U.S. campaign as well as the positive ones. While I have attempted to show balance, I acknowledge that there are additional stories from both U.S. and Iraqi perspectives that would round out a truly holistic history of these events.

The ranks of individuals in the text of the book are listed as the ranks at the time. The list of interviewees in the endnotes includes updated ranks of individuals after their tour in Iraq where applicable and known. The names of Iraqis in the endnotes are alphabetized by first name, as is the Arabic convention.

I have attempted to reconcile discrepancies between versions of the same event presented to me by multiple interviewees. This is an inherent challenge in relaying combat incidents via the recollections of different people. In cases where I judged that it was impossible to reconcile accounts to a requisite degree of comfort, I chose not to include these portions of the narrative. Otherwise, I used my best judgment.

INTERVIEWEES

January and September 2007, Fallujah

Sergeant Richard Arias
Staff Sergeant Tylor Belshe
Major Jason Brezler
Captain Mark Cameron
Richard Crawford, civilian advisor to
  the Iraqi police
Major Eric Dominijanni
Captain Barry Edwards
Colonel Faisal Ismail Hussein
  al-Zobaie
Fallujan *mukhtar,* neighborhood
  leader
Fallujan neighborhood watch
  volunteer 1
Fallujan neighborhood watch
  volunteer 2
Fallujan neighborhood watch
  volunteer 3
Fallujan neighborhood watch
  volunteer 4
Fallujan police volunteer 1
Fallujan police volunteer 2
Fallujan police volunteer 3
Lieutenant Colonel Clayton Fischer
Major Theodore J. Folsome
Tom Gorman, civilian advisor to
  the Iraqi police
Jabbar, Iraqi soldier
Hospitalman Jared Jurgensmier
First Lieutenant Christopher Kim
Captain Lawton King

Major Adam Kubicki
Gunnery Sergeant Jason Lawson
"Leo," Fallujan interpreter for
  the U.S. Army
Major Brian Lippo
Captain Joseph Lizaragga
Sergeant Jonathan Malone
Jody Martinez, civilian advisor to
  the Iraqi police
Staff Sergeant Nicefero Mendoza
"Mohammed," Fallujan police
  officer
Mohaned F., Iraqi soldier
Mohaned N., Iraqi soldier
Chief Warrant Officer 2 Mauricio
  Piedrahita
Major Jeffrey Pool
Lieutenant Colonel Joel Poudrier
Captain Kyle Reid
"Sam," Iraqi interpreter for the
  Marines
Major Tad Scott
Major Pat Semon
Lieutenant Colonel Anthony
  Sermarini
Staff Sergeant Thomas Smith
Lieutenant Colonel J. T. Taylor
Chief Warrant Officer 4 Steve
  Townsley
Corpsman Josh Watson
Lance Corporal Chad Yeager

2008–2010, primarily via telephone or e-mail

First Lieutenant Alex Albrecht

Professor Amatzia Baram, Department of Middle Eastern History, University of Haifa

Gunnery Sergeant Matthew Barrera

Sergeant Major Ken Baum

Staff Sergeant Tylor Belshe

Corporal Robert Blevins

Major Jason Brezler

"C. J." Wadhah Sahib, Iraqi interpreter

Corporal Joshua Clayton

Hospitalman Brian Davis

Staff Sergeant Christopher Dockter

Sergeant Kendrick Doezema

Sergeant Ken Fall

Major William Ghilarducci

Captain Jerome Greco

Lieutenant Commander Eric Greitens

Professor Mary Habeck, associate professor of strategic studies, Johns Hopkins University

Major Jeremy Hoffmann

Gunnery Sergeant Jeremy Howe

Sergeant Matthew Hunt

Sergeant Caleb Inman

Sergeant Ronald Jansen

Sterling Jensen, American translator around Ramadi

Corporal Jared Kimmey

Sergeant David Kopera

Captain Matt Kralovec

First Sergeant Lee Kyle

Captain Robert Lehner

Sergeant Steven Levasseur

Major Brian Lippo

Sheikh Ma'an Khalid Aifan al-Issawi

Keith Mines, U.S. Foreign Service officer in Fallujah

Sheikh Mishael Abdullah Owdeh (Sheikh Shalaan)

Corpsman Ruben Muñoz

Gunnery Sergeant Dave Ogden

Sergeant Brandon Osborne

Corporal Trevor Pickel

Colonel John Pollock

Sergeant Guadalupe Ponce

Lieutenant Colonel Joel Poudrier

Bill Roggio, managing editor, *Long War Journal*

Chief Warrant Officer 5 Jim Roussell

Major Tad Scott

Lieutenant Colonel Anthony Sermarini

Lance Corporal Jeremy Shaffer

Corpsman Raymond Shirkey

Brigadier General Richard Simcock

Lance Corporal Corey Steimel

Staff Sergeant Matt Stout

Sheikh Tha'er Khalid Aifan al-Issawi

A U.S. intelligence official

Lieutenant Colonel Dan Whisnant

Lance Corporal Tyler Williams

Corporal Matthew Zofchak

Lieutenant Commander Andrew Zwolski

2012, primarily via telephone, e-mail, or Facebook

Master Sergeant Michael Abragan
Sheikh Ahmed Mishael Shalaan, son
of Sheikh Shalaan
Sheikh Aifan Sadoun Aifan al-Issawi
(Dark)
Sheikh Bassam "Ama'an" Mishael
Shalaan, son of Sheikh Shalaan
Lance Corporal Craig Bays
Corporal Michael Beemer
Sergeant Daniel Campbell
Second Lieutenant Kelly Carlson
Sergeant Joshua Robert de Bruin
Sergeant Gabe Foerster
Gunnery Sergeant Michael Gillitzer
Sergeant Matthew Hunt
Corporal Chris Jongsma
Thomas Joscelyn, senior editor,
Long War Journal, and senior
fellow, Foundation for Defense
of Democracies
Staff Sergeant Michael Moose
Corporal Eddie O'Connor

Omar Noori Daham Mohna,
Fallujan civilian
Corporal Ernan Paredes
Staff Sergeant Joshua Price
Corporal Dickie Prince
Corporal Edward Przybylski
Sergeant Luke Reames
"Saint One," military intelligence
Marine
Corporal Scott Serr
Kirk Sowell, Arabic-language
researcher and analyst of Iraqi
politics
Major Jodie Sweezey
Commander Edwin Taylor, M.D.
Sergeant Elijah Villanueva
Captain Bryan Welles
Lieutenant Colonel Dan Whisnant
Corporal Jessie Wortman
Corporal Joel Zavalavargas
Corpsman Tony Zermeno

❖ ACKNOWLEDGMENTS ❖

This book was made possible by the cooperation of more than 120 interviewees, including U.S. and Iraqi security personnel, tribesmen, intelligence personnel, and academics. I sincerely appreciate that these men and women gave of their time to be interviewed and that most of them were extraordinarily patient when I first asked for information and then when I verified (and re-verified) basic facts and my interpretation of events. All of the interviewees have my gratitude, and I hope that I've given their story the treatment it deserves. Reporters endeavor to maintain a sense of detachment from their subjects, but I couldn't help but develop immense respect for many of the brave Iraqis and Americans who risked life, limb, and sometimes even loved ones in choosing to do the right thing in war. To them, I say, thank you.

A few individuals warrant special acknowledgment for their assistance with the project. Lt. Col. Dan Whisnant was incredibly forthcoming and helpful in numerous interviews. He was also the key to initially obtaining the cooperation of the Marines who were attached to Alpha 1/24 during 2006–2007. He spent hours on the phone with me to ensure that the story of his Marines made it into print and took the leap of faith that I would attempt to tell their story ethically and honestly. I am honored by his trust.

Capt. Barry Edwards was instrumental in organizing my two trips to Fallujah in 2007 as well as providing crucial support when I began the research for this book. His jokes weren't half bad either. Frank Warner was the manuscript's first reviewer, offering encouragement that compelled me through the first draft. In addition to being a candid interview subject, "C. J." Wadhah Sahib was willing to field questions about Arabic translations and transliterations. Sterling Jensen assisted me in hiring a skilled Arabic interpreter and reviewed Iraqi linguistic concepts; he also shared invaluable insights from his experience as an interpreter and witness to the tribal Awakening in Ramadi. Joshua Clayton provided maps and statistics that helped bring Alpha 1/24's story to light. Jim Roussell, a retired Marine and Chicago cop, was especially informative, delivering fascinating lectures on the key concepts of counterinsurgency and how they were applied around Fallujah.

Maj. Tad Scott, Maj. Brian Lippo, Lt. Col. Joel Poudrier, and all of the personnel with the Fallujah Police and Military Transition Teams in 2007 provided extraordinarily open journalistic access and closely watched out for my safety when I was in the city.

My friend Marty Bielecki reviewed material and offered his unwavering support. My friend Daryl Lee gave helpful feedback on the book's graphics. Jonathan Schanzer at the Foundation for Defense of Democracies patiently walked me through the process of marketing a manuscript. Matt Dupee and Lisa Milord generously donated editing assistance that blew away my writer's block. At the Naval Institute Press, Adam Kane, senior editor and electronic publications manager, made additional revisions, in addition to giving me the opportunity to finally tell this story through a great publisher. Robin Surratt, my copy editor, made this a better book. Claire Noble patiently guided me through the marketing process. Emily Bakely diligently applied final changes to the material. Bill Roggio, my editor at the *Long War Journal*, provided advice, help with editing, and crucial encouragement. I am grateful for his friendship.

In closing, thanks to my family. Research for this book started with trips to Iraq in 2007, and the project began in earnest in March 2009. There were a lot of ups and downs during this process, and my family made sure that I never gave up on my goal. Thank you.

❖ NOTES ❖

Chapter 1. Dark

1. Author interview with Lt. Col. Dan Whisnant.
2. Author interviews with Whisnant, "Saint One" (a military intelligence operative; interviews conducted in confidentiality and the name withheld by mutual agreement), and SSgt. Christopher Dockter for general descriptive details; the latter often accompanied Whisnant on his meetings with local leaders at the house in Zuwiyah.
3. Author interview with Whisnant.
4. Author interviews with Saint One, Lt. Col. J. T. Taylor, and Whisnant.
5. Author interview with Whisnant; Lin Todd et al., *Iraq Tribal Study: Al-Anbar Governorate—The Albu Fahd Tribe, the Albu Mahal Tribe and the Albu Issa Tribe* (n.p.: Global Resources Group and Global Risk, 2006), 4-42–4-44, http://www.comw.org/warreport/ fulltext/0709todd.pdf; Gary W. Montgomery and Timothy S. McWilliams, eds., *Al Anbar Awakening*, vol. 2, *Iraqi Perspectives: From Insurgency to Counterinsurgency in Iraq, 2004–2008* (Quantico, VA: Marine Corps University, 2009), 87–89.
6. Author interviews with Whisnant, J. T. Taylor, Cpt. Lawton King, Sheikh Aifan Sadoun Aifan al-Issawi, Sheikh Mishael Abdullah Owdeh (Sheikh Shalaan); "Leo," interpreter; Colonel Faisal Ismail Hussein al-Zobaie, and others; Todd et al., *Iraqi Tribal Study*, 4-37. The Fallujans are famously tough, insular people. On my first trip to the region, King cited a travel guide to Iraq from about the 1940s that even then advised tourists in the region to steer clear of the area. A Marine intelligence officer remarked that "the first things Fallujans rebuilt after [the Second Battle of Fallujah] were the gated walls surrounding their own houses."
7. Author interview with Whisnant.
8. Todd et al., *Iraq Tribal Study*, 2-41–2-44; author interviews with J. T. Taylor and Whisnant.

9. Author interviews with Whisnant, J. T. Taylor, and Saint One; Khalid al Ansari and Ali Adeeb, "Most Tribes in Anbar Agree to Unite against Insurgents," *New York Times*, September 18, 2006; Bill Roggio, "The Anbar Tribes vs. al Qaeda, Continued," *Long War Journal*, November 22, 2006, http://www.longwarjournal.org/archives/2006/11/the_anbar_tribes_vs.php; Mark Kukis, "Turning Iraq's Tribes Against al Qaeda," *Time*, December 26, 2006.

10. Author interviews with Sheikh Ma'an Khalid Aifan al-Issawi, CWO-5 Jim Roussell, Saint One, J. T. Taylor, and Whisnant.

11. Montgomery and McWilliams, *Al Anbar Awakening*, 2:92; author interview with Sheikh Aifan.

12. Author interviews with Sheikh Aifan, Roussell, Saint One, J. T. Taylor, and Whisnant. Sheikh Aifan said that he had returned home to do the right thing for his people. Americans believed that this was a significant part of his motivation, but also that pragmatic sheikhs saw their influence evaporating during their exile and therefore felt compelled to return.

13. Montgomery and McWilliams, *Al Anbar Awakening*, 2:85, 98.

14. Author interviews with Saint One and Whisnant.

15. Author interviews with Sheikh Aifan, Tha'er Khalid Aifan al-Issawi, Ma'an Khalid Aifan al-Issawi, J. T. Taylor, and Whisnant; Todd et al., *Iraqi Tribal Study*, 4-42–4-44.

16. Todd et al., *Iraqi Tribal Study*, E-14.

17. Ibid., 4-42–4-44.

18. Author interviews with Whisnant and Roussell.

19. Author interviews with Saint One and Whisnant.

20. Author interview with Ma'an Khalid Aifan al-Issawi.

21. Author interviews with Ma'an Khalid Aifan al-Issawi and Sheikh Aifan.

22. Author interview with Ma'an Khalid Aifan al-Issawi.

23. Author interviews with Saint One and Whisnant.

24. Ibid.

25. Author interviews with Sheikh Aifan, Saint One, and Whisnant.

26. Author interviews with Saint One and Whisnant (quotes as remembered by Whisnant, sentiments verified by Saint One); "Report: Abu Sadoon 12 26 06" (intelligence document in the author's possession).

27. Author interview with Ma'an Khalid Aifan al-Issawi. His place in the tribe as a link between Sheikh Khamis Hasnawi Aifan al-Issawi and Sheikh Aifan was verified by Saint One, who said it was a factor that legitimized the younger sheikh in the Americans' estimate prior to this meeting.

28. Author interviews with Sheikh Aifan, Roussell, Saint One, J. T. Taylor, and Whisnant. To be clear, Sheikh Aifan has claimed business motivations were unimportant at the time and that security was the only priority. The Americans believe that business interests were definitely part of Aifan's thinking.

29. Todd et al., *Iraqi Tribal Study*, 2-41–2-42; Montgomery and McWilliams, *Al Anbar Awakening*, 2:97–99; "Report: Abu Sadoon, 12 26 06."

30. Author interview with Sheikh Aifan, Sheikh Shalaan, Whisnant, and Sterling Jensen, a translator for the U.S. Army in Ramadi. Jensen sat in on a meeting with Sheikh Aifan and Sheikh Sattar. Aifan asked Sattar if he could borrow some of his forces, and Sattar agreed on the condition that Aifan place the Albu Issa under the authority of his tribe. The request was a nonstarter, and Aifan demurred, as the Albu Issa was a historically more prominent tribe than the Abu Risha. Whisnant stated that Dark sought his own official license for his forces from the Iraqi government on a trip to Baghdad in March 2007 and also during several later meetings with Fallujah's chief of police.

31. Author interviews with Sheikh Aifan, Saint One, and Whisnant; Montgomery and McWilliams, *Al Anbar Awakening*, 2:97–99; "Report: Abu Sadoon, 12 26 06."

32. Quote as recalled by Whisnant in author interview.

33. Author interviews with Saint One and Whisnant.

Chapter 2. Chasing Shadows

1. Author interview with Whisnant.

2. Author interviews with more than one hundred Marines, including more than 50 with Alpha 1/24 and 3/24, during 2006–2012. An almost universal sentiment expressed by Marines is that they visited the recruiters of several branches of the military, but the Marines

stood out because of their reputation and the difficulty highlighted by the recruiters.

3. Author interviews with hundreds of Marines and U.S. Army soldiers and personal experience. During my first embed in Fallujah, some members of a U.S. Army Military Police unit marveled at how "good to go" and helpful the Marines were compared to Army units they worked with. One man stated his intent to sign up with the Marines as soon as his contract with the Army was finished. An Army infantryman in Afghanistan who had been booted from the Marines for disciplinary problems told several officers that he planned to try and rejoin them if possible, now that he was older and wiser and a Purple Heart recipient. He was adamant that the discipline was like "night and day." Having heard many anecdotes of this nature, and having been embedded with both Marine and Army units, I can say that while there are great Army units and bad Marine units, and vice versa, the average discipline and aggressiveness of Marines—typically because of their tighter culture and extensive training—are a bit stronger.

4. Author interviews with hundreds of Marines and Army soldiers and personal experience. As has been described in innumerable books on the military, many recruits are romantics, who perceive service as a way to achieve something noble and bigger than themselves. This romanticism doesn't always survive contact with the reality of military bureaucracy.

5. Author interviews with hundreds of Marines and Army soldiers and personal experience. During my second embed in Fallujah, active duty artillerymen, infantrymen, and the security element of a Police Transition Team (mentors to Iraqi Police) scoffed at the perceived lack of aggressiveness by their predecessors, who were dubbed "weekend warrior" Reservists. Also, see Evan Wright, *Generation Kill: Devil Dogs, Iceman, Captain America, and the New Face of American War,* Kindle ed. (New York: Putnam Penguin, 2008), location 5356–5435.

6. Author interviews with Capt. Jerome Greco, Maj. Jeremy Hoffmann, Capt. Robert Lehner, Roussell, Saint One.

7. "Playing three-dimensional chess" derives from a U.S. official describing the complexity of trying to stabilize Iraq: Anthony H. Cordesman, "The Tenuous Case for Strategic Patience in Iraq: A Trip Report,"

Center for Strategic and International Studies, Washington, D.C., August 6, 2007, 1; Charles Krulak, "The Three Block War: Fighting in Urban Areas," *Vital Speeches of the Day* 64, no. 5 (1997): 139–41; Charles Krulak, "The Strategic Corporal: Leadership in the Three Block War," *Marine Corps Gazette* 83, no. 1 (January 1999): 18–23; Walter A. Dorn and Michael Varey, "The Rise and Demise of the 'Three Block War,'" *Canadian Military Journal* 10, no. 1 (2009): 38–44.

8. *Counterinsurgency,* Field Manual 3–24, Marine Corps Warfighting Publication 3–33.5, Department of the Army, Department of the Navy, Washington, D.C., December 15, 2006; David Galula, *Counterinsurgency Warfare: Theory and Practice* (Westport, CT: Praeger Security International, 1964).

9. Author interviews with Greco, Hoffmann, 1st Sgt. Lee Kyle, Lehner, and Whisnant.

10. Author interviews with Sgt. Maj. Ken Baum, Cpl. Robert Blevins, Cpl. Josh Clayton, Maj. William Ghilarducci, GySgt. Jeremiah Howe, Kyle, Lehner, SSgt. Michael Moose, GySgt. Dave Ogden, and Whisnant.

11. Author interviews with Sgt. Kendrick Doezema, Sgt. Ken Fall, Ghilarducci, Howe, Kyle, Ogden, Cpl. Trevor Pickel, Whisnant, and HM2 Tony Zermeno.

12. These are paraphrased, typical interactions based on author interviews with 1st Lt. Alex Albrecht, LCpl. Craig Bays, Cpl. Michael Beemer, 2nd Lt. Kelly Carlson, Sgt. Daniel Campbell, Dockter, Sgt. Kendrick Doezema, Sgt. Gabe Foerster, Sgt. Caleb Inman, Sgt. Ronald Jansen, Cpl. Chris Jongsma, Cpl. Jared Kimmey, Sgt. David Kopera, Kyle, Sgt. Steven Levasseur, HM2 Ruben Muñoz, Cpl. Eddie O'Connor, Sgt. Brandon Osborne, Cpl. Ernan Paredes, Sgt. Guadalupe Ponce, Sgt. Luke Reames, "C. J." Wadhah Sahib, Cpl. Scott Serr, LCpl. Corey Steimel, Sgt. Elijah Villanueva, LCpl. Tyler Williams, Cpl. Matthew Zofchak.

13. Author interviews with Campbell, Dockter, Doezema, Greco, Howe, Inman, Kyle, Levasseur, Muñoz, O'Connor, Paredes, "C. J." Wadhah Sahib, Serr, Williams, Cpl. Joel Zavalavargas, and Zofchak.

14. Author interviews with Beemer, Carlson, Foerster, Hoffmann, Howe, Jansen, Jongsma, Kimmey, Kyle, Osborne, Ponce, Steimel, Villanueva.

15. Author interviews with Albrecht, Baum, Beemer, Blevins, Campbell, Carlson, Dockter, Doezema, Fall, Foerster, Ghilarducci, Howe, Inman, Jansen, Jongsma, Kimmey, Kopera, Kyle, Lehner, Levasseur, Moose, Muñoz, O'Connor, Ogden, Osborne, Paredes, Pickel, Ponce, "C. J." Wadhah Sahib, Serr, Steimel, Villanueva, Whisnant, Williams, Zermeno, and Zofchak.

16. Author interviews with Campbell, Dockter, Doezema, Levasseur, Paredes, "C. J." Wadhah Sahib, Williams, and Zofchak.

17. Author interview with Dockter; author used this metaphor in a 2007 blog post to describe an amusingly circular conversation between a Marine and a Fallujan police officer about keeping track of fuel supplies. Some Americans refer to frustrating attempts at communication as the "Iraqi runaround" or similar descriptions.

18. Author interviews with Dockter. The quotes are examples of paraphrased census questions as recalled by Dockter.

19. Author interviews with Dockter, Greco, and Webster.

20. Author interview with Dockter; quotes as recalled by Dockter.

21. Author interviews with Dockter, Ma'an Khalid Aifan al-Issawi, Sheikh Aifan Sadoun Aifan al-Issawi. These village leaders were adamant in interviews that locals who wanted to fight the insurgency could not have done so openly, lest they be mistaken for insurgents by Marines and shot or imprisoned for brandishing a weapon.

22. Lin Todd et al., *Iraq Tribal Study: Al-Anbar Governorate—The Albu Fahd Tribe, the Albu Mahal Tribe and the Albu Issa Tribe* (n.p.: Global Resources Group and Global Risk, 2006), 2-4–2-5, http://www.comw.org/warreport/fulltext/0709todd.pdf.

23. Author interviews with Maj. Jason Brezler, Greco, Hoffmann, Maj. Brian Lippo, Sheikh Aifan, Colonel Faisal Ismail Hussein al-Zobaie, "Mohammed" (a Fallujan police officer; interview conducted in confidentiality and the name withheld by mutual agreement), Sheikh Mishael Abdullah Owdeh (Sheikh Shalaan), "Sam" (an Iraqi interpreter working with the Marines; interview conducted in confidentiality and the name withheld by mutual agreement), Bill Roggio, managing editor of the *Long War Journal*, Roussell, Maj. Tad Scott, and Whisnant; "Report: Abu Sadoon 12 26 06" (intelligence document in the author's possession); Gary W. Montgomery and Timothy

S. McWilliams, eds., *Al Anbar Awakening,* vol. 2, *Iraqi Perspectives: From Insurgency to Counterinsurgency in Iraq, 2004–2008* (Quantico, VA: Marine Corps University, 2009), 89: Said Sheikh Aifan in this interview, "[T]he insurgents, if they had any suspicion that a guy had any relationship with the Americans, they cut off his head."

24. Kopera, among many other interviewees.

25. Author interviews with Greco, Jansen, SSgt. Joshua Price, Villanueva, Cpl. Jessie Wortman, and many others.

26. Author interviews with Clayton, Greco, Hoffmann, Howe, Lehner, and Whisnant.

27. Author interviews with Clayton, Greco, Hoffmann, Howe, and Whisnant.

28. William McCallister, "COIN and Irregular Warfare in a Tribal Society," 14–15, 48, *SWJ Blog,* February 4, 2008, http://smallwarsjournal.com/blog/coin-and-iw-in-a-tribal-society. In most of my interviews with Marines, they asserted that the majority of searches were professional, and this matches my much more limited experience accompanying U.S. military night raids. Some Marines were willing to candidly state, on condition of anonymity, that some Americans were unduly rough when they searched the home of a suspected detainee. Some individuals in small units broke things, made a mess, and were rude to the home's occupants.

29. Author interviews with Albrecht, Baum, Beemer, Blevins, Carlson, Campbell, Dockter, Doezema, Fall, Foerster, Ghilarducci, Howe, Inman, Jansen, Jongsma, Kimmey, Kopera, Kyle, Lehner, Levasseur, Moose, Muñoz, O'Connor, Ogden, Osborne, Paredes, Pickel, Ponce, "C.J." Wadhah Sahib, Serr, Steimel, Villanueva, Whisnant, Williams, Zermeno, and Zofchak.

30. Author interview with Greco; Map of IEDs Found, Map of IEDs Blown, Map of SIGACTS (internal Alpha Company 1/24 documents showing the number and location of each category during the deployment). SIGACTS (significant act) is typically defined as any contact with the enemy, such as small-arms fire (SAF), indirect fire (IDF, i.e., mortars), IEDs found or hit.

31. Author interview with Bays.

32. Author interviews with Bays, Levasseur, and Pickel.

33. Author interviews with Dockter, Doezema, Greco, Howe, Levasseur, Muñoz, Whisnant, Williams, and Zofchak.

34. Author interviews with Albrecht, Baum, Beemer, Blevins, Carlson, Campbell, Dockter, Doezema, Fall, Foerster, Ghilarducci, Howe, Inman, Jansen, Jongsma, Kimmey, Kopera, Kyle, Lehner, Levasseur, Moose, Muñoz, O'Connor, Ogden, Osborne, Paredes, Pickel, Ponce, "C. J." Wadhah Sahib, Serr, Steimel, Villanueva, Whisnant, Williams, Zermeno, and Zofchak.

Chapter 3. COIN

1. Author interviews with Kopera, Muñoz, O'Connor, Serr, and Zofchak.

2. Author interviews with Muñoz, O'Connor, and Serr.

3. Author interviews with Kopera and Muñoz; verified by O'Connor; "Sergeant David Kopera Recommendation for Bronze Star with Valor Device" (document in the author's possession); "Optimized A3A SAF RPG Engagement Main–Watertower 4 Nov 06" (document in the author's possession).

4. Author interviews with Kopera, Muñoz, and Serr.

5. Author interviews with Kopera and Muñoz. Estimates of their relative distance from the village ranged from fifteen to twenty-five meters.

6. Author interview with Muñoz; proximity of the bullet impacts verified by O'Connor, who thought better of running in that direction when he saw the place get "lit up by impacts"; verified by Kopera.

7. Author interview with Muñoz.

8. Author interviews with Kopera and Muñoz; verified by O'Connor and Zofchak.

9. Author interview with Kopera; "Optimized A3A SAF RPG Engagement Main–Watertower 4 Nov 06."

10. Author interview with Muñoz; "Optimized A3A SAF RPG Engagement Main–Watertower 4 Nov 06."

11. Author interviews with Inman, Serr, and Zofchak.

12. Author interview with O'Connor.

13. Author interviews with Inman and Zofchak.

14. Author interview with Serr.
15. Author interview with O'Connor; "Optimized A3A SAF RPG Engagement Main–Watertower 4 Nov 06."
16. Author interview with Zofchak.
17. Author interview with Inman.
18. Author interview with Zofchak.
19. Author interview with Inman.
20. Author interview with Serr.
21. Author interview with Zofchak.
22. Author interview with Zofchak; confirmed by Serr; "Optimized A3A SAF RPG Engagement Main–Watertower 4 Nov 06."
23. Author interviews with Inman, O'Connor, and Zofchak; "Optimized A3A SAF RPG Engagement Main–Watertower 4 Nov 06." The report and testimony differ on the number of outgoing 40-mm grenades shot at insurgents—one versus two or three, respectively. The passage splits the difference, but defaults to the testimony of multiple grenades.
24. Author interview with Kopera; "Optimized A3A SAF RPG Engagement Main–Watertower 4 Nov 06."
25. Author interviews with Inman, Muñoz, O'Connor, and Zofchak; "Optimized A3A SAF RPG Engagement Main–Watertower 4 Nov 06."
26. Author interview with Muñoz.
27. Author interview with Kopera.
28. Author interview with Serr.
29. Author interviews with Kopera and Zofchak; "Optimized A3A SAF RPG Engagement Main–Watertower 4 Nov 06."
30. Author interviews with Greco and Zofchak; "Sergeant David Kopera Recommendation for Bronze Star with Valor Device."
31. "Optimized A3A SAF RPG Engagement Main–Watertower 4 Nov 06"; Muñoz confirms they were told they had "killed some insurgents"; "Sergeant David Kopera Recommendation for Bronze Star with Valor Device"; general American impressions of insurgents efficiently retrieving the dead expressed to this author by multiple interview subjects in Iraq.

32. Author interviews with Kopera, O'Connor, and Serr.

33. Donavan Campbell, *Joker One: A Marine Platoon's Story of Courage, Leadership, and Brotherhood,* Kindle ed. (New York: Random House, 2009), chap. 21; Bing West, *No True Glory: A Frontline Account for the Battle of Fallujah* (New York: Bantam, 2005).

34. Author interview with Kopera, Muñoz, O'Connor, Serr, and Zofchak.

35. Author interviews with Muñoz and Serr.

36. Author interviews with Inman, O'Connor, and Zofchak.

37. Author interviews with Inman and Zofchak.

38. Ibid.

39. Author interview with Zofchak.

40. Ibid.; Kopera described a typical interaction "Usually the oldest woman, or [head of household] would . . . try to make contact with the Marines, while the younger women would go back into the house [or adjoining room]. And usually we would round up everyone into one room. They were kind of used to the routine."

41. Author interviews with Inman and Zofchak.

42. Author interview with Zofchak.

43. Author interviews with Kopera and Muñoz.

44. Ibid.

45. Ibid.

46. Ibid.

47. Ibid.

48. Author interviews with Kopera, O'Connor, and Serr.

49. Author interview with Kopera; "Optimized A3A SAF RPG Engagement Main–Watertower 4 Nov 06."

50. Author interviews with Kopera and Serr.

51. Author interview with Kopera; "Optimized A3A SAF RPG Engagement Main–Watertower 4 Nov 06."

52. Author interviews with Kopera, Serr, and Zofchak.

53. Kopera and Zofchak suspected the buildings; O'Connor recalls Tyink saying he had seen the shooting come from the reeds and that he "thought he hit him."

54. Author interviews with Inman, Kopera, Serr, and Zofchak.

55. Quote as recalled by Zofchak in an author interview.

56. Ibid.

57. Author interviews with Inman, Serr, O'Connor, and Zofchak; Zofchak remembers Kopera finding shell casings; O'Connor recalls finding a "single casing." Inman recalls "casings."

58. Author interview with Zofchak; "Optimized A3A SAF RPG Engagement Main–Watertower 4 Nov 06."

59. Author interview with Kopera; pictures of the house in the author's possession. This residence would later become a permanent patrol base that certain squads nicknamed FOB Dark. Others referred to it as "the patrol base on Main Street and Water Tower [Road]."

60. Author interviews with Inman, Kopera, and Serr; verified by Zofchak.

61. Author interview with Inman.

62. Author interviews with Inman, O'Connor, Serr, and Zofchak.

63. Author interviews with Kopera, O'Connor, and Zofchak.

64. Author interviews with Kopera and Serr.

65. Author interviews with Inman, Kopera, O'Connor, Serr, and Zofchak; "Optimized A3A SAF RPG Engagement Main–Watertower 4 Nov 06."

66. According to Inman, "Auton was under the stairs, getting lit the fuck up."

67. Author interview with O'Connor.

68. Author interviews with O'Connor and Serr; "Optimized A3A SAF RPG Engagement Main–Watertower 4 Nov 06."

69. Author interviews with Muñoz, Kopera, and Zofchak.

70. Author interviews with Carlson, Muñoz, Serr, and Zofchak; author's personal experience.

71. Author interview with Zofchak; Muñoz confirms "Zofchak was returning fire from the side."

72. Author interview with Zofchak.

73. Author interview with O'Connor.

74. Author interview with Muñoz.

75. Author interviews with Dockter, Inman, Kopera, Muñoz, O'Connor, and Zofchak.

76. Author interview with Muñoz.

77. Author interview with Muñoz.

78. Author interviews with Inman, Kopera, and Serr.
79. Author interview with Kopera.
80. Author interview with Serr.
81. Author interview with Inman.
82. Author interview with Serr.
83. Author interview with Kopera.
84. Author interviews with Kopera, O'Connor, and Zofchak; "Optimized A3A SAF RPG Engagement Main–Watertower 4 Nov 06."
85. Author interview with Greco; "Optimized A3A SAF RPG Engagement Main–Watertower 4 Nov 06."
86. Author interviews with Kopera, Muñoz, Serr, and Zofchak.
87. Author interview with O'Connor.
88. Author interview with Zofchak; "Optimized A3A SAF RPG Engagement Main–Watertower 4 Nov 06."
89. Author interview with Kopera.
90. Author interview with Serr.
91. Author interview with Kopera.
92. Author interviews with Kopera and Serr.
93. Author interviews with Kopera, Serr, and Zofchak.
94. Quote as recalled by Zofchak in author interview.
95. Author interview with Muñoz.
96. Author interviews with Kopera, Muñoz, and Zofchak.
97. Author interviews with Kopera and Muñoz.
98. Author interviews with Inman and Muñoz.
99. Author interviews with Muñoz and Serr.
100. Author interview with Muñoz.
101. Author interviews with Kopera and O'Connor.
102. Author interviews with Serr and Zofchak. "They weren't happy about it, but they calmed down after [Muñoz] was trying to help," Zofchak said.
103. Author interview with Inman.
104. Quotes as recalled by Zofchak in author interview.
105. Author interview with Inman.
106. Paraphrased quote as independently recalled by both Serr and Zofchak in author interviews.

107. Quote as recalled by Zofchak in author interview.
108. Author interviews with Kopera and Zofchak.
109. Author interviews with Inman, Kopera, O'Connor, and Serr.
110. Author interview with Kopera.
111. Author interview with Muñoz.
112. Author interviews with Inman, Kopera, Muñoz, O'Connor, Serr, and Zofchak.
113. Author interview with Kopera and Zofchak.
114. Author interview with Dockter.
115. Author interview with Serr.
116. Author interview with Muñoz.
117. Author interviews with Kopera, Muñoz, Wortman, and Zofchak. Williams, who was in a nearby squad, saw the helicopter fly by and is "positive" it was a CH-46.
118. Author interviews with Muñoz, O'Connor, and Zofchak.
119. Author interviews with Inman and Zofchak.
120. Author interviews with O'Connor and Serr.
121. Author interviews with Inman, Kopera, and Muñoz.
122. Author interview with Muñoz.
123. Author interview with Kopera.
124. Ibid.
125. Author interviews with Dockter, Greco, and Kopera; Dockter had several dealings with the woman's husband after the incident. The man seemed grateful to the Americans for caring for his wife, at least outwardly implying that he did not blame them for the shooting. He told Dockter she was in Baghdad and would live; "Optimized A3A SAF RPG Engagement Main–Watertower 4 Nov 06."
126. Author interviews with Inman, Kopera, Muñoz, O'Connor, Serr, and Zofchak.
127. Author interview with Kopera.
128. Author interviews with Inman and Kopera.
129. Author interview with Kopera; "Optimized A3A SAF RPG Engagement Main–Watertower 4 Nov 06"; "Sergeant David Kopera Recommendation for Bronze Star with Valor Device."

130. Author interviews with Muñoz and Zofchak; Zofchak was awarded the Navy and Marines Corps Commendation Medal with Combat "V" for braving fire to save Kopera.
131. Quote as recalled by Zofchak in author interview.
132. Author interview with Zofchak.
133. Author interviews with Greco and Kopera; "Sergeant David Kopera Recommendation for Bronze Star with Valor Device."

Chapter 4. Alliance

1. Author interview with Whisnant.
2. "Report: Abu Sadoon 12 26 06" (intelligence document in the author's possession).
3. Author interviews with MSgt. Michael Abragan, Brezler, Scott, Whisnant, and many others.
4. Author interview with Roussell.
5. Author interviews with Maj. Eric Dominijanni, SSgt. Nicefero Mendoza, Roussell, Sheikh Aifan Sadoun Aifan al-Issawi, Saint One, Whisnant, Colonel Faisal Ismail Hussein al-Zobaie; Phil Williams, *Criminals, Militias, and Insurgents: Organized Crime in Iraq* (Carlisle, PA: Strategic Studies Institute, U.S. Army War College, 2009), chaps. 2, 3, 4, 5, and 7.
6. Author interviews with Capt. Joseph Lizaragga, Roussell, Colonel Faisal Ismail Hussein al-Zobaie; Jeffrey Azarva, "Is U.S. Detention Policy in Iraq Working?" *Middle East Quarterly* 16, no. 1 (Winter 2009): 5–14.
7. Author interview with Roussell.
8. Author interviews with Abragan, SSgt. Tylor Belshe, Brezler, Howe, Lippo, Saint One, Maj. Tad Scott, Whisnant.
9. Author interviews with Brezler, Roussell, Scott, and Whisnant.
10. Author interviews with Roussell and Saint One.
11. Author interview with Roussell.
12. Author interviews with Clayton, Howe, Lippo, Roussell, Scott, and Whisnant.
13. Author interviews with Roussell and Whisnant.
14. Author interview with Roussell.

15. Author interviews with Saint One and Whisnant; "Report: Abu Sadoon 12 26 06."

16. Author interviews with Maj. Jim Hayes, Roussell, Saint One, and Whisnant.

17. Author interview with Hayes.

18. Author interviews with Roussell, Sheikh Aifan, Saint One, and Whisnant.

19. Quote as recalled by Whisnant in author interview.

20. Author interviews with Roussell, Saint One, and Whisnant; "Report: Abu Sadoon 12 26 06."

21. Quote as recalled by Whisnant in author interview; sentiment also summarized in "Report: Sheikh Khamis and Abu Sadoon: 1.06.07" (intelligence document in the author's possession).

22. Author interviews with Roussell, Sheikh Aifan, Saint One, and Whisnant.

23. Author interviews with Colonel Faisal Ismail Hussein al-Zobaie; Sterling Jensen, an American interpreter in Ramadi who witnessed meetings between Sheikh Sattar and Sheikh Aifan.

24. Sheikh Khamis Hasnawi Aifan al-Issawi's opinion on the *takfiris* was recounted indirectly by his nephew Ma'an Khalid Aifan al-Issawi in an interview with the author.

25. Author interviews with Roussell, Saint One, and Whisnant; Lin Todd et al., *Iraq Tribal Study: Al-Anbar Governorate—The Albu Fahd Tribe, the Albu Mahal Tribe and the Albu Issa Tribe* (n.p.: Global Resources Group and Global Risk, 2006), 4-39–4-40, http://www.comw.org/warreport/fulltext/0709todd.pdf.

26. Author interviews with Roussell, Saint One, and Whisnant; "Report: Sheikh Khamis and Abu Sadoon 1.06.07."

27. Quote as recalled by Whisnant in author interview.

28. Author interviews with Roussell, Sheikh Aifan, Saint One, and Whisnant.

29. Author interviews with Roussell and Whisnant; "Report: Sheikh Khamis and Abu Sadoon 1.06.07."

30. Quote as recalled by Whisnant in author interview.

31. Gary W. Montgomery and Timothy S. McWilliams, eds., *Al Anbar Awakening,* vol. 2, *Iraqi Perspectives: From Insurgency to*

Counterinsurgency in Iraq, 2004–2008 (Quantico, VA: Marine Corps University, 2009), 100–101; author interviews with Howe, Roussell, and Whisnant. I have noticed this trend as an embedded journalist: the six- to seven-month deployments of many Marine units—compared to the twelve- or even fifteen-month Army deployments—seem ideal for the Marines, especially in areas presenting a great deal of combat stress, but it is not ideal for building the long-term relationships required in counterinsurgency campaigns. Relationships with locals and continuity of strategy suffer with the shorter deployments and turnover of personnel.

32. Author interviews with Colonel Faisal Ismail Hussein al-Zobaie, Lt. Col. Clayton Fischer, Tom Gorman, an international police liaison officer and civilian law enforcement advisor to the Iraqi Police, GySgt. Jason Lawson, Lippo, Lt. Col. Joel Poudrier, Maj. Pat Semon, Scott, LCpl. Chad Yeager.

33. Author interview with Sheikh Aifan.

34. Author interview with Whisnant; "Report: Sheikh Khamis and Abu Sadoon 1.06.07."

35. Montgomery and McWilliams, *Al Anbar Awakening,* 2:94; author interview with Roussell; Roussell's assessment is correct, but incomplete. Dark was an organizer, but he was undoubtedly involved in some direct fighting, as he has said in interviews and as verified by others. For example, Saint One recalled in an interview with the author that Dark once called him on his cellphone as gunfire raged in the background. Dark was in the midst of a running gunfight with insurgents and wanted U.S. assistance.

36. Montgomery and McWilliams, *Al Anbar Awakening,* 2:100.

37. "Report: Sheikh Khamis and Abu Sadoon 1.06.07."

38. Author interviews with Roussell, Saint One, and Whisnant; "Report: Sheikh Khamis and Abu Sadoon 1.06.07."

Chapter 5. The *Diya*

1. Author interviews with "C. J." Wadhah Sahib and Greco.

2. Author interview with Greco.

3. Author interview with Sheikh Aifan Sadoun Aifan al-Issawi.

4. Author interviews with Whisnant and Roussell.

5. Author interviews with Dockter, Greco, and Campbell.

6. Author interviews with Dockter and Greco.

7. Author interviews with Dockter, Greco, and "C. J." Wadhah Sahib.

8. Author interviews with Campbell, Dockter, Greco, Muñoz, Paredes, and Williams.

9. Author interview with Campbell.

10. Author interview with Williams.

11. Author interviews with Campbell, Dockter, Greco, Muñoz, Paredes, and Williams.

12. Author interviews with Dockter, Greco, Muñoz, Prince, and Williams.

13. Author interviews with Campbell, Dockter, Greco, Muñoz, Paredes, Prince, and Williams.

14. Author interview with Muñoz.

15. Author interviews with Campbell, Dockter, Greco, Muñoz, Paredes, Prince, and Williams. All of the Marines but Campbell recall hearing a long burst of fire, possibly indicating a PKM machine gun. Campbell said he only heard short bursts from an AK-47.

16. Author interviews with Campbell, Dockter, Paredes, Prince, and Williams.

17. Author interviews with Campbell, Dockter, Greco, Muñoz, Paredes, Prince, and Williams. These "scattered bangs" could have been return fire from the house that was initially attacked and may have been the lighter fire initially heard by Campbell.

18. Author interview with Paredes.

19. Author interviews with Dockter, Paredes, and Williams.

20. Author interview with Dockter.

21. Author interviews with Dockter, Paredes, and Williams.

22. Author interviews with Dockter, Paredes, and Williams; stilted Arabic quote as recalled by Dockter in author interview.

23. Author interview with GySgt. Michael Gillitzer.

24. Author interviews with Campbell, Dockter, Greco, Muñoz, Paredes, Prince, "C. J." Wadhah Sahib, and Williams.

25. Author interview with Dockter.

26. Author interview with Paredes.

27. Author interview with Dockter.

28. Author interviews with Dockter, Prince, and Paredes.

29. Author interviews with Dockter, Paredes, and Williams.

30. Author interview with Dockter.

31. Author interview with Williams.

32. Author interviews with Mishael Abdullah Owdeh (Sheikh Shalaan), and J. T. Taylor; Peter Bouckaert, Fred Abrahams, and Marc Garlasco, "Violent Response: The US Army in al-Falluja," *Human Rights Watch Iraq*, June 2003, 6–17; "Fallujah," GlobalSecurity.org, http://www.globalsecurity.org/military/world/iraq/fallujah.htm.

33. Author interview with Campbell.

34. Author interviews with Campbell, Dockter, Greco, Muñoz, Paredes, Prince, "C. J." Wadhah Sahib, and Williams.

35. Author interview with Tha'er Khalid Aifan al-Issawi. The quotes are Tha'er's paraphrased recollection of the sentiments he and his fellow militiamen were shouting at the Americans.

36. Author interview with Whisnant.

37. Author interviews with Greco and Whisnant.

38. Author interview with Greco.

39. Author interviews with Greco, Muñoz, and "C. J." Wadhah Sahib.

40. Author interview with "C. J." Wadhah Sahib.

41. Author interviews with Albrecht, Dockter, Greco, "C. J." Wadhah Sahib, and Whisnant.

42. Author interview with "C. J." Wadhah Sahib.

43. Quote as recalled by Muñoz in author interview.

44. Author interviews with Dockter, Greco, Muñoz, and "C. J." Wadhah Sahib; previous quotes as recalled by Muñoz and Greco in author interview, respectively.

45. Author interviews with Dockter, Greco, and Muñoz.

46. Author interview with Dockter.

47. Author interview with Paredes.

48. Author interview with Prince.

49. Author interview with Greco.

50. Interviews with Dockter, Greco, and Muñoz.

51. Interview with Greco.

52. Interviews with Ma'an Khalid Aifan al-Issawi, Tha'er Khalid Aifan al-Issawi, and Sheikh Aifan.

53. Author interviews with Campbell, Dockter, Greco, Muñoz, Paredes, "C. J." Wadhah Sahib, and Williams.

54. Author interview with Greco.

55. Author interview with "C. J." Wadhah Sahib.

56. Author interviews with Campbell, Dockter, Greco, Muñoz, Paredes, Prince, "C. J." Wadhah Sahib, and Williams.

57. Author interviews with Dockter and Greco. Quotes are according to their recollections in author interviews.

58. Author interviews with Campbell, Dockter, Greco, Muñoz, Paredes, "C. J." Wadhah Sahib, and Williams.

59. Author interviews with Dockter and Greco.

60. Author interviews with Campbell, Muñoz, Paredes, and "C. J." Wadhah Sahib.

61. Author interviews with Campbell, Dockter, Greco, and Prince.

62. Author interview with Campbell.

63. Author interviews with Muñoz and Williams.

64. Author interviews with Campbell, Dockter, Greco, Prince, "C. J." Wadhah Sahib, and Williams.

65. Author interviews with Dockter, Greco, and Whisnant.

66. Author interviews with Campbell, Dockter, Greco, Muñoz, Paredes, Prince, "C. J." Wadhah Sahib, and Williams.

67. Author interview with Dockter.

68. Author interview with Sheikh Aifan.

69. Author interviews with Dockter, Greco, and Whisnant.

70. Author interviews with Campbell, Dockter, Greco, Muñoz, "C. J." Wadhah Sahib, and Williams; cigarette anecdote from Campbell.

71. Author interviews with Gillitzer and Greco.

72. Author interviews with Greco, Roussell, and Whisnant.

73. Author interviews with Campbell, and Greco.

74. Author interview with Greco.

75. Gary W. Montgomery and Timothy S. McWilliams, eds., *Al Anbar Awakening*, vol. 2, *Iraqi Perspectives: From Insurgency to Counterinsurgency in Iraq, 2004–2008* (Quantico, VA: Marine Corps University, 2009), 87.

76. Author interview with Dockter.

77. Author interview with Ma'an Khalid Aifan al-Issawi.

78. Interview with Tha'er Khalid Aifan al-Issawi.

79. Author interview with Sheikh Aifan.

80. Lin Todd et al., *Iraq Tribal Study: Al-Anbar Governorate—The Albu Fahd Tribe, the Albu Mahal Tribe and the Albu Issa Tribe* (n.p.: Global Resources Group and Global Risk, 2006), 2-31; Cullen Murphy, "Inshallah," *American Scholar,* autumn 2007, http://theamerican-scholar.org/inshallah; IslamicDictionary.com, s.v. "Inshallah," http://www.islamic-dictionary.com/index.php?word=inshallah. More than any secondary reference, my interpretation of *insh'allah* is based on my travels in Iraq, especially my experience embedding with Americans training Iraqi security forces. The Americans alternately admired and deplored the concept. Some were impressed when it sparked an instance of exceptional bravery or allowed an Iraqi to endure hardship. Many more were frustrated by how the concept caused a disregard for personal safety or obviated punctuality and precision among those they were trying to train.

81. Hussein Hassan, "Iraq: Tribal Structure, Social, and Political Activities," Congressional Research Service Report for Congress, Library of Congress, Washington, D.C., March 15, 2007, 1–4; Todd et al., *Iraq Tribal Study,* 2-39, 2-46–2-51; *Encyclopædia Britannica,* online ed., s.v. "diyah."

82. Author interview with Tha'er Khalid Aifan al-Issawi.

Chapter 6. Pulling Threads

1. Author interviews with Clayton, Howe, Roussell, Saint One, and Whisnant.

2. Author interview with Whisnant.

3. Author interviews with Howe and Whisnant.

4. Author interviews with Clayton, Howe, and Whisnant.

5. Author interview with Clayton.

6. Author interviews with Clayton, Howe, and Whisnant.

7. "SALTRs—IEDs Found 10/2006–3/2007" and "SALTRs—IEDs Blown 10/2006–3/2007" (intelligence reports in the author's possession).

8. Author interviews with Clayton, Howe, Saint One, and Whisnant.

9. Author interviews with Clayton, Howe, Price, Roussell, Saint One, Scott, J. T. Taylor, and Whisnant.

10. Author interviews with Clayton, Howe, Saint One, and Whisnant.

11. Author interviews with Hayes and Whisnant.

12. "Detainee graph" (intelligence report in the author's possession).

13. Author interviews with Clayton and Howe.

14. Quotes as recalled by Whisnant in author interview.

15. Author interviews with Lt. Cdr. Eric Greitens and Whisnant.

16. Author interview with Whisnant.

17. Eric Fair, "An Iraq Interrogator's Nightmare," *Washington Post*, February 9, 2007.

18. Author interviews with Clayton, Howe, Jongsma, Lippo, Poudrier, Roussell, Saint One, Scott, and Whisnant. Said Poudrier, a Marine advisor to the Iraqi Army, on the impact of the Abu Ghraib scandal, "I'm not going to lie, that really hurt us."

19. Author interviews with Clayton, Howe, Lippo, Roussell, Saint One, Scott, and Whisnant; Michael J. Totten, "The Dungeon of Fallujah," February 18, 2008, http://www.michaeltotten.com/archives/2008/02/the-dungeon-of.php; personal observations of the jail in the Fallujah district police headquarters.

20. Quote as recalled by Whisnant in author interview.

21. Author interview with Jongsma.

22. Gary W. Montgomery and Timothy S. McWilliams, eds., *Al Anbar Awakening*, vol. 2, *Iraqi Perspectives: From Insurgency to Counterinsurgency in Iraq, 2004–2008* (Quantico, VA: Marine Corps University, 2009), 96.

23. Author interviews with Brig. Gen. Richard Simcock, Scott, and Whisnant.

24. Author interview with Whisnant.

25. "Mullah Fallah Hamadi Salih al-Isawi Analyst Assessment" (intelligence report in the author's possession).

26. Author interviews with Ma'an Khalid Aifan al-Issawi, Sheikh Aifan Sadoun Aifan al-Issawi, and Sheikh Shalaan.

27. Author interviews with Clayton, Howe, and Whisnant.

28. Author interviews with Clayton, Hoffmann, Howe, Saint One, and Whisnant.

29. Author interviews with Colonel Faisal Ismail Hussein al-Zobaie, Capt. Joseph Lizaragga, and Roussell; Jeffrey Azarva, "Is U.S. Detention Policy in Iraq Working?" *Middle East Quarterly* 16, no. 1 (Winter 2009): 5–14; Montgomery and McWilliams, *Al Anbar Awakening,* 2:89: Said Sheikh Aifan in this interview: "[T]he insurgents, if they had any suspicion that a guy had any relationship with the Americans, they cut off his head."

30. Author interviews with Clayton, Howe, Roussell, Saint One, and Whisnant; quote by Howe.

31. Author interviews with Clayton, Howe, Saint One, and Whisnant.

Chapter 7. Adilah

1. Author interviews with Albrecht, Kimmey, Hoffmann, and Jongsma.

2. Author interview with Albrecht.

3. Author interviews with Beemer, Carlson, Foerster, Hoffmann, Howe, Jansen, Jongsma, Kimmey, Kyle, Osborne, Ponce, Steimel, and Villanueva.

4. Author interview with Albrecht.

5. Author interviews with Albrecht, Hoffmann, and Kimmey.

6. Author interviews with Albrecht, Hoffmann, Jongsma, and Kimmey. Hoffmann remembers one child and that the woman was in her "early to mid-twenties"; the other Marines estimated late twenties to mid-thirties.

7. "Adilah" is a pseudonym to insulate the young woman from possible retribution by any remaining insurgent groups in Iraq.

8. Author interviews with Albrecht, Jongsma, and Kimmey.

9. Author interviews with Albrecht and Kimmey; a mixture of quotes as recalled by Albrecht and Kimmey.

10. Author interviews with Albrecht and Kimmey; quote as recalled by Kimmey.

11. Author interviews with Albrecht, Beemer, Carlson, Foerster, Jongsma, and Kimmey.

12. Author interview with Kimmey.

13. Author interview with Albrecht.

14. Author interviews with Albrecht and Kimmey; quotes as recalled by Albrecht in author interview.

15. Author interview with Kimmey.

16. Author interviews with Albrecht, Beemer, Carlson, Jongsma, and Kimmey.

17. Author interviews with Albrecht, Jongsma, and Kimmey.

18. Author interview with Kimmey.

19. Author interviews with Albrecht, Carlson, Greco, Hoffmann, Jongsma, and Kimmey; quote as recalled by Carlson.

20. Author interviews with Albrecht, Carlson, Greco, Hoffmann, Jongsma, and Kimmey.

21. Author interviews with Albrecht, Carlson, Jongsma, Kimmey, and "C. J." Wadhah Sahib.

22. Author interviews with Albrecht and Kimmey; quote is a mixture of recollections by the two Marines.

23. Author interviews with Albrecht, Hoffmann, and Kimmey.

24. Author interviews with Albrecht and Greco.

Chapter 8. Civil Affairs

1. Author interviews with Belshe, Brezler, Edwards, King, Lippo, and Scott; Bing West, *No True Glory: A Frontline Account of the Battle of Fallujah* (New York: Bantam, 2005), part 4 and epilogue; Patrick O'Donnell, *We Were One: Shoulder to Shoulder with the Marines Who Took Fallujah* (Cambridge, MA: Da Capo Press, 2006); Dahr Jamail and Ali al-Fadhily, "Fallujah Again in the Line of US Fire," *Asia Times Online*, September 13, 2006; John Patch, "Operation al Fajr: Enduring MOUT Principles Make the Fight for Fallujah a Success," *Marine Corps Gazette*, http://www.mca-marines.org/gazette/article/ operation-al-fajr; Geoff Ziezulewicz, "Iraqi Inaction in Fallujah Has Stalled Reconstruction of Local Businesses," *Stars and Stripes*, March 2, 2008; IRIN, "Focus on Reconstruction in Fallujah," May 24, 2005.

2. Matthew McAllester, "After Fallujah Falls, Seabees Set To Tackle Reconstruction," *Newsday*, November 4, 2004; Joel Wing, "Fallujah Waste Water Treatment Plant, A Tale of U.S. Reconstruction in Iraq Gone Wrong," Kurdistan News Agency, November 30, 2011; IRIN,

"Focus on Reconstruction in Fallujah; U.S. Department of Defense, "Defense Department Briefing on Progress of Reconstruction Work in Iraq; Plans For Reconstruction in Fallujah," November 19, 2004.

3. Author interviews with Abragan, Belshe, Brezler, Colonel Faisal Ismail Hussein al-Zobaie, Lippo, Scott, and Maj. Jodie Sweezey; Anne Garrels, "Long-Awaited Fallujah Rebuilding Shows Promise," NPR, January 23, 2008; Hannah Allam, "Iraqi Insurgents Taking Cut of U.S. Rebuilding Money," McClatchy, August 27, 2007.

4. Author interviews with Abragan, Brezler, Poudrier, and Sweezey

5. Author interviews with Abragan, Belshe, Brezler, SSgt. Mauricio Piedrahita, Sweezey, and CWO Steve Townsley.

6. Author interview with Colonel Faisal Ismail Hussein al-Zobaie.

7. Author interviews with Abragan, Belshe, Brezler, and Sweezey.

8. Author interview with Abragan.

9. Author interviews with Abragan, Belshe, Brezler, and Cpl. Edward Przybylski.

10. Author interviews with Abragan, Belshe, Brezler, Przybylski, and Sweezey.

11. Author interview with Belshe.

12. Author interviews with Abragan, Belshe, Brezler, Przybylski, Roussell, and Sweezey.

13. Author interview with Sweezey.

14. Author interviews with Abragan, Belshe, and Brezler.

15. Author interviews with Abragan, Belshe, Brezler, Sweezey, and Whisnant.

16. Author interview with Brezler.

17. Author interview with Belshe.

Chapter 9. *Wasta*

1. Author interviews with Clayton, Howe, and Whisnant.

2. Author interviews with Brezler and Whisnant.

3. William McCallister, "COIN and Irregular Warfare in a Tribal Society," 30, *SWJ Blog*, February 4, 2008, http://smallwarsjournal .com/blog/coin-and-iw-in-a-tribal-society.

4. Lin Todd et al., *Iraq Tribal Study: Al-Anbar Governorate—The Albu Fahd Tribe, the Albu Mahal Tribe and the Albu Issa Tribe* (n.p.: Global

Resources Group and Global Risk, 2006), 2-42, http://www
.comw.org/warreport/fulltext/0709todd.pdf; McCallister, "COIN
and Irregular Warfare in a Tribal Society," 26–32; Hussein Hassan,
"Iraq: Tribal Structure, Social, and Political Activities," Congressional
Research Service Report for Congress, Library of Congress,
Washington, D.C., March 15, 2007, 2–4.

5. Todd et al., *Iraqi Tribal Study,* ES-4–ES-5, 3-17–3-37, 5-42–5-54;
   McCallister, "COIN and Irregular Warfare in a Tribal Society," 27;
   Hassan, "Iraq," 3–4.

6. Author interviews with Colonel Faisal Ismail Hussein al-Zobaie,
   Capt. Matt Kralovec, Sheikh Aifan Sadoun Aifan al-Issawi, J. T.
   Taylor; Todd et al., *Iraqi Tribal Study,* 4-19–4-26, 4-32–4-35, 4-42–
   4-44; Gary W. Montgomery and Timothy S. McWilliams, eds.,
   Al Anbar Awakening, vol. 1, *American Perspectives: From Insurgency
   to Counterinsurgency in Iraq, 2004–2008* (Quantico, VA: Marine
   Corps University, 2009), 18–137.

7. Todd Pitman, "Sunni Sheiks Join Fight vs. Insurgency," Associated
   Press, March 25, 2007.

8. Phil Williams, *Criminals, Militias, and Insurgents: Organized Crime in
   Iraq* (Carlisle, PA: Strategic Studies Institute, U.S. Army War College,
   2009), chaps. 2, 5, 6, 7, and 8.

9. Author interviews with Kralovec, "Leo," Roggio, Saint One, J. T.
   Taylor, Whisnant, and a U.S. intelligence official speaking on
   condition of anonymity; "A Dark Side to Iraq 'Awakening' Groups,"
   International Herald Tribune, January 4, 2008; "Q&A: Iraq's
   Awakening Councils," *BBC News,* July 18, 2010.

10. Author interviews with Roussell and Whisnant.

11. Author interview with Brezler.

12. Author interviews with Belshe, Brezler, Sweezey, and Whisnant.

13. Author interviews with Brezler and Whisnant.

14. Shane Bauer, "The Sheikh Down," *Mother Jones,* September/October
    2009; Sam Dagher, "Will 'Armloads' of US Cash Buy Tribal Loyalty?"
    Christian Science Monitor, November 8, 2007; Dahr Jamail, "Iraq's
    'Teflon Don,'" *Huffington Post,* February 12, 2009.

15. Author interviews with Brezler, Sheikh Aifan, Ma'an Khalid Aifan
    al-Issawi, Sheikh Shaalan, and Whisnant.

16. Author interviews with Belshe, Brezler, Fallujan neighborhood watch volunteer 1, Fallujan neighborhood watch volunteer 2, Fallujan neighborhood watch volunteer 3, Fallujan neighborhood watch volunteer 4, Fallujan police volunteer 1, Fallujan police volunteer 2, Fallujan police volunteer 3, "Leo," Mendoza, Poudrier, Price, Roussell, J. T. Taylor, and Whisnant.

17. Author interviews with Belshe, Brezler, Roussell, and Whisnant.

18. Author interviews with Belshe, Brezler, Kralovec, Roussell, Saint One, Whisnant, and a U.S. intelligence official speaking on condition of anonymity.

19. Author interviews with Mishael Abudullah Owdeh (Sheikh Shalaan), and Whisnant.

20. Author interview with Whisnant.

21. Author interviews with Belshe, Brezler, Roussell, and Whisnant.

22. Author interview with Roussell.

23. Author interviews with Belshe, Brezler, Roussell, and Whisnant.

24. Author interviews with Belshe, Brezler, Roussell, and Whisnant; Bauer, "The Sheikh Down."

Chapter 10. A Macy's Thanksgiving Day Parade

1. Author interviews with Belshe, Brezler, and Whisnant.

2. Author interviews with Sheikh Bassam "Ama'an" Mishael Shalaan, one of Sheikh Shalaan's sons, Belshe, Brezler, Omar Noori Daham Mohna, a nephew of Sheikh Khamis, Piedrahita, Sweezey, and Townsley. An interesting anecdote from Sweezey is that bananas were apparently a luxury item before the war, so much so that one of President Saddam Hussein's wives used to send them as gifts to honor individuals. Thus, when Iraqis encountered American food supplies, the "bananas were like gold," according to Sweezey.

3. Author interview with Brezler.

4. Author interviews with Baum, Brezler, and Omar Noori Daham Mohna.

5. Author interviews with Belshe and Brezler.

6. Author interviews with Abragan, Belshe, Brezler, Przybylski, Sweezey, and Whisnant.

7. I've witnessed the enthusiasm with which Fallujans received items from care packages sent from the United States. Everything from snacks and magazines to personal hygiene products were luxuries in the area.

8. Author interviews with Abragan, Belshe, Brezler, Przybylski, Sweezey, and Whisnant.

9. Author interviews with Abragan, Belshe, Brezler, Przybylski, Sweezey, and Whisnant; photographs of the event in the author's possession.

10. Author interviews with Belshe, Brezler, Przybylski, Sweezey, and Whisnant.

11. Author interviews with Belshe, Brezler, Przybylski, Sweezey, and Whisnant.

12. Author interviews with Belshe, Brezler, Piedrahita, Przybylski, Sweezey, Townsley, and Whisnant. This characterization is also via my attendance at civil affairs missions in January and September 2007. Different Marines take to the "non-kinetic" activities with different levels of enthusiasm.

13. Author interviews with Belshe and Przybylski; quote as recalled by Belshe.

14. Author interviews with Belshe and Przybylski; quote as recalled by both men.

15. Author interviews with Belshe, Przybylski, and Sweezey.

16. Author interview with Belshe.

17. Author interviews with Baum, Belshe, Brezler, Kimmey, Omar Noori Daham Mohna, Sheikh Bassam, and Sweezey.

18. Author interviews with Baum and a number of Alpha Company Marines. The first thing most of them brought up was some version of a chuckle, followed by, "You know he got kicked in the head by a horse, right?"

19. Author interviews with Baum, Beemer, Foerster, and Kimmey.

20. Author interviews with Baum, Beemer, Foerster, and Kimmey. Most of the section is from Baum's recollection; many of the Americans agreed that the women usually did much of the household chores and tended the animals. Notably, Kimmey disagrees with the opinion that local women did a great deal more work than the men; he thinks

the sentiment, while true to some extent, is overstated by American observers.

21. Author interview with Baum.

22. Author interviews with Baum, Beemer, Foerster, and Kimmey.

23. Quote as recalled by Baum.

24. Author interviews with Baum, Foerster, and Kimmey.

25. Anecdote as recalled in author interview with Baum; Foerster can't specifically recall the mortars, but says that some might have exploded; Whisnant asserts that there was "definitely" a mortar attack in the area that day.

26. Author interviews with Belshe, Brezler, Przybylski, Sweezey, and Whisnant.

27. Author interviews with Belshe, Brezler, Przybylski, and Sweezey; photos of the anecdote in the author's possession.

28. Author interviews with Belshe, Przybylski, and Sweezey; most of the detailed descriptions and quotes are as recalled by Belshe.

29. Author interviews with Belshe, Przybylski, and Sweezey; most of the detailed descriptions and quotes are as recalled by Belshe.

30. Author interview with Belshe.

31. Author interview with Hoffmann.

32. Author interview with Marine who provided the anecdote in confidentiality and whose name has been withheld by mutual agreement.

33. Author interview with Captain Bryan Welles, who served on the peninsula with Golf Company of the 2/7 Marines in 2005. His unit spent roughly three months on the northern peninsula before rotating to a different area for the remainder of the tour; such a short window of time does not make it easy to build relationships with locals.

34. Author interviews with Ghilarducci, Greco, Hoffmann, Kimmey, Ponce, Roussell, Whisnant, and many others. It seems to be a commonly held article of faith among the interviewees from Alpha 1/24 that they conducted counterinsurgency operations differently than their predecessors. Some are critical of this fact, while others laud the approach of Alpha 1/25; Jim Garamone, "Army, Marines Release New Counterinsurgency Manual," American Forces Press Service, December 18, 2006; "General Petraeus's Opening Statement," *New York Times*, January 23, 2007 (delivered before a Senate Armed

Services Committee hearing on his nomination to be the commander of U.S. forces in Iraq); George Packer, "The Lesson of Tal
Afar: Is It Too Late for the Administration To Correct Its Course in
Iraq?" *New Yorker*, April 10, 2006. It is widely accepted that General
Petraeus' co-authorship of a new counterinsurgency field manual
and appointment to head U.S. forces in Iraq marked a holistic implementation of counterinsurgency strategy in Iraq, whereas previously
the doctrine was applied to varying degrees by individual commanders at their knowledge and discretion. Perhaps the most famous
example of successful COIN strategies in Iraq prior to this shift
was the experience of Col. H. R. McMaster and the U.S. Army's 3rd
Armored Cavalry Regiment in Tal Afar in 2005.

35. Author interview with Welles.

36. Author interviews with two Marines who offered their candid assessments on condition of anonymity. In a fair number of interviews,
a portion of them conducted after I had established a rapport with
the Marines, some of them acknowledged the negative aspects of the
execution of their mission; they usually centered around treatment
of detainees or suspected insurgents. A large majority of interviewees
earnestly expressed, however, that their team, squad, or platoon had
maintained respect and professionalism in their interactions with
Iraqis.

37. Author interviews with Jensen, the interpreter "Leo," Poudrier,
Roussell, and J. T. Taylor; Gary W. Montgomery and Timothy S.
McWilliams, eds., *Al Anbar Awakening*, vol. 2, *Iraqi Perspectives: From
Insurgency to Counterinsurgency in Iraq, 2004–2008* (Quantico, VA:
Marine Corps University, 2009).

38. Author interviews with Fallujan mukhtar, Fallujan neighborhood watch volunteer 1, Fallujan neighborhood watch volunteer 2,
Fallujan neighborhood watch volunteer 3, Fallujan neighborhood
watch volunteer 4, Colonel Faisal Ismail Hussein al-Zobaie, "Leo."

39. Author interviews with Brezler and Whisnant; paraphrased quotes as
recalled by Whisnant.

40. Author interviews with Brezler, Roussell, Sweezey, and Whisnant.

41. Author interviews with Sheikh Aifan Sadoun Aifan al-Issawi,
Brezler, and Whisnant; Lin Todd et al., *Iraq Tribal Study: Al-Anbar*

Governorate—The Albu Fahd Tribe, the Albu Mahal Tribe and the Albu Issa Tribe (n.p.: Global Resources Group and Global Risk, 2006), 4-42–4-44, http://www.comw.org/warreport/fulltext/0709todd.pdf.

42. Author interviews with Sheikh Aifan, Brezler, Roussell, and Whisnant; quote as recalled by Whisnant.

43. Author interview with Whisnant.

44. Author interviews with Brezler, Roussell, and Whisnant.

45. Author interview with Whisnant.

46. Quotes as recalled by Whisnant in author interview; Alpha Company electronic newsletter, March 6, 2006.

Chapter 11. Down by the River

1. Author interviews with Clayton, Howe, Saint One, and Whisnant.

2. Author interviews with Howe and Whisnant; quote as recalled by Howe.

3. Author interviews with Clayton, Howe, Saint One, and Whisnant.

4. Author interview with Saint One.

5. Questions paraphrased from description of questioning by Howe in author interview.

6. Author interviews with Howe and Whisnant

7. Author interview with Howe; quote by Dark as recalled by Howe.

8. Author interview with Saint One.

9. "Optimized A4 Engagements 08 Feb 07" (intelligence document detailing the engagement in the author's possession); author interviews with Hoffmann, Jansen, and Osborne.

10. Author interview with Moose.

11. Author interview with Howe.

12. Author interviews with Clayton, Hoffmann, Howe, Saint One, Whisnant.

13. Ibid.

14. Author interview with Howe.

15. Quote as recalled by Whisnant in author interview.

16. Author interviews with Howe and Whisnant.

17. Ibid; quote as remembered by both Howe and Whisnant.

Chapter 12. Hawa

1. Author interviews with Clayton, Dockter, Greco, Hoffmann, Howe, Jansen, Lehner, Osborne, Ponce, Villanueva, Whisnant, and Wortman.
2. Author interviews with Greco, Hoffmann, Howe, and Whisnant.
3. Author interviews with Greco, Hoffmann, Howe, Jansen, Lippo, Scott, and Whisnant. According to a number of Americans, insurgents didn't like to operate in bad weather. The predictability led to jokes among the team advising police in Fallujah that mortars always came in at "10 and 2." Members of a unit advising the Iraqi Army fretted about driving home to Fallujah in the late afternoon after a trip to Habbaniyah because the timing was within "afternoon rush hour," the typical window of the day's second wave of roadside bombings. The first wave occurred in the mornings.
4. Author interviews with Hoffmann, Jansen, Osborne, Ponce, Wortman, and Zavalavargas.
5. "Optimized A4 Engagements 08 Feb 07" (intelligence document in author's possession detailing the engagement); author interviews with Hoffmann, Jansen, Osborne, Ponce, and Wortman.
6. Author interviews with Hoffmann, Jansen, Osborne, and Ponce; Ponce was the lance corporal who disagreed with Hoffmann and believed the Marines were too far from support to conduct an attack.
7. Author interview with Jansen.
8. Author interviews with Jansen, Osborne, Ponce, and Zavalavargas.
9. Author interview with Ponce.
10. Author interviews with Jansen and Ponce.
11. Author interviews with Jansen, Osborne, and Ponce.
12. Author interview with Osborne.
13. Author interviews with Osborne and Wortman; quote as recalled by Wortman in author interview.
14. Quotes as recalled by Osborne in author interview.
15. Author interviews with Jansen, Osborne, and Wortman.
16. Author interviews with Jansen, Osborne, and Wortman; "Hawa Op [3/03/2007]" (intelligence document detailing the incident in the author's possession); descriptions from interviews and pictures of

the shooting's aftermath in the author's possession; phonetic Arabic ("Shufuni idak!") as recalled in author interview with Jansen.

17. Author interviews with Jansen, Osborne, and Ponce.

18. Author interviews with Jansen, Ponce, Wortman, and Zavalavargas; quote as recalled by Ponce.

19. Quote as recalled by Ponce in author interview.

20. Author interviews with Jansen, Osborne, Ponce, and Wortman.

21. Author interviews with Jansen and Osborne.

22. Author interviews with Jansen and Osborne.

23. Quote as recalled by Jansen in author interview. The insurgent's identity remains a mystery.

24. Author interviews with Hoffmann, Jansen, Osborne, Ponce, Wortman, and Zavalavargas; "Hawa Op."

25. Author interviews with Jansen, Osborne, Ponce and Wortman.

26. Author interviews with Hoffmann and Jansen.

27. Author interview with Jansen.

28. Author interviews with Hoffmann, Jansen, Osborne, Ponce, and Villanueva.

29. Quotes as recalled by Jansen in author interview; Hoffmann's quote also as recalled by Zavalavargas in author interview; Hoffmann's quote confirmed by Ponce.

30. Author interview with Villanueva.

31. "Hawa Op 02 [3/03/2007]" (intelligence document detailing the incident in the author's possession); pictures of the cargo in the author's possession.

32. Author interviews with Hoffmann, Jansen, Osborne, Ponce, and Villanueva (primarily via interview with Jansen).

33. Author interview with Jansen; "Hawa Op 02"; descriptions also from pictures of the men in the author's possession.

34. Author interview with Jansen.

35. Author interviews with Hoffmann, Jansen, Osborne, Ponce, and Villanueva; "Hawa Op"; "Hawa Op 02."

36. Author interviews with Howe and Whisnant; quote as recalled by Howe.

37. Author interviews with Howe, Moose, and Whisnant.

38. Author interviews with Dockter and Howe; quote as recalled by Howe.

39. Author interviews with Dockter, Howe, and Moose; quote as recalled by Howe in author interview.

40. Author interview with Moose.

41. Quote as recalled by Howe in author interview.

42. Author interviews with Howe and Moose.

43. Author interviews with Dockter, Howe, and Moose; quote as recalled by Howe.

44. Author interviews with Jansen, Osborne, and Villanueva.

45. Author interviews with law enforcement professional Richard Crawford, Roussell, and Scott.

46. Author interviews with Hoffmann, Jansen, and Osborne.

47. "Hawa Op"; "Hawa Op 02."

48. Author interview with Hoffmann.

49. If there hadn't been additional evidence indicting him, this wouldn't have been a bad excuse. Americans often detained Iraqis who tested positive for bomb residue on their hands, and sometimes they were honest men who, in the local tradition, fished with explosives.

50. Author interviews with Hoffmann, Jansen, and Osborne.

51. Quote as recalled by Osborne in author interview; verified by Jansen.

52. Author interviews with Jansen and Osborne.

53. Author interview with Whisnant.

Chapter 13. Score

1. Author interviews with Albrecht, Beemer, Carlson, Foerster, Hoffmann, Kimmey, and Steimel.

2. Author interviews with Hoffmann and Whisnant.

3. Author interviews with Albrecht, Beemer, Carlson, Foerster, Hoffmann, Kimmey, and Steimel.

4. Author interviews with Foerster and Steimel.

5. Author interview with Albrecht, Foerster, Hoffmann, and Kimmey.

6. Author interview with Albrecht.

7. Author interviews with Albrecht, Beemer, Carlson, Foerster, Hoffmann, Kimmey, and Steimel.

8. Author interviews with Albrecht, Jongsma, and Kimmey.

9. Author interviews with Albrecht, Carlson, Hoffmann, Jongsma, and Kimmey; video of Jongsma's medevac in author's possession.

10. Author interviews with Albrecht, Beemer, Carlson, and Kimmey.

11. Ibid.

12. Author interviews with Albrecht, Beemer, Carlson, Foerster, Kimmey, and Steimel.

13. Author interviews Albrecht, Beemer, Foerster, Kimmey, and Steimel.

14. Author interview with Carlson; "A4B Engagement 070311" (engagement report in the author's possession).

15. Author interviews with Albrecht and Kimmey; "A4B Engagement 070311."

16. Quote as recalled by Albrecht in author interview.

17. Author interviews with Albrecht, Beemer, Carlson, and Kimmey; "A4B Engagement 070311."

18. Author interview with Albrecht.

19. Author interviews with Albrecht and Carlson; quote as recalled by Albrecht.

20. Author interviews with Albrecht and Kimmey; quotes as recalled by Albrecht; "A4B Engagement 070311."

21. Author interviews with Albrecht, Beemer, Carlson, and Kimmey.

22. "A4B Engagement 070311"; descriptions based on pictures of the aftermath in the author's possession.

23. Author interviews with Albrecht, Carlson, Foerster, Hoffmann, and Kimmey; "A4B Engagement 070311."

24. Author interview with Kimmey.

25. Author interview with Carlson.

26. Author interviews with Albrecht, Beemer, Carlson, Foerster, Hoffmann, Kimmey, and Steimel.

Chapter 14. "Because the Language They Use Is Killing"

1. Anthony H. Cordesman, "Success or Failure? Iraq's Insurgency and Civil Violence and US Strategy: Developments through June 2007," Center for Strategic and International Studies, Washington, D.C., July 9, 2007; "The List: The Future of the Insurgency," *Foreign Policy*, June 19, 2006, claims that al Qaeda in Iraq was responsible for 5 percent

to 10 percent of insurgent attacks by the time of Zarqawi's death. Roggio, in an author interview, disputes this, saying such figures merely considered analysis of insurgent public relations statements and that some of the groups affiliated with AQI were not counted in the total. He believes that the portion of attacks stemming from al Qaeda were significantly higher.

2. Author interview with Sheikh Aifan Sadoun Aifan al-Issawi, Ma'an Khalid Aifan al-Issawi, Mishael Abdullah Owdeh (Sheikh Shalaan); Lin Todd et al., *Iraq Tribal Study: Al-Anbar Governorate—The Albu Fahd Tribe, the Albu Mahal Tribe and the Albu Issa Tribe* (n.p.: Global Resources Group and Global Risk, 2006), 4-44, http://www.comw .org/warreport/fulltext/0709todd.pdf.

3. Author interview with "C. J." Wadhah Sahib, Jensen, the interpreter "Leo," and the military intelligence Marine Saint One.

4. Frederick W. Kagan, "Al Qaeda in Iraq: How to Understand It. How To Defeat It," *Weekly Standard,* September 10, 2007.

5. Author interviews with "C. J." Wadhah Sahib, Jensen, and Saint One.

6. Edmund L. Andrews, "Bremer Told Bush of Plan To Dissolve Iraqi 'Military and Intelligence Structures,'" *New York Times,* September 4, 2007; Michael R. Gordon, "Fateful Choice on Iraq Army Bypassed Debate," *New York Times,* March 17, 2008. The idea that the dissolution of the Iraqi Army fed the Sunni insurgency has been repeated to this author in innumerable interviews and offhand remarks by both Iraqis and Americans with experience in Iraq.

7. Author interview with Prof. Amatzia Baram, Department of Middle Eastern History, University of Haifa; David R. Smock, "The Role of Religion in Iraqi Politics," United States Institute of Peace, Washington, D.C., December 2003; "Iraqi Islamic Party," GlobalSecurity.org, http://www.globalsecurity.org/military/world/ iraq/iip.htm; David Blair, "Saddam Has Koran Written in His Blood," *Telegraph,* December 14, 2002; Michael Slackman, "Hussein Putting His Mark on Islamic Faith," *Los Angeles Times,* November 4, 2001.

8. Council on Foreign Relations, "Q&A: What Is the Fedayeen Saddam?" *New York Times,* March 25, 2003.

9. Author interview with "Mohammed" (Iraqi police officer interviewed on condition of anonymity); Bill Ardolino, "'Because the

Language They Use Is Killing': An Interview with a Fallujan Police Officer," *INDC Journal*, January 5, 2007.

10. Author interviews with two intelligence experts interviewed on condition of anonymity and Roggio; Evan F. Kohlmann, "State of the Sunni Insurgency in Iraq: August 2007," NEFA Foundation, 2007; "The List."

11. Jon Lee Anderson, *The Fall of Baghdad* (New York: Penguin Press, 2004); "Colonel Gerard Leachman: Iraq 1920," Cambridge Forecast Group Blog, March 26, 2008, http://cambridgeforecast.wordpress. com/2008/03/26/colonel-gerard-leachman-iraq-1920; Borzou Daragahi and Louise Roug, "Sunni Cleric's Arrest Sought," *Los Angeles Times*, November 17, 2006; Bobby Ghosh, "Al-Qaeda Loses an Iraqi Friend," *Time*, May 14, 2007; Bill Roggio, "The Sunni Civil War," *Long War Journal*, March 27, 2007.

12. Laura Parker, "What Exactly Happened That Day in Fallujah?" *USA Today*, June 11, 2007.

13. Rajiv Chandrasekaran, "Key General Criticizes April Attack in Fallujah: Abrupt Withdrawal Called Vacillation," *Washington Post*, September 13, 2004.

14. Dick Camp, *Operation Phantom Fury: The Assault and Capture of Fallujah, Iraq* (n.p.: Zenith Press, 2009), 79–80; "Complex Environments: Battle of Fallujah I, April 2004," report by the U.S. Army National Ground Intelligence Center, March 31, 2006, 6, 13–14; Bing West, *No True Glory: A Frontline Account of the Battle f or Fallujah* (New York: Bantam, 2005), 90–93: "In the absence of countervailing visual evidence presented by authoritative sources, *Al Jazeera* shaped the world's understanding of Fallujah without having to counter the scrutiny of informed skeptics. The resulting political pressures constrained military actions . . . against Fallujah."

15. Camp, *Operation Phantom Fury*, 81–84; Todd Zeranski, "U.S. Wins Fallujah Cease-Fire, Spokesman Senor Says (Update2)," Bloomberg, April 19, 2004.

16. Camp, *Operation Phantom Fury*, 81–84; Zeranski, "U.S. Wins Fallujah Cease-Fire."

17. Ibid.; author interview with Colonel Faisal Ismail Hussein al-Zobaie.

18. Tao-Hung Chang, "The Battle of Fallujah: Lessons Learned on Military Operations on Urbanized Terrain (MOUT) in the 21st Century," *Journal of Undergraduate Research* 6, no. 1 (Fall 2007): 34; John F. Sattler and Daniel H. Wilson, "Operation al Fajr: The Battle of Fallujah, Part II," *Marine Corps Gazette,* July 2005,14, 18, 20; Dexter Filkins, "With Airpower and Armor, Troops Enter Rebel-Held City," *New York Times,* November 8, 2004; Benjamin Harris, "Fallujah—Looking Back at the Fury," *MarinesMag,* June 29, 2010; Tony Karon, "The Grim Calculations of Retaking Fallujah," *Time,* November 8, 2004; Charles Recknagel and Kathleen Ridolfo, "From Fallujah to Qaim," *Asia Times Online,* May 13, 2005; Doug Sample, "Fallujah Secure, but Not Yet Safe, Marine Commander Says," American Forces Press Service, November 18, 2004.

19. Thomas E. Ricks, *Fiasco: The American Military Adventure in Iraq* (New York: Penguin Books, 2007), 400.

20. "Analysis: Battle for Iraq," *PBS Newshour,* November 15, 2004; "Senior Fighters Escape Fallujah," *Washington Times,* May 4, 2004; "Key Insurgents May Have Already Fled Fallujah," ABC News, November 9, 2004; Kirk Semple, "Iraq Issues Warrant for Arrest of Sunni Cleric," *New York Times,* November 17, 2006.

21. The violent rise of al Qaeda in Iraq to prominence is well documented in a number of news articles and was discussed with me by numerous Iraqi and American interview sources, including two intelligence experts speaking on condition of anonymity, Capt. Matt Kralovec, Ma'an Khalid Aifan al-Issawi, Col. John Pollock, Sheikh Shalaan, J. T. Taylor, and others. For a straightforward and informative open source account of the arc of Iraq's insurgency, see Gary W. Montgomery and Timothy S. McWilliams, eds., *Al Anbar Awakening,* vol. 1, *American Perspectives: From Insurgency to Counterinsurgency in Iraq, 2004–2008* (Quantico, VA: Marine Corps University, 2009), and *Al Anbar Awakening,* vol. 2, *Iraqi Perspectives: From Insurgency to Counterinsurgency in Iraq, 2004–2008* (Quantico, VA: Marine Corps University, 2009). The introductions of each and interviews provide critical insight into American and Iraqi perceptions of events. The introduction of volume two, pages 1–13, provides an excellent summation of Anbar's insurgency.

22. Author interview with Abragon, Belshe, Brezler, Dominijanni, Colonel Faisal Ismail Hussein al-Zobaie, Lippo, Mendoza, Pollock, Scott, and Sweezey; Jim Michaels, "Al-Qaeda in Iraq Relying More on Bank Heists," *USA Today,* September 7, 2010; "Iraqi Insurgents Taking Cut of U.S. Rebuilding Money," McClatchy, August 27, 2007; Bill Roggio, "An Interview with the 'Lion of Arab Jabour,'" *Long War Journal,* September 22, 2007; Phil Williams, *Criminals, Militias, and Insurgents: Organized Crime in Iraq* (Carlisle, PA: Strategic Studies Institute, U.S. Army War College, 2009), chaps. 2, 5, 6, 7 and 8.

23. Author interviews with Baram, Mary Habeck, associate professor of strategic studies, Johns Hopkins University, and Thomas Joscelyn, senior editor of the *Long War Journal* and senior fellow at the Foundation for Defense of Democracies.

24. Author interviews with Baram and Habeck; Bruce Livesey, "The Salafist Movement," *Frontline,* January 25, 2005; the term *Salafist-jihadists* (sometimes *jihadi Salafists*) was coined by Gilles Kepel, a professor at the Institute of Political Studies, Paris.

25. Dale C. Eikmeier, "Qutbism: An Ideology of Islamic Fanaticism," *Parameters,* Spring 2007.

26. Ibid.; Paul Berman, "The Philosopher of Islamic Terror," *New York Times Magazine,* March 23, 2003; John Calvert, "The Afterlife of Sayyid Qutb," *Foreign Policy,* December 14, 2010; Robert Siegel, "Sayyid Qutb's America: Al Qaeda Inspiration Denounced U.S. Greed, Sexuality," NPR, May 6, 2003; *Encyclopedia of World Biography,* 2004, s.v. "Sayyid Qutb" (Encyclopedia.com, http://www.encyclope dia.com/doc/1G2–3404705757.html); *Columbia Encyclopedia,* 6th ed. s.v. "Sayyid Qutb" (Encyclopedia.com, http://www.encyclopedia .com/doc/1E1-QutbSyyd.html); David Von Drehle, "A Lesson in Hate: How an Egyptian Student Came To Study 1950s America and Left Determined To Wage Holy War," *Smithsonian,* February 2006. As a young educator, Sayyid Qutb had visited the United States, from 1949 to 1952, traveling extensively and studying education administration in institutions in Washington, D.C., Colorado, and California. Qutb came away from the experience acknowledging the charms of the West: "[T]he New World . . . is spellbinding," he wrote, but he was also repulsed by Western materialism, immorality, and what he termed "its drought of sentimental sympathy." In subsequent writ-

ings, he proclaimed the vapidity of the United States, while railing against the seductive wiles of its women. Upon his return to Egypt, Qutb embraced extreme religious conservatism and a particularly aggressive philosophy of violent jihad.

27. Author interviews with Baram, Habeck, and Joscelyn; Eikmeier, "Qutbism"; Fawaz A. Gerges, "The Far Enemy: Why Jihad Went Global," *Foreign Affairs*, November/December 2005: The "internal enemy" and "external enemy" constructs are often stated by journalists and academics as the "near enemy" and the "far enemy," although, as Habeck counters, it is an inexact representation of al Qaeda's writings.

28. Author interview with Fallujan neighborhood watch volunteer #2 and "Leo."

29. "Zarqawi and the 'al-Qaeda link,'" BBC News, February 5, 2003; Mary Ann Weaver, "The Short, Violent Life of Abu Musab al-Zarqawi," *Atlantic*, July/August 2006.

30. Hannah Allam, "Fallujah's Real Boss: Omar the Electrician," Knight-Ridder Newspapers, November 22, 2004.

31. Anthony Shadid, "Iraqi Fighters Keep Up Attacks: Sunni Cleric Says Fallujah Attracted Hundreds of Recruits," *Washington Post*, December 12, 2004; for Abdullah Janabi's "inflammatory sermons," see West, *No True Glory*, 34.

32. Author interview with Brezler; West, *No True Glory*.

33. Peter Grier, "Iraq's bin Laden? Zarqawi's Rise: CIA Says the Jordanian-Born Terrorist Leader Is the Person Shown Killing a US Civilian on Video," *Christian Science Monitor*, May 14, 2004.

34. Ellen Knickmeyer and Jonathan Finer, "Insurgent Leader al-Zarqawi Killed in Iraq," *Washington Post*, June 8, 2006.

35. Author interview with Roggio; Kohlmann, "State of the Sunni Insurgency in Iraq."

36. Kohlmann, "State of the Sunni Insurgency in Iraq."

37. Lydia Khalil, "Leader of 1920 Revolution Brigades Killed by al-Qaeda," *Terrorism Focus* 4, no. 9 (2007).

38. Author interview with "Mohammed.".

39. Fallujah insurgency intelligence document 1, Fallujah insurgency intelligence document 2, Fallujah insurgency intelligence docu-

ment 3, and Fallujah insurgency intelligence document 4 (documents detailing the organizational structure of the insurgency in the author's possession).

40. Author interview with Colonel Faisal Ismail Hussein al-Zobaie, "Mohammed," Pollock, Roussell, J. T. Taylor, and Whisnant.

41. Joseph Felter and Brian Fishman, "Al-Qa'ida's Foreign Fighters in Iraq: A First Look at the Sinjar Records," Combating Terrorism Center at West Point, Department of Social Sciences, U.S. Military Academy, 2007.

42. Author interview with Whisnant.

43. Fallujah insurgency intelligence document 1.

44. Author interview with Whisnant; Fallujah insurgency intelligence document 1.

45. Author interviews with an American intelligence official, Pollock, Roussell, Saint One, Simcock, and Whisnant.

Chapter 15. Gas

1. Author interviews with Bays, Doezema, Greco, Levasseur, and Reames.

2. Author interviews with Doezema, Greco, and Levasseur; "BBG SVBIED on GBG 16–17 Mar 07" (intelligence document in the author's possession).

3. Author interview with Levasseur.

4. Author interview with Levasseur.

5. Author interviews with Bays, Doezema, Levasseur, and Reames; quotes as recalled by Levasseur. Doezema recalls someone hearing a gunshot before the explosion.

6. Author interview with Tha'er Khalid Aifan al-Issawi as interpreted by Omar Jabouri; Tha'er's presence and general events were confirmed by Ma'an Khalid Aifan al-Issawi, Sheikh Shalaan (Mishael Abdullah Owdeh), Bassam "Ama'an" Mishael Shalaan, and Ahmed Mishael Shalaan; "BBG SVBIED on GBG 16–17 Mar 07."

7. Author interview with Tha'er Khalid Aifan al-Issawi.

8. "BBG SVBIED on GBG 16–17 Mar 07."

9. Author interviews with Levasseur and with Tha'er Khalid Aifan al-Issawi as interpreted by Omar Jabouri.

10. Author interview with Tha'er Khalid Aifan al-Issawi.
11. Author interviews with Cdr. Edwin Taylor, Whisnant, Lt. Cdr. Andrew Zwolski.
12. Author interview with Lehner.
13. Author interviews with Bays, Doezema, Greco, Levasseur, and Reames.
14. Author interviews with Dockter, Doezema, Kopera, Levasseur, Reames, and Zofchak.
15. Author interview with Bays.
16. Author interviews with Doezema and Greco.
17. Author interview with Levasseur.
18. Author interviews with Doezema and Levasseur; quotes as recalled by Levasseur.
19. Author interviews with Bays, Doezema, Greco, Levasseur, and Reames; quote as recalled by Doezema in author interview.
20. Author interviews with Doezema, Greco, and Levasseur; most of the section and set of quotes as recalled by Levasseur.
21. Quotes as recalled by Greco in author interview.
22. Author interviews with Doezema and Levasseur; quote as recalled by Levasseur in author interview.
23. Quote as recalled by Reames in author interview.
24. Quote as recalled by Levasseur in author interview; Greco doesn't recall disbelieving the squad's initial assessments of a chemical attack, but Doezema and Levasseur do.
25. Author interview with Greco.
26. Author interviews with Doezema, Greco, and Levasseur; confirmed by Bays and Reames.
27. Quotes as recalled by Doezema in author interview.
28. Author interviews with Greco and Lehner.
29. Quotes as recalled by Doezema and Greco in author interviews.
30. Author interview with Doezema.
31. Author interviews with Greco and Doezema.
32. Author interview with Greco.
33. Author interviews with Doezema, Greco, and Lehner; "BBG SVBIED on GBG 16–17 Mar 07."

34. Author interview with Ghilarducci.

35. Author interview with Whisnant; quotes as recalled by Whisnant.

36. Author interview with Ghilarducci.

37. Author interviews with Ghilarducci, Ogden, Whisnant, and Zwolski.

38. Author interview with Cdr. Edwin Taylor; "Summary of Action: 16 Mar 07 Local National Mass Casualty Event Resulting from Reported SVBIED with Suspected Chemical Agents Involvement" (after-action report filed by Zwolski).

39. Author interviews with Baum, Greco, Sheikh Shalaan, Tha'er Khalid Aifan al-Issawi, and Whisnant.

40. Author interview with Sheikh Shalaan.

41. Author interviews with Bays, Doezema, Greco, Levasseur, and Reames.

42. Author interviews with Doezema, Greco, and Levasseur.

43. "BBG SVBIED on GBG 16–17 Mar 07."

44. Author interviews with Bays, Doezema, Greco, and Levasseur; photographs of the aftermath in the author's possession.

45. Author interview with Greco.

46. Author interview with Doezema.

47. Author interviews with Bays, Greco, and Reames.

48. Author interview with Greco.

49. Author interviews with Doezema and Greco.

50. Author interview with Lehner; quotes as recalled and paraphrased in part by Lehner.

51. Author interview with Lehner; quotes as recalled by Lehner.

52. Author interview with Greco.

53. Author interviews with Bays and Levasseur; quotes as recalled by Levasseur in author interview.

54. Author interviews with Doezema, Greco, Levasseur, and Reames.

55. Author interviews with Doezema and Levasseur; number of initial wounded via "17 Mar 2007a: Civilian Mass Casualty" (after action report filed by the regimental combat team surgeon, Cmd. Edwin Taylor).

56. Author interviews with Doezema, Levasseur, and Zermeno; "BBG SVBIED on GBG 16–17 Mar 07."

57. Author interview with Doezema.
58. Author interview with Levasseur.

Chapter 16. MassCas

1. Author interviews with Fall, Pickel, Edwin Taylor, Whisnant, and Zwolski; quote by Taylor.

2. Author interview with Corpsman Raymond Shirkey and Edwin Taylor; "17 Mar 2007a: Civilian Mass Casualty" (after-action report filed by the regimental combat team surgeon Edwin Taylor); "Summary of Action: 16 Mar 07."

3. Author interview with Edwin Taylor; profile of the creator of weaponized chlorine gas, "Fritz Haber," Chemical Heritage Foundation, http://www.chemheritage.org/discover/online-resources/chemistry-in-history/themes/early-chemistry-and-gases/haber.aspx; "Facts about Chlorine," Centers for Disease Control and Prevention, http://www.bt.cdc.gov/agent/chlorine/basics/facts.asp; "Weapons of War: Poison Gas," firstworldwar.com, http://www.firstworldwar.com/weaponry/gas.htm; extract from Arthur Hurst, "Gas-Poisoning," *Medical Diseases of the War*, 1917, chap. 10, www virtual library, http://www.vlib.us/medical/gaswar/chlorine.htm.

4. Author interviews with Davis, Muñoz, Shirkey, Edwin Taylor, and Zwolski; "HN Davis Statement for SVBIED HSM 16 Mar 07" (after-action report); "Cpl. Pickel" (after-action report); "17 Mar 2007a: Civilian Mass Casualty"; "Summary of Action: 16Mar07"; "BBG SVBIED on GBG 16–17 Mar 07."

5. Author interviews with Fall, Ogden, Pickel, Edwin Taylor, Whisnant, and Zwolski; quote by Taylor; "17 Mar 2007a: Civilian Mass Casualty"; "Summary of Action: 16Mar07"; "BBG SVBIED on GBG 16–17 Mar 07."

6. Author interviews with Dockter and Zofchak.

7. Author interview with O'Connor.

8. Author interview with Dockter.

9. Author interviews with Dockter and O'Connor; quote by O'Connor.

10. Author interviews with Baum, Dockter, Fall, and Ogden.

11. Author interview with Ogden.

12. Author interview with Sheikh Shalaan.

13. Author interviews with Edwin Taylor and Zwolski.

14. "BBG SVBIED on GBG 16–17 Mar 07."

15. Author interview with Zwolski; "BBG SVBIED on GBG 16–17 Mar 07"; "Summary of Action: 16Mar07."

16. Author interviews with Shirkey and Zwolski; quote as recalled by Zwolski.

17. Author interview with Baum.

18. Author interview with Fall.

19. Author interview with Pickel; "Cpl. Pickel."

20. Author interview with Muñoz.

21. Author interviews with Muñoz and Edwin Taylor.

22. Author interview with Muñoz; "Summary of Action: 16Mar07"; "HN Davis Statement for SVBIED HSM 16Mar07."

23. Author interview with Muñoz.

24. "17 Mar 2007a: Civilian Mass Casualty"; "Summary of Action: 16Mar07."

25. Author interview with Muñoz.

26. Author interview with Edwin Taylor; "Summary of Action: 16Mar07."

27. Author interviews with Edwin Taylor and Zwolski.

28. Zwolski adamantly gives Edwin Taylor credit for making the convoy happen.

29. Author interview with Edwin Taylor.

30. Author interviews with Edwin Taylor and Zwolski; quote as recalled by Taylor.

31. "BBG SVBIED on GBG 16–17 Mar 07."

32. Author interviews with Muñoz, Pickel, and LCpl. Jeremy Shaffer; "Cpl. Pickel."

33. Author interview with Edwin Taylor; "Summary of Action: 16Mar07"; "HN Davis Statement for SVBIED HSM 16Mar07."

34. Author interview with Edwin Taylor.

35. Author interview with the interpreter "C. J." Wadhah Sahib.

36. "Cpl. Pickel."

37. Author interview with Zermeno; assessment of Zermeno's skill by Muñoz and Whisnant.

38. Author interviews with Fall, Ghilarducci, and Shaffer.

39. Author interview with Zermeno. Other Marine documents and testimony indicate that HN Brian Davis and LCpl. Jeremy Shaffer also treated gravely ill children on other convoys to Camp Fallujah.

40. "17 Mar 2007a: Civilian Mass Casualty"; "BBG SVBIED on GBG 16–17 Mar 07."

41. Author interview with Pickel.

42. Author interviews with Sheikh Shalaan (Mishael Abdullah Owdeh); sentiments also expressed by Sheikh Aifan Sadoun Aifan al-Issawi, Baum, Pickel, the military intelligence Marine Saint One, Whisnant, and others.

43. Author interview with Sheikh Shalaan.

44. Author interview with Sheikh Aifan and Sheikh Shalaan; confirmed by Whisnant and several other Marines; Gary W. Montgomery and Timothy S. McWilliams, eds., *Al Anbar Awakening*, vol. 2, *Iraqi Perspectives: From Insurgency to Counterinsurgency in Iraq, 2004–2008* (Quantico, VA: Marine Corps University, 2009), 94; "Letter of Recommendation for Aifan Sadun Aifan al Issawi and Family to Become U.S. Citizens" (document from Regimental Combat Team 6).

45. Author interviews with Edwin Taylor, who was responsible for tracking the patients. While unable to specifically confirm that the child who died was the child Zermeno treated, testimony and reports indicate that only one male toddler was transported, and Edwin Taylor indicates that one male toddler died. The approximate tally was verified by Sheikh Shalaan and Sheikh Aifan in author interviews. Sheikh Aifan said a few died, "including some children."

46. Author interview with Edwin Taylor.

47. Author interview with Brezler.

Chapter 17. Endgame

1. "Monthly Attacks Totals and Averages (2007)," chart released by Regimental Combat Team 6 (document in the author's possession); "OIF—Iraq Significant Activities (SIGACTS)," GlobalSecurity.org, http://www.globalsecurity.org/military/ops/iraq_sigacts.htm; Author interview with Cpt. Barry Edwards.

2. Damien Cave and Ahmad Fadam, "Iraqi Militants Use Chlorine in 3 Bombings," *New York Times*, February 21, 2007; "Chlorine Gas Attacks Hint at New Enemy Strategy," Associated Press, February 22, 2007; "'Chlorine Bomb' Hits Iraq Village," BBC News, May 16, 2007; "Iraqis Killed by Chlorine Bombs," BBC News, March 17, 2007; Bill Roggio, "Al Qaeda's Chlorine Attacks: The Dirty War in Anbar," *Long War Journal*, March 17, 2007, http://www.longwarjour nal.org/archives/2007/03/al_qaedas_chlorine_a.php; Bill Roggio, "Fallujah Government Center Struck by Chlorine Suicide Attack," *Long War Journal*, March 28, 2007, http://www.longwarjournal.org/ archives/2007/03/fallujah_government.php; Bill Roggio, "Al Qaeda's Chlorine War Continues in Ramadi," *Long War Journal*, March 24, 2007, http://www.longwarjournal.org/archives/2007/03/al_qaedas_ chlorine_w.php.

3. Author interviews with Sheikh Aifan Sadoun Aifan al-Issawi, Howe, Iraqi police officer "Mohammed," Sheikh Shalaan (Mishael Abdullah Owdeh), Roussell, and Whisnant.

4. Author interviews with Howe, Lt. Col. Anthony Sermarini, Roussell, J. T. Taylor, and Whisnant.

5. Roggio, "Al Qaeda's Chlorine Attacks."

6. Author interviews with Sheikh Aifan and Sheikh Shalaan. Author interview with Fallujah neighborhood watch volunteer 1: "We woke up to move the bad guy, to push him out, to kill him or to put him in jail. We were waiting for help from the government." Author interview with Fallujah neighborhood watch volunteer 2: "Before [the Iraqi Police] did not have enough cover to hold their city. But right now, they got cover, like what you see: every single IP [Iraqi police] station has Marines with them, to give them support every time the IP want it. Another thing? They didn't have weapons, but right now they have weapons, so they can do the right thing, kill the terrorists and survive." Author interview with Fallujah neighborhood watch volunteer 3: "I think, what made [the] change, [is] the American support, the USA support to the IPs and . . . support to all the western region, and that's what's different from now and then."

7. Author interview with an American intelligence official quoted on condition of anonymity; events verified by Sheikh Shalaan.

8. Author interviews with Roussell and Whisnant; interview with Sheikh Aifan in Gary W. Montgomery and Timothy S. McWilliams, eds., *Al Anbar Awakening*, vol. 2, *Iraqi Perspectives: From Insurgency to Counterinsurgency in Iraq, 2004–2008* (Quantico, VA: Marine Corps University, 2009), 94.

9. Author interview with Sheikh Aifan; "Anbar Councilman's Guard Killed in Falluja," National Iraqi News Agency, January 1, 2010; interview with Sheikh Aifan in Montgomery and McWilliams, *Al Anbar Awakening*, 2:93–97.

10. Sheikh Khamis Hasnawi Aifan al-Issawi would eventually die from cancer in 2011, a fact relayed to the author by Sheikh Aifan in an interview. Bill Ardolino, "Paramount Sheikh of the Albu Issa Survives Assassination Attempt," *Long War Journal*, September 2, 2009, as excerpted from a report in *Aswat al-Iraq*, http://www.longwarjournal.org/threat-matrix/archives/2009/09/paramount_sheik_of_the_albu_is.php.

11. Author interview with Sheikh Aifan, "Mohammed" (Fallujan police officer), Roussell, Sheikh Shalaan, and Whisnant.

12. Author interview with Sheikh Shalaan.

13. Author interview with J. T. Taylor.

14. Author interview with Whisnant.

15. Author interviews with Sgt. Richard Arias, Crawford, Piedrahita, Poudrier, Sermarini, Simcock, and Townsley.

16. Author interviews with 1st Lt. Barry Edwards and J. T. Taylor.

17. Evan Kohlmann, "State of the Insurgency in Iraq: August 2007," NEFA Foundation.

18. Evan Kohlmann, "Iraqi Insurgent Faction Breaks Silence, Accusing al-Qaida of Fanaticism, Torture, and Murder," *Counterterrorism Blog*, October 4, 2007.

19. Coming to the conclusions that the Americans intended to leave Iraq and that the U.S. military did not intent to plunder Iraq's resources was a process for many Sunnis, insurgents or otherwise. Colonel Faisal Ismail Hussein al-Zobaie remarked in an author interview: "Through my [experience as a former insurgent], the way I look at Americans, I look at them and feel like they are occupiers, occupying my country when the invasion happened. But when other parties

showed up—especially the radicals and the Iranian militias, both who are not Iraqis—now I prefer the Americans. I've met [various Americans working for Fallujah]. It is my feeling that [they are] working hard, and [before I knew] you [Americans] I had a different image. Now that I know the Americans, I have a different impression. Now I deal honestly with them and feel they are really working for the benefit of my side. I think the Americans are more for Iraq than the Iraqis themselves." One mukhtar (local leader in the city, sort of like a block captain) made similar remarks in an author interview: "We thought America wanted to steal Iraq. And from our perspective as Muslims, you should fight against thieves. And all the people around the world. . . . It's the same in America. . . . If Iraq went to America to take America, all the people would fight against Iraq. I think we can agree about that. The Americans now are peaceful—more than us [laughs]. They are helpful and give humanitarian support for the people here."

20. Suadad al-Salhy, "Insight: Iraq War Over? Not Where Qaeda Rules Through Fear," Reuters, March 25, 2012; Saad al-Mosuli, "Al-Qaeda Turns to Mafia Tactics in Mosul," Institute for War and Peace Reporting, June 7, 2010; Bill Roggio, "Iraqi forces Capture Two Senior al Qaeda Leaders in Mosul," *Long War Journal*, April 7, 2010, http://www.longwarjournal.org/archives/2010/04/iraqi_forces_capture.php.

21. Rowan Scarborough, "Al Qaeda in Iraq Mounts Comeback," *Washington Times*, March 4, 2012.

22. Bill Roggio, "Al Qaeda in Iraq Claims Nationwide Attacks That Killed More Than 100 Iraqis," *Long War Journal*, July 25, 2012, http://www.longwarjournal.org/archives/2012/07/al_qaeda_in_iraq_cla_2.php.

23. Bill Ardolino and Bill Roggio, "Al Qaeda in Iraq Video Details Deadly Raid in Haditha," *Long War Journal*, August 21, 2012, http://www.longwarjournal.org/archives/2012/08/_the_islamic_state_o.php.

24. Author's personal observation of the way a number of Iraqi cops and security volunteers regarded al Qaeda. "U.S. Officials: Al Qaeda Unpopular and 'Imploding,'" Associated Press, September 16, 2008; Daniel DePetris, "Allies Could End Iraq's al-Qaeda Scourge," *Asia Times Online*, March 30, 2012, who writes, "Fast-forward six years,

and AQI is a degraded group of jihadist 'misfits' whose puritanical version of Islam is rejected by the vast majority of the Iraqi population"; Shibley Telhami, "Hezbollah's Popularity Exposes al-Qaeda's Failure to Win the Hearts," *San Jose Mercury News*, July 30, 2006.

25. Author interview with Sheikh Aifan.

26. Author interview with Roussell, military intelligence officer Saint One, Simcock, and Whisnant.

27. Author interview with Whisnant.

28. Author interview with Roussell, Saint One, Simcock, and Whisnant.

29. Author interviews with Roussell and Whisnant.

30. Dafna Linzer and Tom Ricks, "Anbar Picture Grows Clearer, and Bleaker," *Washington Post*, November 28, 2006; "Weekly Security Incidents: January 3, 2004–August 28, 2009" (chart of security incidents in Iraq published by U.S. Central Command).

31. Author interview with Whisnant.

32. Author interviews with Sheikh Aifan, Roussell, and Whisnant.

33. Shane Bauer, "The Sheikh Down," *Mother Jones*, September/October 2009; Sam Dagher, "Will 'Armloads' of US Cash Buy Tribal Loyalty?" *Christian Science Monitor*, November 8, 2007.

34. Author interview with Roussell.

35. Author interviews with U.S. intelligence official speaking on condition of anonymity, Roussell, and Whisnant.

36. Author interviews with Roussell, Simcock, and Whisnant.

37. "Letter of Recommendation for Aifan Sadun Aifan al Issawi and Family to Become U.S. Citizens" (document from Regimental Combat Team 6).

38. Dahr Jamail, "Iraq's 'Teflon Don,'" *Huffington Post*, February 12, 2009; Bauer, "The Sheikh Down."

39. Montgomery and McWilliams, *Al Anbar Awakening*, 2:98.

40. Author interview with a U.S. intelligence official speaking on condition of anonymity; "Official Says 3 Emirati Men Have Been Freed after Kidnapping in Iraq," Associated Press, December 6, 2010.

41. Anthony Shadid, "Sunnis Go to Polls, This Time, to Retain a Voice," *New York Times*, March 7, 2010.

42. Author interviews with Sheikh Aifan and Kirk Sowell, an Arabic-language researcher and analyst of Iraqi politics. Sheikh Aifan's status

was verified by two other tribesmen, and Sowell filled in the unique circumstances of his ascent to national office.

43. Author interviews with Brezler, U.S. intelligence official speaking on condition of anonymity, Roussell, Saint One, Simcock, Edwin Taylor, J. T. Taylor, Whisnant, and many other Americans; Jamail, "Iraq's 'Teflon Don.'"

44. Author interview with Roussell.

45. Martyrdom posters posted by Aifan's supporters and family members on Facebook; "ISI Claims Assassination of Iraqi MP Issawi, Strikes in Anbar," SITE Intelligence Group, January 20, 2013.

46. Author interview with Sheikh Aifan.

47. Author interview with Howe.

48. Author interviews with Albrecht, Baum, Bays, Beemer, Blevins, Carlson, Campbell, Dockter, Doezema, Fall, Foerster, Ghilarducci, Greco, Hoffmann, Inman, Jansen, Jongsma, Kimmey, Kopera, Kyle, Lehner, Levasseur, Moose, Muñoz, O'Connor, Ogden, Osborne, Paredes, Pickel, Ponce, Reames, "C. J." Wadhah Sahib, Serr, Steimel, Villanueva, Whisnant, Williams, Wortman, and Zofchak.

49. Author interview with Steimel.

50. Author interviews with Albrecht, Baum, Bays, Beemer, Blevins, Carlson, Campbell, Dockter, Doezema, Fall, Foerster, Ghilarducci, Greco, Hoffmann, Inman, Jansen, Jongsma, Kimmey, Kopera, Kyle, Lehner, Levasseur , Moose, Muñoz, O'Connor, Ogden, Osborne, Paredes, Pickel, Ponce, Reames, "C. J." Wadhah Sahib, Serr, Steimel, Villanueva, Whisnant, Williams, Wortman, and Zofchak.

51. Author interviews with Ponce and Reames.

52. Author interview with Ponce.

53. Author interview with Fallujah neighborhood watch volunteer 1; Bill Ardolino, "Operation Alljah: The Swarm," *INDC Journal*, September 8, 2007.

54. Author interview with Fallujah neighborhood watch volunteer 3; Ardolino, "Operation Alljah."

55. Author interview with Ponce.

56. Fadhil al-Badrani, Ahmed Rasheed, and Paul Casciato, "Thousands Celebrate U.S. Withdrawal in Iraq's Falluja," Reuters, December 14, 2011.

❖ INDEX ❖

Abu Ghraib prison, 9, 37, 88, 249n18
Abu Risha tribe, 15, 61, 231n30
Adilah, 93–94, 96–99, 250nn6–7
Aifan al-Issawi, Aifan Sadoun "Dark":
accidental shooting in Albu Aifan,
77–78, 82; Albu Aifan residence
of, 65; alliance and relationship
with Americans, 82, 210, 211–14;
ambition of, 15, 63, 211–12; assassination attempts and threats to life
of, 205–6, 212–15; attack on house
on outskirts of Albu Aifan, 78–80;
authority and influence of, 9, 12,
14, 59, 78, 81, 110, 112; charisma
of, 81, 214; chlorine truck bomb
driver, disposal of remains of, 203;
chlorine truck bomb incident, 181,
182–83, 186; cooperation, offers of,
59, 60; cordon and sweep operations, 90; death of, 214–15, 278n45;
dinner with and spending night at
house of, 125–26; enthusiasm for
action by, 61–63; family of, 125–26;
fear of, 78; Greco, relationship with,
81; gunfighter role of, 63, 244n25;
Hawa, intelligence about insurgents
in, 131, 142–43, 146; IEDs, information about location of, 80–81,
85–86; imprisonment of, 9; insurgency, fighting back against, 13,
14–16, 54–55, 231n28; insurgency,
ties to, 9; insurgency threat to, 166,
171–72; intelligence from, 85–91,
98, 99; Jordan, return from, 10–11,
61, 230n12; kidnapped Iraqi, intelligence from, 128–30; license for
forces, requests for, 231n30; likabil-
ity of, 60; link between Khamis and,
14, 231n27; medical/veterinary civil

action program, 114, 117; mother of,
death of, 203; motivation for cooperating against insurgency, 9, 10–11,
14, 15, 81, 230n12, 231n28; opinions about, 58–59, 63, 214, 244n25;
organizer role of, 63, 244n25; photos
with, 117; promises made to by U.S.,
58–59, 62–64; promises made to
by U.S. in Jordan, 10, 14, 16; reconstruction project contracts, 110–12;
report about meeting with, 54–55;
risks taken by in cooperation with
Americans, 211–15; Sattar, meeting
with and borrowing units from, 15,
231n30; secret meeting request and
theatrics, 11, 13–14; security for,
210; security for tribes in fighting
insurgents, 62–64; U.S. citizenship, recommendation for, 212–13;
Whisnant meetings with, 7–9,
10–11, 12–16, 58–64; widows, event
to support, 124–25; wounding of
during Second Battle of Fallujah, 81
Aifan al-Issawi, Barakat Sadoun, 61
Aifan al-Issawi, Khamis Hasnawi: Albu
Aifan residence of, 65, 67–68; alliance with Americans, 192–93, 210;
assassination attempts, 205–6;
attitude toward assisting Marines,
60–62; attitude toward insurgency,
14, 54–55, 60–61, 243n24; authority
and influence of, 61, 110, 112; chlorine truck bomb incident, 178, 184–
86; death of, 275n10; insurgency
threat to, 166, 171–72; Jordan,
return from, 10–11, 61; Jordan as
refuge for, 10; link between Dark
and, 14, 231n27; paramount sheikh
status, 10; reconstruction project

contracts, criteria for awarding, 112; security for, 210; Whisnant meetings with, 59–64

Aifan al-Issawi, Ma'an Khalid: accidental shooting in Albu Aifan, 77, 78, 82; attack on house on outskirts of Albu Aifan, 79; collaborative relationship with Americans, 82; cordon and sweep operations, 90; dinner with Americans, 125; as host of Whisnant meeting, 12–13; insurgency, fighting back against, 12–13; Khamis attitude toward insurgency, 243n24; role as link between Khamis and Dark, 14, 231n27; Zien-Muzien Game, 128

Aifan al-Issawi, Mushtaq Khalid, 125, 128

Aifan al-Issawi, Tha'er Khalid, 72, 78, 82, 175–77, 221–22

Aifan al-Issawi, Uthman Majid, 90, 125, 126, 128, 170, 205

Air Force, U.S., attitudes of Marines toward, 18

Albrecht, Alex: Kimmey, trust of and relationship with, 94, 95–96; overwatch house and Adilah, 92, 93–94, 96–99; reason for becoming a Marine, 92–93; Route Boston and shooting of sheikh, 148; Route Boston sniper incident, 149–56

Albu Aifan: accidental shooting in, 66, 68–78, 81–82; ambushes and firefights, 29–34, 41–47, 236nn5–6, 237n23; ambushes and firefights, review of and success of, 34, 51–52, 237n31; attack on house on outskirts of, 68, 72, 78–80, 81, 83, 245n15, 245n17; commandeering house for firing position, 35–36, 238n40; information-gathering campaign, 65, 66–68; medical/veterinary civil action program, 114–20, 126–27, 255n7, 256n25; militia, information about, 86; mosque as location of attackers, 30, 32, 33, 39, 238n53; mosque as location of attackers, move toward and investigation of, 33–36, 38–40, 239n57; photos with female Marines, 120–21; roadblock to find insurgents, 40–41, 45, 239n59; sheikhs of, 10; tribal leadership residences in, 65, 67–68; wounded woman, treatment and evacuation of, 47–51, 52, 53, 240n102, 241n117, 241n125. See also Dark, Forward Operating Base (sheikh's house)

Albu Issa: alliance with Americans, 108, 110–12, 192–93; area under control of, 8–9; double-dealing by and successful cooperation with U.S., 11–12, 124; insurgency, support for, 11; intelligence from, 84, 85, 86–91; Islamist radicals, relationship with, 10; Jordan as refuge for tribal leadership, 10–11, 230n12; nationalist stance, 11; organization of, 9–10; promises made to by Whisnant, 202; sheikhs, authority of, 9–10, 110–12; tribal awakening by, 3; tribe members as insurgents, 89–90; war against al Qaeda, 88–89

Alljah, Operation, 207

ambushes and firefights, situational awareness and response to, 43

Ameriyeh, 1, 205

Anbar province, 1, 2–3

Arabic language, 25

arm wrestling and exchange of gifts, 121–22

Army, U.S.: attitudes of Marines toward, 18; COIN strategies, 256–57n34; deployments, length of, 243–44n31; Marines compared to Army units, 232n3

Auton, Steven, 41, 44, 51, 239n66

bananas as luxury item, 254n2

Baum, Ken, 117–20, 194, 255n18, 255–56n20, 256n25

Beemer, Michael, 149, 150, 152, 156

Belshe, Tylor: arm wrestling and exchange of gifts, 121–22; background and experience of, 103;

Brezler and Roussell, relationship with, 107; CAG projects, 105, 106, 110; medical/veterinary civil action program, 114, 115–17; photo with Dark, 117; sunglasses of, Iraqi interest in, 121; Team Yankee civil affairs missions, 103
Benedict, Christopher, 141
bicycles, 122
Bigger, Dave, 148, 149
Bishop, Robert, 173
Black, Forward Operating Base, 8, 21
Blackwater contractors, killing of, 162
Blevins, Jack, 71
blood debt, 83
Boston, Route: overwatch houses on, 148, 149–50, 156; shooting of sheikh in crossfire of firefight, 147–48; sniper incident, 149–56
Brezler, Jason: Awakening and CAG projects, opinion about, 111; dinner with and spending night at house of Dark, 125–26; experience and leadership skills of, 102; high tempo operations, 102, 106; medical/veterinary civil action program, 113, 114; Roussell and Team Yankee taxi service, 107; sheikhs, projects to support authority of, 108, 110–12; Team Yankee civil affairs missions, 102, 104–5, 106–7, 110–12; widows, event to support, 125
Brown, Ryan, 84
Bueno, Brad, 28, 29
burial of dead, Islamic traditions on, 34, 237n31
Bush, George W., 2, 62, 171, 210

Cahir, Bill, 103–4, 110, 111–12, 114, 125–26
Carlson, Kelly, 97–98, 149, 150–51, 150–56
census ops, 23, 24–25, 94, 96
chemical attacks: gas masks, chemical suits, and preparedness for, 180, 181–82, 186–87; poison and chlorine gas attacks, 204, 205, 209;

threat from and likelihood of, 180; weaponization of chlorine gas, 189
chlorine truck bomb: bomber, disposal of remains of, 203, 273n45; deaths from, 203, 273n45; effects of chlorine gas, 176–77, 180–88, 189–90, 194, 269n24; evacuation and transport of casualties, 186, 187–89, 191–92, 195; explosion of, 173–78; militia checkpoint and detonation of, 175–77; preparedness for chemical attack, 180; re-creation of narrative, 221–22; response to, 181–82, 183–88, 190–91; response to and gratitude from civilians, 201–2; second attack from, 204; transport of casualties to Camp Fallujah Surgical, 193–200, 203, 272n28, 273n39, 273n45; treatment of casualties, 189, 190–91, 195–202, 203; weaponization of chlorine gas, 189
civil affairs and Civil Affairs Group (CAG) units: contracts, criteria for assignment of, 112; convoys, targeting of and attacks on, 102, 106; criticism of projects as bribery, 111; effectiveness of and success of, 105, 107; enthusiasm for Marines to participate in, 116, 255n12; high tempo operations, 102; humanitarian and reconstruction projects, 100–101, 104–6, 110–12; military occupation specialty for civil affairs, 101; mobility of units, 106–7; The Regulators, 102; security and intimidation problems related to projects, 100–101, 105; sheikhs, challenges of conducting business with, 111–12; Team Yankee, 102–7, 110–12; volunteers for, 103; wasted effort of projects, 101. See also medical/veterinary civil action program (MEDCAP/VETCAP) mission
Clayton, Josh, 84–85, 128, 143
condolence payments, 78
Conway, James T., 163
cordon and sweep operations, 90

counterinsurgency doctrine (COIN): application of around Fallujah, 4, 209–11; complexity of execution of, 20, 232–33n7; concept of, 20; controversy over and opinions about, 4, 219–20; development of, 2; execution of, differences in between units, 122–23, 209–10, 256–57n34; information and cooperation of Iraqis as key to success of, 8, 20, 22, 38–39; local political changes and success of, 4; Petraeus and field manual on, 219, 256–57n34; protection of people and people as prize, 20, 53; relationship building and length of deployments, 62, 209–10, 243–44n31, 256n33; relationship building and treatment of Iraqis, 122–24, 256–57n34, 257n36; relationship building and U.S. interests, 63; success of, 3, 4, 27–28, 209–11, 215–18, 219–20, 235n30, 256–57n34; tradition of in Corps, 57–58; urban COIN campaign, 207

Dark. *See* Aifan al-Issawi, Aifan Sadoun "Dark"
Dark, Forward Operating Base (sheikh's house): establishment of, 62, 63–64; firefight in area of, 41–47; roadblock near after ambush, 40–41, 45, 239n59
Davis, Brian, 273n39
Dennert, Jacob, 173
Dhari, Harith al-, 161–62, 164, 167
diya (blood price), 83
Dockter, Christopher: accidental shooting in Albu Aifan, 66, 68–74, 75–76, 81–82; Albu Aifan census op, 66; Albu Aifan information-gathering operations, 66–68; appearance of, 23; attack on house on outskirts of Albu Aifan, 78, 79–80; augmentation of 1/24 with men from 3/24, 23; captured weapons and insurgents, transport back to FOB, 143; chlorine truck bomb incident, 191; commu-

nication with helicopter, 50; experience, patience, and leadership skills of, 23–24; Hawa road, IEDs on, 144; nicknames for, 23; question-and-answer sessions, frustration with, 23, 24–25, 234n17; weapons, confiscation of, 25; wounded woman, treatment and evacuation of, 241n125
Doezema, Kendrick: chlorine truck bomb incident, 173, 174, 178, 179–82, 184–85, 188, 269n24; Levasseur, relationship with, 178–79; nickname for, 178; personality and character of, 178–79; reason for becoming a Marine, 178; wounding and recovery of, 178, 179

Fall, Ken, 194
Fallujah: Awakening and alliance with U.S. to fight insurgents, 2–3, 4, 215–18; Awakening and CAG projects, 111; battles at, brutality of, 1; civilian casualties in, 162–63, 264n14; damage to and destruction of, 100, 101; distrustful relationship with Americans, 124; First Battle of, 1, 162–63, 169; map of, 7; media coverage of events in, 162–63, 264n14; protest at, shooting of Iraqis at, 37, 71; rebellious history of, 124; resistance against foreign forces in, 4; Second Battle of, 1, 19, 27, 57, 81, 100, 163–64, 169; security in, improvement of, 2–3; Third Battle of, 1; tough and strong character of population, 9, 229n6; tourism advisory against visits to, 229n6
Ferris, switching off water to, 106
fishing and use of explosives, 145, 261n49
Foerster, Gabe: medical/veterinary civil action program, 118, 127, 256n25; Route Boston and shooting of sheikh, 148; Route Boston patrol, 149, 150; Route Boston sniper incident, 154
food and supplies distribution, 113–17, 120, 254n2, 255n7

fourth-generation warfare, 20
friend and foe, telling difference
  between, 67

Ghilarducci, Bill, 182–83
Gilbert, Thomas M. "Tommy," 5, 28, 29,
  50, 99
Gillitzer, Michael, 69
Gold, Forward Operating Base, 21
Greco, Jerome: accidental shooting
  in Albu Aifan, 69, 73–74, 75–77;
  Adilah, information from, 99; Albu
  Aifan ambushes and firefights,
  report to on, 33–34; Albu Aifan
  information-gathering operations,
  65, 66, 67–68; Albu Aifan roadblock, 40; appearance of, 21; attack
  on house on outskirts of Albu
  Aifan, 78–80; attacks on Marines,
  volume of, 27–28; chemical attack,
  preparedness for, 186–87; chlorine
  truck bomb incident, 173, 177–78,
  180–82, 184–86, 269n24; combat
  experience of, 19; competition
  between platoons, 21–22; Dark,
  relationship with, 81; experience
  and leadership skills of, 21–22;
  Hawa operations, 132; house for
  patrol base and escape of al Qaeda
  operatives, 73; intelligence reports
  and paper shuffling, 27; medal
  award for Kopera, 53; nickname for,
  22; opinions about, 216; personality and character of, 21–22; platoon
  command by, 19, 21; Reserve units
  and weekend warrior stereotypes
  about, 19; sympathy for noncooperative people, 26; weapons, confiscation of, 25; wounded woman,
  treatment and evacuation of, 48–49,
  53. See also Marine Regiment,
  24th, 1st Battalion (1/24), Alpha
  Company, 3rd Platoon

Hadid, Omar, 167
Hamadi, Fallah, 155, 171–72, 209
Hasa, 52

Hauser, Christine, 120–21
Hawa: attacks and firefights in, 130–31,
  133–34, 259n6; bongo truck incident, 140–42, 145; captured weapons and insurgents, 141, 142–44;
  captured weapons and insurgents,
  transport back to FOB, 143–44;
  early morning arrival, advantage of,
  132–33; IEDs on road to, 132, 143,
  144; intelligence about from Dark,
  131, 142–43, 146; intelligence about
  from kidnapped Iraqi, 128–31; mission to kill or capture insurgents,
  132–44, 146; success of operations,
  146; trials for captured insurgents,
  139, 144–46, 261n49; U-shaped
  house and grenade incident, 135–
  39, 144–45; weapons and ammunition, disposal of, 139–40
Hayes, Jim, 59–60, 86
helicopters: action taken on intelligence
  with, 86–87; communication with,
  48–50; evacuation of wounded
  woman, 48–51, 241n117; Kopera
  injury and evacuation by, 241n125
Hobbits, 84, 89–91
Hoffmann, Jeremy: Adilah, information
  from, 97, 98–99; appearance of,
  21; competition between platoons,
  21–22; experience and leadership
  skills of, 21–22; Hawa operations,
  132, 133–34, 139–40, 259n6; intelligence reports and paper shuffling,
  27; Iraqis, respect and good intentions in treatment of, 140; language
  skills of, 94; opinions about, 216;
  personality and character of, 21–22;
  relationship building with Iraqis,
  importance of, 93; Route Boston
  and shooting of sheikh, 147–48;
  Route Boston patrol, 149, 150;
  Route Boston sniper incident, 152,
  154, 156; training and drilling platoon, 92. See also Marine Regiment,
  24th, 1st Battalion (1/24), Alpha
  Company, Weapons Platoon
Hough, Matt, 173, 174, 180

houses and property: CAG projects, 106; commandeering for firefight positions, 35–36; commandeering of, reaction of residents to, 35–36, 238n40; house for patrol base and escape of al Qaeda operatives, 73; locked houses, 93; overwatch house and Adilah, 92–94, 96–99, 250nn6–7; reactions to firefights around, 36; Route Boston overwatch houses, 148, 149–50, 156; search procedures, 35–36

Howe, Jeremiah: captured weapons and insurgents, transport back to FOB, 143–44; feeling about leaving Fallujah, 215; intelligence about from kidnapped Iraqi, 129; intelligence about Hawa insurgency, 142–43; intelligence analysis role, 84; intelligence operations, preparation for and understanding of, 131; Zien-Muzien Game, 128

human intelligence exploitation team (HET), 97–98, 104

Hussein, Saddam, 108–9, 159–60, 161

"Improvise, Adapt and Overcome" motto, 18

improvised explosive devices (IEDs): attitudes toward Iraqis after troop deaths from, 5–6; cells responsible for planting, detention of, 99; deaths of Marines from, 5–6, 28; factory making VBIEDs, information on location of, 86; foot expedition to locate, 22; on Hawa road, 132, 143, 144; helicopter landing in area known to contain, 50; Iraqis role in hiding, 81, 86; location of, information from Dark about, 80–81; location of, information from Iraqis about, 5–6, 26, 85–86; threat from, 27–28, 235n30

information-gathering campaign and intelligence: action taken on intelligence, 86–91; Adilah, information from, 94, 96–99; Albu Issa tribe,

intelligence from, 84, 85, 86–91; census ops, 23, 24–25, 94, 96; Dark, intelligence from, 85–91, 98, 99; falling in love with sources, 81; Hobbits and analysis of intelligence, 84–85, 89–91; human intelligence exploitation team (HET), 97–98, 104; IEDs, information about location of, 5–6, 26, 80–81, 85–86; information and cooperation of Iraqis as key to beating insurgency, 8, 20, 22, 38–39, 91; kidnapped Iraqi, intelligence from, 128–31; names of insurgents and database to track, 26–27, 90–91, 128, 143; paper shuffling and intelligence reports, 27; poison pen and trust of information, 90–91; preparation for and understanding of intelligence operations, 131; survival instinct, intimidation by insurgents, and cooperation with Americans, 25–26, 27, 38–39, 234–35n23; trust of intelligence information, 90–91, 97, 128–30; Zien-Muzien Game, 128

Inman, Caleb, 30–32, 33, 40, 41, 45–46, 48, 49, 51

insh'allah (God willing), 36, 78, 82–83, 144, 248n80

insurgency and al Qaeda: Albu Issa support for, 11; Albu Issa tribe members as insurgents, 89–90; in Anbar provence, 1; bad weather, operations in, 259n3; burial of dead, 34, 237n31; capture and interrogation of insurgents, 87–89, 205; cell organization of, 169, 171–72; change in attitude toward Americans by, 208, 275–76n19; COIN and halt of growth of, 4; criminal enterprises and gangs, resemblance to, 56; dangerous work of fighting, 28; decline in attacks by, 204–9, 276–77n24; emir of al Qaeda, 155, 171–72, 209; escape of al Qaeda operatives, 73; external enemies, 166, 267n27; Fallujah Awakening and alliance

with U.S. to fight, 2–3, 4, 202–3; foreign fighters in, 170, 202, 206–7; high-value targets, 155; identification of, 55, 60; information and cooperation of Iraqis as key to beating, 8, 20, 22, 38–39, 91; internal enemies, 166, 267n27; killing of insurgents by insurgents, 168–71; names of insurgents and database to track, 26–27, 90–91, 128, 143; negotiations with insurgent groups, 158; al Qaeda, denouncement of, 207–9, 276–77n24; al Qaeda, pariah status of, 202–3; al Qaeda in Iraq, threat from, 157–58, 262–63n1; al Qaeda in Iraq as dominant force, 164–68, 169, 265n21; Ramadi Awakening and alliance with U.S. to fight, 2, 61; reconciliation between tribal leaders and insurgents, 206; revenge against and killing of anyone cooperating with Americans, 12–13, 62–63, 91, 97, 250n29; rush hour for mortar attacks, 259n3; sheikhs, threat to from, 166, 171–72; Shia Iranian help for, 170–71; shooting of Iraqis and growth of in Fallujah, 71; size of, 169–70; success of and popular support for, 20; success of Marines against, 27–28, 235n30; Sunni insurgency, categories and motivations of, 157–62, 263n6; tribes, insurgent threat against, 12–13, 62–63, 91, 97, 250n29; tribes, relationships with, 109–10; tribesmen and citizens, attacks on, 204–9; villagers with weapons, concerns about being mistaken for insurgents, 25, 124n21; warring factions within, 208
intelligence reports and paper shuffling, 27
interrogation of captured insurgents, 87–89, 249n18
Iraq: abuse of civilians and mistakes and public relations disasters after invasion, 36–37, 71, 72–73; Iraqi army, disbanding of, 159, 263n6

Iraqi police and security forces: contributions to security in Fallujah, 3, 207; effectiveness of and success of, 207; interrogation methods of, 88; killing and wounding of, 2; leadership of, 2; rush hour for mortar attacks, 259n3; training and capabilities of, 2, 62, 135, 204–5, 274n6; U.S. strategy for lead role of, 2, 62
Islamic Army in Iraq (IAI), 160–61, 168
Islamic State of Iraq, 10, 109, 168, 171, 202, 206, 208–9
Islamic traditions on burial of dead, 34, 237n31
Ivers, Brian: chlorine truck bomb incident, 183, 185; criticism of, 21; experience and leadership skills of, 21; platoon command by, 21; transport of casualties to Camp Fallujah Surgical, 198. See also Marine Regiment, 24th, 1st Battalion (1/24), Alpha Company, 2nd Platoon

Jansen, Ron: clear conscience over killings, 146; Hawa operations, 133–34, 135–39, 140–42; Iraqis, respect and good intentions in treatment of, 140; trials for captured insurgents, 144–46
Joe (interpreter), 97, 98, 197
Johnson, Andrew, 68, 70–71
Jongsma, Chris, 93–94, 96, 97–98, 149
Jordan: motivation for return from, 10–11, 61, 230n12; promises made to Dark in, 10, 14, 16; refuge for tribal leadership in, 10, 61

Kenny, Tyler, 141
Kimmey, Jared: Albrecht, trust of and relationship with, 94, 95–96; attitude, commitment, and judgment of, 94–96; captured Iraqis, treatment of, 96; language skills of, 94, 96; overwatch house and Adilah, 93–94, 96–99; reason for becoming a Marine, 94–95; Route

Boston and shooting of sheikh, 148; Route Boston sniper incident, 149–56; women, responsibilities of, 255–56n20

Kopera, David: ambushes and firefights, 29–31, 33–34, 45–47, 236nn5–6; ambushes and firefights, review of and success of, 51–52; Bronze Star with Valor Device award, 53; communication with helicopter, 48–50; experience and leadership skills of, 34, 53; interviews with Iraqis on way to mosque, 38–39; Iraqi people, admiration and respect for, 36–37; mosque as location of attackers, 30, 33, 39, 238n53; mosque as location of attackers, move toward and investigation of, 34–35, 36, 38–40; reason for becoming a Marine, 37–38; roadblock to find insurgents, 40–41, 45, 239n59; wounded woman, treatment and evacuation of, 47, 48–51, 52, 53; wounding of, 52, 242n130

Krulak, Charles, 20

Lehner, Rob: chlorine truck bomb incident, 177, 186–87; experience and leadership skills of, 21; Hawa operations, 132; platoon command by, 21. See also Marine Regiment, 24th, 1st Battalion (1/24), Alpha Company, 1st Platoon

Levasseur, Steven: chlorine truck bomb incident, 173–75, 178, 179–80, 187, 188, 269n24; Doezema, relationship with, 178–79

Lippo, Brian, 3

livestock: responsibility of women for, 118, 255–56n20; veterinary aid program, 117–20

long ops, 22, 23, 73

Manis, Gabe, 148, 149

Marine Corps, U.S.: attitudes toward Iraqis after wounding and killing of friends, 5–6; COIN tradition in, 57–58; contributions to security in Fallujah, 3; culture and training of, 17–18, 232n3; cynicism in, 18; deployments, length of, 62, 243–44n31, 256n33; happiness of Marines, 23; motto of, 18; patience and professionalism to cement alliance to stop insurgency, 5–6; reasons for joining, 17–19, 37–38, 231–32nn2–4; romanticism and reasons for joining, 18–19, 232n4; security improvements and activities of, 2–3; unofficial motto of, 18

Marine Corps Reserve, U.S.: advantages of units, 19–20; commanders of units, 19–20; experience and skills of Reservists, 19–20; reason for joining, 17–19, 231–32nn2–4; weekend warrior stereotypes about units, 19, 232n5

Marine Regiment, 6th, 3rd Battalion, Kilo Company, 209–10

Marine Regiment, 24th, 1st Battalion (1/24), Alpha Company: attacks on, volume of, 27–28, 235n30; civilian lives of men in, 17; competition between platoons in, 21–22; deployment rotations of, 38; deployment to Fallujah, opting out of, 38; feeling about leaving Fallujah, 215–18; home for, 17; infantry training of, 19; operational pace and schedule, 22–23; organizational structure of, 20–21; Reserve status and reason for becoming Marines, 231–32nn2–4; Reserve status and reason for joining Reserves, 17–19; success of, 209–11, 215–18; task assignments, 20–21

Marine Regiment, 24th, 1st Battalion (1/24), Alpha Company, 1st Platoon: chlorine truck bomb incident, 186; Hawa operations, 132, 143; Lehner command of, 21. See also Lehner, Rob

Marine Regiment, 24th, 1st Battalion (1/24), Alpha Company, 2nd

Platoon: chlorine truck bomb incident, 183, 185, 186–88; Ivers command of, 21; transport of casualties
to Camp Fallujah Surgical, 198. *See
also* Ivers, Brian
Marine Regiment, 24th, 1st Battalion
(1/24), Alpha Company, 3rd
Platoon: Adilah, information from,
99; chlorine truck bomb incident,
173–78, 186; competition between
platoons, 21–22; Dockter command
of 2nd Squad, 23; Greco command
of, 19; Hawa operations, 132; patrol
and interview operations, 99. *See
also* Dockter, Christopher; Greco,
Jerome
Marine Regiment, 24th, 1st Battalion
(1/24), Alpha Company, Weapons
Platoon: competition between
platoons, 21–22; cordon and sweep
operations, 90; Hawa operations,
130, 132–42; medical/veterinary
civil action program, 114–20; overwatch house and Adilah, 92–94,
96–99, 250nn6–7; patrol and
interview operations, 92–99; Route
Boston riot, 147–48; Route Boston
sniper incident, 149–56; task assignments, 20–21; training and drilling
platoon, 92. *See also* Hoffmann,
Jeremy
Marine Regiment, 24th, 1st Battalion
(1/24), Charlie Company, 86, 97–98
Marine Regiment, 24th, 2nd Battalion
(2/24), 56
Marine Regiment, 24th, 3rd Battalion
(3/24): augmentation of 1/24 with
men from, 17, 23; end of deployment for, 215; home for, 17; reason
for becoming Marines, 231–32nn2–
4; Reserve units and weekend warrior stereotypes about, 19, 232n5
Marine Regiment, 25th, 1st Battalion
(1/25), Alpha Company, 122–23,
256–57n34
McAlinden, Jeff, 41–42, 44
McCarty, Brandon, 42

McMaster, H. R., 256–57n34
medical/veterinary civil action program
(MEDCAP/VETCAP) mission:
arm wrestling and exchange of
gifts, 121–22; food and supplies
distribution, 113–17, 120, 254n2,
255n7; local send-off of Marine
convoy, 126–27; photos with female
Marines, 120–21; veterinary aid
program, 117–20, 256n25; widows,
event to support, 124–25
Mejeur, Curtis, 84
military services, U.S.: individual decisions by service members and
outcome of war, 3; patience and
professionalism to cement alliance
to stop insurgency, 5–6; personalities, importance of in shaping
course of war, 4
Moose, Michael, 5, 143–44
Morris, Steve, 148, 149
mosques, standard operating procedure
for respect for, 39
Muñoz, Ruben "Doc": accidental shooting in Albu Aifan, 73–74, 75–77, 82;
Albu Aifan information-gathering
operations, 68; ambushes and
firefights, 29–30, 31–32, 33, 42–43,
44–45, 236nn5–6; ambushes and
firefights, review of and success of,
51; chlorine truck bomb casualties,
treatment of, 196; coffee, love for,
44; communication with helicopter,
49–50; Kopera injury, 52; Marine
service of, 45; Navy service of, 44,
45; nickname for, 44; opinions
about, 44–45; personality and character of, 44–45; wounded woman,
treatment and evacuation of, 47–51,
240n102

Navy, U.S., attitudes of Marines toward,
18
Neal, Jacob H., 5–6

O'Connor, Eddie, 31, 32, 33, 41, 44, 191,
238n53, 239n57

Ogden, Dave, 192
Ophoff, Steven, 187
orders, explanation of rationale behind, 23–24
Osborne, Brandon, 133, 135–39, 144–46
overwatch house and Adilah, 92–94, 96–99, 250nn6–7

Panasuk, Mike, 134, 141–42
paper shuffling and intelligence reports, 27
Paredes, Ernan, 68, 70–71, 77
patrol and interview operations: operational pace and schedule, 23, 28; question-and-answer sessions, 23, 24–25, 234n17
Petraeus, David: coalition, command of by, 2, 210; COIN doctrine and field manual, 219, 256–57n34
Phantom Fury, Operation (Second Battle of Fallujah), 1, 19, 27, 57, 81, 100, 163–64, 169
Pickel, Trevor, 195, 197, 198, 201–2
Ponce, Guadalupe: background of, 134–35; Hawa operations, 134, 138–39, 141, 259n6; opinion of Whisnant, 217; reason for becoming a Marine, 134–35; sympathy for Fallujans, 217
Prince, Dickie, 77
Przybylski, Edward "Ski": arm wrestling tournament, 121–22; background and experience of, 103; medical/veterinary civil action program, 115–17; photo with Dark, 117; Team Yankee civil affairs missions, 103

Qaeda, al. See insurgency and al Qaeda
Qutbists (Qutbiyyun) and Sayyid Qutb, 165–66, 266–67n26

raids: cordon and sweep operations, 90; Dark's cooperation on, offers of, 59; respect for house occupants during, 27, 235n28; success of, 27
Raleigh Area of Operations (AO): CAG detachment, 101–2, 106; insurgent attacks in areas around, 1

Ramadi, Awakening and alliance with U.S. to fight insurgents, 2, 61
Reames, Luke, 180, 216–17
The Regulators (CAG Team 1), 102
Reist, David G., 10
research methodology, 221–22
Robinson, Matt, 84
Roussell, Jim: Albu Issa tribe, intelligence from, 84; analysis of Iraqis, 58; Awakening and CAG projects, opinion about, 111; background and experience of, 55–57; COIN and success of Alpha Company, 210; COIN tradition in Corps, 57–58; Dark, assessment of, 58–59, 63, 214, 244n25; Dark meetings with, 59–63; deployment volunteering for, 56–57; dinner with and spending night at house of Dark, 125–26; falling in love with sources, 81; influence of, 57–58; intelligence gathering operations, 106–7; opinions about, 56–57; reconstruction project contracts, criteria for awarding, 112; retirement of, 55, 56; sheikhs, relationship with, 57; Team Yankee taxi service, 106–7
rules of engagement (ROE), 57, 68
rush hour for mortar attacks, 259n3

Sady, Omar al-, 104
Sahib, Wadhah "C. J.," 65, 74–75, 78, 98, 197
Salafist-jihadists, 165–66, 167
Salah, Sa'ad, 175–77
Sattar, Abdul, 15, 61, 171, 231n30
Serr, Scott, 32, 40, 41, 45–46, 239n57
Shaffer, Jeremy, 273n39
sheikhs: alliance with Americans, 192–93, 202; authority and influence of (wasta), 9–10, 12, 14, 59, 61, 108–12; authority of, projects to support, 108, 110–12; challenges of conducting business with, 111–12; double-dealing by and successful cooperation with U.S., 11–12, 124; fake sheikhs, 109; insurgency threat

to, 166, 171–72; Jordan, return
from, 10–11, 61, 230n12; Jordan as
refuge for, 10, 61; manipulation of
tribal system by Saddam, 108–9;
meetings of, 57; reconciliation
between insurgents and, 206
Shia Muslims: as internal enemies, 166;
manipulation of tribal system by
Saddam, 108–9; police and security
forces as, 2, 62
Shirkey, Raymond, 193–94
shoot and scoot attacks, 34, 147
Siekman, Josh, 149
Simcock, Richard, 106, 210, 212–13
situational awareness, 43
sniper attacks, 5, 25, 103, 147, 149–56
Steimel, Corey, 148, 149, 216
Stout, Matt, 193
Sunni Muslims: change in attitude
toward Americans by, 208,
275–76n19; manipulation of tribal
system by Saddam, 108–9; Shia
security forces, response to, 2, 62
supplies and food distribution, 113–17,
120, 254n2, 255n7
surge of United States forces, 2, 62,
171–72
Sweezey, Jodie: bananas as luxury item,
254n2; CAG team leader, 101; damage to and destruction of Fallujah,
101; dinner with and spending
night at house of Dark, 125–26;
dress of Irqais, 115; medical/veteri-
nary civil action program, 115–16;
photos with Iraqis, 120–21; The
Regulators Civil Affairs missions,
102, 105–6

Taylor, Edwin: chlorine truck bomb
incident, 177, 189, 190–91; transport of casualties to Camp Fallujah
Surgical, 193–94, 196–97, 272n28,
273n45
Teesdale, Matthew, 5
Thornsberry, Jonathan B., 5, 28, 29, 50, 99
three-dimensional chess, 20, 232–33n7
tribal blood debt, 83

tribesmen and Iraqi citizens: abuse of
and mistakes and public relations
disasters after invasion, 36–37, 71,
72–73; alliance with Americans, 61;
arming of Iraqis, 12, 62–63, 65; bad
bad guys, 58, 60, 64; civil war and
firefights between tribesmen, 65–66,
81; civilian casualties, 162–63,
264n14; COIN and relationship
building with Iraqis, 122–24,
215–18, 256–57n34, 257n36; commandeering of houses, reaction of
residents to, 35–36, 238n40; criminal and civil code to settle disputes,
83; cultural differences and communication with, 25; culture and
willingness to forgive tragedy, 78,
82–83, 248n80; dress of, 115; failure to warn about IEDs, 5–6, 26;
Fallujah Awakening and alliance
with U.S. to fight, 2–3, 4; fear as
motivating factor, 78; firefights,
reactions to, 36, 38–39; friend and
foe, telling difference between, 67;
good bad guys, 58; information and
cooperation of Iraqis as key to beating insurgency, 8, 20, 22, 38–39, 91;
Islamist radicals, relationship with,
10; motivations and interests of, 4,
58; organization of tribes and subtribes, 9–10; question-and-answer
sessions with, frustration of, 23,
24–25, 234n17; relationship building and length of deployments, 62,
243–44n31, 256n33; relationship
building and U.S. interests, 63;
relationship building with Iraqis,
importance of, 93, 127; respect and
good intentions in treatment of,
36–37, 93, 96, 123–24, 140, 257n36;
revenge against and killing of anyone cooperating with Americans,
12–13, 62–63, 91, 97, 250n29;
risks taken by in cooperation with
Americans, 61–63; risks taken by in
stand against criminals and radicals, 4–5; security for in fighting

insurgents, 62–64, 91; shame and honor, living by code of, 37; survival instinct, intimidation by insurgents, and cooperation with Americans, 25–26, 27, 234–35n23; sympathy for Fallujans, 217; villagers with weapons, concerns about being mistaken for insurgents, 25, 124n21; weapons, confiscation of from, 25; weapons, permits to openly carry, 63, 82; women, responsibilities of, 118, 255–56n20; wounded civilians, treatment and evacuation of, 47–51, 52, 53, 240n102, 241n117, 241n125

Tyink, Andrew, 32, 42–44, 84, 238n53

VanSlyke, Bufford "Kenny," 5
vehicle-borne improvised explosive devices (VBIEDs), 86
veterinary aid program, 117–20, 256n25
Villanueva, Elijah, 5, 6, 141, 144–46

wasta, 108–12
Webster, Alan, 25
Wells, Bryan, 256n33
Whisnant, Dan: Albu Issa tribe alliance, 108, 110; Albu Issa tribe, intelligence from, 84; Awakening, role in, 3, 202; Awakening and CAG projects, opinion about, 111; background of, 16; chlorine truck bomb incident, 177, 182–83; COIN and success of Alpha Company, 209–11; Dark, report about meeting with, 54–55; Dark meetings with, 7–9, 10–11, 12–16, 58–64; dinner with and spending night at house of Dark, 125–26; experience and leadership skills of, 19–20; FOB Black command, 8; Hawa operations, 132, 142–43; information-gathering campaign, 23, 87–89; intelligence, action taken on, 86; intelligence operations, preparation for and understanding of, 131; intelligence reports and paper shuffling, 27; Iraqi leaders, meetings with, 229n2; Iraqis,

importance of getting to know and cooperation with, 8, 127; Khamis meeting with, 59–64; local send-off of Marine convoy, 126–27; medical/veterinary civil action program, 114; opinions about, 216–17; promises made by, 202; reconstruction project contracts, criteria for awarding, 112; Route Boston sniper incident, 156; Zien-Muzien Game, 128

widows, event to support, 124–25
Williams, Tyler, 67, 68, 70–71
Witteveen, Brett A., 5
Wortman, Jessie, 134, 136, 138–39

Yankee, Team, 102–7, 110–12

Zarqawi, Musab al-, 166–68, 262–63n1
Zavalavargas, Joel, 134
Zermeno, Tony "Doc," 188, 195, 198–201, 221–22, 273n39, 273n45
Zobaie, Faisal Ismail Hussein al-, 3
Zofchak, Matthew: ambushes and firefights, 29, 30–33, 42–44; ambushes and firefights, review of and success of, 51; chlorine truck bomb incident, 191; commandeering house for firing position, 35–36, 238n40; communication with helicopter, 49; fire superiority, 33; firefights between tribesmen, 66; Kopera injury, 52, 242n130; mosque as location of attackers, 32, 39, 238n53; mosque as location of attackers, move toward and investigation of, 39, 239n57; Navy and Marine Corps Commendation Medal with Combat "V" award, 242n130; wounded woman, treatment and evacuation of, 48, 49, 50, 240n102
Zwolski, Andrew: chlorine truck bomb incident, 177, 189, 190–91; dinner with and spending night at house of Dark, 125–26; transport of casualties to Camp Fallujah Surgical, 193–94, 196–97, 272n28

ABOUT THE AUTHOR

Bill Ardolino is an associate editor/overseas correspondent for the *Long War Journal*. His reporting includes embeds with the U.S. Marine Corps, the U.S. Army, the Iraqi Army, and the Iraqi police in Fallujah, Habbaniyah, and Baghdad in 2006, 2007, and 2008. He traveled to Afghanistan in 2010 to embed with the Marine Corps, the Afghan police, and the Afghan Army in Helmand province, and with the U.S. and Afghan air forces in Kabul, and returned in 2011 to embed with the U.S. and Afghan armies in Khost province.

His reports, columns, and photographs have been published in the *Washington Examiner, Wired, Small Wars Journal,* and the *Weekly Standard.* His reporting has focused on combat operations, the development of indigenous security forces, civil affairs work, and Iraqi politics. He has also been a guest on *The Dennis Miller Show, The John Batchelor Show, The Charles Adler Show,* and Al Jazeera English. He lives in Washington, D.C.

The Naval Institute Press is the book-publishing arm of the U.S. Naval Institute, a private, nonprofit membership society for sea service professionals and others who share an interest in naval and maritime affairs. Established in 1873 at the U.S. Naval Academy in Annapolis, Maryland, where its offices remain today, the Naval Institute has members worldwide.

Members of the Naval Institute support the education programs of the society and receive the influential monthly magazine *Proceedings* or the colorful bimonthly magazine *Naval History* and discounts on fine nautical prints and on ship and aircraft photos. They also have access to the transcripts of the Institute's Oral History Program and get discounted admission to any of the Institute-sponsored seminars offered around the country.

The Naval Institute's book-publishing program, begun in 1898 with basic guides to naval practices, has broadened its scope to include books of more general interest. Now the Naval Institute Press publishes about seventy titles each year, ranging from how-to books on boating and navigation to battle histories, biographies, ship and aircraft guides, and novels. Institute members receive significant discounts on the Press's more than eight hundred books in print.

Full-time students are eligible for special half-price membership rates. Life memberships are also available.

For a free catalog describing Naval Institute Press books currently available, and for further information about joining the U.S. Naval Institute, please write to:

Member Services
U.S. Naval Institute
291 Wood Road
Annapolis, MD 21402-5034
Telephone: (800) 233-8764
Fax: (410) 571-1703
Web address: www.usni.org